An Ethic of Innocence

SUNY series, Studies in the Long Nineteenth Century
———————
Pamela K. Gilbert, editor

An Ethic of Innocence

Pragmatism, Modernity,
and Women's Choice Not to Know

KRISTEN L. RENZI

Maurice Brazil Prendergast (1858–1924). *Large Boston Public Garden Sketchbook: A woman in a veiled hat*, 1895–1897. Robert Lehman Collection, Metropolitan Museum of Art, NY.

Published by State University of New York Press, Albany

© 2019 State University of New York

All rights reserved

No part of this book may be used or reproduced in any manner whatsoever without written permission. No part of this book may be stored in a retrieval system or transmitted in any form or by any means including electronic, electrostatic, magnetic tape, mechanical, photocopying, recording, or otherwise without the prior permission in writing of the publisher.

For information, contact State University of New York Press, Albany, NY
www.sunypress.edu

Library of Congress Cataloging-in-Publication Data

Names: Renzi, Kristen Lucia, author.
Title: An ethic of innocence : pragmatism, modernity, and women's choice not
   to know / Kristen L. Renzi.
Description: Albany : State University of New York Press, [2019] | Series:
   SUNY series, studies in the long nineteenth century | Includes bibliographical
   references and index.
Identifiers: LCCN 2018045848 | ISBN 9781438475974 (hardcover) |
      ISBN 9781438475967 (pbk.) | ISBN 9781438475981 (ebook) Subjects: LCSH:
             American literature—19th century—History and criticism. |
   American literature—20th century—History and criticism. | Women in
   literature. | English literature—19th century—History and criticism. |
   English literature—20th century—History and criticism. | Knowledge,
   Theory of, in literature.
Classification: LCC PS217.W64 R46 2019 | DDC 810.9/3522—dc23
LC record available at https://lccn.loc.gov/2018045848

10 9 8 7 6 5 4 3 2 1

To Debbie, Cecilia, and Lucy,
three primary role models in my life;
and to Josephine Jane,
who is already an excellent teacher

Contents

Acknowledgments ix

Introduction: The Problem of Modern Female Innocence 1

PART ONE
NEGOTIATED LIVING

Chapter One
A Pragmatist's Dilemma: The Collusion between Myth and Reality in the Tale of the Hull House Devil Baby 37

Chapter Two
Coming of Age via Critical Complaint: Reading Women's Choices Not to Know in Realist Bildungsroman 71

Chapter Three
A Failure of Sympathy or of Narrative? Naturalism's Jaded Women and the Narrative Cycle of Domestic Violence 105

Chapter Four
The Legacy of Naturalism, a Cycle of Leaving: Reading Agency in the Passive, Empty Woman 135

PART TWO
PRAGMATIC FANTASIES

Chapter Five
Are Women People? Discourses of (Non)Personhood in Suffrage Poetry and Protest 159

Chapter Six
Making Women, Making Humans: Fantasies and Melancholic
Mourning in Modern Sex Changes and Sex Losses   193

Chapter Seven
Allowing Innocence? Belief, Knowledge, and the
Modern Community   227

Notes   249

Works Cited   261

Index   279

Acknowledgments

This book emerged from work I first pursued in my dissertation at Indiana University, under the direction of Jennifer Fleissner. Our conversations over the years about innocence, female agency, and fin-de-siècle literature pushed this project in directions I could not have taken it alone, for which I am grateful. I am also deeply indebted to Shane Vogel for his years of mentorship, both on this project and in my graduate and early career work in general—his support and careful critique have made me a better thinker and writer. I also benefited immensely from the reading and commentary of other dissertation committee members—Ranu Samantrai, Judith Brown, and Ross Gay—and a handful of peers who helped me in many stages of the project, particularly Lee Anne Bache, Carrie Sickmann Han, Elizabeth Hoover, and Michael Lewis. In addition, I am grateful to Indiana University's College of Arts and Sciences, its English Department, and the Wertheim family for providing me with fellowship funding to focus on this project in its early stages.

I am also grateful for the readership and advice of colleagues of mine at both Michigan State University and Xavier University who have helped me to develop this manuscript, in particular Zarena Aslami, Gabriel Gottlieb, Ellen McCallum, Jennifer McFarlane-Harris, and Natalie Phillips. Special appreciation and thanks also go to my faculty mentor at Xavier University, Norman Finkelstein, for his help and support in readying the book for submission, and to the members of the research support group for early-career female faculty at Xavier: Shannon Lafayette, Wendy Maxian, Mollie McIntosh, Niamh O'Leary, and Annie Ray. I am also grateful for a Faculty Development Leave granted to me by Xavier University in Spring 2017, which provided me with the concentrated time needed to finish this manuscript. In addition, I appreciate the support of my editor, Amanda Lanne-Camilli; series editor Pamela K. Gilbert; and the SUNY Press staff in bringing this manuscript to press. I would also like to express my appreciation for my two anonymous reviewers, whose careful commentary and useful critique on this manuscript have allowed me to revise it for the better.

I thank the journal *SubStance* for allowing me to reprint part of an article I published with them in 2013—"Safety in Objects: Discourses of Violence and Value—The *Rokeby Venus* and *Rhythm 0*" (41.1, no. 130: 120–45). I also thank the University Press of Florida for allowing me to reprint part of my chapter, "On Jane Addams's Feminist Pragmatism," published in 2018 in *American Literary History and the Turn toward Modernity*, edited by Melanie Dawson and Meredith Goldsmith.

In addition to the extensive support of the academy that I have been lucky enough to receive, I also want to acknowledge the other realms of support that have been crucial to the development of the project's core theoretical ideas and to bringing this book to fruition. In particular, my volunteer work at Bloomington, Indiana's Middle Way House, a rape crisis and domestic violence center, during my years as a graduate student at Indiana University deeply influenced the conceptual framework of this project; special thanks to Toby Strout, Leila Wood, Tina Cornetta, Lauren Taylor, and the many other Middle Way House staff, clients, and volunteers, whose influence contours these pages.

The support of my close friends and family, who have been kind enough to listen to many iterations of these ideas and to continue to help me refine them, deserves more thanks that I can express: love and appreciation to Michael Lewis, Lee Anne Bache, Jonathan Lund, Carrie Sickmann Han, John Han, Natalie Phillips, Suparna Chatterjee, Amit Sen, Debbie and Tony Renzi, Steve and Una Renzi, Cecilia and Stan Tomaszewski, and Lucy Renzi. Finally, I would not have been able to complete this manuscript in its current form without the support, love, and intellectual engagement of my husband, Gabriel Gottlieb, who has buoyed both the philosophical discourse of the project and my spirits when the work has seemed overwhelming. As I sit on our couch, nestled between him and our two-week-old daughter, Josephine Jane, I am grateful for the comfort and security of home that they, and our four-legged companions, provide to me. It is my hope that the world Josephine will one day inhabit will offer more generous options for comfort and security to women than it does today: materially, emotionally, and, of course, epistemically.

Chapter 1 modifies and extends a chapter published previously in *American Literary History and the Turn Toward Modernity* (2018) edited by Melanie V.

Dawson and Meredith L. Goldsmith, 144–71. It is reprinted with permission by the University Press of Florida.

Chapter 5 modifies and extends an article published previously entitled "Safety in Violence" that is reprinted with permission by Johns Hopkins University Press. Copyright © Board of Regents, University of Wisconsin System. This article was first published in *SubStance* 42.1 (2013), 120–45.

Introduction

The Problem of Modern Female Innocence

> I find it very pleasant not to know. A swift carriage, of a dark night, rattling with four horses over roads that one can't see—that's my idea of happiness.
>
> —Henry James, *Portrait of a Lady* (235)

Not-knowing—the who, what, when, where, why, and how of it—anchors this study. Which means, of course, that knowledge also grounds it. As with any binary, knowledge intimately connects and relates to its opposite of ignorance, and the study of one entails the study of the other. That scholars in multiple disciplines who are concerned with knowledge have not, as a matter of course, also developed comprehensive theories of not-knowing is unsurprising only if we acknowledge an epistemophilic bias that pervades traditional epistemology, much scholarly enterprise, and—arguably—modernity itself. As defined by philosopher Cynthia Townley in *A Defense of Ignorance: Its Value for Knowers and Roles in Feminist and Social Epistemologies* (2011), epistemophilia is an "excessive love for knowledge" that "tends to take all ignorance to be remediable, and best remedied, so the proper response to ignorance is to replace it with knowledge" (xii, xiii). To understand why this bias has been so pervasive, we must merely highlight our negative associations with tradition and ignorance, associations that are noncoincidentally also deeply linked to gendered, racialized, and classist prejudice.[1] And yet, this neglect cannot be ascribed solely to not-knowing's negative inflection; Townley notes that other fields within philosophy (such as moral philosophy) often study positively inflected terms alongside their negative counterparts (virtues alongside vice, for instance) (xvi–xvii). Something peculiar has gone on in the study of knowledge that has unnaturally, and fairly comprehensively, suppressed the concomitant exploration of not-knowing. Thus, a study of not-knowing that would be open to its nonnegative aspects appears particularly odd, even uncomfortable.

And yet, this book is such a study. *An Ethic of Innocence* explores not-knowing as an epistemological practice that is not inherently negative through the figure of the fin-de-siècle woman. She, I argue, marks a turning point in the transatlantic literary-cultural representation of women from seeing female innocence as acceptable, if childish/naïve, to viewing women who choose not to know as antimodern, antifeminist, regressive fools. While the who, what, when, where, why, and how of this study are essential to my project's thesis, they are not necessary to an exploration of not-knowing. That is, there is nothing necessarily modern (the when) or transatlantic (the where) or female (the who) about not-knowing. Nor do the types of not-knowing (the what), the ways not-knowing is expressed (the how), or the reasons not-knowing is claimed, sustained, and embraced (the why) that I cover in this book encompass the necessary or total whats, hows, and whys of epistemologies of ignorance. Instead, my book tells a very particular story—that of the modern female subject as she has been represented within literature and art—in an unconventional way: by exploring the ways in which she has been shaped, circumscribed, opened, and misunderstood through practices of not-knowing.

Using an array of interdisciplinary discourses, including feminist and queer theory, social and feminist epistemologies, and philosophical pragmatism, in concert with literary critical, historical, and feminist cultural scholarship, *An Ethic of Innocence* traces the trope of female choices not to know—what I term an "ethic of innocence"—through a variety of literary and cultural manifestations in the late nineteenth and early twentieth centuries. Though gender and not-knowing are the threads I use to weave these texts together, my analysis is intersectional and treats, in particular, race, class, and national identity of characters as crucial complications to these threads. While this book responds to an overarching story of modern female representation within the transatlantic literary canon that in and of itself reflects significant bias toward white, middle-class, and heterosexual representations of women, the story of not-knowing that my manuscript engages is not limited to such a narrow view of women. Here, the transatlantic nature of the project requires my engagement with related, albeit distinct, canonical relationships to identity and difference. For instance, the early American lineage of indigenous or enslaved voices is importantly divergent from the British canon's engagement (or lack thereof) with the perspective of the colonial other; meanwhile, these literary traditions' engagement with the topics of immigration, class stratification, and national relationship is likewise discrete and requires text-specific contextualization.[2] However, one of the more important arguments of this book is that this literary period contains representations of women from a variety of identity backgrounds—some privileged, some decidedly not, many complicated—engaging with strategies of not-knowing. The engagement may look different and have different costs and benefits based on a woman's identity features, but my chapters show that choosing not to know is not a privilege reserved merely for the elite; it is, rather, a flexible epistemic tool that can be, and has been, used to diverse ends by very differently situated characters and persons.[3]

This practice of not-knowing that this book traces is something I call an "ethic of innocence"; I define this as a system or tactic by which an agent (often, though not exclusively, female) makes a choice against knowledge in favor of a suspended stance of not-knowing. Though I will further unpack this terminology later on in this introduction, I will signal just a few key things about it here. First, I use the term "innocence" rather than "ignorance" to emphasize that this refusal of knowledge is chosen as a particular *gendered* strategy of epistemic negotiation. Discourses of innocence, as the literary canon attests, have been deployed strategically to control women's access to knowledge (women should not know certain things), to infantilize them (women, like children, should be pure and innocent), and to define their sexual worth (women should be virginal and innocent until marriage, as well as chaste afterwards). Of course, the "shoulds" in the parentheticals above also make clear that such discourses surrounding innocence have been used to differentiate "proper" or "good" women from their fallen, racially or economically othered, or questionably worldly sisters. As I will make clear later on in this introduction, these valuations of female propriety that include but exceed consideration of intellectual knowledge alone make the term 'innocence,' rather than 'ignorance,' a ripe one for my study of the ways in which women choose not to know in this era. Second, I have yoked innocence to the term "ethic" in order to emphasize the reasoned, epistemic, and sociomoral dimensions of this choice not to know. In doing so, an "ethic of innocence" breaks from a linear understanding of innocence's temporality (as a state that precedes but can never follow knowledge or experience). We are, I suspect, used to thinking of innocence as something one *is*; through the composite "ethic of innocence," I posit innocence as something one *adopts, has,* or *does.*

As a segue to further exploration of an ethic of innocence, I offer the following portrait of what I consider to be a characteristic fin-de-siècle non-knower, a character whose very freedom to choose anything in her life is made possible, and then cut short, by her gendered choices not to know. Indeed, her tale's title, including its indefinite "a," suggests that if not an everywoman, Isabel Archer, of Henry James's *The Portrait of a Lady*, is at least a discernable, turn-of-the-century *type*. *An Ethic of Innocence* argues that this fin-de-siècle female type is not defined merely by the uses to which she puts her choice not to know; just as, if not more, important to this book's analysis is the way in which such a choice (and its uses) has been misunderstood and mischaracterized, by other characters and readers alike.[4] For, crucially, the fin-de-siècle/modern woman's choice not to know has been judged, not merely as an epistemic lack but also as a sociopolitical failing.

Not-Knowing as *Trope-cum-Trap*

Isabel Archer, the protagonist of James's 1880–81 novel, embodies a paradox that faced many an intelligent, educated, middle-class women on the cusp of modernity: she knows that to obtain the (classed, raced, gendered) status of "lady," she must marry and adopt the role of wife and mother but fears that by marrying she will lose her independence and agency. Isabel is no ignorant socialite; early on, she is characterized as a "prodigy of learning," evincing a palpable, distinct "love of knowledge" that differentiates her from the "horridly ignorant" other girls (66, 27, 62). Yet Isabel's knowledge is affectively and experientially limited; as her cousin Ralph puts the matter, she is fond of "happy knowledge—of pleasant knowledge" but has not yet acquired "miserable knowledge" through personal suffering (64). Instead, Isabel demonstrates "a fixed determination to regard the world as a place of brightness, of free expansion, of irresistible action" (68). Yet such determination evidences no mere Pollyannaesque romanticism; Isabel clearly understands that the independence her class in particular permits her indulgence in this worldview. Therefore, despite perceiving Casper Goodwood, her first suitor, as "the finest young man she had ever seen," she refuses to marry him in order to maintain her independence (47).

The Portrait of a Lady's narrative trajectory painstakingly charts Isabel's failures to keep both her independence and the merely happy knowledge to which it is linked. In the face of social pressures to marry, the connivance of false friends, the *laissez-faire* attitude of her family, the corrupting force of money, and her own naïve stubbornness, Isabel soon opts to marry a man who neither truly sees nor respects her and who curtails her worldview and her freedom with gusto—a marital fate many critics have abhorred.[5] But before this tragic narrowing of her fate, Isabel does experience a period of independence, partially financed by an inheritance from her rich uncle but also partially purchased by an embrace of a very curious phenomenon for this passionate lover of knowledge: a series of choices not to know.

The quote that opens this introduction is said by Isabel Archer to her friend, Henrietta Stackpole, when Henrietta asks what Isabel plans for her future. This conversation occurs directly after Henrietta discovers Isabel has rejected (for the second time) the suit of Casper Goodwood. Henrietta sees this rejection as a grave error, asking Isabel accusingly, "[D]o you know where you're drifting? (235). Isabel's response, "No, I haven't the least idea," is followed by the cheeky claim that she "find[s] it very pleasant not to know" (235). Henrietta's dismayed reply to Isabel's perversity, that she is behaving "like the heroine of an immoral novel," expresses both the (negative) moral inflection such "drifting" has and also the sentiment that it is only in an unrealistic, even fictional, world in which such "drifting," for a leading lady, is permissible. It might be tempting to dismiss Henrietta's reply as mere reactionary conservatism that sees no path for women aside from marriage; such a dismissal is troubled, however, by the clear New Woman attributes Henrietta also represents; she is introduced as a career journalist who does not find her equal footing with men to be at odds with a "duty" to marry and who "smell[s]" so much "of the Future" that "it almost knocks one down" (127, 131). Indeed, Henrietta even declares, in the same conversation, that if Isabel decides to marry an Englishman she will "never speak to [her] again" (234). So, something else in Isabel's reply other than the mere rejection of marriage must be irking Henrietta.

Seen in light of questions of knowledge, Isabel's reply might trouble Henrietta as an immoral rejection of reality, in that it describes Isabel's abdication of intellectual control. The vision Isabel imparts of happiness as "a swift carriage, of a dark night, rattling with four horses over roads that one can't see" provokes a romantic dream of being carried off, without active volition but in forward motion (235). The multiple rather than singular invisible roads over which the carriage trundles mark out a meandering and unconscious path, in stark opposition to the planned, directional use to which roads are often put. The nocturnal nature of the trip, further obscuring its traveler's knowledge of the journey's path, hints at the not merely risky but also risqué nature of such a journey (despite its clear disengagement from coupling with Goodwood, whom Isabel tellingly terms the "stubbornest fact she knew") (162). Passion and happiness, for Isabel, happen via not-knowing: choosing to divest oneself of sight and control and instead moving unwilled and alone, at the whim of machines and beasts rather than human logic and fact.

How do we make sense of this eminently intelligent, learned, and sensible woman turning away from fact and embracing the choice not to know? And why does she need to do so in order to claim her independence, both bodily and intellectually, from the burgeoning modern world? An exchange between Isabel and her aunt early in the novel gives us one clue. When Isabel claims that she "always want[s] to know the things one shouldn't do," in response to her aunt's query as to why—"so as to do them?"—she instead responds: "so as to choose" (93). Here, the idea of choosing (rather than knowing) takes on the privileged position and moral valence; rather than seeking the distinction between should and should not as moral instruction, Isabel seeks the distinction in order to engage a different binary: choosing vs. obeying. For Isabel, to choose is a value in and of itself; I suggest that it is this insistence on enacting her agency via choice rather than via knowledge that troubles Henrietta.[6] Here, Henrietta's judgment, that Isabel "live[s] too much in the world of [her] own dreams," can be read not as a critique of dreaming but of rejecting "contact with reality" when dreams better suit one's desires (310).

The gendered, raced, and classed expectations of her late nineteenth-century marital reality clamp down firmly upon Isabel when she finds that the marriage she believes she has chosen has instead been brokered by a woman she thought was her friend in order to shore up the fortune of that woman's illegitimate daughter with Isabel's now-husband Osmond.[7] When these secrets are revealed to Isabel by Osmond's sister, Osmond's sister expresses incredulity at Isabel's ability to "succeed in not knowing" and to maintain her "innocent ignorance" (365). These two phrases seem to work in tension with one another; an "innocent" ignorance would seem to be not-knowing through some kind of naïveté, but the idea of "succeeding" in an enterprise of not-knowing constructs the act of not-knowing as an effort and accomplishment. Isabel herself is contradictory in her expressions of her lack of knowledge. She says she "had no idea" and that she "do[es] not] know" these secrets, but she then also claims that "things *have* occurred to me, and perhaps that was what they all meant" (365). Isabel constructs herself oppositionally as both unknowing and as having ideas (albeit without concluding on their meaning). Perhaps here, we see the culminating illustration of how, for Isabel, "the love of knowledge coexisted in her mind with the finest capacity for ignorance" (284).

With this contradictory picture of Isabel in mind, it is possible to understand the novel's tragic trajectory as a result not of Isabel's inability to choose her independence, but rather her inability—after choosing independently to get into the swift carriage of happiness—to continue to choose not to know, within the bounds of her particular embodied identity, when one of these choices has been to marry. Though Osmond's sister sees her act of illuminating Isabel as to the true relationship between Osmond and his mistress as a freeing good, in the way that her own realization of her husband's limitations was "a wonderful simplification," she accuses Isabel of rejecting such simplicity (362). And indeed, Isabel is not happy to have obtained this information, though she recognizes she is "much obliged to [Osmond's sister]." "I suppose I ought to know," she says to her, "but I'm sorry" (371). We as readers are only able to take the full measure of her meaning at the novel's close, where once again Isabel is offered the love (if not the hand) of Casper Goodwood. Goodwood's final moments with Isabel in the novel are filled with his own attempt to jump into that swiftly moving carriage of happiness. Upon realizing how unhappy Isabel has been in her marriage, Goodwood offers her the following alternative reality, which seems in many ways to echo Isabel's own previous embrace of pleasure and dreams:

> Why shouldn't we be happy—when it's here before us, when it's so easy? . . . It would be an insult to you to assume that you care for the look of the thing, for what people will say, for the bottomless idiocy of the world. . . . We can do absolutely as we please; to whom under the sun do we owe anything? What is it that holds us, what is it that has the smallest right to interfere in such a question as this? Such a question is between ourselves—and to say that is to settle it! Were we born to rot in our misery—were we born to be afraid? (434–35)

The questions Casper asks betray his willingness (and also his identity-based ability) to reject the knowledge of convention, propriety, of even community and shame for the more productive choice of happiness. Isabel is tempted by Casper's offer, and his vision of their cares-to-the-wind rejection of social mores strikes her as both rapturously beautiful and deadly dangerous. For Isabel, to believe in Casper's worldview is no longer the unknowing happiness of a surrender to nighttime freewheeling in a carriage; it is, instead, "the next best thing to her dying"—a strange bit of phrasing that equates happiness with death, unhappiness with life (435). No wonder, then, that she escapes her moment of temptation—the "white lightning" of his kiss—into a darkness that once again signals freedom but not, as before, happiness (436). During Isabel's flight across her uncle's lawn to the safe banality of the house, she might have "s[een] nothing," but in this final dark journey, she embraces knowledge that cannot be described as anything but miserable. We find that "she had not known where to turn; but she knew now. There was a very straight path" (436). No longer careening across unseen roads, Isabel is now fully a knower who sees the singular, straight (perhaps even the proverbially narrow) path in front of her and whose knowledge most likely returns her to her unhappy, unfree marriage. Not-knowing, no longer viable, has been relinquished as a strategy, and as a character, Isabel (along with the fin-de-siècle "lady" she represents) is the worse for its loss.

At root, *An Ethic of Innocence* asks why: Why has not-knowing (instead of knowledge) been a site of female happiness and/or resistance at the turn of the century for this lady and so many both like and unlike her? Why has this pattern been so difficult for readers and critics to comprehend? And, most centrally, why has the relinquishment of knowledge, despite its concomitant affective or even material loss for these women, been generically, and morally, required?

Epistemologies of Not-knowing, Ethics of Innocence

The topics of not-knowing, subjects' negotiation of sociocultural spaces, and gendered epistemology have emerged in recent scholarship as natural interdisciplinary bedfellows. Even so, the notion that not-knowing might be a necessary, even ethical, component of epistemology has not lost its controversial edge. For example, when, in a 1975 talk given at the National Symposium on Genetics and the Law, Italian-born microbiologist, US immigrant, and Nobel laureate Salvador E. Luria advocated the balancing of the commonplace, modern, socially sanctioned "right-to-know value, that is, the ethics of knowledge" with what he termed "the ethics of innocence," he understood his idea's radical thrust (3). Indeed, we might see the "right-to-know" paradigm Luria invoked as a warped version of the post-enlightenment emphasis upon the pursuit of knowledge, one that has turned knowledge acquisition into a moral, ethical, and epistemic mandate. As a result, rather than viewing knowledge acquisition as a mere tool among a variety of others, this false elevation of the pursuit of knowledge lends a metaphysically absolute value to the attempt "to know" that modernity has come to equate with goodness, virtue, rightness, or even moral superiority. The extension, of course, is that knowledge's opposite, not-knowing, evidences vice, small-mindedness, wrongness, and moral inferiority.

Such pejorative treatment of not-knowing works, in Luria's provocative view, as a form of "obscurantism and oppression" that impedes the integrity of any knowledge pursuit (5). Recent developments in the field of epistemology have taken this view to heart. Increasingly, interdisciplinary scholarship in feminist theory, cultural studies, race studies, and philosophy have begun to interrogate not-knowing—what this literature terms "ignorance"—as an epistemic field that is no mere empty opposite to, but rather complex interlocutor with, epistemologies of knowledge. A basic tenet of such inquiry holds that ignorance is neither a lack nor a unified state, but rather can itself be studied epistemically. Recent scholarship looks at both the methodological questions at stake in ignorance (ways in which one might not know) and the varieties of ignorance one might study (for instance, ignorance as a descriptor of a state of not having access to certain facts or as a descriptor of a refusal of facts that one has been presented with). In short, rather than thinking about ignorance as merely an absence of knowledge, studies that theorize an epistemology of ignorance seek to understand the various presences that not-knowing occupies in our cultural reality. In Robert N. Proctor and Londa Schiebinger's 2008 edited anthology *Agnotology: The Making and Unmaking of Ignorance*, their introduction makes clear that the space not-knowing occupies can be one "made, maintained, and manipulated" in order to strategically maintain doubt or ignorance in a population (what might be seen as akin to the "fake news" brouhaha of the early days of the Trump presidency), but it can also be embraced as part of a strategy of "resistance or moral caution" on the part of the powerful or, fascinatingly, the oppressed (8, 20). In both examples, however, these engagements with ignorance emphasize the social, not objective, sphere in which the production of both knowledge and not-knowing takes place.

Landmark studies of the epistemologies of ignorance have integrated interdisciplinary and intersectional approaches to knowledge in order to construct readings of invested ignorance that expose its conservative, even obstructionist, foundations. For example, the philosopher Charles Mills argues, in his article "White Ignorance" (included, in modified form, in both *Agnotology* and another anthology on not-knowing, *Race and Epistemologies of Ignorance*), that racial hierarchies and racist beliefs are anchored, in part, by a normatively produced ignorance, including the suppression of facts that would counter racialized stereotypes, blindness to racially inflected embodied differences in experiences, and even liberal-identified expressions of color-blindness (Sullivan and Tuana 20–28). This "cognitive tendency" toward ignorance on the part of the hierarchically advantaged toward the disadvantaged is "not the only kind of privileged, group-based ignorance," Mills argues; he goes on to name "male ignorance" specifically as another "doxastic disposition" requiring critical unpacking (22, 23). Likewise, literary theorist Eve Sedgwick has argued that ignorance alongside knowledge plays an essential role in Western legal regulations of sexuality and gender privilege, claiming that "inasmuch as it matters not at all what the raped woman perceives or wants just so long as the man raping her can claim to have not noticed," our laws "privilege at the same time men and ignorance" and that the "male receives careful education" in this confluence (5). Here, both Mills and Sedgwick make clear the odd reality that social configurations help us learn not-knowing just as we learn to know; furthermore, Mills claims, without attention to ignorance's social construction and meaning, we will never be in a position "to reduce or eliminate it" (Sullivan and Tuana 23).

And yet, the reduction/elimination of all types of ignorance cannot be our only impetus to study not-knowing. Not only have scholars started to study epistemologies of ignorance to understand sustained ways in which oppression operates via the use of chosen ignorance *to* injustice (on the part of the oppressor) and enforced ignorance *of* information (on the part of the oppressed), but—and this is key—we have also started to think through the myriad ways in which marginalized subjects have appealed to ignorance in order to resist dominant power structures, carve out spaces of resistance, or simply make their lives more livable. Linda Martín Alcoff argues in her essay "Epistemologies of Ignorance: Three Types" that

> members of oppressed groups also have specific reasons to maintain their own ignorance about the social order; for example, reasons based on the need to maintain civil relations with other people with whom they may have to work, [or] to avoid the emotional distress of having to acknowledge the full weight of one's oppression or the humiliation of one's family members. (Sullivan and Tuana 44)

Alison Bailey's work, "Strategic Innocence," extends Alcoff's insight to explore more robustly the "strategi[c]" "wield[ing]" of ignorance by oppressed groups in order to "gai[n] information, sabotag[e] work, avoi[d] or dela[y] harm, and preserv[e] a sense of self" (77). For an example, she turns to Frederick Douglass's autobiography to explore, as a strategic form of ignorance, the way he describes "play[ing] dumb as a means of gaining information" (88). Such an example—which involves exploiting a form of white ignorance simultaneous to the performance of ignorance on the part of the black person—helps to show the complications that arise when knowledge and ignorance are analyzed with attention to the intersectional identity attributes (race, gender, class, etc.) that condition epistemology in the first place. Ignorance, like knowledge, is not solely a tool of the privileged; indeed, such scholarship begins to explore the way in which strategic not-knowing can work to resist dominant epistemic structures, not merely enforce them.

This is one reason why, although this book's focus is on the relationship between gender and knowledge/ignorance, the readings I turn to in the following chapters explore the various other intersectional strands woven into character representations that affect the ways in which these characters and texts embrace and reject knowledge. For instance, chapter 1 treats immigrant voices alongside middle-class, white ones; chapter 2 focuses upon lower-class women's experiences, both white and black; chapter 3 takes as its subjects lower-middle-class white and Chicana women; chapter 4 focuses upon lower-class, African American women's experiences; and chapters 5–7 primarily focus on white experiences, but the classes of these individuals vary widely. Attention to intersectional analysis also helps make sense of the sometimes-surprising critical reception such characters and texts have received. Thus, though this book demonstrates that individual women of many distinct identities are represented as strategically employing innocence within this period, it also makes clear that the way in which their choices are received—by other characters and by readers alike—are contoured by racial, class-based, and other identity-based biases.[8] Any continuities I trace in tactics of not-knowing across identity lines in these fin-de-siècle and modern women is not, in short, an attempt to flatten their identity differences. Indeed, while work in feminist epistemology has taken as foundational the interdependent nature of knowing, its more radical work has added insights from feminist and gender theory, as well as other intersectional approaches to identity, in order to study not only the power differentials attending knowledge production, distribution, and uptake but also the alternative forms of knowledge that gender bias, combined with other forms of bias, has rendered less visible or credible.[9]

Another avenue for thinking about modes of not-knowing is through the types of knowledge that might be judged too risky, socially, to try to know for *any* modern human, not merely women. For literature enthusiasts, such invocation smacks perhaps of the religious and/or supernatural warnings about knowing that proliferate in early science fiction. Take, for example, Frankenstein's caution to his interlocutors about the hazards that attend the hubristic knowledge-at-all-costs seeker in Mary Shelley's 1818 novel, *Frankenstein, or The Modern Prometheus*. His command to the hearer/reader of his tale to "learn from me, if not by my precepts, at least by my example, how dangerous is the acquisition of knowledge" comes with the simultaneous, almost wistful claim that "the man . . . who believes his native town to be the world" is immeasurably happier "than he who aspires to become greater than his nature will allow" (Shelley 932). Lest we move too quickly to dismiss this representation as the bogeymen of scientific progress (on one hand) or the humanist's corrective to the mad scientist (on the other), I would like to return us to the key insight from which epistemological studies of ignorance emerges: the pursuit (or rejection) of knowledge is, above all, a socially determined value that is neither inherently positive nor negative, but rather gains moral valence from the effects, consequences, and discourse surrounding its pursuit.

To unpack this socially determined aspect of the value of choosing not to know, epistemic treatments of ignorance draw on the work of both feminist and social epistemology; Townley credits both for insights that have been crucial to breaking down the presumed equally and autonomously available good of knowing.[10] Social epistemology in particular takes as foundational the interdependent nature of knowing—we know not within a vacuum but as one in a community of knowers with whom we interact epistemically as well as civically, morally, ethically, and so on. Thus, it follows that any socially inflected ethics of knowing/not-knowing balances the desire to gain new information with an attention to the social impact, both negative and positive, that such new information will have (5). For example, Luria suggests that "genetic research on race difference in intelligence," even if possible to pursue in a manner that avoids reaffirming social biases about race within the study's design itself, might not be worth knowing within a social sphere in which racial equity has been, on the one hand, a desired goal and, on the other, a persistently difficult one to attain (2–3). Such scholarship suggests that it is not merely or primarily our attempts to play God in groundbreaking feats of scientific prowess that we should curb, but rather the seemingly innocuous practices of knowledge acquisition that mask more insidious, systemic harm to those who are already socioculturally disadvantaged.

Of course, we need not be limited to reading contemporary philosophical concepts back onto fin-de-siècle and modern texts; provocatively, the philosophical work in epistemology I reference above cites the nineteenth-century philosophical pragmatist movement as one of its orienting approaches to knowledge. Pragmatism's emphasis on methodology, process, and the discursive, interdependent nature of truth complements the feminist and social investments in revising assumptions about knowledge that make an inquiry like mine possible. This fin-de-siècle philosophical movement is not only useful to *An Ethic of Innocence* because it emerges contemporaneously to the literary texts I treat; it also, at its core, takes on the modern predilection to view knowledge asocially. Pragmatism's social orientation toward epistemology—that it deems "true" or "factual" what is socially, collectively determined to be not *objectively correct* but, instead, *subjectively useful*—might at first appear to be unscientific, anti-intellectual, or wishy-washy—a soft humanism at odds with modernity. Yet if what we mean here by pragmatism's humanism—its acknowledged acceptance of the inextricability of human bias from what we perceive of as reality—remains suspect within a modern purview that has emphasized structuralism, mechanization, and a certain logic of coldness, it would behoove us to note the ways in which Luria, an internationally renowned, respected, and rewarded modern scientist, promotes theories that share in pragmatism's "humanistic" bent.[11] For Luria's framework—one in which "values are not given but chosen, partly consciously, partly unconsciously, and are adhered to or modified or abandoned in the continuing effort of each individual to create a moral identity," one in which "values are only norms for human interaction," and one in which "morality does not exist in a vacuum"—looks, through its emphasis on social interdependence and exchange; values and morals that are contingent and changing rather than absolute and steadfast; and socially determined, continually negotiated sense of "right/wrong" or "true/false," very much like American Pragmatism (1, 4).

Pragmatism has not traditionally been a lens through which we have read literature, which should not surprise; though philosophy has often been used to study literary texts, pragmatism's particular tenets have caused it to sit uneasily within the discipline of philosophy and be viewed, in early pragmatist William James's words, as more of a "method" than a "dogma" (*Pragmatism* 38).[12] Thus, pragmatism has been seen as a philosophy that offers not new ideas but rather new ways of organizing, connecting, and working through old ones, which has meant to certain critics, most notably renowned American pragmatist Richard Rorty, that pragmatism has little to offer to literary critics as they search for ways to understand the stories we continue to turn to and tell (Rorty, *Take* 125). And yet, Rorty's own attention to language, politics, morality, and society within his version of pragmatism indicates some of what the pragmatist method might offer literary critics.[13] More importantly, his essay "Feminism and Pragmatism" (to which I will turn in the book's latter half) compellingly argues that pragmatism is of value for feminists who seek to insist on the social distinctiveness of female experiences within broadly patriarchal cultures, while neither reducing all individual female experiences to a unitary whole nor arguing that patriarchal cultures have oppressed women's essentialized rights.[14] As such, he defends pragmatism's particular use for contemporary feminist criticism that seeks to incorporate post-modern, poststructuralist views of the de-essentialized, fluid, and hypercontextualized self into its purview—aims that many contemporary literary critics concerned with feminist theory share.

Indeed, adding a feminist perspective to pragmatism enables further pluralization and contextualization of the already complicated way in which pragmatism has understood subject positions. Doing work similar to what Cornel West has done in *The American Evasion of Philosophy* (1989) to merge racial politics and spirituality with pragmatism, scholars such as Charlotte Haddock Seigfried, Ann Clark, Heather E. Keith, Marjorie C. Miller, Shannon Sullivan, and James Livingston have begun to write about connections between pragmatist and feminist thought, both historically and contemporaneously (Sullivan, *Living* 171).[15] For instance, in her book *Living across and through Skins*, in which Sullivan uses Dewey's idea of "transactional" bodies to describe the porous, imbricated nature of person-to-person relationships, she outlines some of the major tenets of pragmatism that could lend themselves to feminist analysis. Such potential commonalities include an emphasis on real life or a lived reality, a rejection of a neutral or "God-like" point of view, and an "inclusive and collaborative" style of thinking, writing, and working (Sullivan 5). Pragmatism—which emphasizes the intersubjective, work-in-process nature of "reality"; material, lived experience; and mediation of old and new forms of knowledge—provides one turn-of-the-century model by which readers could take choices not to know seriously without rejecting feminist politics.[16]

Glossing Not-Knowing

All of these more neutral or positively inflected understandings of ignorance as tool or method, drawing from pragmatism, feminist theory, social and feminist epistemologies, and epistemologies of ignorance, help to frame the trope of female choices not to know that *An Ethic of Innocence* studies. This chosen female ignorance, or "ethic of innocence," is not represented uniformly within modern literature and art in terms of the situations in which the choice arises, the types of knowledge refused, or the effects of such refusals, but rather in the means by which not-knowing was deployed to negotiate social dynamics for characters with distinct identity attributes. In other words, the pattern this book traces in fin-de-siècle and modern literature is not in the content but rather the methodology of choosing not to know. I use the term "ethic" to insist that (1) the methods of enacting innocence are multifaceted, containing strategies of forgetting, projecting, fantasizing, lying, refusing, and dreaming, to name a few, and that (2) these methods, like any system of ethics, form a coherent means of approaching one's intersection with reality. As such, a reader must understand that there is nothing essentialized about the innocence I want to discuss, nor do I want to associate innocence primarily with characterological goodness, purity, or religiosity, however socially or personally defined. Indeed, these are the traditional readings of innocence that I would seek to oppose.

Thus far, the theoretical claims I have outlined that structure this book are not particularly literary or artistic. Indeed, the above claims might also be made about persons, as in the fields of epistemology, philosophy, and many disciplines within feminist studies. But two aspects of my approach to not-knowing mark this project as definitively literary. The first is the vocabulary I use to name the form of not-knowing I trace; though my philosophical peers investigate the idea of not-knowing under the terminology of "ignorance" or "agnotology," and though "ignorance" might be a more natural corollary term for knowledge than innocence, I have chosen to use the term "innocence" for its literary and artistic epistemic resonance. One, if not the, dominant arena of knowledge-gender-ethical confluence that the field of literature has invested in is intimate, bodily, worldly, and sexual knowledge. Particularly within the literary-artistic shift between the Victorian and the modern periods, the extent to which representations of women's epistemic participation within the public sphere show them to be fully embodied, sexual beings has dominated our critical conversations about gender within modernity. The historically hallowed representation of "innocent" female literary figures, by contrast, features at once sexual and epistemic purity. Indeed, in the nineteenth century, to be able to speak knowledgeably about one's body and sexuality was tantamount to demonstrating one's sexual experience: chastity was not merely of the body but also of the mind. And yet, the idealized innocence of female minds problematically links women to another nineteenth-century discourse of childhood and innocence. As Robin Bernstein points out, during this century, "sentimental culture had woven childhood and innocence together wholly" (4); this new weave of concepts could be used to not only value but also infantilize the innocent adult female, which was understood all too keenly by some Victorian feminists (such as Frances Power Cobbe) who decried the middle-class Victorian social order, which "ke[pt] its females perpetual children, sexually innocent, financially dependent, adorably helpless" (Nelson 72).[17] By using "innocence" rather than "ignorance" to refer to the state of not-knowing that the female characters I study choose, I mean to make evident this literary conflation between knowing, sexual experience, public-sphere activity, infantilization, and idealized femininity within the Victorian and modern eras. That these concepts are not neutrally applied to all women but rather include significant class, race, national, and other identity-based biases is also key to my project's understanding of the way in which innocence, and its various literary-cultural valences, have been used to value, control, define, and contain women.[18]

The other means by which this book announces itself as a literary-artistic study is through the types of knowledge that I chart female subjects choosing to reject. Some forms of knowing that I study (that one's abusive partner is likely to batter again, for instance) are literary representations of human experience and thus could be studied from a philosophical, psychological, or sociological perspective as well as a literary one. But I am also interested in the forms of literary knowledge that are rejected by the representations I engage: knowledge about newly popular versus outmoded genres, for instance, as well as knowledge of reality versus fantasized alternatives. Here, I study not only the ways characters choose not to know, but also how those who write these representations choose not to know and/or engage in generic formulations that are deemed "ignorant" rather than "knowledgeable." This expansive, even metaphorical, use of knowledge might seem, to some, to be a stretch; indeed, to call sentimental narration in all its maudlin presence a form of not-knowing is potentially strange. But this is precisely the point that epistemologies of ignorance would make about not-knowing in general: that not-knowing is not mere lack; it is, or at least can be, a substantive epistemic engagement on its own. In claiming that an outmoded literary genre within modernity like the sentimental is a form of not-knowing, I am insisting that we look at the content as well as the action of not-knowing in order to study its use-value to modern female subjects.

Alongside characterological and literary rejections of knowledge that would often read as backward or conservative, *An Ethic of Innocence* also treats, in its latter chapters, more radical rejections of knowledge—refusing to "know," for example, that women are people or that maleness and femaleness are inescapable binary opposites. Just as these rejections of knowledge are more radical, some of the texts I turn to that showcase such rejections—suffrage protest, fantasy, and speculative fiction—and their fantasized alternatives to knowledge are not regularly treated as a part of a conservative, feminine archive. And yet the throughline of chosen female innocence, I argue, is there, in both these radical texts and their more conservative kin. Part of the stakes of this project are, thus, to understand what such a continuity means: how these strategies of choosing not to know can be deployed so disparately, what the fantasies are constrained by, and where the conservative might be more risqué than we suppose or vice-versa: what, ultimately, contours and defines a fin-de-siècle female ethic of innocence.

This book focuses its study on literature, art, and critical work from the later nineteenth century (starting in the 1870s/1880s) through the early twentieth century (extending to the 1930s/1940s) on both the British and the American sides of the Atlantic divide. In doing so, I treat a period that has, within literary studies and with the exception of work on new women writers, traditionally been split into studies of the nineteenth century and early twentieth century, or modern, studies, as well as treating together two national traditions that literary studies have tended to keep discrete. Recent developments in the field of literary studies have begun redrawing these boundaries, through long nineteenth-century studies (which treats work at the turn of the century and the first few decades of the twentieth century) and longer views of modernism (that locate the field's beginnings in the midnineteenth century). Exciting developments in scholarship have emerged at the interstices of these temporal and national boundaries; for example, *Recovering the New: Transatlantic Roots of Modernism* (Edward S. Cutler, 2003), *Atlantic Citizens: Nineteenth Century American Writers at Work in the World* (Leslie Eckel, 2013), *American Literary History and the Turn toward Modernity* (Melanie V. Dawson and Meredith L. Goldsmith, 2018), and *Virginia Woolf and the Nineteenth-Century Domestic Novel* (Emily Blair, 2007) each reach across one or both of these traditional divides for their critical thrust. This book joins such efforts to reap the intellectual insights that redrawing canonical boundaries sows. Particularly at the juncture of fin-de-siècle literature and gender studies, a transatlantic approach—for instance, like the one taken by the recent anthology *Transatlantic Conversations* (edited by Beth Lueck, Sirpa Salenius, and Nancy Lusignan Schultz, 2016)—leverages the dialogue between British and American feminisms that was already taking place in the late nineteenth/early twentieth centuries to make legible continuities and tensions beyond the limits of nation. And though the argument this book proposes straddles both nineteenth century and modern literary studies, it couches the chosen innocence it studies as, alternatively, a fin-de-siècle or modern phenomenon—not to segregate this trope from the nineteenth century but rather serve as a corrective to the already-segregated temporalities it seeks to breech.

In the brief reading of James's Isabel Archer—herself a transatlantic creation (as an American transport to England and then Italy)—I have hoped to mark out some of the ways in which Isabel's embrace of not-knowing might signal the unique nature of gendered not-knowing at the fin-de-siècle. To start, Isabel is intelligent and loves knowledge (that is, she is neither stupid, nor does she reject epistemology altogether). Then, too, Isabel reads and questions things (that is, she is not childlike or complacent in her acceptance of the world). And finally, like many "new" or modern women, Isabel seeks independence and values choice (that is, she is concerned with maintaining her freedom and will). In all these ways, Isabel Archer distinguishes herself as a competent, intelligent, and thoughtful—perhaps even modern—subject. And yet, she chooses not to know in specific moments because, for her, to *not know* is what exemplifies happiness when the structures of the world seem to preclude it. The narrative trajectory of this novel is also instructive for my study: our female protagonist moves from choosing not to know in order to negotiate her independence and make her life more livable to feeling trapped, via knowledge, into obeying sociocultural mandates for married ladies that render her miserable. On the cusp of modernity, our "lady" finds herself unable to sustain her practice of not-knowing as an independent, intellectual move; on the contrary, her resistance to knowing is deemed, toward the novel's conclusion, not only futile but also indicative of her "innocent ignorance." And, make no mistake, her gender is of tantamount import: not only is the knowledge she rejects rife with gendered obligation, and not only is the term "innocent" flush with gendered, literary meaning, but—most strikingly—her male beau, Casper Goodwood, endures none of the narrative foreclosure or characterological condemnation for his similar efforts not to know.

No, the kind of knowledge rejection that Isabel Archer so aptly displays in *The Portrait of a Lady* is inseparable from her identity as a turn-of-the-century woman. For, though the female ethic of innocence *An Ethic of Innocence* studies is rife within late nineteenth- and early twentieth-century literature, modernity's representational ideologies—for a variety of reasons I will begin to sketch out below—have disparaged and cast this trope aside as outmoded Victorian residue. Women's choices not to know have been repressed within modern representation—and this study returns our attention to them within modernity: where they have always, even if unknowingly, been.

Not-Knowing as Fin-de-Siècle Story, Gendered Story

In the late eighteenth and much of the nineteenth centuries, the female innocent—so long as she was also white, middle-class, and heteronormative—might have seemed, to observers, to embody a romantic faith, childish hope, and sheltered ignorance to life's harshness deemed essentially (and unproblematically) feminine. A few such touchstone characters (all of whom can be read with greater or lesser levels of complexity) include Madame de Tourvel from Choderlos de Laclos's *Les Liaisons Dangereuses* (1782), Jane Bennet from Jane Austen's *Pride and Prejudice* (1813), Georgiana from Nathaniel Hawthorne's "The Birthmark" (1843), Amelia Sedley from William Thackeray's *Vanity Fair* (1847–48), and the March girls (particularly Beth) from Louisa May Alcott's *Little Women* (1868–1869). More radically, later nineteenth-century texts, such as George Eliot's *Middlemarch* (1871–1872) and Henry James's *Daisy Miller* (1878), often present heroines (again, white, economically comfortable, and straight) who display nascent feminist impulses by refusing to abide traditionalist, masculine-centered knowledge.

For example, Eliot's *Middlemarch* tells the story of main character Dorothea Brooke, an intelligent woman who remains "willful[ly]" blind to the affections of her suitors; instead, she chooses to marry the elderly, pedantic "scholar" Edward Casaubon, who she believes is engaged in great work, a book entitled *The Key to All Mythologies* (35). Once married, however, Dorothea shortly discovers that her husband's supposed great work is nothing but an endless sham of a project, doomed to failure, and that her husband, far from being a great man, is petty and belittling. Nonetheless, she remains loyally by his side, even after she develops romantic interest in another character, the young artist Will Ladislaw. Casaubon, while dying, asks Dorothea to promise to continue with his work in his stead; she puts off answering him, and, before she can agree to his bidding, he dies. After his death, she is able to put aside his instructions, the "Synoptical Tabulation for the Use of Mrs. Casaubon," and go on with her life free from "his cold grasp" (479). Dorothea thus not only literally rejects knowledge by rejecting the key to the scholarly project that she "had no belief in" (521), but she also paves a path by which she continues to reject more socially constructed "knowledge" for the sake of her own happiness. Though Casaubon makes a provision in his will that should Dorothea marry Will, she will lose her inheritance, Dorothea gives up this money and risks her reputation by marrying him anyway. Ultimately, Dorothea's various rejections of knowledge work in her favor; as the text explains it, "[S]he was blind, you see, to many things obvious to others—likely to tread in the wrong places . . . yet her blindness to whatever did not lie in her own pure purpose carried her safely by the side of precipices where vision would have been perilous with fear" (363). Female innocence in *Middlemarch* thus becomes a tool by which such a woman can evade patriarchal and social control.

James's *Daisy Miller*, which tells the story of young American Daisy Miller's flirtatious relationship with (among others) the older, richer, more sophisticated Winterbourne, depicts a similar use for female innocence; however, *Daisy Miller* more clearly depicts the themes of sexual and moral purity at stake in such representations of choosing not to know. In the course of James's novella, many of the main characters argue over whether Daisy's flouting of social conventions in her behavior toward the texts' men is evidence of her "exceedin[g] innocen[ce]" or, rather, shows her to be "a designing, an audacious, an unscrupulous young person" (12). Her seeming "mixture of innocence and crudity" allows her to take liberties, such as spending time alone with men she does not know well, without enduring immediate condemnation from the others in the text, as they are not able to ascertain if she is truly morally reprehensible or merely ignorant (or both) (30).

The novella is careful to suggest, despite the "is she/ isn't she" dialogue it depicts, that Daisy is not merely unknowing. For instance, when Daisy's friend Mrs. Walker tries to get her to mend her ways as she is "old enough to be talked about," Daisy refuses to listen to Mrs. Walker on the basis of chosen innocence: she claims, "I don't think I want to know what you mean . . . I don't think I should like it" (43). Here, though Daisy explicitly chooses to reject "knowing" what Mrs. Walker means, she also exhibits her knowledge about what she chooses not to know; otherwise, there would be no way for Daisy to articulate this knowledge as something that she shouldn't like. Daisy's shrewdness, as depicted in this exchange, is not lost on other characters for long; as the novella's characters come to decide that Daisy merely "played an injured innocence," they also shun her from society (60). Yet at the novella's end, when Daisy turns out to have died, it is society, not Daisy, who seems to be truly condemned by this tragic trajectory. Winterbourne ends by feeling he has "done her injustice"; the final pronouncement upon Daisy, that she was "the most innocent," seems both an ironic comment on Daisy's behavior (that she does, in fact, know what she's doing) and a condemnation of Victorian gendered oppression (that what she does should not, in fact, signal a moral failure at all) (64, 63).

Middlemarch and *Daisy Miller* both present female characters who manipulate and refuse knowledge—who pretend not to know—as a way to negotiate a social environment that they experience as oppressive. As such, these later nineteenth-century female characters' embrace of innocence moves beyond merely accepting a possible feminine posture to seeking opportunities to fulfill personal desires at odds with "proper" femininity. Of course, their successful leveraging is not incidental but rather a product of combined gender disadvantage with other identity-based privileges; as Robin Bernstein's *Racial Innocence: Performing American Childhood from Slavery to Civil Rights* (2011) and Claudia Nelson's *Precocious Children and Childish Adults: Age Inversion in Victorian Literature* (2012) make clear, the attribution of innocence even to children has historically been not merely a gendered but also a racialized and classed phenomenon on both sides of the Atlantic. Certainly, too, the type of epistemic injustice that studies of strategic innocence focus upon would not only help extend Bernstein's concept of racial innocence to discourse on race, slavery, and adult innocence in the nineteenth century, or Nelson's discussion of girls as adults to Victorian-era discourse around child labor, prostitution, and respectability; it would also help clarify the various ways in which the protected types of innocence I have noted above are particularly white, middle-class instantiations. And yet, while the depiction of the nineteenth-century white, middle-class, and straight heroine might have been able to be seen as embracing a feminist agenda alongside her innocence, with the advent of fin-de-siècle feminism, many modern texts that critics have historically dubbed "feminist" instead depict women's increasing access to knowledge and power within the twentieth century's public sphere, an access bolstered by women's newly gleaned rights, in the late-nineteenth and early-twentieth centuries, within the workplace, the university, the marital sphere, and the voting box. Yet this unparalleled access was neither uniform across female identities nor unchallenged by opposition; it did not enact any sure bar against female oppression.

Modern white, moneyed women's increasing ability to enter into the public, heretofore male sphere in educational and professional capacities was met with the public's increasingly hostile response to old forms of "feminine" activity. At the same time, however, these women were also met with a public demand that the New Woman still approximate recognizable femininity. Thus, as literary critic Rita Felski notes in *The Gender of Modernity*, turn-of-the-century feminists embodied a markedly schizoid temporality: suffragettes, for example, dramatized their own sense of alienation from the givenness of tradition while simultaneously "view[ing] the past as a potential source of inspiration and symbolic strength" (166). For Felski, the way in which such women positioned themselves as a part of modernity was always simultaneously opened and limited by such discursive categories. To argue for a positive construction of women's knowledge, both real women and authors at times found it helpful to insist, to some extent, on the power of a traditionally defined female moral innocence. For example, Felski points out that twentieth-century feminist discourses and suffragist rhetoric often had to weave a complicated path between socially accepted roles of the feminine and the revolutionary potential of those same "feminine" women—a path that redefined the knowledge or power women could have while not quite giving up their ties to the home and moral superiority through purity.[19]

Of course, the opening of a new social sphere for women also marked another one's closing: historian Caroll Smith-Rosenberg's "The Female World of Love and Ritual" argues that for many women, the twentieth century "cut short homosocial ties" between women, ushering them into an alienating heterosexual landscape that was less "flexible and responsive" to some women's needs (27, 29). This alienation might also be one of nation, language, age, and/or culture, as is the case with the immigrant women in Chicago at the turn of the century discussed in chapter 1. Many turn-of-the-century female scholars who were hopeful of pursuing academic careers in the changing university landscape found only frustration. As historian Rosalind Rosenberg documents, their "work was celebrated in graduate school," but these women later "could find no academic position in which to carry on their research"; instead, they were pushed out into the still "feminine" spheres of social work and direct action. Indeed, in some ways, as my discussion in chapter 1 will detail, Jane Addams's work at Hull House is a perfect exemplar of the compromised professional life of many modern women: she articulated her space as a type of "civic housekeeping" and "saw much of her work as a translation of the family claim into the world and work of the social claim" (Deegan 232). Meanwhile, the population with which Addams works demonstrates that this struggle to find one's place within modernity is shared by women in a variety of social positions, many of whom lack the comparative sociocultural and economic advantages of Addams.

When modern women do attain more unconditional access to the public sphere, to knowledge, and to the vote (even or especially while still experiencing significant identity-based oppression based on gender, race, class, etc.), it becomes harder to advocate for "innocence" as a viable, feminist subject position. Even if such innocence is akin to an ethic of innocence—performed, nonessentialized—to claim it runs the risk of misreading by those who are unable or unwilling to see a difference between *being innocent* and *opting not to know*. As a result, the fin-de-siècle and modern figures who seem willfully nonknowing that this book treats have been read by critics neither as progressive nor particularly feminist but rather regressive and conservative. In short, we find ourselves occupying a modern textual landscape in which critics and readers show particular discomfort either reading texts that depict women who refuse knowledge through a feminist lens or interpreting such moments as sensible, even powerful, even as they feel comfort with representations of white, middle-class, and straight modern men doing the same thing.[20]

Indeed, representations of women within modernity seem, from the fin de siècle onward, to be newly and narrowly judged negatively for what they do not know in a way that does not mirror the treatment of modern male representations. In Rebecca West's *The Return of the Soldier* (a text to which I will return in this book's final chapter), Chris Baldry suffers shell-shocked amnesia and, as a result, relives his youthful love affair with Margaret Allington, a woman who has gone on in the fifteen years since their liaison to marry and have a life of her own. One might argue that, psychologically, Chris does return to a state of "innocence" that is more childlike—rather than choosing to relive this time in his life, he does so inadvertently through memory loss.[21] Margaret more unambiguously is depicted as choosing not to know and *performing* her own return to innocence to complement Chris's. She knows full well what year it is, that she is married to another man, and that Chris is a soldier who has been wounded in the war. Margaret wishes to remain in this performance, one launched against "the whole hostile reasonable world," but she is not allowed to do so, for the sake of Chris (86). Her "ethic of innocence" is not sustainable because it would make Chris "not be quite a man" (88). Thus, we see that not only is West's heroine (like James's Isabel Archer before her) unable to sustain her ethic, but she must refuse to sustain it in order to protect the man she loves (without attending to her own best interests or desires in the scenario).

Not-knowing:
Feminist Irritant or Surprising Salve?

If fin-de-siècle and modern female not-knowing has disturbed readers and critics alike because it seems like a lack, a blankness, or a stupidity, then this seems to presuppose that these readers and critics think that this lack emerges where there should be an actively knowing, knowledgeable subject. In short, they view women as capable of knowing and are upset when they do not. Yet this has not always been the case. Given the way female characters have frequently been portrayed and viewed as "innocents"—sentimental, child-like, morally pure, or domestic and unworldly—or, when "knowledgeable," deviant or manipulative, often perversely sexual in their manifestations of such knowledge, it is certainly understandable why modern literature that has an interest in seeing women as the equals of men might have turned away from such dichotomous positioning and why most feminist critics might turn away from "innocence" as a viable critical term. For feminists working intersectionally, the viability of something like female innocence is even more fraught, due to the compounding discourses of race, nation, class, and so on, each of which have their own additive biases and stereotypes related to not-knowing.

Critical discourse surrounding modern novels has, indeed, overtly commented on some of these issues of female complacence, compliance, and passivity that have made female innocence so difficult for modern critics to affirm, particularly from an intersectional feminist theoretical perspective. In her analysis of Gwendolyn Brooks's 1953 novella *Maud Martha* (a text I treat in more detail in chapter 2), Karen Iker acknowledges the conundrum that critics with feminist investments have traditionally encountered when treating a text that seeks to work within, rather than to explicitly oppose or challenge, the societal constrictions on the female subject. Iker's focal text for this comment, *Maud Martha*, charts the life story of its title character, a young black woman, in vignettes that expose everyday scenarios of racism and small household joys, juxtapositions that move from daily interactions with her husband and daughter to extreme life incidents such as childbirth and death. Throughout, Maud Martha Brown displays an anger that almost always dissolves into a cheerier affect, a dissolution into optimism that allows her to perceive hope rather than doom in the moments in which she is overlooked due to her skin color by her husband, her family, and others in town. This hope, however, has also resulted in the novella's critical conundrum, even condemnation, since the lead character's cheer presents an innocent face to the harsh realities of a Jim Crow racial landscape and midcentury America's gender discrimination.

Though Brooks's Maud Martha experiences instances of knowing and makes choices not to know that are particular to her race, class, physical beauty, marital status, and historical context, the issues that critics have faced when treating her character's innocence—an innocence marked by her insistent cheeriness, her seeming passivity to racism and sexism, the limited sphere in which she finds happiness—are similar to many other characterological and narrative traits which spark broader feminist concerns regarding female innocence that this introduction has discussed. Iker articulates one potential crux of these concerns in the following manner:

> To determine a domestic hero is to possibly valorize a space and an ideology which has been oppressive to women. How can Maud Martha be a feminist hero in a space which she does not designate, or, in Hortense Spillers' words, in a space which is "the heart of dailiness, or the mundane and the unglamourous . . . [of] carefully circumscribed ambition?'" (96)

Iker's answer, that Maud Martha might be viewed as a feminist heroine by "redefin[ing] what constitutes the heroic," understandably sits uneasily with feminist critics who worry that to read agency and intellect in a figure like Maud Martha *while also taking her happiness seriously* is tantamount to overlooking or even sanctioning the oppressive circumstances of Maud Martha's life (96).

Such happiness displayed by oppressed individuals, and particularly by women, has been viewed suspiciously in modernist literary criticism of recent decades. Though theorists such as Leo Bersani and Lee Edelman provided exciting discussions regarding alternative strategies by which subjects might deploy and enjoy nonnormative bodies, such work often privileges knowledge and experience as the emancipatory root by which normativity is rejected.[22] And though these theorists often privilege "knowing" and knowledge as a more powerful, potentially revolutionary, and certainly nonconcessional mode, the affect that often accompanies such "knowing" is not a happy one; indeed, Michael D. Snediker terms it "queer pessimism" (4). For critics like Snediker and myself, such a tendency within literary-critical analyses of gender and sexuality to eschew happier affective stances in favor of a theoretical "current of enchantment that has privileged 'suffering' and 'dereliction'" has meant that a host of experiences that do not fit comfortably within this current have been either jettisoned from critical discourse or disparaged as anti-intellectual or unrealistic when they are treated (Snediker 4).

In particular, and of note as it arises specifically at the juncture of feminist and queer theory, Lauren Berlant has taken on the issues of conventionality, optimism, and concession in *The Female Complaint*. Here, Berlant critiques, for instance, what she calls femininity's "love affair with conventionality" and its problematic narratives that "keep people attached to disaffirming scenarios of necessity and optimism in their personal and political lives" (2). Berlant understands these attachments—to making due, to finding value in the horrible—as a means by which individual protagonists (often women) can complacently avoid having to rock the status-quo, regardless of how detrimental this status-quo might be to their ultimate emotional, intellectual, and/or material welfare. In Berlant's formulation, the positive affective stance of optimism not only contributes to one's entrapment within a limited mode of reality but also signals one's mental or intellectual inferiority.

The opening pages of Snediker's *Queer Optimism* clearly set up this link between optimism and anti-intellectualism; "in the vernacular," he writes, "optimism often is imagined epithetically as 'premature; as though if the optimist at hand knew all that she might eventually know, she might retract her optimism altogether" (1). The other epithet Snediker points to for optimism is the even less enabling "woeful," for describing one as "'woefully optimistic' . . . implies that the knowledge that would warrant optimism's retraction might never arrive" (1). Either formulation—the optimist as one who does not yet know or who will never know—situates the "innocent" figure as an individual who is not, for some reason, operating at full adult intellectual capacity, one who thus does not deserve serious consideration from readers or critics *as an intellect*. Even in the literary genre most at ease with such formulations of female innocence, the sentimental, critical disparagement or "contempt" has been, according to Faye Halpern, a longstanding, if often unacknowledged, affective mode with which we have engaged such literature (137).[23] This problematic is only exacerbated when turning to other genres in the *fin de siècle*/modern era that (at least purport to) eschew sentimentality.

This book's argument intervenes in the above critical trajectories; Snediker's call for a "reconceptualization of optimism itself" heralds, as does my project, a way of attending to a set of characters, figures, and texts that would necessitate not only a revision of the way in which critical discourse has interpreted these figures and texts but also a revision of the terms of the discourse itself (2). In this way, *An Ethic of Innocence* investigates what has been overlooked when innocence (especially if feminized) is stigmatized as backward or conservative. In doing so, I am well aware that the fear of losing feminist ground by acknowledging both innocence and its incongruous positive affects as a mode cultivated by female characters in order to engage reality rather than as a mode to be avoided for the woman's own sake has both theoretical and material concerns. I do not use this book to dismiss this fear as false, nor do I use it to ignore this fear. Rather, I attempt to show how facing this fear head-on, while still taking women's choices to embrace innocence seriously, can actually put feminist critics in a better (not a weaker) position to challenge the oppressive circumstances to which Iker, via Spillers, alludes.

Eve Sedgwick's landmark *Epistemology of the Closet* (1990) functions as an important forerunner to this study, both in terms of the valuable energy it exerts in outlining the complex relationship between knowledge and sexuality that literature of the late nineteenth and early twentieth centuries traces and in terms of the general stakes in alternative epistemologies—including epistemologies of ignorance—that it evinces. In her introduction, Sedgwick takes to task the epistemology-as-knowledge-only paradigm to which many of us have fallen prey as the "unexamined Enlightenment assumptions by which the labeling of a particular force as 'ignorance' seems to place it unappealably in a demonized space" (7); without examining this assumption-ridden space, Sedgwick argues, we are wont to equate "a political fight" with "a fight against ignorance" (7). In fact, Sedgwick writes, and though we are loathe to acknowledge it, "ignorance and opacity," far from merely opposing or defining knowledge in negative, "collude or compete with knowledge in mobilizing the flows of energy, desire, goods, meanings, persons" (4). In this formulation, Sedgwick opens the same rich space for investigating not-knowing and ignorance as does the study of epistemologies of ignorance for philosophy, albeit fifteen to twenty years after *Epistemology of the Closet* is published. In Sedgwick's colorful wording: "If ignorance is not—as it evidently is not—a single Manichaean, aboriginal maw of darkness from which the heroics of human cognition can occasionally wrestle facts, insights, freedoms, progress, perhaps there exists instead a plethora of *ignorances.*" (8) Countering the dualistic assumption that innocence is knowledge's opposite, as well as and alongside the tellingly primitivist, racist language upon which such problematic simplifications of not-knowing rest (invocations of the "dark ages" before Enlightenment's bright rescue alongside the animalistic "maw" conjoined with and possessed by the racially inflected "of darkness" moniker), is no easy task, and Sedgwick's gesture toward a multitude of ignorances is a potential that her text leaves largely unexamined. Yet it seems worth pointing out that, foundational to this key, literary critical study of the open secret of closeted sexuality within modernity is a basic willingness to set knowledge and ignorance free from their traditional binary moorings. Without ignorance's presence, it seems, we lose our ability to see important contours of modernity, contours that have had not only literary effects but also material consequences on individual lives.

Indeed, one real feminist power of analyzing epistemic choices not to know is that it allows one to study not only a protagonist's response of "making do" but the social structures and communal bargains that police, limit, and make possible whatever options a protagonist has. As Ellen Peel notes in *Politics, Persuasion, and Pragmatism*, "pragmatists' optimism stems from their conviction that we do not always need certainty, for what matters about a belief is not whether we are certain it is true but whether it works well (with 'working' to be broadly construed), helps us cope with the world, and stands the test of experience, of practice" (9). Thus, though the type of pragmatic innocents this book treats have features in common with those Lauren Berlant describes in both *The Female Complaint* (2008) and, more overtly, in her 2011 book *Cruel Optimism*, my formulation is meant to first and foremost expand the range of this pragmatism beyond a repression of the past or an emphasis on optimism's "cruel" effects that describe "compromised conditions of possibility" (24). Many texts I consider demonstrate ways in which memories can be used powerfully as a site of productive social negotiation and change. And while *Cruel Optimism* points to the necessary complications of what might seem a passive tactic like an ethic of innocence—one that, in some instances, replaces revolution with mere survival, if even that—I resist the assumption that "the conditions of ordinary life . . . are conditions of the attrition or the wearing out of the subject" (28); even though, in many cases, this might seem undeniably true, this book also investigates how such ordinary conditions might also be the means by which (not only in spite of which) some women come to generate moments of happiness in lives circumscribed by danger, prejudice, difficulty, or banality. Indeed, I am specifically interested in the innocent fictions pragmatism breeds, fictions that allow individuals to successfully negotiate, even modify, harsh realities.

By studying the trope of female innocence, however, I do not want to stray toward an easy idealization of what I reread; that an ethic of innocence entails costs and possibilities alike will be a foundational understanding of this book. In the pages that follow, I will analyze both emancipatory, hope-filled possibilities of an ethic of innocence and the crucial risks of choosing against knowledge. Thus, when I claim that this volume seeks to map out a means by which critics (feminist and otherwise) could affirm female figures' and texts' embrace of innocence, I walk a fine line: doing this without advocating that women (or the texts concerning them) *should* reject knowledge and without suggesting any simple equation between women and innocence.

An Ethic of Innocence

Each of this book's chapters studies a figure of innocence alongside a particular artistic genre or mode; I take on the aging yet idealistic mother in the context of the mythic fable in chapter 1, the frustrating feminist "failure" in the context of the realist coming-of-age story in chapter 2, the repeatedly battered women in the context of naturalist determinism (chapter 3) and its descendent, modernist pessimism (chapter 4), the objectified women in relation to political performance art in chapter 5, the sex-changing body within fantasy texts in chapter 6, and the female community sustaining others' epistemic innocence from the modern to the postmodern period in my final, concluding chapter. Throughout, I attend to the distinctions that class, race, nation, sexuality, and other identity categories make in their representations.

To best study such figures' dynamism, I compose an archive for this book that pairs canonical and noncanonical works; literature with performance art, film, nonfictional memoir, and political protest; and historic with current feminist movements in order to show the throughline of powerful female choices not to know in otherwise disparate texts. By linking, for example, the primly chaste Victorian social-purity movement (discussed in chapter 3) with the political protest poetry of suffragist Alice Duer Miller (analyzed in chapter 5) or the writings of canonical realist Sherwood Anderson with the radical work of fantasy author Katharine Burdekin (both studied in chapter 6), I show the continuity of epistemic innocence in texts that have been treated by scholars as both "conservative" and "radical," sentimentally antimodern and challengingly avant-garde. I ultimately hope that this volume's generic diversity can provide a means by which scholars, feminist and otherwise, can rethink our assumptions about what makes a "feminist" narrative or a "feminist" attitude toward the *fin de siècle* and/or the modern, to epistemology, and to political and social advancement, precisely by looking at the similarities by which such categorically disparate texts have confronted the possibilities and dangers for modern women who refuse knowledge.

The material included within the body of this book is loosely divided into two halves: the first, focused on instances of what I'm terming "Negotiated Living" and the second on what I am defining as "Pragmatic Fantasies." Though both halves treat characters and texts that engage dreams alongside reality, the emphasis in the first half is on figures and texts that have been treated largely in reference to their conservative, realist, and/or naturalist modes, while the emphasis in the latter half is on texts whose fantastic, avant-garde, and radical elements have more often been the focus of critical inquiry. Chapters 1 through 4, which together form the section entitled "Negotiated Living," analyze primarily innocent *female figures*. Here, I treat nonfiction, memoir, realist, and naturalist texts from the *fin de siècle* and the modern period. I argue that reading these texts for their figures' ethic of innocence can help make clear what pragmatic work non-realist flights of fantasy, gothic grotesquery, feminine perversity, and contradictory, even self-destructive, impulses are doing in these stories.

Chapters 5 through 7, by contrast, extend these largely character-driven readings of the previous chapters to readings that consider epistemic innocence as something that one might see as enacted not only by the characters within a text but also by *the stance of the text itself*. In these chapters, I analyze the "pragmatic fantasies" within performance art, film, fantasy texts, satirical poetry, political protests, and communal ideologies in order to understand, first, what knowledge the fantasy text refuses and, second, how this refusal is still tied to a pragmatic engagement with everyday, "realist" realities. Each of these chapters engages not only with the possibilities allowed by refusing knowledge for an "ethic of innocence," but also with the risks that adhere to this refusal at the turn of the century, which largely sees knowledge as the moral good, innocence (at least in adults) as the stunted inferior.

Chapter one, "A Pragmatist's Dilemma," begins with the unlikely value that Jane Addams, an eminently modern professional who worked to found the settlement-house movement, modern sociology, and feminist pragmatism, placed in her female Hull House clients' investment in a seemingly "unmodern" tale—that of the "Devil Baby." This chapter not only explores the gendered dynamics of pragmatist philosophy but also argues that Addams's textual depictions of the Devil Baby hubbub in *The Long Road of Woman's Memory* (1916) serve as an exemplary pragmatist-feminist reading model; they reveal not the women's ill-founded credulity but rather the story's mythic capacity to covertly correct domestic ills while pragmatically shielding these women from overtly "complaining" about such men. Working from this reading model developed in the first chapter, Chapter 2, "Coming of Age via Critical Complaint," focuses on three modern coming-of-age texts—Edith Wharton's *Summer* (1917), Zora Neale Hurston's *Seraph on the Suwanee* (1948), and Gwendolyn Brooks's *Maud Martha* (1953)—whose protagonists have traditionally proven difficult for feminist critics to read as agential. Here, I work through some of the key objections critics have had to these texts' protagonists while showing how a consideration of epistemic ignorance, in conjunction with intersectional treatments of gender, race, and class, can resuscitate these protagonists for feminist aims.

Chapters 3 and 4 turn away from the hopeful innocent figure and focus on a more horrific counterpart: a woman who chooses not to know her abusive husband will continue to beat her because she expects nothing better or because his violence is understood as a normative aspect of heterosexual love/sex dynamics. Chapter 3, "A Failure of Sympathy or of Narrative?", studies Frank Norris's Naturalist touchstone *McTeague* (1899) within the context of fin-de-siècle feminist antidomestic violence and social-purity activism in order to suggest the historically located ideological means by which these discourses all deflect attention from potential societal critique (regarding what men do to her) to the woman's agency (what she *allows* men to do to her). In doing so, I chart the arc of Trina McTeague's representation within Norris's novel as one that develops from fin-de-siècle jadedness into a more modern expression of female masochism, in line with turn-of-the-century discourses within psychoanalysis and sexology. In chapter 4, "The Legacy of Naturalism, a Cycle of Leaving," I continue this analysis of the female figure who stays with an abusive partner into the modern era, ultimately focusing on Ann Petry's 1946 novel, *The Street*. Here, I argue that Petry's representation of a seemingly irredeemably passive woman, Min, is actually surprisingly complex, as long as we read this character's supposed ignorance as a choice rather than an essential state. In doing so, I counter traditional readings of Min (which allot agency to her only when she chooses to leave her abuser) by demonstrating the strategic negotiations at work in her choice to both leave and stay. Throughout both these chapters, I challenge the limiting feminist master-narrative that deems leaving as the "reasonable" choice, "staying" the wrong or "innocent" one.

Chapter 5, "Are Women People?" marks *An Ethic of Innocence*'s turn from character-specific studies to investigations of authorial stances of "innocence": here, I take on texts that seem not to know or understand the difference between human beings and objects. This chapter focuses on parody, performance, and protest, particularly the moment, in 1914, when suffragette Mary Richardson walked into the National Gallery in London and slashed a painting of an idealized female nude with a meat cleaver. I use not only the coverage of Richardson's act of iconoclasm but also the poetic parodies of Alice Duer Miller's text *Are Women People?* (1915) and the pragmatist philosophies of Richard Rorty and Judith Butler to suggest that the epistemic innocence these texts portray is deployed strategically and argumentatively to suggest that, in ways concerning political/social rights and freedoms, women do not yet quite fit into the protective category "people." And, counter to critics like Amelia Jones who laud performance art for its potential to encourage "intersubjective" exchange, I look to the demeaning and even deadly treatment of imprisoned, hunger-striking suffragette "subjects" like Richardson in order to ultimately wonder not only if women *are* people but also, more radically, if they should be.

Chapter 6, "Making Women, Making Humans," continues to study texts that radically question fundamental elements of modern knowledge: here, dyadic sex. I juxtapose the joyful tone and full-fledged departure from reality in Virginia Woolf's *Orlando* (1928) against two other modern texts—Sherwood Anderson's "The Man Who Became a Woman" (1923), and Katharine Burdekin's *Proud Man* (1934)—that temper their related fantasies of sex change with an acknowledgment of reality's limitations. Ultimately, I argue that the knowing innocence these texts portray is a type of pragmatic fantasy that works to mark not only the extent of its imaginings but also the important work within reality that such imaginings do.

And finally, in chapter 7, "Allowing Innocence?" I meditate, through close readings of Rebecca West's novella *The Return of the Soldier* (1918) and the postmodern film *Lars and the Real Girl* (2007), upon not only the powerful promise of communal acts of not-knowing, but also (and just as importantly) the limitations, risks, and dangers of too quickly assuming that this promise is all that is needed to imagine and then actualize better worlds. This ultimate turn to community serves, on one level, to provide a crucial counter to what might at times seem to readers to be too-hopeful analyses of troubling texts, particularly as I chart the legacy of gendered epistemic innocence in one post-modern instantiation. More importantly, however, the project's conclusion allows me to address the ways in which not only the communities within the texts I treat but also the communities of critics and readers who treat these texts are implicated in these choices for and against knowing.

As a final note before turning to the body of the project, I would like to speak quickly to the largest stakes that I do—and that I do not—claim for this book. By using pragmatism as a way to frame a literary analysis of innocent female figures and texts that have troubled and continue to trouble feminist attempts to read them, I do not seek to emphasize a pragmatic theory of reading that is different from all other theoretical perspectives. Indeed, this seems counter to the pluralistic roots of pragmatism itself. What I do intend to do is, like James, come back to some old ways of thinking; to bring them newly to and into new light; and to order them in a more visible, more meaningful way that can reconcile feminine postures of not-knowing within the modern era with feminist theoretical and political aims.[24] My interest in doing so is not only scholarly but also deeply personal. As a feminist critic with strong commitments to intersectional analysis, I have found and still find much that troubles me in the portraits of female innocence that this book treats. For instance, the phenomenon of women tolerating or celebrating abuse at the hands of their husbands strikes me, just as it strikes many of the critics that my project critiques, as immensely off-putting and disturbing. Yet via an ethic of innocence, I am able to recognize that my disturbance—my insistence on wondering why women stay with men who abuse them—often focuses on questioning these women's efforts to survive in a way that ultimately fails to hold the husbands accountable for their violation.

In this brief example, and in this book in general, I am not suggesting that an epistemic treatment of innocence can provide any easy or sure-fire answers to literary critics, particularly those working on issues of representation of gender in the modern period. Indeed, these questions of choosing not to know, or of ignoring knowledge, have become particularly fraught in our contemporary American and global context, in which appeals to "fake news" and "alternative facts" have allowed real, material harms to individual bodies to be dismissed, ignored, and disappeared. However, the questions that reading with an openness to the category of ignorance allows one to raise—the assumptions about and normative limits of knowledge it allows one to investigate—do, I insist, earn the study of not-knowing a place within the toolbox of literary analysts. Indeed, I think its permanent presence there has a crucial function: to impede us from accepting an absolute ethics of knowledge at any or all costs, and to prevent us from adhering to our literary interpretive stances, whatever they may be, too complacently.

PART ONE

Negotiated Living

Chapter One

A Pragmatist's Dilemma

The Collusion between Myth and Reality in the Tale of the Hull House Devil Baby

> Calling something "superstition" means declaring the currency to which it belongs worthless. Used among equals, the word expresses tolerance for illogical foibles; given a racist or sectarian edge, however, it can mark an unwillingness to consider those to whom it is applied as fully human.
>
> —Angela Bourke, *The Burning of Bridget Cleary* (153)

In 1913, as Jane Addams recalls, three Italian women burst into Chicago's Hull House and demanded to be shown an infamous guest the settlement house was supposedly sheltering: the Devil Baby. Though Hull House residents adamantly denied the child's presence, the three women refused to believe them, since they "knew exactly what he was like": in addition to his "cloven hoofs," "pointed ears," and a "diminutive tail," the creature was able to speak upon birth, indeed to be "most shockingly profane" (Addams 2–3). Yet this colorful description failed to secure them a sighting of the child, even as Hull House's denial failed to counter the women's certainty that the Devil Baby both existed and lived at Hull House.

This mutual impasse turned out to be but a portent. Over the next six weeks, Addams writes, "from every part of the city and suburbs the streams of visitors to this mythical baby poured in all day long and so far into the night that the regular activities of the settlement were almost swamped" (3). Addams claims that for days, she could overhear Hull House staff fielding scores of calls that sought confirmation of the baby's existence and queried the admittance fees and visiting hours for the presumed Devil

Baby "exhibit" (5–6). Origin stories varied along ethnic lines: in the Italian version of the myth, the Devil Baby is the product of paternal blasphemy. Here, a pious Italian girl wed an atheist husband, who, while removing a holy picture his wife had hung in their home, claimed he would prefer "a devil in the house to such a thing"—never assuming, one supposes, that his wish would be actualized via his own progeny. In the Jewish variant, another ill-tempered husband blasphemously states his preference for the devil's presence over his current reality, though in this case it is the potentially female fetus with which his wife, mother of six girls already, was currently pregnant that brings on this comparison. Despite these ethnic variations, it became clearer with every inquiry that each individual's certainty that the child was real depended on his or her knowledge of a particular descriptive story with a core similarity: some bad behavior on the part of the husband toward his pregnant wife that led to the couple being cursed with a devil child in lieu of a human infant.

That the variations on the core Devil Baby story were often divided along ethnic lines suggested to Addams that what she deemed an "old wives' tale" has its roots in already existent folklore and mythology and indeed "might have been fashioned a thousand years ago" (4). Yet the oldness of this particular tale lends suspicion rather than gravitas to its contemporary utility. Indeed, Addams disparages some of the baby-seeking throng's intelligence, arguing that such a strong response to what was tantamount to a fairytale gave evidence of the "thousands of men and women in modern society who are living in a corner of their own, their vision fixed, their intelligence held by some iron chain of silent habit" (5). Fittingly for a tale as flimsily substantiated as a rumor, the transmission of the Devil Baby story took place via "the old method of passing news from mouth to mouth" rather than through the press's more accredited and publicly sanctioned versions of intelligence transmission. In this damning portrait of antimodern, sentimental attachment as an ignorance stubbornly clung to within the modern world, the "primitive" individual (again, Addams's term) who inquires after something like a devil child possesses a mind enslaved by tradition rather than a mind that is allowed to flourish in "the tremendous tonnage of current writing," for (so the logic goes) no one exposed to the light of modern reason or publishing would give credence to a story as absurd as the devil manifesting himself in the form of a baby (5).

Despite Addams's admission that "visitors to the Devil Baby included persons of every degree of prosperity and education," by concentrating her retelling of the incident on the visitors identified by ethnicity who lacked formal education, Addams contrasts the modern, intellectual purview of her settlement house (a Progressive Era darling) with the limited, emotion-driven perspective of the unmodern clients her establishment served. And yet, in this same period, Addams began to grapple more fully with the realization that the Devil Baby hubbub might bespeak more than mere myth. First, an easy dismissal of the stream of visitors to Hull House is made difficult by Addams's recognition of these "primitive" people's potentially serious investment in the tale. While Addams strongly condemns those individuals who seem to seek out the Devil Baby as spectacle or entertainment alone (claiming she "quite revolted against" their "vapid" curiosity seeking), she has an opposite response—indeed, an attraction—to those who viewed the child as a potential site of knowledge, regardless of how old fashioned such a perspective was (7). For "such primitive people," Addams notes, "the metaphor [of the Devil Baby] is still the very 'stuff of life'" (5).[1]

In this sentence, Addams' understanding of the story—a metaphor, a myth—meets and struggles with the rumor's popular understanding: a real manifestation of an old story tantamount to the "stuff" or essence of "life itself." Addams adopts the social scientist's observational tone that creates distance between herself and the people she studies, positioning herself as an intellectual attempting to unearth the crumb of reason in a wild bit of gossip. Not a surprising rhetorical move (Addams self-identified as a sociologist and even published one of the first versions of her account of the Devil Baby incident in a journal of sociology), her condescension regarding the intellectual practices (if not potential) of Hull House's clientele clearly marks these "primitive" persons as the object of her more sophisticated study. Her tone also, however, suggests these folks are *worthy* of study, putting her in a position to learn and glean knowledge from the myth's popular importance. Addams's attitude toward the "primitive" people that she serves—one that values even as it belittles, or vice-versa—might at first appear to anticipate some of the intellectual negotiations that later modernist interest in the primitive relied upon. However, whereas modernists often sought to remedy aspects of modernity gone awry via recourse to "primitive" values, Addams's inquiries into the primitive seem ultimately to concern the productive entwinement of the two.

As Addams finds the tale's popular import demands her attention, if not respect, she gives particular attention to the influx of old women who seem transformed through their interest in the Devil Baby into "alive and eager" beings (7). Addams is unable to reject these women based on either the Devil Baby's certain fictionality or her own tendency to renounce the brouhaha as evidence merely of the intellectual enslavement of Chicago's disenfranchised. Instead, she describes herself as being "irresistibly interested" in the "high eager voices" of these old women, so much so that she habitually dropped her work and "left anything [she] might be doing in order to listen to them" (7). The mysterious power these women held over Addams due to their expressions of belief in the Devil Baby's authenticity does not merely spark Addams's sociological interest; in a very real way, their pursuit of the Devil Baby spawns Addams's own complicated belief—one she attempts to chart throughout the first half of *The Long Road of Women's Memory* (1916)—that there is wisdom to be gained regarding the way in which women's memories and voices work through a serious consideration of what might at first seem fantastical, ridiculous, and distinctly unmodern.

In short, Addams's evolving rationale for valuing the insights of the women seeking the Devil Baby is one that morphs over the course of *The Long Road of Woman's Memory* from the moral grounds of mutual respect to the epistemic grounds of alternative knowledge production purchased, ironically, at the price of not-knowing. Through this consideration of the unlikely value placed by the eminently modern, professional Addams on this old wives' tale—and on the old wives who tell it—I will argue that we can find an exemplary pragmatist-feminist reading of an ethic of innocence, one that reveals not women's ill-founded credulity but rather a story's mythic capacity to intervene in domestic and social ills. Both temporally and ideologically, critics often situate Addams at the threshold of modernity; her work looks both backwards and forwards, exhibiting ties to both nineteenth-century femininity and twentieth-century new womanhood. Using literary-critical insights to attend to the gendered dynamics at work in Addams's engagement with the Devil Baby tale, I will suggest why this reading model, this feminist-pragmatism, and this valuation of the fantastical, ridiculous, and unmodern both allows Addams a means to value the tale and prevents this valuation from seeming to offer much to modern readers. Both Progressive Era endeavors and the stories we've told about this era via literary history have foregrounded developmental narratives; as such, an analysis of Addams that instead privileges her teleological resistance is primed for exclusion.[2] In addition, Addams's narrative techniques, writings, and modes of exploring "knowledge"—her ability to not only tolerate but also find value in what is, explicitly, an old wives' tale—engage what modern literature has stereotyped as "feminine" and ready her gender-inflected pragmatism for mainstream dismissal.

Thus, I will argue that it is not Addams's ideas themselves, but rather their root in female individuals/minds and expression through what is, at least in part, seen as "feminized" prose, that both the early pragmatists and a modern critical landscape found questionable.[3] In her treatment of the Devil Baby tale, Addams not only overtly analyzes the ways in which women experience, remember, and give meaning to their gendered realities but also uses the tale to think through the limitations and power of her own "threshold" position. In doing so, Addams offers a specifically gendered understanding of her position as a turn-of-the-century writer—not quite Victorian, not quite modern—that relegation to either nineteenth or twentieth-century norms occludes. Her equal investment in both new, modern possibilities for women and old, explicitly feminine forms of knowledge is not only, I argue, one reason she's been largely ignored by canonical pragmatism; it also provides us with a model of feminist recovery that, far from objectifying the products of its "recovery" as relics of the past, demonstrates the contemporary sociopolitical needs and possibilities that can only be understood and addressed through a pragmatic turning backward.

Progressive Blinders and Settlement Tensions

It may seem counterintuitive that Jane Addams, the impassioned early advocate of universal education and cultural exposure for even the most economically destitute, would not only entertain but also find value, even power, in the superstitious fiction of a "Devil Baby" running rampant in Hull House halls for a six-week period one year. After all, as a co-founder (in 1889) of the Chicago settlement house, Jane Addams worked at the forefront of the Progressive Era's social reforms.[4] These reforms, of which the settlement-house movement was a part, were ushered in by the industrial revolution's urban development and immigrant influx that contributed to the immense economic, social, and environmental changes in American society between the end of the nineteenth century and World War I.[5] Such settlement houses, despite having been explicitly created to assist and address the needs of the urban working class, often functioned, as Shannon Jackson notes, as simultaneously "a symptom, reaction, haven, and self-styled antidote" to the ever-shifting ground that was Progressive Era America (Jackson 4).

The settlement-house movement, in which philanthropically minded middle- and upper-class Americans relocated themselves from their comfortable surroundings in order to live and work amid the working-class poor, enjoyed great popularity in the fin-de-siècle United States, though it in fact started oversees in London, England. Five years after she visited the original settlement house, Toynbee Hall, during a European tour, Jane Addams—a young, unmarried, educated, and economically advantaged woman—partnered with her friend-cum-lover Ellen Gates Starr to create an American settlement house based on its model. Even from its inception, gender was a hallmark distinction between the two: while Toynbee Hall provided a university- and religiously affiliated experience in "Christian Socialism" for male graduate students to live near and work firsthand with the poor, Addams and Star's Hull House began without university or religious affiliation and as an all-female endeavor (Addams, *Twenty*, x–xi). Though its gender-exclusive foundation would be short-lived, Hull House remained a largely female-led space throughout its first years of existence.[6]

The female-centric space of Hull House must have appeared to some to be in keen contrast with its working-class environs. Based in the old Charles Hull mansion on Chicago's Halsted Street, the area at the turn of the century was impoverished; home to immigrants from Ireland, Germany, Russia, Italy, and Poland; and "lined with dingy saloons, pawnshops, and—on the side streets—houses of prostitution" (Addams, *Twenty* xii). The settlement house offered classes for adults and children in sewing and other handiworks, as well as social and practical clubs for all ages; eventually, it housed "an art museum, a theatre, a music school, [and] a gymnasium" (66–69). The house was designed, Addams explained, to provide opportunities for the poor of the neighborhood to play, act, draw, and dance, as well as to furnish companionship and shelter for the lonely, unemployed, pregnant, and even those "on the run" (Addams, *Twenty* 66–69, xii).

Despite Addams's insistence that Hull House was "opened on the theory that the dependence of the classes on each other is reciprocal," the reality of Hull House demonstrates both the democratic idealism and problematic hierarchical bias endemic to many such Progressive Era reforms: projects where individuals earnestly sought to help the less advantaged without fundamentally challenging the class structures that maintained such disadvantage and that, in historian Rivka Shpak Lissak's words, "assigned the working class [and immigrant population] a passive role in American society" in relation to their so-called helpers (Addams, *Twenty* 59; Lissak 23). Further, the settlement-house movement's emphasis on "cultural" reform is critiqued by Lissak and others, such as Mina Carson, as assimilationist.[7] According to Louise W. Knight, this led to a system in which "the settlement was potentially conservative and radical, condescending and democratic, all at the same time" (86). No mere social service initiative, the settlement-house movement can be viewed as a historical barometer of the aims and limits of a progressive, democratic, but ultimately nonradical scene.

Addams and the Hull House project have been criticized along similar lines; tensions within the era (broadly) and the movement (specifically) can be seen in Addams's conflicting treatment of those seeking the Devil Baby as both primitively gullible and also authentically interesting.[8] Angela Bourke, a scholar of oral culture and literature, characterizes the Progressive Era somewhat more polemically: "[T]he progressive mind of the late nineteenth century advocated a ruthless hygiene that would exterminate—or at least remove from use by potential subversive—everything not dreamt of in its own philosophy" (189). Superstitions, rumors, and stories of mythological creatures such as fairies and changelings were the type of concepts exterminated, according to Bourke. Perhaps, one might suggest, this makes Addams's engagement with the Devil Baby tale typical rather than exceptional. I will argue, however, it is precisely Addams's tension-filled, but ultimately serious investment in analyzing the complicated, emotional, and very intellectual ways in which the Devil Baby tale sustained individual Hull House clients that marks her unique orientation toward her clientele, on one hand, and that exposes her *own* complicated subjectivity as a turn-of-the-century professional woman, on the other. Put another way: if Addams is an exemplar, it is as a model of a particular turn-of-the-century gendered and epistemic engagement with pragmatism and narrative, one that is difficult to appreciate within traditional temporal and canonical distinctions.

For instance, the list of Hull House services—classes, clubs, and recreational facilities—might, at first, seem to support Addams's critics, especially if we read these services unidirectionally: drawing on the moneyed to benefit the impoverished. In fact, though, the opposite dynamic can be seen in Addams's articulation of the original idea for her settlement house:

> I gradually became convinced that it would be a good thing to rent a house in a part of the city where many primitive and actual needs are found, in which young women who had been given over too exclusively to study might restore a balance of activity along traditional lines and learn of life from life itself; where they might try out some of the things they had been taught and put truth to "the ultimate test of the conduct it dictates or inspires." (55)

While the neighborhood's perceived and actual needs give Hull House its purported reason for being, what is most intriguing about Addams's articulation above is that the primary benefactors of Hull House are not the needy neighborhood residents. Instead, what comes to the foreground are the needs of the "young women"—women, we must suspect, like Addams herself—who require the practical and real-life benefit of settlement-house work to test, validate, and expand their book-heavy educations.[9] Here the "primitive" needs of a people, whose later excitement about a Devil Baby would result in them, too, being labeled by Addams as primitive, are aligned (once again) with "life itself," in a position privileged in relation to those young women who have yet to learn about this "life" and the type of truth with which it aligns. Noting Addams's rationale for the Hull House project does not exonerate her from charges of exhibiting elitism or patronizing the poor in her charity work; what it does do, though, is question her employment of a "benevolent" handout model as the primary means by which this elitism and patronizing took place by focusing on her project's selfish interest in how the poor could help members of her own social class. In fact, it might be more accurate to think of the charitable purpose of Hull House as one that was initially theorized as of benefit to the wealthy rather than the poor.

Thus, in a very basic way, the Hull House project was, from its inception, entwined with education and a sense of mutual dependence between residents and clients, rich and poor. In the early years of the settlement house's existence, its residents—most notably Alice Hamilton, Florence Kelley, Alzina Stevens, and Julia Lathrop—quickly expanded upon a theoretical articulation of this mutuality by bringing more expansive, radical, and egalitarian ideas of democracy with them. These women significantly augmented Hull House's interdependent model. Seigfried notes, "Addams credited Julia Lathrop with helping her realize that she [Addams] should not set the agenda for Hull-House but instead should meet the needs of the neighborhood" (78). Relatedly, Florence Kelley pushed Hull House toward its eventual status as a site for broad social reform by engaging politically in the Hull House neighborhood; she actively campaigned against child labor throughout her Hull House residence and, in 1893, was appointed to a four-year governmental position of chief factory inspector for Illinois (Bryan 23). As time went on and the neighborhood residents became more trusting of the Hull House residents' desire to listen to the neighborhood's needs, new services were introduced. Bryan and Davis note that "there was a need for a kindergarten, so [Hull House residents] started one," they "invited labor unions to meet at the house," and they "organized a cooperative residence for working girls" (6). Mary Kenney, a union organizer from the neighborhood, noted not only her skepticism about Addams's motives upon first meeting her, but also her quick revision of this attitude when Addams inquired about her union work and asked, "Is there anything I can do to help your organization?" (Bryan 22). With such a simple question engaging Kenney's passions and not her own, Addams proved her commitment to reciprocal and interdependent, rather than assumption-laden and unidirectional, reform.

Thus, the community-centered, experience-based methodology that Hull House residents both used to run their home and offered as a possible model to other settlement-house programs, educational movements, social theorists, and philosophers more generally found its core agenda in a "reject[ion] [of] top-down patrician political reform" (Seigfried 78). Instead, by first investigating the community's own sense of its needs and afterwards designing Hull House programming to address those needs, Addams and the house's other residents advocated a reform model through not only their theorization but also their direct community work that privileged mutually constructed political action, a reform model that "provided a means not just of understanding experience but of transforming it" (Seigfried 78). This pragmatic emphasis on community participation and ever-changing contexts was a key contributor to Hull House's longevity and continued relevance to Chicago's urban poor.

Pragmatist Principles and the Genres of Jane Addams

In the same decade that Hull House and the University of Chicago were founded, the discipline of "academic sociology," according to Thomas L. Haskell, began to systematize and professionalize what had until then been social science's "eclectic and diffuse" work to connect individuals, address experience's subjectivity, and promote volunteerism (191). As a discipline, sociology took shape in response to the same societal changes and debates about social progress to which the settlement-house movement and other Progressive Era reforms were indebted (Calhoun 10). Haskell argues that a key feature of social science's early work was an implicit acknowledgment of society's increasing interdependence; this interdependence, however, was not "captured . . . in thought" until "the young scholars of the 1880's and 1890's . . . put it to use in an energetic if unsystematic way as an analytic tool" (252).

Haskell's key exemplar of these young scholars is John Dewey, the man he calls "the preeminent philosophical spokesman for modern social science" and, through sociology, societal interdependence (253). Indeed, Dewey and fellow academics George Herbert Mead and Albion Small were key contributors to what Craig Calhoun calls "America's single most influential sociology department" at the University of Chicago (14). Founded by Small as the university itself was founded, the diversity of the involved faculty's professional specializations led to this department combining "philosophy," "the history of social thought," "social reform," "Christian socialism," and "ideals of ethically informed action"—a litany that speaks to the new discipline's focus on interdependence, even at the level of its own professional makeup (Calhoun 20). What Calhoun calls "an enduring question for sociologists since the discipline's founding"—that of what the relationship should be between scientific study and social action—was, at least at the Chicago department's inception, a lesser issue; all of the men listed above, as well as others, were active at Hull House (17). Addams herself, though not an academic, was active in the discipline of sociology; her published works were regularly reviewed in the *American Journal of Sociology* (*AJS*), and she even published five articles in that journal. Rosalind Rosenberg writes that Jane Addams was so frequently at the University of Chicago that she "became a virtual adjunct professor in sociology" (33). Many of these same individuals, including Addams, Mead, and—most prominently—Dewey would also contribute to the burgeoning field of philosophical pragmatism.

Pragmatism in general and Addams's own pragmatic work more specifically insist, like sociology, "that knowledge is given in social rather than individual experience" (Calhoun 189). Indeed, the centrality of social interdependence to both one's experience of reality and the production of knowledge is a key component of pragmatism, as is an emphasis on material, lived experience as opposed to metaphysical contemplation. For example, founding pragmatist Charles Sanders Peirce suggests evaluating ideas not by so-called objective criteria, but rather by their ability to be understood and accepted by a community (Thayer 79).[10] John Dewey would most famously extend Peirce's articulation of the social origin of philosophical knowledge production with his theory of transaction; however, as early as 1917, Dewey argues that experience, rather than being simply a unidirectional "knowledge-affair," is "assuredly" an "affair of the intercourse of a living being with its physical and social environments" (*Philosophy* 61).[11] Like Hull House's movement from unidirectional philanthropy to mutually constructed reform agency for both Hull House clients and residents, Dewey articulates a philosophical shift in which interdependence complicates a simplified view of reality, the simple view that emanates from what Dewey terms the "ancient spectacles" of unchanging subjects who only *acquire* knowledge (*Philosophy* 61).

Pragmatism's rejection of traditional models of knowledge production (including discipline-centered ones), keyed to its methodological stance of interdependence, positions it sympathetically, at least theoretically, toward feminist epistemologies. Seigfried writes that "it is axiomatic to both feminism and pragmatism that knowledge is developed interactively among communities of inquirers and given conditions" (4). Historian James Livingston even goes so far as to claim that the early pragmatists' epistemic challenges to the traditional philosophical epistemology that privileges a disembodied, rational mind/subject "was in effect a challenge to male supremacy" (71). As well, Hull House itself provided an epistemological model that the early pragmatists found useful, even essential to their own work. For example, John Dewey cites his use of "Hull-House as his 'working model'" for his own ideas and even dedicated his Liberalism and Social Action (1935) "To the Memory of Jane Addams" (Seigfried 77, 45). As well, William James designated Addams's first book (*Democracy and Social Ethics* [1902]) as "one of the great books of our time"; this same book was taught by Dewey to University of Chicago students and even resulted in Addams guest-lecturing for him on its contents (Seigfried 228).[12] And yet, Addams's influence on these pragmatist philosophers is largely discussed only in scholarship on Addams, not within work on Dewey and James. One might reasonably wonder: if pragmatism is sympathetic to alternative forms of knowledge and feminist agendas, and if it even draws upon Addams's own work for its incipient theorization, why have Addams's written works on such alternative epistemic models been largely dismissed from pragmatism's canon?

In important ways, pragmatism itself both enables and inhibits Addams's intellectual import. In particular, one of pragmatism's key tenets—the close tie that pragmatist philosophy, despite its future orientation, maintains to the past—sets the stage for writers like Addams to fail to be received in a like manner to their "masculinized" peers. "New truths," William James writes, "are resultants of new experiences and of old truths combined and mutually modifying one another" (103). Elsewhere, he notes that a new idea "preserves the older stock of truths with a minimum of modification, stretching them just enough to make them admit the novelty, but conceiving that in ways as familiar as the case leaves possible" (41–42). Jane Addams is not the only pragmatist, then, to notice the specter of the "old" in the modern era; James, too, notes that "the most primitive ways of thinking may not yet be wholly expunged" (104). Such hopes of productive intertwining between past and present, however, are hampered in Addams's case not by virtue of the "oldness" of the tales she values but by the gendered form this knowledge takes. The "old" ideas to which James draws pragmatic continuity tap into a tradition of philosophy that retains a respected, even privileged, place in an intellectual lineage. By contrast, Addams—as a woman who values women's myths and makes use of "feminized" forms within her written work—retains access to "old" ideas that are stigmatized in a modern landscape by virtue of their connection to an outmoded nineteenth-century femininity.

Indeed, by looking at Dewey's and James's methods of valuing Addams, we might notice a problematic trend, in which Addams is narrowly relegated to feminized modes of knowing and contributing. Such troubling relegation to the feminine most clearly appears in Seigfried's discussion of a review William James wrote of Addams's book *The Spirit of Youth and the City Streets* (1907). James writes, "[Addams] simply *inhabits reality*, and everything she says necessarily expresses its nature. She *can't help writing truth*" (qtd. in Seigfried 135, original emphasis). Regarding this quote, Seigfried argues that while this is at once "highest praise from James," the man who sought throughout his life to reach a "oneness with reality" through "rational means," it is simultaneously a means of "appropriat[ing] women's insights by transforming them into masculinized rational discourse"—namely, privileging women's power to experience but also necessitating the interpretive power of men (135). I would additionally note that here, while James is reviewing a book written by Addams, his comments pertain not to her intellectual or theoretical contributions but rather to her embodied state, her ability to *inhabit* truth and reality, as though the words she writes come to exist mystically through the vehicle/mediator of her body and not through the reasoned thoughts born of her reflections on experiences she has had. Thus, an older idea of the woman as exemplar of nature, the nonthinking being, infiltrates and even overtakes the review, even as James seeks (even potentially believes) to compliment a woman he admires. In this light, Dewey's dedication to Addams reads as suspect even before later, critical versions of the text erase it. By dedicating his text to Addams's memory, rather than to Addams herself or to a particular text she had written, Dewey essentially claims ownership over Addams, mediating her through his own mind and thereby claiming the right to use and articulate her according to his own intellectual needs.

It is only by recognizing the distinctly gendered expressions of past forms of knowing that we are able to understand why certain modes of pragmatist temporal-epistemological mediation were championed as ideally modern while others, such as Addams's, were dismissed and relegated firmly to an uneducated, unmodern, feminine past. In doing so, we can better ascertain why not only Addams but also the forms of "old knowledge" she writes within and about have been largely excluded from pragmatism's purview. For while Siegfried's work uses Jane Addams as an example of the ways in which female pragmatists, by virtue of the limitations they encountered due to their embodied sex, have been excluded from the canon, I am more invested in the epistemic dimensions of her exclusion. If pragmatism is able to work as a "mediator," "reconciler," and methodological go-between because, as James Livingston rearticulates from William James, "it accommodate[s] both past and future by mediating between previous truths and novel facts," then this tendency to both "annu[l] and preserv[e]" does female pragmatists like Addams a disservice in the modern critical landscape (James, *Pragmatism* 53; Livingston 7, 9). Pragmatism's accommodating tendencies acknowledge women's ability to contribute intellectually and professionally to cutting-edge theoretical positions; simultaneously, however, these tendencies help to disavow women's ability through recourse to older models of femininity which value women's ability to *be* rather than to *think* (one kind of epistemic injustice) and which connect to gendered narrative modes that were also, in the Progressive Era, viewed as backward-looking (yet another form of unjust epistemic exclusion).

As nineteenth-century literature's generic emphasis on the sentimental and Gothic gave way to new genres like realism, naturalism, and eventually, modernism, these earlier generic modes were dismissed. Not simply outmoded, they were also denigrated as particularly feminized genres to which the newer, more masculinist genres served as a corrective. Michael Davitt Bell, for instance, argues that America's preeminent advocate of realism, William Dean Howells, defined that genre through "a denigration of 'style' in the interest of 'truth' " in large part in order to "obscure" an image of the writer as a feminized artist divorced from the "world of men's activities" (21, 33, 34). The literary success of writers' attempts to compromise between older, feminized forms and newer, masculinized ones was further hampered by the instability of the binaries that divided the old from the new, and thus the feminine from the masculine. As Suzanne Clark notes in *Sentimental Modernism*, these divisions are created "again and again—not as a continuity but in a series of repetitions" (19). In Clark's view, the "feminized 'other' discourse" is repeatedly reinscribed on older literary forms that obscure earlier generic distinctions; she argues, for instance, that while "romanticism [originally] arose as an opposition to a feminized sentimentality," modernism later "constituted itself by conflating the romantic with the sentimental and the popular" (19). This oppressive history—in which the location of the threshold might shift but the association of privilege with the male never alters—demonstrates that, for modern women, the struggle to "unsettle the terms of the cultural gendering which oppressed them" while still retaining ties to a sense of history and tradition was not only a cultural struggle, but also a generic one (38).

Recent scholarship on Addams's writing has begun to focus on the multiple and varied generic traditions that she made use of in her books and essays. Viewing these literary-critical arguments within the cultural/generic struggle outlined above helps us understand why Addams was so easily dismissed as a writer and a thinker by her contemporaries. At root, these critics argue that Addams strategically manipulates genre, obscuring her philosophical and sociological investments by employing the "feminized" prose her readers would find most palatable. Though Addams published eleven books and hundreds of articles during her lifetime, almost all critical treatments, literary or otherwise, of her written work focus on the first of her autobiographies, *Twenty Years at Hull-House* (1910). And in this body of criticism, scholars have critiqued Addams's use of genre to de-emphasize her defiance of gender norms and normalize her chosen professional life. For instance, Heather Ostman argues that Addams's use of the "sentimental daughter" trope in her autobiography—the loyal, obedient, ever-loving domestic daughter—is a "textual persona [that] embodies nineteenth-century constructions of womanhood," which allows Addams to "ingratiate [her] autobiographical persona with [her] audience and to persuade [her] readers to support [her] social activist causes" (60, 61). This ingratiation, however, necessarily masks Addams's lack of follow-through in regard to this trope; though she may depict herself as a sentimental favorite, an obedient daughter who loves and honors her father through the ethics by which she lives her life, Addams refuses the transfer of her dutiful affection to another male figure when she never marries and instead remains as a public-sphere worker for the duration of her adult life. Debra Hotaling also speaks about Addams's manipulation of sentimental tropes, though she does so by discussing *Twenty Years* through its rhetoric of illness.[13] She argues that Addams emphasizes the connection of her personal illness to her work in order to sublimate her ambition and portray her work as therapeutic. As such, Hotaling claims that Addams was "able to circumvent the criticism which would inevitably surround a woman writing her own life story" (38). These two critics provide ways of understanding Addams's seemingly nineteenth-century rhetoric as the politically savvy vocalization of a New Woman. At the same time, however, they also suggest the ways in which this savvy can be ignored by readers who are entrenched in the ideologies of traditional femininity that the sentimental genre employs.

The genre of Addams's writings, much like the person of Addams, is deeply divided in terms of critical interpretation, both despite and because of her pragmatism's refusal to invest in such a division. Intersecting with Addams's own story in *Twenty Years* and in her other texts concerning social issues are the stories she tells about others—mainly other women. These stories, in contrast to Addams's sentimentalizing techniques, work within the genres of sensationalist journalism and literary naturalism. Katherine Joslin argues that in these vignettes, Addams "unabashedly employs titillating details," even as she seeks to rouse social consciousness of the injustices these individuals face ("Experimental" 6). At first glance, the presence of this "sensational" speech in Addams's tales might seem to undermine an argument that entrenches her in traditional femininity. After all, the subjects and stories that Addams takes up—depictions of sexuality, prostitution, spousal abuse, domestic violence, crime, and grotesque poverty—clearly depict her distance from a domestic, insular, unworldly womanhood by showing her to be an observer of these phenomena. Indeed, Addams's use of the colorful vignette works explicitly to underscore her public-sphere knowledge; these stories make use of her pragmatist emphasis on experience as a governing factor in any theory of truth.

Yet the gap between sentimental domesticity and sensational worldliness is quickly closed in Addams's critics' eyes; her emphasis on the vignette, rather than demonstrating pragmatic engagements with knowledge, opens up Addams to critique based on the scholarly merit—the professionalism—of her writing about Chicago's poor. Her choice to emphasize story and thus her "refusal to use the rational logic and statistical data of male-designed sociology" functioned, in Jill Conway's words, "to tie [her] identity as a social critic to acquiescence in the traditional stereotype of women" (qtd. in Joslin, "Experimental" 1). So what is both entrenched in a new articulation of epistemology (experience as a vehicle toward knowledge) and in a demonstration of worldly understanding is also read by Joslin and Conway as a renunciation of intellectualism by her use of "tales" that "subvert the sociological discourse" (Joslin, "Experimenta'" 5). Addams focuses on the story—which is individualized, idiosyncratic, and artistically/ aesthetically rendered—rather than on the statistic—which is collective, normative, and scientifically verifiable—when she composes her texts. In doing so, she may better entertain her readership; however, Conway and Joslin suggest that she also sacrifices a goal of bringing broad public awareness to social ills in need of attention. Here, Addams can be seen as a writer who supports the female anti-intellectual stereotype that women have gossipy tongues, rather than scientific brains.

Rather than attempting to mediate between these compromises and divergent claims in Addams's work and her work's reception history, for the purposes of this study, it will be most useful to dwell in and among Addams's contradictory tethers that pull alternately forward and backward toward publicity and obscurity, sentiment/sensation and objectivity, scholarship and experience, femininity and masculinity, nature and intellect, and canonical theories and unorthodox ideas. For many feminist critics, Addams is truly a New Woman who performs a version of the nineteenth-century woman, a thoroughly modern thinker who uses the guise of the antiprogressive domestic woman as it suits her needs.[14] Though such interpretations of Addams's agency provide an important corrective to readers who might otherwise dismiss her as simply the latter (as the pragmatist canon has tended to do), they do not take seriously the pragmatist focus on combining old and new, on specifically *not* letting go of the past, a key tenet of the philosophy to which Addams had such an intimate, if complex, connection.

By emphasizing Addams's specific textual mediation between old and new forms of knowledge in *The Long Road of Woman's Memory*, I contend that she be considered as a turn-of-the-century figure engaged in practicing an epistemic model open to an ethic of innocence. In doing so, we might take her engagement with the Devil Baby tale as an exemplary expression of the fin-de-siècle's complex relationship to gender, genre, and knowledge. Further, I argue that tensions can be seen (through recourse to Addams's work) as crucial test cases for modern feminist theory rather than as antitheses to its ends. Addams's writing suggests not only that the past might be usefully incorporated into the present and future, but also that doing so entails a certain risk—a risk of being misread, misunderstood, or ignored: condemned to an ignorant acceptance of the past rather than useful transformation of it. Her work also makes evident how texts marked with an ethic of innocence are never *either* literary *or* social, but rather always story *and* cultural script. By viewing her work in this way, it should cease to surprise us that Jane Addams wrote a modern, intellectual book about a wild, sensational/sentimental story. Instead, this feminist pragmatist seems the ideal figure to give credence to fanciful rumors she knew, always, to be false, if only because her own experiences being misread may have allowed her to sympathize with a tale and its tellers who were, by their very social status, age, class, and gender, also easily dismissed and overlooked.

The Devil Baby Tale: Old Magic Meets New Protest

Through *The Long Road of Woman's Memory*'s in-depth engagement with the Devil Baby episode, Addams theorizes a pragmatic understanding of alternative, feminine modes of knowing and not-knowing. Lest such a privileging of this incident seem out of place given Addams's breadth of writings and contributions to pragmatist as well as feminist issues, I note that the episode is one that held a place of prominence in Addams's intellectual life. Addams uses the Devil Baby incident in three discrete writings: it was first analyzed in an article that was published in both the scholarly *American Journal of Sociology* (July, 1914) and the popular *Atlantic Monthly* (October, 1916); next, as part of a longer meditation in *The Long Road of Woman's Memory* (1916); and, finally, in vignette form in her second autobiographical work, *The Second Twenty Years at Hull-House* (1930). For the purposes of this chapter, I focus on the tale as it is treated within *The Long Road of Woman's Memory*, a largely critically neglected book that combines anecdotes, personal memoir, philosophical meditation, and political protest into what Katherine Joslin calls her "most literary," even modernist project (*Jane* 169).[15] Though this book, drawn from incidents that occurred during more than twenty years of Hull House's operation, is more broadly concerned with the many kinds of overlooked experiences of older, poor women, Addams roots its first two chapters in in-depth intellectual investigation of the Devil Baby episode, and this story grounds the beginning of the third and fourth chapters as well. Thus, what might have been a forgotten episode becomes a pivot, an exemplar, in Addams's writing that challenges the meaning and value of female forms of knowledge at the fin de siècle.

In doing so, Addams seems to take the emphasis pragmatism places on transactional, communal learning to an almost illogical point; she suggests that one can learn not only from nonscholastic sources but also from interactions with fictional stories or people whose very behaviors seem to advocate the avoidance of knowledge. Whereas pragmatism's coining philosopher, Charles Sanders Peirce, would articulate that what passes for true or credible is always that which can be proven via a methodologically regular, experimental method, Addams suggests that something not only unverifiable but, indeed, *verifiably false* could "urg[e] its credibility upon [her]" and, in doing so, tap into a type of "wisdom which becomes deposited in the heart of man by unnoticed innumerable experiences" (*Long* 9).[16]

These innumerable experiences to which Addams points, every day in nature and unacknowledged in their frequency, predominantly attest to the neighborhood women's experiences of poverty, sexism, brutal violence in the home, and neglect at the hands of their own families. The Devil Baby story itself demonstrates the difficulties women faced in their relationships with men by depicting a husband character who rejects his wife's religious beliefs, rages violently against her, and/or curses their unborn, tellingly female, child; at the same time, the Devil Baby story also pinpoints, through positing the husband's comeuppance in the body of a baby that is carried in his wife's womb and birthed by her, the very inextricability of the woman from these scenarios of domestic abuse and hardship. Thus, the tale ends by launching the baby-turned-devil—and the social/moral condemnation such a figure inspires—against not only the father who "deserved" it but also the mother who bore it.

The very fact that it tells a narrative of both male and female entrapment and guilt, however, allows the Devil Baby story to be used covertly as a "taming" device aimed at "recalcitrant husbands and fathers" without this taming being linked overtly to the wives and mothers who instigate it (26). Women thus use the words of the tale as a sort of protective weaponry wrought of its supernatural appeal; Addams notes that "shamefaced men [were] brought . . . by their women folk to see the baby" (26). Since the wife in the Devil Baby scenario is herself also a "victim" of the changeling child, the story aligns the husband's and wife's fates by presenting them as dual victims, which might in turn breed an alliance, rather than further conflict, between the spouses. Thus, the Devil Baby tale ideally serves as a corrective to male behavior, one that seems to stem from an extramarital source (supernatural sanctions) rather than an internal one (a wife's complaints). Such a corrective might force the husband to amend his behavior to his wife according to her desires while at the same time shielding her from the violence that might result if she were to ask more directly for what she wanted. Hence, the scenario reminds Addams that "for thousands of years women had nothing to oppose against unthinkable brutality save 'the charm of words,' no other implement with which to subdue the fierceness of the world about them" (29). At their best, such words work their magic by erasing the presence of the female magician.

This use of the Devil Baby tale, however, also highlights the distance between its words' magic charms and the reality they are summoned to redress. These same men "ill concealed their triumph" when Hull House workers found it necessary to deny the existence of the Devil Baby, therefore suggesting to the Devil Baby seekers that "there proved to be no such visible sign of retribution for domestic derelictions" (26). The world of Addams's fin-de-siècle Chicago must have seemed especially harsh at this moment, since the Devil Baby tale's protective charm fails at the threshold of rationality—a threshold that is simultaneously and literally the entrance to a home that the neighborhood women had been encouraged by Addams and her coworkers to think of a refuge from their difficulties (29).

The irony that Jane Addams, a clear sympathizer with and advocate for these women, was just as clearly, by refusing to confirm the Devil Baby story, the instrument by which these women might once again become unable to "tame" their husbands is certainly not lost on Addams herself. Several times in *The Long Road of Woman's Memory*, Addams mentions the guilt that attended her role as the debunker, saying that she "found it hard to take away [a woman's] comfort in the belief that the Powers that Be are on the side of the woman" (42). Addams even notes an instance when, faced with one "eager old woman aroused to her utmost capacity of wonder and credulity," she contemplated the possibility of confirmation. She justifies this temptation to lie by likening it to an act of charity, writing:

> If the object of my errand had been an hour's reading to a sick woman, it would have been accounted to me for philanthropic righteousness, and if the chosen reading had lifted her mind from her bodily discomforts and harassing thoughts so that she forgot them all for one fleeting moment, how pleased I should have been with the success of my effort. But here I was with a story at my tongue's end, stupidly hesitating to give it validity, although the very words were on my lips. (19–20)

Here, we can see Addams's pragmatic struggle, not between rationality and myth but between two modes of rationality—one that would reject the supernatural by confirming the natural order of the world, and one that would reject the injustice found at the nexus of gender, class, and age by confirming the belief of the old woman. Addams links the woman asking for the Devil Baby tale's confirmation with the sick woman being read to through the device of the story, a comparison demonstrating that stories are believed to be good and proper medicine in certain scenarios only—namely, when they are meant to comfort through distraction or amusement, not through irrational belief. In this scenario, Addams is herself on the verge of becoming a woman telling a Devil Baby tale, and only what she disparages as a "stupi[d] hesita[tion]" prevents this leveling between Addams and the women she serves.

It is, though, precisely by being "on the verge" that Addams is able to see why belief in this story might matter to this woman. Certainly, the meaning of the Devil Baby tale or the means to which this tale was put varied for each woman with whom Addams dealt. But for the older women, in whom Addams was most interested, it seemed to rectify a lack of inclusion in a largely unfamiliar land, amidst a younger generation who spoke of newer topics in a foreign language at a speed that rapidly outpaced them. The Devil Baby tale, by contrast, represented the kind of "material with which they were accustomed" (8). Such women might have sought Addams's confirmation of the tale in order to give credence to their own worth or social importance, which—given their status as elderly immigrants—was often in question. So when Addams hesitates to affirm the Devil Baby story, she is also hesitating to value the insights of a woman who is already epistemically undervalued, particularly in the very foreign, modern, American landscape that enabled Jane Addams the professional in the first place.

Addams's own personal threshold—the twentieth-century theorist with the nineteenth-century tongue—puts her in a position in which to speak in either direction (confirmation or denial) would betray her position as the pragmatist mediator. Then, too, the very tensions of Hull House itself—both a domestic space and a public project, run by a woman at once a matriarch and a professional—intensify the contradictions of Addams's position. Addams's job at Hull House pits her at once as domestic caregiver and social reformer, as both the layperson who ministered to the neighborhood and the academically invested theorist who used her experiences as a catalyst for broader social analysis. Therefore, it is no wonder that her tongue hesitates to deny the supplicant just as it hesitates to affirm her. Rather than either dismissing or accepting this woman's understanding of the Devil Baby tale's power, Addams sits, pragmatically, at the threshold of that decision.

Ultimately, though, Addams finds that in the modern epistemic landscape, a hesitation—a silence—is a type of speech aligned against superstition, and through superstition, against antiquated forms of female wisdom. She writes, "[B]ut, as in the case of many another weak soul, the decision was taken out of my hands, my very hesitation was enough, for nothing is more certain than that the bearer of a magic tale never stands dawdling on the door-step" (20). Although a tongue full of confirming words could offer support to the old woman, no such verbose opposition is necessary to deny it to her. The burden of proof favors the "rational" minds of both women rather than either the old woman's fantastical hope in her chosen innocence or Addams's pragmatic attentiveness to situational truth that would seek to split the difference. By denying the Devil Baby tale, Addams cannot, at least in person, remain "dawdling on the door-step" of belief and logic, but she is instead forced off the threshold via the act of dawdling itself.

Thus, *The Long Road of Woman's Memory* can be read as a way for Addams herself to make peace with her inability to remain on the threshold and support these female seekers of the Devil Baby; her book, in contrast to her actual life, dwells on the doorstep in regard to these tales and gives her the means to more fully engage her pragmatic mediation. The space she opens up in *The Long Road of Woman's Memory* for this kind of deferral of a final decision—for the textual proposition that she take seriously something she's already, in life, denied—has the potential to be read as a failure of will, a byproduct of the wishy-washiness of a pragmatism that, "as a mediator between tough-mindedness and tender-mindedness," foregrounds dialogue rather than forward progress (James 164).

Yet the pragmatic methodology, through its emphasis on dawdling and keeping the either/or choice firmly at bay, can also be read as granting intellectual attention to an insistent present. Rather than declaring ourselves unable to deal with the present moment with intellectual soundness because of our intimacy with it, pragmatism suggests that it is this very intimacy, our inability to remove ourselves and become "objective," that we should use to inform any intellectual engagement. Unlike academic distinctions, cultural validation, or even settlement-house work, pragmatism by definition "has no dogmas, and no doctrines save its method," and its method is one of postponing conclusions in favor of dialogue, what Livingston calls "not so much a new event in the story of Western philosophy as a new way of relating, of narrating previous events" (James 38; Livingston 118). Thus, in one sense, this pragmatic dawdling, far from being wishy-washy, might come as close as possible to approximating objectivity because of the pragmatist's insistence on engaging in dialogue with diverse voices before stepping one way or another. But from a literary standpoint, this dawdling fractures the reader's narrative expectations. Rather than illustrating problems and proposing solutions, Addams's prismatic narration complicates the problem's context, provides alternative interpretations of scenes, and increases the lines of connectivity between the figures in her stories—ultimately challenging the readers' sense of what might even *be* a proper ending.

The Long Road of Woman's Memory is very much a pragmatist retelling of "reality," one that neither forgets the closed-off lived narrative (in which a woman's hopes end in Addams's denial) nor uses this closure as the ending of the tale Addams tells. Rather, Addams renarrativizes the event of her denial, using it as a hub from which to explore not only her own silence and implication in the forces that deny Devil Baby seekers' comfort but also the insistent tongues that wag despite her own speechlessness. For one of the peculiarities about the Devil Baby story that most fascinates Addams is that it acts beyond its mythic capacity to covertly correct domestic ills and becomes a catalyst for other tales—personal stories that emerge seemingly spontaneously from the mouths of the female Devil Baby seekers.

Inspired by the Devil Baby: Generic and Affective Gaps

For many women—often old, quiet, and mild-mannered; always poor—the hubbub surrounding Hull House's demonic infant resulted in their increased willingness to communicate about their own lives. These were individuals Addams had known for years, but the Devil Baby story seemed to release "new volubility" and new details in the autobiographical stories the women told for public consumption (Addams, *Long* 9). The Devil Baby story itself appears to have a clear, if covert, use value for the women who tell it; however, in the broader stories of the women's lives that the Devil Baby tale brings about, a more mysterious strain of attachment to the story prevails. Many a woman found that the neighborhood talk about the baby inexplicably "loosened [her] tongue" about painful, seemingly unrelated life circumstances that she had vowed never to publicly discuss (41). One woman, for instance, found herself discussing, for the first time, her alcoholic son who repeatedly spent any money he had on liquor rather than on his mother's support; she, in turn, had to scavenge his pockets while he was asleep for any loose change with which to feed them. Even as she tells Addams about him, the woman signals her "shame" and reluctance to tell this tale—as it turns out, she had previously been informed by a nurse at Hull House that her son "could be arrested for [the mother's] non-support" and as such, had determined to be "awful close-mouthed" (41). Here, the supernatural power of the Devil Baby tale extends beyond the circumstances of the tale itself and its practical domestic correctives to the mouth of the mother, who seems to suddenly, at the end of her story, find that her lips are working against both her will and her motherly instinct to protect her son at all costs.

Addams depicts many other such unexpected revelations in fragmented story snippets that give the reader insight into the type of tales the Devil Baby myth had loosed: tales "of premature births, 'because he kicked me in the side'; of children maimed and burnt because 'I had no one to leave them with when I went to work' "—as well as comparatively fuller narratives, such as "My face has had this queer twist for now nearly sixty years; I was ten when it got that way, the night after I saw my father do my mother to death with his knife" and "Yes, I had fourteen children; only two grew to be men and both of them were killed in the same explosion. I was never sure they brought home the right bodies" (35, 10). Like the Devil Baby tale proper, these are Gothic stories of horror and violence occurring within the domestic space of the home, ones that very often place men in the villains' roles. In contrast to the myth, however, these Gothic tales are of everyday life, in which the supernatural is far off, and the women, if they cared to, could often produce the flesh-and-blood evidence to support the bodily transformations these tales enact. And for those, such as the mother of fourteen, who experienced a failure of bodily evidence, that failure speaks not to the disembodied mystery of a ghost story but to a strange and confusing modernity: a world of "explosions" that could confirm a son's death and yet remain unable to reconstruct and identify his dismembered body. Such Devil Baby–inspired stories bear witness to the continued relevance of the seemingly archaic Gothic mode to these women's modern experiences of male violence and poverty, but it also draws a clear distinction between the supernatural tale that starts these conversations and the grotesque but distinctly earthly narratives to which it leads.

The fragmentary form in which Addams gives us these women's stories seems to echo her own admittedly incomplete understanding of the Devil Baby's secondary, generative storytelling phenomenon. Why tell these stories, and why via this catalyst? Through the genre of the Gothic as well as the character similarity within the narratives, we might most readily *thematically* link the women's tales and the Devil Baby myth via male violence and "deviltry." And, indeed, one attempted explanation Addams gives is that for these women, whose own life circumstances have cheated them out of receiving any justice for their poverty and difficult domestic relations, the desire to see proof of the Devil Baby's existence stems from "a longing to see one good case of retribution before they died (34). The Devil Baby tale, then, works as a generically fitting, narrative solution to the material, embodied, and very real difficulties these women face and relate in the personal narratives they come to tell.

Through this simile, Addams aligns the adult women seeking assurances about the Devil Baby with vulnerable children dependent on the future, along with its promise of maturation and increased power, in order to see their dreams of revenge come to fruition. This comparison troubles, however, as the women of whom Addams speaks are already not only "grown," but aging. Any fantasy of the future ability to deal a "crushing blow" thus becomes even more fantastical for the Hull House frequenters than for the child in Addams's example who hopes to grow up and attain a different social circumstance, not only because the Devil Baby does not exist but also because the future it promises is thus already marked as impossible. Unlike the child, who will age, these real women are relegated by Addams's comparison to a perpetual present, one in which their hope in the supernatural makes them always both children and victims. The "ending" that any longing for retribution signals is in this way staved off for an indeterminate—and likely unreachable—future.

Thankfully, Addams immediately retracts this simile as a broadly applicable statement, writing in the same sentence, "but I think, on the whole, such an explanation was a mistake" (34). Instead, she claims that the story itself was, in a sense, its own explanation, that it was "one of those free, unconscious attempts to satisfy, outside of life, those cravings which life itself leaves unsatisfied" (34–35). Of all the uses of the Devil Baby story to which Addams makes reference, this one seems the most intriguing. Here, the very nonreality, the fictionality, of the Devil Baby tale is neither inconsequential nor impediment; rather, it is crucial to these women that the tale *be* a fiction, and thus bigger than their lives. The very limited nature of their own lived reality demands as much, for if the Devil Baby tale were to take its place among their own experiences, it would never hold a place more prominent than a lie or an old wives' tale. The social circumstances in which these women lived did not permit an embittered husband to be subdued by a miracle demon child or any other such physical bar against the social ills they faced daily. Most often, these ills went unnoted or unpunished, even (or even especially) by the victims themselves. So this story, which necessarily tells a lie—even if it is a lie about what should happen—also provides a safe space for women to rethink the silences that they have taken on in their own lives, both voluntarily and otherwise. If a Devil Baby had been born in Hull House, Addams's book would have had to focus directly on such an extraordinary circumstance; because the story instead remained a fiction, most likely overtly untrue and at the very least unproven, these women's lives as told in the Devil Baby–inspired tales are able to become her focus—a public attention gained only by way of a twisted route through a fictional investment.

Just as the Devil Baby story itself works surreptitiously by allowing the woman to argue her case against her husband without seeming to do so, the Devil Baby–inspired tales work covertly to announce and argue these women's cases against the men and circumstances which do them harm. But whereas the Devil Baby tale speaks silently and intimately between a husband and wife without disclosing the particulars of their domestic experience to any audience, the Devil Baby–inspired tales are public tellings of domestic particulars, explored in the presence of the female-dominated Hull House audience. Yet these inspired tales also work through what is *not* said. For though the genre of these tales might be Gothic, their tone is matter-of-fact, indeed even inexplicably romantic or happy, and only briefly, unobtrusively, and momentarily punctuated by "baffled desires, sharp cries of pain, [and] echoes of justices unfulfilled" (35). Rather than overtly announcing their complaints, these narratives' complexities are rendered visible when one reads, as many feminist literary critics do, the textual gaps and silences alongside that which is explicit.[17] Here, Addams *the reader* emphasizes and uses silence pragmatically to mediate competing tensions in a way that Addams *the Hull House professional* was not able or permitted to do, even as she must implicitly admit that such silence requires a sympathetic reader for its interpretation.

One such moment of silence met with sympathetic reading can be seen in Addams's account of an old woman who "evidently obtain[ed] inscrutable comfort from the story of the Devil Baby even after she had become convinced that [Hull House] harbored no such creature"; indeed, she continued to come to Hull House "many times to tell of her longing for her son, who had joined the army eighteen months before and was now stationed in Alaska" (37). The woman's distress seems to center around the idea of the spring thaw, when she thought it possible for him to "get out" of Alaska and come back to her (37). Her narrated "worry" escalates with a series of increasingly unlikely thoughts—she begins by imagining that her son can get out, but that the officers won't let him, which then moves her into thinking that he might run away, which then prompts her to imagine her son being shot, all of which culminates with her fear that she'll never get to see him again before she dies (37–38). The woman herself notes that she has a history of mental illness and "was once in the Insane Asylum for three years at a stretch," but she seems to think that having her son back would solve everything, even her history of mental disease; she claims that "without this worry about him [her] mind would be alright" since he could "[earn] money and [keep] [her]" (37, 38).

At first pass, this woman's narrative might seem the simple tale of a doting mother's worry, even as it also exposes a background of mental illness and poverty that have likely caused her considerable suffering. The information Addams adds, via personal knowledge of the old woman and her family, complicates this sentimental story. Addams explains to us as readers that this woman's son was a "vagabondish lad" who had never supported his mother, had been "arrested twice," and was now likely being disciplined and looked after by the army in a way his mother never could have. Addams even attempts to persuade his mother that life in the army—where he was clothed, sheltered, given work (hard to come by at the time in Chicago), and kept out of trouble—might be better for him in the long run (38–39). The response the woman gives is as follows, after which she falls silent: "That wouldn't make any real difference to me—the work, the money, his behaving well and all that, if I could cook and wash for him. I don't need all the money I earn scrubbing that factory. I only take bread and tea for supper and I choke over that, thinking of him" (39).

This illogical response of a mother who wants, at any cost, to care for a son who is perhaps better off being looked after by the army signals to Addams the "eternally unappeased idealism which, for her, surrounded her son's return"—a habit of mind so dear to the woman that it leaves her "overcome by a thousand obscure emotions which could find no outlet in words" (39). As the narrative breaks off, we are left with a sentimental impression of a woman who romantically sustains her hope in her son's goodness beyond even her capacity to speak to it.

Addams subtly gestures toward another complicating explanation for the mother's silence. This view stems from the mother's "realiz[ation]" that "the facts in the case, to one who had known her boy from childhood, were far from credible," since the loving son of whom she painted a portrait was not a person of whom any of her neighbors and friends had seen evidence. The son the mother constructed and worried about was, to them, a fantasy son, as unreal perhaps as the Devil Baby himself. By professing her belief in this son, Addams suggests, the mother is thus essentially expressing a belief in a mythological being. The anecdote ends with Addams's comment that the woman "was even afraid to say much about it, lest she should be overmastered by her subject and be considered so irrational as to suggest a return to the Hospital for the Insane" (39).

Motherly love here risks turning the woman into not only a fool but a lunatic, one who needs to be locked up for either society's protection or her own. Likewise, hope, far from being simply this old woman's salvific, sustaining affect, becomes a dream to which she cannot give voice for fear of being condemned for her audacity. Affecting ignorance about her son's true characteristics and history thus puts this woman at significant risk, even though this same insistence on not-knowing is what allows this woman to imagine a way out of her "worries"—namely, escape via the dream of the son's return. The sentimental narrative is punctuated by realism as a reader recognizes that this mother continues to sustain herself by employing what appears to be a successful two-part coping strategy: a secret allegiance to the dream coupled with a self-imposed silence as a means to sustain the dream's possibility.

That this allegiance remains largely a public secret, if also a public confession to Addams, speaks to the mother's rationality as well as her romanticism. The fact that she closes her narrative in a flood of "obscure emotions" and breaks off her confession for fear of being thought insane supports the notion that there is not just motherly love at stake here; rather, her self-silencing suggests that the mother knows she is being illogical and yet continues to embrace the nonrational anyway. The silence that exposes this paradox could also be read, moreover, as a means by which the woman calls our attention to her "baffled desire" or to "justices unfulfilled" because it highlights the fact that the mother's love for her son will most likely remain unrequited and that she knows the hope that sustains her is also a hope that others find so impossible as to qualify her as insane. The mother's silence, then, bears witness to the social norms (of which, in some sense, Addams's own response to the mother is a part) of questioning the intelligence of the woman who copes in a fashion that we might find distasteful or feel helpless to comprehend within traditional epistemic bounds. But it also focuses a critical eye away from the woman herself and onto the circumstances that imprison hopefulness and love within either a silence that disallows the mother's voice or a presumed insanity that is worthy of institutionalization. Ironically, it is within the gap—the emotional "obscurity" that silences this mother's story—that the psychical and social power of fiction finds its voice.

A second illustrative moment of silence and choosing not to know is related by Addams via the story of yet another old woman with a wayward son who had come to Hull House in a "desperate effort" to see the Devil Baby (49). This second woman, gravely ill, also longs to see her son before she dies; he, however, was serving a life sentence in prison for murdering his prostitute wife's madam because she had been withholding too much of his wife's earnings. As with the last mother, Addams had known this woman for years; unlike the other woman, this mother had previously told the sensational, "hideous story" of her son's crime to Addams, and Addams is also "familiar" with what she terms her "vicissitudes," the domestic circumstances that inflect it (49–50). So Addams relates to her readers the difficulties of this woman's life—married to a "shiftless, drinking husband" and having a "large family of children, all of whom had brought her sorrow and disgrace" (50). Addams's logical assumption, perhaps also a readers', seems to be that the mother could not easily overlook the crime of her youngest son, Joe, no matter how much she may have wanted to do so. Yet Addams once again depicts her marvel at the seemingly senseless hopefulness that the mother exhibits, arguing that the woman, rather than rejecting her son, mocking her own longing, or even just treating him with complacency, "put all the vitality she could muster into his defense" (51).

Here, too, Addams walks her readers through the at-once fantastical and logical ways in which this defense of the son is staged. The first line of defense: Joe gallantly marries Lily, despite the fact that she had been "so long in that life [prostitution] that few men would have done it" (51). Then, this same "gallant" man found himself forced to become Lily's "protector," as "everybody" would cheat "such a girl" if she did not have someone to occupy this position (51). An implication of this arrangement, noted here by Addams but not the mother, is that Lily, not Joe, financially supports both of them by continuing to work as a prostitute. Even Lily, according to the mother, maintained her son's goodness after the murder, declaring that "he was the kindest man she ever knew" and that the murder was essentially her fault because she had told Joe about her madam's miserly ways, and Joe had no other option but to protect her through violence (51). These last details of Lily's justification not only highlight Joe's goodness and worth, but they do so covertly by displacing the character testimony, via attributive tags, from the mother onto the wife. Like the Devil Baby tale itself, then, this inspired story works by articulating its voice of protest from the mouth of another—though, again, the Gothic disembodiment merges with modern reality, as the protesting voice in this Devil Baby–inspired tale becomes not that of a supernatural child but that of a real, if also somewhat demonized, whore.

A final piece of evidence that the mother offers in order to defend Joe's goodness is the most striking, however, and it helps us most fully explore the story's link to silence and choosing not to know. This evidence takes the form of a defense issued from the position as well as the voice of the "gasping" mother herself, and it is quoted in full, rather than summarized by Addams: suggesting that there is something about this *specific* retelling of the tale that offers particular insight to the study of these Devil Baby–inspired stories. Here, following Addams's lead, I quote in full in the mother's words: "He was always that handsome and had such a way. One winter, when I was scrubbing in an office building, I'd never get home much before twelve o'clock, but Joe would open the door for me just as pleasant as if he hadn't been waked out of a sound sleep" (51). Addams understandably points out the absurdity of this supposed compliment, in which the mother's evidence of the son's "goodness" is simultaneously the evidence of both his laziness and his mother's victimization at his hands. Again, we have a covert social corrective at work; the gap between the mother's emotional response to this remembrance and the literal details it uses to convey this emotion allow the listener to understand and condemn the abuse of the son without the mother, again, ever voicing a complaint. But, actually, the woman does not appear to be complaining at all, covertly or otherwise, even though she can barely speak this defense. Addams claims that the woman appeared so excited, "so triumphantly unconscious of the incongruity" between the mother's evidence's literal content and the meaning she interprets from it, that the listeners imposed silence upon themselves at the close of her narrative (51). Addams writes that "her auditors said never a word, and in silence we saw a hero evolved before our eyes" (52). As they keep this silence, this woman's fiction—her refusal to know—moves from a privately held dream to a witnessed event, and, in the process, Addams reverses the kind of psychic disempowerment of the Devil Baby seekers that her previous silence toward another old woman enacted. This time, through silence, the group not only performs their own innocence to the son's true colors, but they also do something that I would argue is much more valuable—they give the woman the benefit of the doubt that her "unconscious[ness]" is perhaps partly chosen, or at least not theirs to disabuse.

Reading like Addams:
Pragmatism, Knowledge, and the Turn-of-the-Century Woman

Would these women's lives be better if they could find their sons to be evil, irresponsible, or at the very least not the heroes they talk about them as being? One of the most compelling aspects of Addams's text is that she never asks this question. Instead, by refusing to examine this issue, Addams implicitly advocates leaving these women's choices not to know alone, for these seem to be, in some sense, all they have. Here, we can see Addams's faith in the efficacy of coping strategies that might look like foolishness and ignorance to an observer. For the silences that maintain them also mysteriously allow for the "transmutation," to use Addams's own term, of the Gothic domesticity these women suffer into a secret yet sustaining fiction. As these women's experiences were brought tumbling forth by the Devil Baby, Addams experienced a "crystalli[zation] [of] thoughts and impressions" regarding these women that had before remained either unacknowledged or idiosyncratic, without a unified theory to render them coherent and communicable (9). *The Long Road of Woman's Memory*, I argue, puts forth such a theory.

Addams opens *The Long Road of Woman's Memory* with a hypothesis on the place of narratives of past experiences in women's lives, the first two paragraphs of which I quote here in full:

> For many years at Hull-House I have at intervals detected in certain old people, when they spoke of their past experiences, a tendency to an idealization, almost to a romanticism suggestive of the ardent dreams and groundless ambitions we have all observed in the young when they recklessly lay their plans for the future.
>
> I have, moreover, been frequently impressed by the fact that these romantic revelations were made by old people who had really suffered much hardship and sorrow, and that the transmutation of their experiences was not the result of ignoring actuality, but was apparently due to a power inherent in memory itself. (ix)

Several things stand out in this opening gambit. First of all, Addams describes the imparted memories as inherently unrealistic, calling them "idealistic," "romantic," "dreamy," "reckless," and "groundless," characteristics that we certainly might second after considering the two representative (and not exceptional) maternal memories depicted above. These descriptors are not particularly unique; after all, memories are often discussed as being idealized and romanticized. Addams makes a more surprising move, however, by comparing memory's nostalgic power to a state or view of youthfulness that emphasizes youth's impracticality and unfettered dreams; we might expect that such a view would appear to those older and wiser to be rife with flawed logic, ignorance of reality, even foolishness. Addams herself acknowledges the potential foolishness of this youthful view in her own thesis when she admits that the truth-content of the remembered experiences does not hold up under scrutiny of the rememberer's hard, sorrowful life. Viewing these older rememberers as childlike "innocents" rather than as the adult, experienced women they are, as Addams seems to do here, risks not only disenfranchising them from having intelligent control over their own lives but also casts them as willing participants in their victimization by fate's (and men's) bullying behavior.

Despite her admission of memory's incongruity with reality, however, Addams does not charge these women with foolishness or argue that they display a propensity for "ignoring actuality." Instead, she contends, their seeming return to youth through memory makes clear the strange "power" that memory inherently possesses. Temporal slippage is born of these old women's memories—they are likened to youths when they remember, but youths who significantly have already experienced lives. Likewise slippery, remembering the remote past is explained via comparison to future plans. These outmoded women, dismissed as ignorant, Old-World thinkers by their families, are able to gain a purchase not only on the present but also on the future through recasting their experiences through the lens of youth's innocence. Here we see at work the pragmatist principles of mediating between views that would otherwise seem irreconcilable—age is likened to youth, and experience is made over through not-knowing into a type of sustaining fiction. The necessarily linear life is thus coupled with a cyclical memory that not only highlights the potential connection of mindsets across generational divides but also emphasizes that experience, like a natural resource, can be recycled and reused.

For Addams, memory, as demonstrated in the Devil Baby–inspired tales, does not merely work to ameliorate past ills and injustices by recasting antiquated sentimentality in a more positive light; it also provides a platform for those who have experienced "monstrous social injustices" in their lives to publicly acknowledge these injustices through mutual storytelling and reminiscing (xiii). These two roles of reminiscence speak to the power of the Devil Baby–inspired tales, which function pragmatically as a meeting ground of reality and fiction, one that psychically supports the rememberer while also allowing her to stage publicly, through deferral and silence, domestic complaints and social injustices. Even when the affect of the rememberer seems untouched by the horror or tragedy of the memory, its story remains as a record of life circumstances that a Hull House worker like Addams—wealthier, better educated, but also a woman caught between the old and new types of knowledge available to her at the turn of the century—could evaluate, even acknowledge as a story related to her own.

It is not coincidental but essential that, once again at the end of this discussion of and around the Devil Baby tale, we find ourselves left mulling over the figure of the listening Jane Addams, the complex and contradictory feminist pragmatist, who both takes an active role in these narratives of domestic strife and illogical dreams and simultaneously stands outside of them as a social worker, audience member, and philosopher. Addams's textual persona combines the roles of listener, reader, and narrator; it is a decided strength of Addams's pragmatist feminism that her refusal of either old or new forms of knowledge extends, in *The Long Road of Woman's Memory*, to her representation of herself. If *The Long Road of Woman's Memory* is a peace-seeking text, one in which Addams attempts to reconcile the way in which her professional role as the leader of Hull House did not make room for these women's voices, then she also uses it to subtly make room for her own story.

Addams narrates her own understanding of the Devil Baby incident through the genre of tragedy; through it, she documents her individuated sympathetic response to these women along with a broader social need that she argues their stories demonstrate both to her and, through her, to her readers. By calling the Devil Baby–inspired tales "tragic reminiscences," Addams seems at first to situate herself once again as the professional sociologist, the advocate for social justice documenting these women's stories and then threading them into her text as a call for public awareness and action (*Long* 52). This collected and communicated set of female experiences, here named "tragic," calls to mind Kathleen M. Sand's definition of tragedy as a form of ritualized narration. Sand argues that "tragedy, as an aesthetic form, consigns trauma to a ritual space where, rather than being silently reenacted, it is solemnly voiced and lamented" (Felski, *Rethinking* 83). If we think of *The Long Road of Woman's Memory* as such a voice of lament, its public nature is particularly important to understanding both these women's pain and Addams's role as witness. As textually narrated tragedies, these stories emerge from obscure individuation into the modern public eye through the communal female space that an older world, the Devil Baby mythology, opens. Their narrator, Addams—an interlocutor—translates between these two temporalities and makes these women's tragedies available to a modern audience.

Where Addams oversteps her professionalized sociological stance is where the more interesting aspect of her relationship to her text lies. As Addams's relation of the Devil Baby incident begins to personally reflect the more theoretical sense of epistemic and pragmatic interdependence, her understanding of the incident involves something more than the ritualized tragedy above. The tragedy that, on one hand, fuels her cry of social justice for her Hull House clients also seems, she notes, to sustain these women. She phrases her understanding like this:

> In the midst of the most tragic reminiscences, there remained that something in the memories of these mothers which has been called the great revelation of tragedy, or sometimes the great illusion of tragedy; that which has power in its own right to make life palatable and at rare moments even beautiful. (52)

Revelation or illusion, the revelation that is borne out of or as part of the illusion, it is the transformative power of memory and its concomitant refusal to know at least a part of the harshness of these mothers' lived circumstances that becomes their future possibility. Addams begins her chapters with fantasies about a demon child and ends with fantasies about real ones, and in the process, her portrayal of both the Devil Baby story and the women surrounding it suggests that things—mythological tales, old women, silences, innocence—are not always what they seem. Born from tragedy, then, Addams speaks to a power that *exceeds*, one that can be defined by the reality of a "revelation" or the fiction of an "illusion," but is—in either sense—"great." By once again refusing a choice, by here invoking both revelation and illusion, Addams refuses judgment about the intellectual quality of these women's memories and instead focuses her attention on what these memories accomplish—the power they have for the women who use them.

The critical neglect of the gender-inflected pragmatic root of Addams's engagement with the Devil Baby–incident has tended to simplify the mutual implication of teller and listener in determining the affectively sustaining, sociocritical uses of narrative, rumor, and women's myths. Indeed, though the tensions that the Devil Baby episode and Addams's theoretical exploration of it reveal in regard to genre, professionalization, age, fictionality, realism, femininity, social awareness, and intelligence are many, they all boil down to issues of how female knowledge and experiences are both displayed and hidden in a public sphere, both within the walls of Hull House and in the broader world of Addams's readers. Without an understanding of epistemic alternatives to modern traditions of rational knowledge, both Addams's subjects and Addams herself risk being oversimplified by readers. The genres in which these tales are told and the affect with which they are performed might overly determine an estimation of these tales' speakers; similarly, a listener's silence or denial might too often mirror Addams's more damaging dawdling and reject the women it hopes to protect.

It may seem that it is both good modern literature and good feminist philosophy to dismiss the fictional attachments and romanticized, sentimental mythology of the Hull House Devil Baby seekers, but the danger in endorsing an either/or choice, in either easily dismissing or accepting these narratives, is that readers run the risk of denying the social conditions that structure narratives like the Devil Baby myth and the tales that circle around it in the first place, just as they risk dehumanizing those who circulate such tales.

To read, by contrast, with these tensions intact and unresolved is to understand the immense seriousness with which Addams considered these women's fantastical hopes—in the face of both devil children and real domestic deviltry—and the potential she saw in their stories to ameliorate personal suffering while also advocating for social change. It is also to acknowledge that the only means by which these women's stories can reach their dual potential is through implicating an audience—not just listeners but also readers—in not only the harsh realities but also the fantastical hopes they contain. By refusing (on our part) to decide whether Addams is truly a New Woman or a nineteenth-century sentimental throwback—that is, by reaping the value that comes from acknowledging that she is neither, both, or something quite unique—we set the stage for these stories' full potential to be reached and to reach us. And if readers can learn to read them pragmatically—to displace the either/or and see these stories as strategically entered into as alternative epistemic choices—they could be prompted to inquire about the social circumstances that require epistemic alternatives on the part of the tale's teller.

Chapter Two

Coming of Age via Critical Complaint

Reading Women's Choices Not to Know in Realist Bildungsroman

It is not surprising but, rather, fitting that our talisman of feminist pragmatism, chosen innocence, and Jane Addams's catalyst for bringing to light women's hidden memories and stubborn hopes thus far has come in the form of the Devil Baby—a strange comingling of godlike (albeit evil) wisdom and pure (albeit immature and untested) innocence. For the presence of such comingling in the mythical form of a Devil Baby gestures toward the mythic within the "innocent" woman ideology. If a baby could be infused at birth with the noninnocence of the devil, then surely it is farcical to imagine that a mentally competent human woman could attain "innocence," even if she were to want to do so, in any way other than through a chosen rejection of knowledge and/or a misreading of her actions as ignorant. Though the Devil Baby myth does not necessarily counter the cultural *ideal* of feminine innocence, it does expose the complicated *reality* of female innocence—a posture always attended by some form of knowledge that can be exposed by reading these women's rejection of knowledge as a choice rather than an inevitability.

Yet, as we have also seen in the previous chapter, the Devil Baby story seems to simultaneously and contradictorily point to a sense of women's fate and loss of agency. For the mythology of the Devil Baby speaks to a sort of inborn or early-learned evil that could squash a woman's hope of change, resilience, or even simply futurity. Here, the open-ended storytelling strategy of pragmatism, the room it leaves for narrators to inhabit their own stories, is thwarted by a particular narrative formation of epistemic tragedy—the coming of age of the fin-de-siècle woman into a modern environment not yet ready to accept her on her own terms. As much as critics comment on Addams's adoption of sentimental and other literary generic forms within her nonfiction to convey her points and mask her own ambitions in a world convinced that men had professions and women ran homes, she is still professing to write about reality by recounting real events. By contrast, the authors I will treat in this chapter make no such generic commitment to telling "true" stories of women's lives; their way of writing about reality, as realists, depends on fictional tales designed to express reality without confessing it. In seeking to use Addams's portrayal of the Devil Baby scenario as a model for reading fictional texts, I am arguing that something like the Devil Baby tale, in epistemic effect and outcomes, can be found in some forms of realist fiction.

In the following chapter, I will turn my attention to three such realist novels whose depiction of their female protagonists' silences, "bad" decisions, and seeming ignorance have caused critical discomfort and consternation. The focus of chapter 1 on Addams's *The Long Road of Woman's Memory* demonstrated that Addams—via recourse to the alternative epistemological models and forms that her pragmatism, her feminism, and her awkward embodiment of turn-of-the-century tensions primed her to embrace—was able to mine the female narratives surrounding the Devil Baby hubbub for intellectual, emotional, and theoretical value. Yet, I hope this previous chapter's discussion also demonstrated that Addams's ability to value these tales was not commonsensical but rather indebted to the confluence of her unique experiential, temporal, intellectual, and personal attributes. Even then, it took Addams a book-length reflection on these experiences—as well as her regret concerning her in-the-flesh discrediting of these women—in order to capture her revised evaluations of what she wishes she had done or had seen earlier. I do not judge Addams; I note her early failures alongside her requirements of time and reflection to see these women more clearly in order to demonstrate just how difficult it has been and is to understand such female engagements with knowledge as strategic modern practices rather than useless, primitive holdovers.

The texts to which I will now turn—three realist coming-of-age narratives featuring poor female protagonists—all share the ambiguous honor of proving intractably problematic for feminist critics to interpret in a way that can both acknowledge the agency and intelligence of these texts' female protagonists and also refuse to allow such acknowledgment to serve as tacit advocacy for the decisions these characters make. At root, the model of an ethic of innocence made evident in the Devil Baby story has several basic characteristics, as follows:

1. it offers an alternative epistemological model;

2. this alternative epistemology is utilized within specific confluences of gender and genre;

3. it operates unclearly, remains unknowable or unprovable, and employs silence;

4. it puts its epistemic agents at risk of being viewed as pejoratively ignorant within traditional epistemic norms.

It is this model that I trace within Edith Wharton's *Summer* (1917), Zora Neale Hurston's *Seraph on the Suwanee* (1948), and Gwendolyn Brooks' *Maud Martha* (1953). Addams asks overtly within *The Long Road of Woman's Memory*: What epistemic value does the Devil Baby story open up for the women who engage it? These three realist novels ask instead: What reality does these novels' protagonists' ethic of innocence allow them to ignore? The questions, of course, are not unrelated or even opposed, and both have a place in teasing out the complicated issue of choosing "innocence" at some cost. But this chapter's key question has the side effect of painting these protagonists as "ignorers," a label which easily slips into condemning them as constitutionally "ignorant" and "innocent." It is this downspin into "innocence" as a state of being, and not the question itself of what innocence ignores, that critics have found challenging to move beyond.

Wharton's *Summer* tells the story of Charity Royall, the eighteen-year-old, free-spirited ward of Lawyer Royall. Once, earlier, Lawyer Royall drunkenly entered Charity's room at night and attempted to sleep with her, which she rebuffed. Though Charity afterward despises him throughout most of the novella, her summer romance with Lucius Harney ends with her pregnant, abandoned, and—ultimately—married to Lawyer Royall. Hurston's *Seraph on the Suwanee* follows the coming into adulthood of Arvay Henson, a poor white woman, as she engages in a long and complicated relationship with Jim Meserve. Early in the novel, Jim rapes Arvay in order to ensure that she will marry him; though he belittles and dominates her throughout their life together, he also at times appears to love and need her. Arvay is depicted as alternatively loving, hating, resenting, treasuring, and ultimately coming to peace with their relationship. And Brooks' *Maud Martha* tells the story of its title character, a young black woman, in vignettes that expose specific moments throughout her life, from girlhood to adulthood. These vignettes include everyday moments of racism and small household joys and juxtapose daily interactions with her husband and daughter with extreme incidents such as childbirth and death. Throughout, Maud Martha Brown displays anger that almost always dissolves into a cheerier affect, one that allows her to perceive hope rather than doom in the moments in which she is overlooked due to her skin color by her husband, her family, and other townsfolk. Each of these women's coming-of-age tales is marked by her choice to turn away from the knowledge of her limited reality in some way, and each has been critiqued on these grounds by critics as a feminist failure.

Critics have tended to read these texts as regressive on the part of these authors, as texts that present female protagonists who are annoying, frustratingly passive, or incomprehensibly cheery in the face of terrible living conditions. As such, they have posed problems in terms of coming up with nuanced readings that defend feminist political values while also respecting the agency of their female characters. While recent modernist scholarship such as Sianne Ngai's *Ugly Feelings* has made much of resuscitating what she terms the "fundamentally ambivalent" negative affects entwined within modern texts, their hopeful correlates have seemed harder to recognize as retaining a like ambivalence at their root (5). Instead, for instance, *Summer's* critics have seemed troubled by the ethical and political ambiguities not only of Charity's hope but also of the text's overarching narrative itself, specifically regarding the concluding marriage between Charity and Lawyer Royall. For example, Kathleen Pfeiffer's attempts to redeem Charity Royall as a heroine, if failed ones, are contingent upon her disavowal of Charity's marriage compromise at the novel's end; she laments that "Charity's most feminine quality—her capacity for sympathetic compassion—proves to also be her most self-destructive one," as it is "this compassion" that "causes her to compromise her own integrity by transcending her disgust for Mr. Royall's sexual advances" (147). Meanwhile, a fully redemptive reading runs the risk of affirming a marital relationship that seems troubling at best. For instance, Kathy Grafton's reading of Charity's consent to marriage as evidence of "her maturity and clear vision," which follows from realizing "her true feelings for Mr. Royall," problematically glosses over the issue of Mr. Royall's ephebophilia and naturalizes the strange power dynamics in their relationship. Brooks's critics, in turn, have developed intersectional critiques that consider race alongside gender and that have very clearly condemned Maud Martha as both a woman and a mother for her seeming passivity toward racism. Readings of her character have tended, as Valerie Frazier notes, to concentrate exclusively on either her overt sunny side or her under-the-surface anger, without attempting to reconcile the two usefully (133).

And critics of *Seraph on the Suwanee*, according to Janet St. Clair, have "almost unanimously faulted [Hurston] for turning her back on her own racial heritage and feminist convictions in this novel" through her depiction of a white woman who tolerates some sexist, degrading treatment (38). By this statement, St. Clair points to a critical feminist difficulty in affirming Arvay's choice to stay with, even love, her rapist and abuser.[1]

Rather than reading these texts as realist tragedies that reject feminist political power, and rather than reading these female characters as depictions of individuals who are either trampled by oppressive circumstances or blissfully ignorant of the way they are being trampled, I will show how reading their rejection of knowledge as a *choice*, or an ethic of innocence, can help us to resee the stories of these characters in a way that affords them dignity and intelligence but that does not obscure or normalize the circumstances that they find themselves negotiating. In the close readings that follow, I hope to demonstrate how a pragmatic ethic of innocence helps heal the critical division between being ignorant of one's reality and being oppressed by reality's bleakness that these texts' receptions have evidenced. I will use the epistemic treatment of ignorance as a way not only to read against an assumption that women enact innocence toward unhappy realities because they cannot (not will not) do otherwise but also to turn our attention toward the survival strategies of those whose lives contain a bleakness that might easily appear all-oppressive.

Critical Complaints:
Loving, Choosing, and Living Wrongly

Why have the three focal texts of this chapter proved such a bane to critics? Any answer we might give is multipronged and convoluted. Though the three authors of the texts I treat—Edith Wharton, Zora Neale Hurston, and Gwendolyn Brooks—are all major figures in American literature in the modern period, the texts upon which this chapter focuses have not historically been lauded in the same way as other texts by these same authors. Lack of critical attention cannot be attributed to lack of quality alone or to authorial disinvestment. For instance, though Wharton herself named *Summer* as one of "her five personal favorites among her fiction," her own regard for the novel was not mirrored by critics (qtd. in Pfeiffer 142); Kathleen Pfeiffer notes that in R. W. B. Lewis's 592-page biography of Wharton, this novella receives only three pages of attention (141). Both historical and contemporary critics have demonstrated this critical discomfort. Nancy A. Walker's explanation is that *Summer* "has either been largely ignored or relegated to the position given it by early reviewers: a less tragically powerful and therefore less significant work than *Ethan Frome*" (107).[2] Indeed, the review literature does often pair the two, and to *Summer*'s disadvantage. *The Bookman* begins its September 1917 review of *Summer* by focusing on both novellas' depictions of New England, while the *Times Literary Supplement* reflects Wharton's own penchant for referring to Summer as "the hot Ethan" in its opening remarks: "Summer it is, indeed, as much as 'Ethan Frome' was winter" (*Times Literary*). Most illustrative, perhaps, of Walker's point, the substantial book review of *Summer* featured on July 8, 1917, in the *New York Times* concludes its evaluation by ceding *Ethan Frome*'s superiority: "Summer is not in any way a big book; it ranks with the author's lesser tales, not with 'Ethan Frome' or 'The House of Mirth' and their fellows" (*New York Times* 58).

The status of the novel within an author's oeuvre has also dogged the reception of Brooks's *Maud Martha* and Hurston's *Seraph on the Suwanee*. Not only was Brooks primarily known as a poet rather than a novelist (already a critical disadvantage for her fictional work), but the text's formal construction—short, episodic chapters; linguistic attention to description rather than narration; little overt connection between chapters; no overarching plot—confuses its generic departure from poetry even further, while also making it difficult to comprehend within analytical structures normally attached to fiction, even modernism's experimental forms of the genre. Indeed, Mary Helen Washington, Valerie Frazier, and Patricia H. and Vernon E. Lattin have all commented on the "critical voice" surrounding Brooks's only fictional work, which cannot seem to be easily placed within a clear literary lineage or generic grouping. In Hurston's case, the critique of her novel comes not from its generic but rather its racial idiosyncrasy among her other works. *Seraph on the Suwanee*'s main characters are white southerners who frequently espouse racist views; if the text's initial reviews neglected this racism, remarking instead that "Miss Hurston knows her Florida Negro as she knows her Florida white," it was not due to the lack of racist language depicting black Floridians but rather to the biased racial attitudes of those reviewing the novel (Hedden 35). Claudia Tate has commented on *Seraph*'s race-specific history of reception, claiming that when it was originally published, "Hurston's white reviewers were much more amenable to her writing about white folks, whom she called 'Crackers,'" . . . than black scholars would be over the next four decades" (161). Indeed, recent critics have either responded harshly to the novel's "embarrassing characterizations," criticized Hurston's move away from depicting black folks to white ones, or simply ignored the book altogether (St. Clair 56).[3] Delai Capraroso Konzett sums these critical attitudes up well, claiming that "these critics find it difficult to come to terms with a xenophobic, insecure, and whimpering heroine, seemingly the exact inverse of her most popular character, the vital and towering Janie Crawford of *Their Eyes Were Watching God*" (134). In this view, *Seraph of the Suwanee* is an embarrassing blip in an author's otherwise politically forward-looking oeuvre.

This critique of Hurston's novel based on racial representation raises the importance of the political and affective dimensions of each of these three texts in relation to its lack of critical treatment. For while the critique of Hurston's work is most overtly political, it is easy to argue that political, rather than generic, reasons for *Maud Martha's* critical obscurity are also most salient. Maud Martha's critics have tended to undertreat, nonadvantageously compare, and flatten ambiguities in the text, reading Maud Martha Brown as a female protagonist who is either passively angry or incomprehensibly cheery in the face of racist living conditions, without attempting to usefully reconcile the two (Frazier 133). For instance, upon the novella's 1953 publication, the *New York Times* review remarked chiefly on the book's "freshness" and "warm cheerfulness" (Creekmore BR4). This review, tellingly entitled "Daydreams in Flight," posits Maud Martha's narrative as one of success and triumph over negativity, in which "she still can feel, in an affirmation of vitality, that life is good, and people, though often ridiculous, will continue—as she puts it—to be grand, glorious, and brave" (Creekmore BR4). Such a description bears little resemblance to those analyses that privilege the "scraps of baffled hate" that haunt the text in momentary flares before Maud Martha's cheeriness returns, a passive experience of anger that emphasizes and reifies Maud Martha's own impression that her hate had "not much voice" (Brooks 176). Due to this bifurcated response, *Maud Martha* has posed problems in terms of generating nuanced readings that both respect feminist, antiracist political principles and value the agentic choices of its female lead character.

While *Maud Martha's* cheeriness has been welcome to some (albeit for reasons more likely to do with racist desires to erase evidence of white privilege than to any actual political value they find in Maud Martha's optimism), Wharton's *Summer* has been condemned for its unrelenting gloom. In a 2003 article by Pascha Antrece Stevenson, the unfavorable comparison between *Ethan Frome* and *Summer* is coupled with a critique of both texts' affective despair. Stevenson writes: "Edith Wharton singles out Ethan Frome and *Summer*'s Charity Royall to suffer the most unromantic of miseries, penning not a final tableau of suffering terrible in its beauty, but a vision of banal misery which is so repulsive it barely elicits our sympathy" (11). What fascinates about this critique is the emphasis not merely on tragedy but on the "banal" terribleness that the novellas depict. Stevenson seems to suggest that tragedy, unhappiness itself, is not to be condemned as long as its generic packaging makes it affectively palatable; however, this review claims that there is something in *Summer*'s packaging of its protagonist's pain that repels rather than attracts a feeling reader. If we follow Sianne Ngai's lead and consider the peculiarly "unsocial" nature of disgust, in which "disgust explicitly blocks the path of sympathy," then *Summer*'s rendering of Charity Royall troubles precisely because it alienates its protagonist from the social sphere of traumatic bonding, instead placing her beyond the pale of affective communion with a readership (335). This repulsion is based not on the depiction's over-the-top nonsensicalness, but rather its "banal" entrenchment in what one reviewer complains is a representation "so real that one finds one's self questioning her actions" (Wharton, "Mrs." 58). The very realism of this realist text seems to create its negative affective pull.

It is easy to see what might strike a reader as banal, miserable, and "so real" about the journey to adulthood that Wharton pens for *Summer*'s protagonist. Charity Royall, neither bookish (she refers to the library where she works as her "prison-house") nor mild-mannered, begins the book passionate and hopeful; this affective state is vividly drawn, as is her "deep disgust" when Lawyer Royall, the man who has acted as her guardian for most of her life, attempts to enter her bedroom and sleep with her (Wharton 5, 16). That she ends the book married to this same man has often been read as her sad relinquishing of passion and will to fight. Ngai's discussion of disgust locates its utility in its diagnostic reach: its ability to point "powerfully" to the display of "social powerlessness" that, she argues, is at the root of the persons/scenarios/objects to which we react with disgust (353). And indeed, critics have attempted to read *Summer* as a critique of the "so real" that repulses its readers by understanding the novella as one that questions received ideologies about women's roles and limitations. Susan L. Hall gestures toward such a reading through her argument that *Summer* reads as an exemplum of Wharton's own skepticism toward a model of marriage and romantic love that "required that a woman sacrifice her personal freedom" yet offered "few alternatives to marriage" to fin-de-siècle American women (16). This reading offers the palliative that if Charity pays the price of a banal, miserable end, she at least serves as a warning and a social corrective. Yet I hope to show that this mode of redeeming *Summer*, like *Maud Martha* and *Seraph on the Suwanee*, is contingent upon a troubling flattening of the protagonist's epistemic dynamism, one that hinges upon not characterological affect but rather suspect attachments.

By positing the nexus of critical rejection of these protagonists' intellectual acumen as their "suspect attachments," I mean to highlight the way in which critical discourse about each of these female lead characters has gotten hung up in the attempt to parse out exactly why they remain enmeshed in relationships that critics and readers deem suspicious. In Charity Royall's case, her attachment to her guardian-cum-husband, Lawyer Royall, has caused the most consternation, though her relationship to her lover, Lucius Harney—particularly her desire to shield him from the knowledge that he has gotten her pregnant—has its share of detractors. Unhappiness regarding the marital pairing of Lawyer Royall and Charity is widely evidenced in *Summer*'s critical literature. S Kathryn Voorhees-Whitehead, finding support in Elizabeth Ammons, condemns the marriage as "unquestionably a 'bad' thing" (24).[4] Other critics scan their marriage as a morbid enactment of the realist novel's generic endgame: an inevitable tempering of dreams into the compromised "knowledge" of reality (women need husbands; babies need fathers), the sort of narrative closure of desire and closeting of the desirous protagonist that Leo Bersani charts in *A Future for Astyanax*. Jennie A. Kassanoff gestures toward such a reading when she dismisses the more sentimental or romanticized "Kate-Chopin-like image of the 'broken wing' that hinders Charity's final fugitive 'impulse of flight' " and instead argues that "Charity's commitment to generational continuity trumps her desire for feminist individualism" (148). The romantic symbol of the caged bird might be there, Kassanoff argues, but it is a "resigned" bird, not an enslaved one, that closes the novel by a return to reality from a romantic flight of fantasy.

Even in more positive readings of the marital pairing, such as Nancy Walker's affirmation of the relationship as a movement toward the "only natural [option]," the specter of limitation haunts the interpretation (114). Indeed, in many critiques, the language of ensnarement reigns. Pfeiffer reads the conclusion of the novel as both a literal and a symbolic closed door "which [Charity] had so significantly opened in the first line of the novel" (151). William E. Hummel claims that the end of the text finds Charity "trapped, no doubt forever, under the rubble and waste of Lawyer Royall's once glorious self" (232). And John W. Crowley argues that not only does the book's ending mark "the death of her summer daydreams" but also

Charity's "final entrapment in the dependent childish identity from which North Dormer permits her no escape" (95). In these critics' views, Wharton's novel confines its protagonist to a kind of depressing Peter Pan scenario, in which she will not only never grow up but also never escape to an otherworldly land that gifts children with power over their lives and destiny.

Indeed, characterological passivity in the face of a limited or shuttered reality is a commonplace of critical displeasure, interestingly in tension with the charge that these protagonists simultaneously cling to problematic attachments. For example, Maud Martha's attachment is to an optimistic mode of moving through life that does not mesh well with the racism she regularly encounters, to the chagrin of critics who would have her do more to voice her anger rather than contemplate injustice in silence. Though both Nancy Gerber and Mary Helen Washington agree, for instance, that Maud Martha moves toward vocalizing her discontent in the latter part of the novella, while the former uses this trajectory to claim that Maud Martha becomes "an outspoken mother-artist," the latter argues that even at the book's close, neither the "problem of Maud's anger [nor] her silence" in the face of racism is solved (Gerber 36; Washington, "Taming" 466). Yet neither Charity nor Maud Martha has been met with the degree of attachment-focused critique as has been leveled at Arvay Henson, protagonist of *Seraph on the Suwanee*. Here, critics once again take issue with the marital choice of the female lead; however, whereas Charity at least begins her novella hating Lawyer Royall, Arvay Henson seems always at least somewhat sympathetic to the sexist, violent Jim Henson.

Even when Jim rapes her, Arvay's "total submission to Jim," coupled with her "feminine insecurity" has made it difficult for critics to view her sympathetically—and this does not even take into account the troubling representations of race that proliferate within the text, making both Arvay and Jim even more difficult to pity (Comprone 152, 145). Konzett goes so far as to claim the book has proven "a bane to feminists, particularly black feminists," not only due to the distinct opposition between Arvay and Janie Crawford (as mentioned above), but also, and more problematically, because "the husband of the heroine establishes his dominance in their relationship through rape and violence, acts that the novel does not condemn but depicts as motivated by love" (134). Though it is worth noting that perhaps Konzett implicitly idealizes Janie Crawford's marital situation in this comparison (after all, Tea Cake hits Janie in his own effort to establish control over her), what the above most clearly evidences is the difference that Hurston's presentation of the *women* makes in the critical reception of their life stories.

Janie Crawford seems vital and towering, in part because she does escape not one but two bad marriages; thus, we might give her (and her power of discernment) the benefit of the doubt when, after the love of her life abuses her, she still clings to him. In Arvay's case, she chooses to stay with a man who first rapes her and then claims, "You're going to keep on getting raped" for the rest of her life (57). Rather than disgusting Arvay, these words seem to be moved beyond, even forgiven; over twenty years later, after Jim has left her, and she has a chance to make her own way, she goes back to her marriage with him, declaring that "it was her privilege to serve him" (351). Such capitulation to, even delight in, an abusive relationship has proven to critics to be a near-impossible pill to swallow.

Critics of each of these protagonists—Charity Royall, Maud Martha, and Arvay Henson—have seemingly sought an explanation for their problematic affects and attachments by critiquing their intelligence. Maud Martha is a character who displays "intense inwardness," and her coming-of-age story charts a character whose growing knowledge and awareness of herself lacks a public or professional outlet (Iker 91–93). Without the benefit of hearing (or, in the novella's case, reading) Maud Martha's never-voiced knowledge, she would run the risk of appearing completely ignorant. And yet, whereas some critics take advantage of this unique perspective Brooks's text offers—being both inside Maud Martha's thoughts and also outside them, even sometimes inside other characters' thoughts looking down at her—the seeming lack of knowledge that directs Maud Martha's actions can be viewed simultaneous to the knowledge and understanding that undergirds and even constructs her seeming not-knowing. Even so, the novella is still often critiqued based on Maud Martha's dialogic silence: such critics appreciate her intelligence, but not the strategic masking of it.

Yet understanding Maud Martha as playing dumb is a far cry from the readings of Charity Royall and Arvay Henson, where "playing" has nothing to do with the dumbness most critics cite. In the case of Arvay, far too many critics have reaffirmed Jim's own assessment of Arvay, when, after their first fight, he comes to the conclusion that she must be "a trifle dumb" (66). For instance, Lillie Howard's commentary regarding Arvay's mental facilities begins by critiquing Jim's denigration of Avray's intelligence, calling it "chauvinistic and unflattering to women everywhere," but then goes on to express her sympathy with his undervaluation of Arvay's mind in the astonishing evaluation that follows: "but Arvay's consistent actions are a poor defense against the charge [that his understanding far exceeds hers]. Not only must most things be explained to her, but they often must be explained without her seeking an explanation or even knowing that she should" (271). Ignorance, then, to the goings-on around her and her need for a teacher fuse with another sense of her ignorance: that of her inability or lack of desire to extricate herself from what must strike an outside viewer as an abusive and sexist husband.

Likewise, Charity is also conceived of as an unlearned woman whose ignorance dogs her in both intellectual and relational matters. Woven throughout the critical readings of *Summer*, for instance, which I reference above, are associations between Charity's relationships and her lack of intelligence or childlike innocence. Many critics, whether they defend or pity Charity, view the "knowledge" of the text to be outside of Charity's person. Some emphasize Charity's intellectual ignorance, noting she dislikes books and is not university educated, to explain her inarticulateness with her lover, Lucius, and to delimit what power she has as bodily rather than intellectual.[5] Stevenson even reads Charity's lack of knowledge as part of her character and Wharton's class prejudice, comparing Charity to a "noble savage" who is "genetically selected to be uncouth and uncivilized" (420). Crowley is most polemic here; in contrast to readings such as Kathy Grafton's and Deborah Hecht's, which posit Charity's acquiescence to marriage as a direct result of her maturation, Crowley highlights Wharton's language in the novel's final chapter of "infantile helplessness" to argue that the marriage is "profoundly regressive," expressive not of "the adult love of a woman for a man but the pathetic cry of a battered child for a nurturing parent" (94).[6] This final return to innocence for Crowley does not reinvigorate Charity with the lightness and purity of a lost youth but instead condemns her to a life led in an epistemic void. Charity's lack of knowledge—whether essentialized or regressive—is what allows Charity's choice of Lawyer Royall's hand to exist and what allows her critics most clearly to question it.

By engaging this extensive analysis of the common sources of critical difficulties these three texts share, I hope to have clarified the very seriousness with which such critical qualms need to be taken. The critical frustrations these texts have produced stem from critical and social investments that are real and that I share. For example, when Claudia Tate warns that *Seraph on the Suwanee* "engages Hurston's female readers with . . . internal conflict" because "women readers find themselves in the awkward position of feeling like traitors to their sex if they like this novel," her words do not read as mere hyperbole (164). I would hope, for instance, that any reader, male or female, would be disgusted by Jim's assertion that marriage to him will be, for Arvay, a series of continual rapes (Hurston 57). And yet, by focusing on these women's weaknesses and reading their choices as regressive portrayals of ignorant women rather than as active female agents choosing not to know, we risk overlooking the circumstances of their lives, in their limitations and violence, which require such choices. Indeed, readers' own attempts to comprehend the challenging choices of these texts' women have resulted in their revisions or dismissals of the serious violence with which the women are visited. For example, despite the explicit language of rape used in the text by Jim himself to describe his assault on Arvay, Frank G. Slaughter's *New York Times* review of the book refers to Arvay's rape as "an episode," while Worth Tuttle Hedden, of the *New York Herald Tribune*, names it "a seduction" (Gates, Jr.). In trying to understand *Seraph on the Suwanee* as a romantic tale—by trying to make sense of Arvay's love for Jim—these reviews end up excusing sexual violence and with it, perhaps, the patriarchal prejudices that, in 1948 when these reviews were written, had no legal name for rape within marital bonds and offered little recourse for an abused woman. Conversely, the same tendency to view these women as passive innocents blandly flattens any potential positive depictions of female strength. For when Hurburt Creekmore highlights Maud Martha's uplifting message by emphasizing its protagonist's optimistic, life-sustaining cheer via the novella's ending question—"What, *what*, am I to do with all of this life?"—he does so without acknowledging that much of the life of which Maud Martha speaks has not been received by chance but rather has been created by Maud Martha herself (Creekmore BR4). Overlooking either type of complication is an unacceptable narrowing of critical possibilities. It is this narrowing that a theory of an ethic of innocence can help us, as critics and readers, avoid. To demonstrate this, I will use the next sections of this chapter to read a few key moments of each of these texts through the ethic-of-innocence lens in order to demonstrate the nuanced possibilities such a lens asks us to attend to in textual detail and privilege in our interpretation.

Pessimistic Optimism: Charity's Choice of Agency over Affect

Like many critics, I, too, wish to question Charity's final choice of marriage, but on terms that pay tribute to Charity's independence, resourcefulness, and intelligence. Here, I find the reading of *Summer* by Barbara A. White instructive; while White argues that *Summer* breaks Wharton's pessimistic mold since it "works within the essentially optimistic plot of women's fiction," she also acknowledges the "co-existence" of both optimism and pessimism at the conclusion of *Summer*. This "doubleness," White claims, is "built into the structure of women's fiction," a structure in which the heroine, when reaching her "reward" of marriage, "shrinks" from her earlier growth, "ending up a child" (234). Once again, the "innocence" Charity betrays through her choice of Lawyer Royall is associated with a childlike state, no doubt helped along by Wharton's own language. But what if we were to view this "innocence" in a way that respects both the desire to read power into Charity's decision and the feminist need to point out the problems with such power? Reading via an ethic of innocence, I think it is possible to understand Charity's final choice to marry as one that displays neither an innocence of Mr. Royall's questionable behavior nor hopeless acquiescence to an impossible situation. Rather, such a reading serves to emphasize not only that marrying Lawyer Royall before Charity's "condition" is made public is the best choice available to her in a culture in which to be pregnant and unmarried is a socially stigmatized position, but also that in order to make this marriage possible, she must perform an innocence about her negative feelings toward Lawyer Royall, even to herself.

Moments at the end of the text show Charity's struggle to enact innocence in order to make her marriage to Lawyer Royall livable. Whether a changing or a dawning attitude, a move from hatred to acceptance or a shift from the Charity who "*thinks* she hates and despises" Lawyer Royall only to find, in the end, that she doesn't, critics have often emphasized Charity's changing feelings toward Lawyer Royall as the crucial precedent of the marriage (White 231, emphasis mine). Yet I also think it is instructive to look at just how carefully, even rationally, Charity chooses her own affective responses. Certainly, Charity and Lucius are broken up at the moment when Charity discovers her pregnancy, but this does not automatically make Charity feel helpless and abandoned. After confirming her pregnancy at an abortionist's office, Charity is actually calmed by the thought that "she no longer had any difficulty in picturing herself as Harney's wife now that she was the mother of his child" (Wharton, *Summer* 151). In fact, Charity feels a sense of power in their relationship for the first time via the knowledge that she can force Lucius's return to her: as she puts it, "she knew she had it in her power" to "make things hard," that she "held his fate in her hands" (156). And, in looking closely at the narrative arc, it is actually this power of pregnancy's embodied knowledge, not the body's doomed surrender, that allows Charity to choose, whether generously or selfishly, to let Harney go forward with his marriage to another woman without the knowledge that he is expecting a child with Charity. Harvey remains ignorant through Charity's choice to withhold knowledge—a state that might perhaps be easier on Harney in the long run but one that also preserves, for Charity, her power to reject Harney on her own terms (rather than accept a forced marriage to him or to be rejected anew, on terms only Harney could decide).[7]

Indeed, in making any decisions toward the end of the novella, Charity weighs all of her options—even the ones that seem initially distasteful to her. Once she decides that she does not want to force Lucius to marry her, she reconsiders an abortion. At the abortionist's office, Charity experiences extreme anger at being taken "for a miserable creature like Julia," an infamous townswoman who works as a prostitute and to whom an unwanted pregnancy would prove no real dilemma, as long as the abortion was affordable (150). But at the moment of decision and in the privacy of her own room, Charity acknowledges her newfound understanding of the other woman's decision. Though "her soul recoiled" when she imagined working in Julia's profession, Charity admits that she "had always understood Julia Hawes's refusal to be snatched" into an unwanted marriage under the town's derisive eye (156). Through this moment, we might understand Charity's subsequent flight to the mountain, where she was first born, as her own attempt to evade "snatching" or capture: a true escape from social norms rather than pejoratively escapist fantasy. And yet when the mountain proves more dehumanizing than the alternatives from which Charity was running, she does determine upon a career in prostitution, one in which she could still envision being able to make enough money to keep her baby "cleaned and combed and rosy" and "bring it pretty things to wear" (174). So when Lawyer Royall's carriage arrives on the mountain trail and Charity makes the choice to get in, it is not clear at all that we are meant to read this as a moment in which she is saved from the fate of sex work: rather, we might read this marriage as the most comfortable form of selling herself that Charity sees available. For when Lawyer Royall asks Charity to marry him yet again, and Charity protests, "Oh, I can't," the reader is told that "she was not sure if she was rejecting what he offered, or already struggling against the temptation of taking what she no longer had a right to" (180). That she does "take" his offer might signal her temptation, but it also might signal her re-evaluation of what exactly was being offered: as a prostitute, she certainly would have a right to the economic recompense for access to her body, regardless of that body's reproductive state.

Whereas the logic behind Charity's choice to marry remains unclear, Lawyer Royall's offer is not depicted as salvific or benevolent on his part, but rather as a culmination of desire. Indeed, he is "persuasive" in his tone and feels no compunction in declaring his desires; whereas Charity struggles to finish the sentence "I want," Lawyer Royall does not hesitate to dismiss her wants in favor of declaring his own (180). Lawyer Royall takes advantage of his position of power over his ward throughout the book—attempting the seduction, controlling her movements, berating her for her relationship with Lucius, and doggedly pursuing and harassing her despite her refusal of his affections. That Charity herself feels more powerful than Royall, that she "had always thought of him—when she thought of him at all—as of someone hateful and obstructive, but whom she could outwit and dominate when she chose to make the effort"—does not make his actions either just or defendable (183). It does allow us to dig into the ambiguity of Wharton's text. Perhaps Charity's silence and acquiescence to Lawyer Royall before her marriage is not that of the obedient child but that of the naughty liar—the silence of a woman who hopes to find refuge for herself and her unborn child in a marriage that she can see a promising possibility of pulling off—if only she can keep quiet and not acknowledge the pregnancy to her suitor.

After the marriage, Charity again feels "the old impulse of flight," the one that took her to the mountain, but nothing comes of it, as "it was only the lift of a broken wing" (187). Life has clearly harmed Charity; however, a broken wing is not a razed one, and Charity is able, we see, to negotiate this relationship through choosing to reject knowledge she has previously relied upon. She begins by recasting Lawyer Royall's character—calling to mind his address at Old Home Week in an attempt to see him again, as she did then, as "another being, a being so different from the dull-witted enemy with whom she had supposed herself to be living" (183–84). Though the "illusion" that Lawyer Royall is "her lover with the leafy arch of summer bending over them" remains "faint and transitory," Charity takes refuge in it while she can (182).

This ethic of innocence, which can transmute an enemy into a refuge, makes a future with Lawyer Royall possible for Charity to envision. Charity's final statement to Lawyer Royall, "I guess you're good, too," seems not to be an admittance of new understanding but rather of a decision made and enacted (194). She is not an innocent, as evidenced by her continued fear and regret; after the wedding, Charity even displays remorse and terror at her own actions and silences, asking, "What have I done? Oh, what have I done?" (188). However, she puts her fear aside by convincing herself that Royall "knew" what her state was when she married him, that "it was because he knew that he had married her," and that his actions (not joining her in the marriage bed) were meant "to show her she was safe with him" (189). There is no corroborating evidence from Lawyer Royall's point of view, and Charity may well be making up this kinder version of her guardian-turned-husband (as well as this kinder version of her own potential secret-keeping). But she enacts innocence to her previous feelings and continuing judgments through her belief in these bits and pieces of her new tale of Lawyer Royall's character, and her pretense is enough to satisfy him and allow her to get what she wants—respite and a future for herself and her baby.

That staying married to Lawyer Royall appears to be the best choice to Charity should not lead to simple condemnation of what might appear, under the auspices of feminist knowledge, to be a weak acquiescence to social norms (or women's fiction's plot structures) on the part of either Charity's character or the text's depiction of this character; rather, it should be a starting point for our understanding of the difficulties of the circumscribed self (whether a literary self or a human self), especially the self of the modern (poor) female. Yet such understanding of these difficulties, exhibited in either literary works or in nonfictional accounts like Addams's, is hampered by the silent and silenced routes in which such doing (especially, again, female doing) often takes place. As a complement, then, to the silence that accompanies much of Charity's decisions at the end of *Summer*, I turn to Gwendolyn Brooks's *Maud Martha*, a novella whose story line consists of a jumble of words that, first and foremost, "transpire within Maud's mind" (Iker 93).

Veiled Sass: Maud Martha's Covert Protests

Brooks's *Maud Martha* is a *bildungsroman* and a *kunstlerroman* in which, as Karen Iker notes, both personal and artistic developments differ from the traditionally male course by occurring largely in private, unacknowledged to any character outside the consciousness of Maud Martha Brown (91–93). When reading such a female-centered development narrative for moments of epistemic choice, our focus must shift from the moment of actual speech to the multiplicities of intelligence and communication that silence and reflection, even "playing dumb," display. Some of the clearest places in which Maud Martha exhibits the dynamic nature of her choice not to know occur in moments in which the text depicts racist commentary or treatment she faces as part of her everyday reality. For instance, in the chapter "tree leaves leaving trees," Maud Martha and her daughter, Paulette, make a visit to Santa Claus in the Toy Department. Maud Martha encourages Paulette to "tell Santa what [she] want[s] for Christmas," something her little girl has been wanting to do, only to find that when Paulette does approach him, Santa ignores her (Brooks 173). Something as seemingly lighthearted as an encounter with a department store Santa Claus becomes an ideal site from which to view such dynamism, in large part because it allows Maud Martha to successfully voice public resistance to racism, even though she simultaneously promotes her daughter's innocence toward this racism.

Maud Martha addresses the injustice visited upon her daughter by this Santa by understanding his racism as, first and foremost, a type of blindness. Indeed, Maud Martha notices that Santa is "unable to see either mother or child" and so speaks to him both to get his attention and to point out his disregard for her daughter: "'Mister,' said Maud Martha, 'my little girl is talking to you'" (173). Santa eventually does respond to Paulette, though he does so grudgingly; Brooks writes that his neck "turned with hard slowness" and his face was "unwilling" to even add a "question mark at the end" of his only words to the girl: "And what—do you want for Christmas" (173). Maud Martha intervenes in his disinterest and directs Paulette to cut her wish list short, because "Santa Claus is through" with Paulette long before her daughter is with him (174). Outside, once the two have left, Paulette asks her mother about Santa Claus's behavior: "Why didn't Santa Claus like me?" (174). Maud Martha denies the truth—that Santa was a racist—in her reply, insisting that Santa liked her daughter; Paulette rejoins that he did not like her, though, and continues to provide evidence to support her impression until Maud Martha tells her daughter a story. This "innocent" story—what we might also call a lie—that rejects the knowledge of racism in favor of a fantasy of universal love, is strikingly, as Gerber notes, Maud Martha's longest speech in the novella (32). It goes as follows:

> Listen, child. People don't have to kiss you to show they like you. Now you know Santa Claus liked you. What have I been telling you? Santa Claus loves every child, and on the night before Christmas he brings them swell presents. Don't you remember, when you told Santa Claus you wanted the ball and bear and tricycle and doll he said "Um-hm"? That meant he's going to bring you all those. You watch and see. Christmas'll be here in a few days. You'll wake up Christmas morning and find them and then you'll know Santa Claus loved *you too*. (175, original emphasis)

Understandably, Maud Martha's lie to her daughter has caused critical conflicts. Gerber acknowledges the dispute even as she praises Maud Martha's speech, arguing that "the fact that Maud Martha does not say that Santa Claus loves only white children does not diminish the heroism of her voice" (Gerber 33). Gerber goes on to indicate that what Maud Martha does is invested with motherly, rather than political, care, arguing that "while the language of political struggle is not yet available to Maud Martha, there is nonetheless a maternal voice that struggles simultaneously to be heard—'Hey, mister!'—and to comfort—'Santa Claus loved you, too' " (33). Conversely, Washington condemns the scene because she sees these words as "still part of [Maud Martha's] subterfuge" that squelches her anger at injustice and chooses instead to play nice (Washington, "Taming" 462). Worse still in Washington's evaluation is that Maud Martha's illusions threaten to silence her daughter; Washington writes that "the honest voice in the chapter is Paulette's" and that Maud Martha, rather than supporting such honesty, problematically "insists that Paulette deny her own perception of Santa's cold indifference" (462). Washington's point is crucial here, as it troubles the inherent goodness of a motherly love that advocates lies and innocence over reality and shows it as a bankrupt means of buying only temporary reprieve at the cost of full participation in the world.

Certainly, I would agree that desire to keep Paulette from being hurt by the world informs Maud Martha's decisions in the chapter. Patricia H. Lattin and Vernon E. Lattin note that her primary thought is "of protecting her child's innocence"; as Maud Martha frames it, she'd like to "keep her that land of blue!" (Lattin 184; Brooks 176). This blue land of ignorant innocence is markedly different from the chosen innocence I have been discussing thus far; it is a child's fantasy land, populated by good fairies and evil witches, with no complicating crossovers or conflations. With this exclamation, "[K]eep her that land of blue!" one could read Maud Martha's desire to keep Paulette indefinitely from the knowledge of a racist reality. In this reading, though Maud Martha is clearly aware of the racism behind Santa's hatred of her child and chooses to pretend otherwise, she would choose to keep Paulette from this knowledge if she could, denying her a choice not to know by enforcing ignorance instead.

Such enforced innocence could lead down a troublingly oppressive path for her daughter, one that would likely teach her (as cultural ideology has taught many women before her) that her value lies in her innocence and she must deny reality to sustain it, thus squelching a type of voice that Maud

Martha herself regrets not having. Maud Martha calls the quietness of her anger in the face of her own and her daughter's oppression her "hungriest lack," the aspect of her affect she "especially regretted" (Brooks 176). To keep her daughter in her childlike innocence would be to trap her in a position even worse than Maud Martha's—for Paulette would lack not only a voice to express her anger, but also a consciousness with which to acknowledge it.

We see, however, that Maud Martha is not merely "naïve" as some criticism suggests; indeed, she has no illusions about keeping Paulette in an innocent state forever. After she tells the "Santa loves you" story/lie, Maud Martha looks "furtively" at her daughter and wonders, "Was Paulette believing her?" (176). In doing so, Maud Martha hopes that "the little creature wasn't ready" to confront the reality of racism she would inevitably uncover upon trying to "think" and "find out answers" to the Santa episode (176). Her fervent hope, "some other night, not tonight," makes it clear to a reader that Maud Martha knows that her child's eventual disbelief in the mother's protective lie is inevitable—indeed, that such knowledge may even have already been gleaned—and that one night, Maud Martha will have to meet her daughter's own readiness to face the world with her own ready mind. In some sense, then, we can understand Maud Martha's wish for Paulette's yet-untarnished innocence as at once indicative of a mother's protective love and also acknowledgment that a mother's duty is not merely to protect her daughter but, more importantly, to help her cope with the world once she meets it. To "keep her that land of blue," then, might be understood not as Maud Martha's desired place of innocence in which to keep her daughter, but rather as a symbol of a more general ability to find hope and joy in the world despite her daughter's new knowledge. The "land of blue" might be Maud Martha's alternative of "choosing not-knowing"—a place, a mindset, to which Paulette could return, could keep, even after she "understands."

To place too much emphasis on Maud Martha's maternal protective instincts here, then, is to dismiss her "knowing innocence's" political bent. Not only does Maud Martha attempt to protect her daughter from discovering one truth, but she also tells a political story of hope for her daughter that can continue to exist even when said truth is discovered. This story of hope, though a fiction, is as much practical as it is fantastical. Maud Martha's proof of Santa's love may well be a rejection of knowledge in favor of an innocent story, but it is a fable she has carefully constructed so that she can, in fact, create a reality for Paulette as she herself describes it. Maud Martha's fable recycles Santa's own words in order to reread them for her daughter, telling Paulette that his "Um-hm" was an indication of his care for her (in the form of remembering her presents) rather than his disregard for her (in the form of a silencing utterance of inattention). She then indicates that the proof of this will arrive on Christmas morning, when the promised presents do actually appear. We can surmise that in Maud's world, as in ours, there is no mythic Santa who physically brings gifts to children: it will be Maud Martha who makes Santa's love come alive. Gerber's insistence that we not deny Maud Martha's speech because she does not tell the "truth" about racism remains as essential as Washington's critique; however, the remarkable thing about the tale is not, as Gerber states, that it is based "on a false promise" to her daughter regarding the world's goodness; rather, what is remarkable is that it has been designed to fulfill the promise it makes (33). Indeed, Maud Martha crafts a fiction she can realize and, in realizing, grab control over the racist environment that might otherwise encompass her daughter and ingrain in her its dehumanization.

Paulette may not hear the truth of racism from her mother's mouth, may have this truth in fact obscured if not overtly denied, but she does hear another truth from her mother, one that proclaims that she is loved "too," on par with and the same as the others. We learn early in the novella that Maud Martha's darker skin prohibits her from hearing this same message from her own parents, who "were enslaved [by], were fascinated" with, and preferred her lighter-skinned sister, Helen. Here, the knowledge-rejecting story allows Maud Martha an opportunity to communicate obliquely to her daughter how much she is loved. Yes, Maud Martha invests in an innocent fantasy rather than the truth that would confirm her daughter's suspicions of Santa's hate, but because of this, the societal hatred that Paulette notes in her questions is never reflected back to Paulette in her mother's voice.

Such silences, then, might be read as something other than the desire "to lapse into a state of mind absent of thought or imagination, a state of passivity and indifference" (Iker 93). In the chapter "the self-solace," Maud Martha is present in a beauty salon when a white saleswoman, Miss Ingram, tells Sonia Johnson, the black owner of the shop, that she, Miss Ingram, "work[s] like a nigger to make a few pennies" (Brooks 139). This statement gets Maud Martha's immediate attention; we read that her "head shot up," and she immediately watches Sonia (139). As Sonia doesn't respond, Maud Martha is led to believe that she "must have been mistaken. [She] was afraid [she] heard that woman say 'nigger.' Apparently not. Because of course Mrs. Johnson wouldn't let her get away with it. In her own shop" (139). With repeated reassurances to herself that the racist word had not actually been uttered, Maud proceeds to imagine all the things she herself would have done had this actually happened. Here, we see the chosen innocence (nothing racist happened here) being spun at the same time this tale is subtly acknowledged as a fiction (here is how I would deal with a racist remark being said because it likely happened here, and it will certainly happen again). Far from passively accepting or turning away from reality, we see Maud Martha using a choice of not-knowing as a way to process and contemplate possible responses to her racist environment. Indeed, when Maud Martha looks at Sonia, we read that "she forced her smile to stay on," indicating that she is aware and working against reasons why her smile might need to come off (139).

When Sonia later engages Maud Martha in an explanation of her choice not to say anything to censor Miss Ingram's racism, Sonia makes her own dynamic epistemologies evident, a dynamism that has also been critically simplified. Gerber, for instance, understands Sonia's argument for feigning innocence as "it is better to agree with white people than to risk their anger by talking back" (31). Certainly, the avoidance of "mak[ing] enemies" is one of the things that Sonia notes in her explanation (142). But her reasons are more varied and complex than simply being agreeable; she cites both epistemic ignorance of white people as to the true meaning of the term and black oversensitiveness as two reasons for her response; most interestingly, however, she argues that the racist term doesn't apply to her because it "means to them [white people] something bad, or slavey-like, or low," a category from which Sonia is exempt (141). Sonia even goes so far as to say that "a white man can be a 'nigger,' according to their meaning for the word, just like a colored man can" (141). Without apologizing for the racism of others, and without going so far as to let the white woman off the hook for her own ignorance, this exchange makes it possible to read Sonia's silence as one that rejects racism not by denial of its presence but by an epistemic acuity that refuses to be identified with it. For through this latter refusal, Sonia also demonstrates a more complex and superior understanding of language and connotation than the white Miss Ingram. We may be suspicious of Sonia Johnson's actions and might have plenty of answers to her final defense of her silence—"What would be the point"—but Sonia herself clearly sees her chosen stance as complexly empowering rather than simplistically helpless (142).

For her part, Maud Martha does three things of note throughout this scene. First, she clarifies with Sonia that the word "nigger" really was spoken. Then, she explains her need for clarification by saying that she'd thought she "must have been mistaken" because Sonia wasn't "getting after her" (141). Finally, Maud Martha enacts her own silence. After Sonia's defense of her nonconfrontational choice, we as readers are left without access to Maud Martha's interiority. All we get is three sentences of wordless response: "Maud Martha stared steadily into Sonia Johnson's irises. She said nothing. She kept on staring into Sonia Johnson's irises" (141). Is Maud Martha's silence similar to Sonia's? Gerber reads it as evidence that Maud Martha "silently rebels," but as we have just discussed, Sonia also articulates her own silence as a way to reject a racist name and thus rebel in her own way (31). We also are not privy to the whole course of the conversation or relationship between Sonia and Maud Martha. If Maud Martha eventually responded, or if Sonia's protests or clarifications continued, we might have a better idea of how Maud Martha's silence is understood by Sonia as either sympathetic or disapproving or something different altogether. We might also further understand the scope of Maud Martha's silence if she were to quit the beauty salon, never to return, as she does when dealing with another racist encounter while working for Mrs. Burns-Cooper. None of these narrative arcs is filled out for us in the text, so any confirmation of our suspicions remains elusive. All I would suggest is that if Maud Martha does have a desire to "lapse" into indifference to racism, as Karen Iker suggests, this desire is not realized in this chapter (93). Maud Martha sees "fighting" racism like this as "plain old ugly duty" on her part, and yet her chosen refusals of knowledge allow her to feel it is okay, from time to time, if she is "too relaxed to fight today" because there's no need for her life to be constructed *only* of such fights (Brooks 140). Though this means of solacing the self might prevent Maud Martha from "fighting" with the saleswoman overtly, I do not think it means she does not "fight." Indeed, Maud Martha fights—epistemically, affectively—to retain the right *to not fight* all of the time, to relax, and to yet remain vigilant to the racism that would try to disallow her leisure. If Sonia refuses the derogatory term, so does Maud Martha, and on the terms the saleswoman sets out; rather than constantly working for pennies, Maud Martha relaxes—and perhaps saves up for when she, not another, might decide it counts.

Far from demonstrating a lack of agency, Maud Martha's deployment and sustaining of innocence within the Santa and beauty-shop episodes work to position her as an active subject, one with the power to literally reauthor a dominant, racist text. Rather than reading her hopeful storytelling or stubborn silences as ironic commentaries on the reality of racism, through an ethic of innocence, we might see Maud Martha's rejection of racist knowledge as a political action designed not to reject reality but to change it. Richard Rorty, a leading contemporary pragmatist philosopher, writes in "Feminism and Pragmatism" that he sees the promise of pragmatist feminism (and we might add antiracist pragmatism) in its efforts toward "trying to actualize hitherto undreamt-of possibilities by putting new linguistic and other practices into play and erecting new social constructs" (47). Rejection of knowledge via choosing a knowing innocence, then subsequently creating a fiction from within this innocent stance, does not deny but rather *shifts* reality, in a move that helps to create the world it imagines. *Maud Martha*'s undertow of pragmatism founds its title character's optimism in action rather than daydreams, for it provides the possibility of yoking what can be imagined with, through process, what can be realized.

Maud Martha's pragmatic "knowing innocence" presents a feminist/antiracist politics of hope; as such, Brooks's novella demonstrates the way in which the dynamism of pragmatism can be used to inform what might otherwise seem to be a text that posits either a complete rejection of reality or a critique of reality without providing a practical way of realizing the utopic alternatives demonstrated in Maud Martha's fantasies. As much tool as coping strategy, Maud Martha's engagement with innocence suggests a way in which we can expand our understanding of the commitment to social justice Gwendolyn Brooks demonstrated in her work, in which to imagine a blue land—alongside a clear recognition that this land is indeed imagined—is the first step to attaining it.

Recasting Trauma: Arvay's Mental and Bodily Manipulation

For feminist readers, Wharton's *Summer* may be a realistic tragedy for its conclusion, which traps Charity in an incestuous marriage, and Brooks's *Maud Martha* might be a book worth lauding for its insistence on personal, rather than marital fulfillment, what Karen Iker calls "not a fulfillment but a rejection of the Romance plot" (98). But Hurston's *Seraph on the Suwannee*, which comes between these two in terms of publication year, also separates them by virtue of its strange and complex tale of its own protagonist, Arvay Henson, and her chosen innocence. By way of conclusion of this chapter, I want to turn briefly to *Seraph on the Suwanee* to investigate just a few of the nuances it can add to our understanding of the choice to enact innocence—and of what ignoring such a choice's existence might also help us to ignore. For Hurston's text is undoubtedly a love story that ends by seemingly fulfilling Arvay's desires, though chief among these realized dreams is Arvay's happiness in her marriage with her rapist-turned-husband.

In order to trouble the common critical notion that Arvay is, at worst, ignorant of her oppressive life conditions or, at best, a stark example of the "hopelessness" that "women—whether black of white—had at the time," I will suggest that she, too, makes use of epistemic innocence in order to navigate the affective and material dimensions of her marriage (Comprone 152). Yet such epistemic innocence is not simply a strategy Arvay develops in order to deal with Jim Meserve. I will show how, looking at the opening of the novel, these choices not to know are actually a cornerstone of Arvay Henson's way of life (and perhaps even of other townswomen who share Arvay's limited life options). For the "hysterical neurotic" that one original reviewer, Frank Slaughter, terms the pre-marital Arvay Henson could be productively understood as a woman already enmeshed in an ethic of innocence. Hurston's novel opens with the information that five years previously, at age sixteen, "Arvay had turned her back on the world and all its sins and snares" in favor of becoming a missionary (3). To compound matters, at eighteen, Arvay developed "hysterical seizures" or "fits" that manifested at moments of public exposure to courting rituals, often after church and "usually when some extra brash young gallant had forced himself upon her to the extent of seeing her home" (6). Arvay's fits were only cured by a dose of turpentine and sugar and the exit of "the embarrassed would-be suitor," events that happened with less and less frequency as "one by one the more brash were discouraged and the timid never tried" (7). Here, Arvay's "sickness" produces the antisocial effect of discouraging potential marital mates, an effect that, it turns out, is much to Arvay's liking.

These hysterical fits play on notions of innocence both directly and indirectly by detailing Arvay's piety and insinuating her sexual prudery; yet readers quickly discover that Arvay, if "innocent," is hardly naïve. Her denouncement of the world in favor of the church follows after her first love, the town minister named Carl, marries her sister. Arvay "plan[s]" to be "sent far off to some foreign land" by way of her religious vocation, hoping that this will spur Carl to acknowledge his own secret love for her and leave her sister to follow her (11). In the same vein, Arvay's fits begin when Carl and her sister start having children. Rather than a case of hysteria, it appears that what Arvay has is a keen sense of what will keep other men away from her as she alternately treasures her secret love for Carl and mourns the loss of actualizing it. That Arvay convinces the town, who regard her as "queer, if not a little 'tetched,'" perhaps not only pays tribute to Arvay's performative skill but also makes evident the extent to which a woman rejecting her suitors was seen as perversion (6). Interestingly, though the book does not go into this much further, we learn that Arvay is not the only woman in the novel who has these strange fits. The narrator tells us that "the old heads recalled that Maria Henson had been given to fits and spasms in her girlhood the same way that Arvay was" (6). This history, paired with the townsfolks' claim that "marriage would straighten her [Arvay] out," might suggest that Mrs. Henson, like Arvay, attempted to strategically employ her hysteria until she was able to choose her marriage, was forced into marriage, or was, like Arvay, exposed as a "fraud." In this, we can see the seeds of a resistance practice enacted by townswomen when they, like Arvay, are looking for a way to keep their own antisocial desires in play without directly countering the community's social scripts.

That Arvay's father, Brock Henson, is so "deeply impressed" by Jim's turpentine-in-the-eye solution to Arvay's fits, which he terms the "quickest cure for spasm-fits I ever did see," further suggests that Brock Henson is himself familiar with such fits and the ways in which men (perhaps even himself) have attempted to "cure" them (33). Jim Meserve's "cure" of dropping turpentine in Arvay's eye not only dispels this instance of female resistance, but it also demonstrates from the start his willingness to be cruel in the pursuit of his desires. Not only is he willing to cause Arvay physical pain, but he is also more than happy to expose her performance for what it is—a pretense of hysteria—without considering that such a performance might be enacted reasonably, for a reason. To Jim, Brock, and perhaps other townsmen, Arvay's fits indicate only bodily response: she is a sexually "high-charged woman," who, "in place of looking things in the face" and acknowledging her bodily needs, instead "blinded [her] eyes and took up with that old missionary foolishness to make believe that [she] was much too nice to feel natural" (263). They understand Arvay's fits as performative, then, but do not believe her to have made an epistemic choice in enacting them.

Thus, when looking at the rape scene, we should consider the qualities not only of the Jim-Arvay relationship trajectory but also of the past knowledge given about how Arvay has manipulated her past presentation of herself. To fully comprehend Arvay's choices within the larger narrative trajectory in which she marries her rapist, we need to mind this history of fits and turpentine in order to understand the success and limits of Arvay's agency when it comes to her own romantic and sexual desires. When Arvay and Jim become engaged, Arvay is not simply flattered or forced into the relationship; after Jim makes his intentions clear, Arvay "thought and asked questions of herself" while alone in her room, enabling her to ask, "if Jim really wanted her, what about herself?" (35). Even this early in their relationship, she is canny enough to acknowledge Jim's sexism, realizing that he will never value her mind and "had just as good as excused the woman he married from all worry and bother" (35). Far from being a bar to the marriage, Arvay's understanding of Jim's limited expectations for her allows her to acquiesce to the engagement, after she extracts his promise that he will "drop no more teppentime in [her] eye" (40). This understanding upon which their engagement is founded, however, is broken metaphorically if not literally when Jim, two weeks before their wedding, convinces a shy but trusting Arvay to take him into her secret place under a mulberry. There, in Arvay's sanctuary, he rapes her.

That the scene depicts a rape seems unquestionable, both due to the language of the scene itself and both characters' judgments of the scene afterwards. In the scene itself, Jim commands Arvay to let go of the tree limbs she's swinging on, though she "held onto the limbs desperately" as he drags her down to the ground (51). She attempts to call for help but finds herself unable to do so: she "opened her mouth to scream, but no sound emerged" (51). The next sentence in the rape scene is read by Janet St. Clair as evidence of "even more outrageous complicity" on the part of Arvay in her own rape. Though St. Clair's reading typically supports Arvay and condemns Jim for his sexism and violence, she cannot countenance the following: "Her mouth was closed by Jim's passionate kisses, and in a moment more, despite her struggles, Arvay knew a pain remorseless sweet" (51). Rather than reading her final three words, "pain remorseless sweet," as indicative of Arvay's own enjoyment of the rape, if the sentence is taken in whole we must acknowledge that whatever sweetness Arvay feels occurs while she is still struggling to fight off her attacker. It seems perfectly plausible, given what we now know of the body's physiological responses, that Arvay might have become physically aroused during her rape while also, at the same time, remaining unconsenting—a biological possibility that, far from indicating Arvay's silent complicity with her rapist, calls forth further sympathy toward a woman whose very body might seem to be working against her will in such a circumstance.

After the rape, Arvay's primary feeling is fear. In her words, "she had been taken for a fool, and now her condition was worse than before . . . What was to become of her now? Where would she turn for refuge? Not to her folks, certainly. She would get no sympathy there." (51–52). Arvay's response to her rape seems neither ignorant nor idealized. She is immediately pragmatic and quick to realize how a rape has changed her circumstances from an engaged and eligible young woman to a "ruined" prospect, despite the fact that it is her intended who has assaulted her. And though we might have disgust at these social scripts, which would fault a victim of sexual assault rather than the perpetrator, Arvay's understanding of the situation is verified when her mother, seeing Jim and Arvay dash off and fearing astutely that Jim might be "dragging our girl off somewhere to rape her and then leave her on our hands" acknowledges not anger at Jim but rather the resigned acceptance of potential consequences for Arvay: "a young 'un without no name for us to look after and feed and raise" (55). Arvay's mother, like Arvay, sees the only hope for this situation in marriage; she urges her husband Brock to "take that shot-gun and get on your horse and overtake 'em. Make him marry her before the sun go down" (55). Both women see marriage as a way to protect Arvay's ability to live unshunned in her community, a means that ironically, and not uncommonly, requires yoking her to a man who has violated her.

Whereas Brock scoffs at their ability to make Jim marry Arvay, saying that "Arvay wasn't hollering or nothing" and thus they "couldn't swear to a thing," no swearing appears necessary to make Jim admit he has raped Arvay (55). In a remarkable passage that takes place while Jim and Arvay are riding into town after the rape, Jim declares to Arvay that she is "a married woman now" (56). At Arvay's incredulity, Jim insists "why, sure you're married, Arvay. Under that mulberry tree" (56). Arvay's response is far from passive; instead, she clearly and precisely claims her own understanding of what has happened: "All I know is that I been raped" (56). Jim's response, "You sure was," both acknowledges Arvay's interpretation and also tries to paint rape as akin to marriage—which it very well may be in Jim's understanding. For Arvay, the news that Jim is marrying her in addition to raping her comes as a comfort rather than a fresh signal of entrapment. She believed, it seems, that her possible rape and then abandonment were heavenly punishment for her "secret sin" of still loving her sister's husband; in fact, Arvay's initial understanding is that "she had paid under that mulberry tree" for her previous sinful thoughts (57). When she finds out she will be able to marry Jim, she interprets this as evidence of penance paid that shows her she's been forgiven, not a continuing punishment that abandons her to cruel social prejudices. While this interpretation of events might justly cause feminist readers consternation that a female character would live under social conditions that have taught her to believe that her most private thoughts could deserve punishment through physical violation, it also shows that Arvay is no fool and fully comprehends the crime that has been committed against her.

Finding herself married to her rapist, and happy to have gotten that much from him, however, is no easy epistemic and emotional shift to make. From the moment of her marriage onward, Arvay grapples with the project of making it tolerable to herself. As such, Arvay begins to enact an ethic of innocence toward Jim's violence and sexism. One key moment of rejecting what she knows, and recasting this knowledge as something else, can be seen in her shifting representations of the rape under the mulberry tree. When Arvay returns home in order to visit her family after several years of marriage, she goes out to her old safe place. She finds herself "dazed by the feelings that swept over her," but far from feeling the trauma of the rape, or her "penance" again, she feels this time only the remembrance of her success in marrying Jim and escaping ostracization, here transmuted into a joyful sexual experience. Arvay now calls her recollection "a memory inexpressibly sweet. No injury that she could conjure up could stand up beside the ecstasy that she had felt here. God, please have mercy on her poor soul, but she was a slave to that man!" (134). Though Arvay has a fight with Jim that prefaces her return to the mulberry tree, her memory of the rape does not corroborate but rather counters her anger, and the "slave" state Arvay feels seems, in Arvay's estimation, to be born of her desire, not Jim's violence. Late in the novel, during Arvay's final return to the mulberry tree, the memory that is sparked is one of "violent ecstasy" that also marks the beginning of what she terms—for better or worse—her "real life" (305). Her epistemic refusal of Jim's criminal encroachment on her body in these later years may be a strategy Arvay employs to live in her reality with some measure of happiness, and it may even coexist with her knowledge of her rape, but it does not erase the fact of her knowledge.

Arvay's attachment to the man who rapes her has caused critics to characterize either Arvay or the relationship in various ways that obscure her victimization. For Lillie Howard, Arvay is best described as a "sick woman" who only at the close of the novel is able to appreciate what her loving, if chauvinistic, husband does for her (Gates 277). Claudia Tate reads the complexities of Arvay and Jim's relationship as indicative of "sadomasochistic bondage" that the two are only able to work through by sating their desire in a sort of peaceful living death (174). But I think it is equally plausible to read Arvay as neither sick nor desirous of pain but as an eminently pragmatic woman. It is the pragmatic woman that I see when I watch Arvay burn her family's old home to the ground after her husband leaves her until he might "see any signs of [Arvay] coming to be the woman [he] married [her] for" (Hurston, *Seraph* 267). I agree with Janet St. Clair that Hurston's text is not simply conformist but more accurately read as "the thinly veiled story of a woman who," after her husband leaves her, "resists victimization, throws off oppression, chooses the burden that she will carry, and takes it up with courage, dignity, and delight," but I think that this action happens from the start of the novel through both of Arvay's performances of innocence rather than just in the last hundred pages of the novel, as St. Clair argues (40). Again, making this marriage palatable requires hard epistemic and emotional work on Arvay's part. That it takes over twenty years for Arvay to fully endorse her own choice to stay with her rapist is not surprising; what is surprising is that she can do it at all.

In this reading, it makes sense why Arvay is only fully comfortable and happy when she chooses to return to Jim and their marriage at the end of the novel; here, she realizes that she has power over him because she now sees that Jim "had his doubts about holding her" (348). This piece of knowledge, a "wonderful and powerful thing to know," becomes the seed of Arvay's next performance of innocence; as she puts it, in order to keep this power, "she must not let him know what she had perceived" (348). Jim's power in their marriage has been enacted by force; Arvay's, we surmise, will be hidden away and enacted in silence, but it will allow her a measure of control and comfort that she was previously missing and that will hopefully provide Arvay with the happiness in her marriage that at least she, if not Jim, deserves.

Suspect Optimism, Grievable Lives

What I hope my readings of these three protagonists has demonstrated is the intelligence and awareness that each shows for her circumstances and social position, as well as the way a performance of innocence allows these female characters to inhabit their limited choices. Whether to make the best of a marriage of convenience, to deal with racism while protecting both one's self and one's children, or to deal with the trauma of a rape and subsequent marriage to this rapist, Charity Royall, Maud Martha Brown, and Arvay Henson use their performances of innocence in order to preserve and carve out something other than hopelessness for themselves. Yet these choices not to know are endeavors that risk alienating those watching our protagonists—other characters, critics, general readers—from seeing these endeavors as *chosen*. As discussed in the previous chapter, Addams's dynamic endorsement of an ethic of innocence's use value for Hull House clients was a literary-theoretical response to her failure to endorse such dynamism in these women's real lives. Yet when all we have is the literary-theoretical with which to work, the danger of a similar failure to endorse characterological dynamism is twofold. One, it simplifies what is an active epistemic choice not to know into a passive epistemic lack. And yet the alternative—simply endorsing a woman's choice not to know without questioning the conditions that structure this choice—runs the risk of denying the social ills to which our protagonists' choices so emphatically point. Janet St. Clair's reading of Arvay's final choice to stay with Jim is ambivalent but uplifting; she argues that "there is a price to pay for her choice, of course, and she pays it; her willingness to pay asserts her belief in the dignity of her decision" (56). This reading is valuable in that it understands Arvay's action as a choice that she makes with attention to costs and benefits, and yet its characterization of Arvay's payment as "willing," yoked as it is to "dignity," seems to validate Arvay at a cost this reader, at least, is unwilling to pay: that of ignoring the confines that structure the options she might choose, the content of the costs and benefits, in the first place. What I seek, and what I think an ethic of innocence can make possible, is a mode of reading that *by* believing in Arvay's dignity is able to conceive of something more to offer her. This wish for "something more" resonates with critical responses to the close of *Summer*, when Wharton gives us Charity's thoughts on the recompenses of her marriage: "Mr. Royall seldom spoke, but his silent presence gave her, for the first time, a sense of peace and security. She knew that where he was there would be warmth, rest, silence; and for the moment they were all she wanted. She shut her eyes, and even these things grew dim to her" (182). Barbara White writes astutely of this ending, "if marriage to Royall is Charity's best option, we applaud her learning to take it; yet what kind of world allows women such limited choices in the first place?" (233). It is this final question that is at the heart of understanding the performative dimension of innocence in these realist, modern texts. For if readers see these women's choices not to know as intelligently and pragmatically entered into rather than blindly believed in, they could be prompted to ask why such choices are necessary, rather than turning away their own blind eyes.

I remind us: not-knowing, in and of itself, advocates no particular ideological or political agenda. Nowhere is this clearer than in *Summer*, when the backstory surrounding Lawyer Royall's middle-of-the-night proposition of his ward allows us to see Charity glimpse first the promise, then the failure, of her town's female authorities to protect her from male sexual predation. After the incident, Charity's initial disgust turns into "a belated sense of fear" when she becomes conscious that she has only temporarily held off his sexual advances (16). Because of this fear, Charity turns to Miss Hatchard, a town elder and—later—her boss at the library, for assistance. And indeed, Miss Hatchard had previously hinted to Charity about Lawyer Royall's suspect desires, followed by her assurance to the girl that "[she] shall always do what [she] can for [Charity]; and in case . . . in case . . . [Charity] know[s] [she] can always come to [Miss Hatchard]" (14). Though this blank is filled only by Miss Hatchard's blush at the time, after Lawyer Royall approaches Charity as a "lonesome man," Charity fully comprehends Miss Hatchard's hints (16). But when Charity actually does ask her for help in leaving Lawyer Royall, in the form of a job that would enable Charity to "earn enough money to get away," Miss Hatchard's response teaches her that despite what they suggest, even other women will not protect her against a future sexual advance or assault (17). More disturbingly, Miss Hatchard accomplishes this denial not through explicit refusal of an explicit accusation but through choosing not to know what Charity suggestively implies—the same strategy Charity later relies upon to make her inability to get away tolerable.

There is a deep and troubling irony in noting that an ethic of innocence both condemns Charity to further misery and saves her from this same misery's depths. When Miss Hatchard asks Charity to confirm that she wants to leave Lawyer Royall, Charity's "resolute[e]" and blunt response—'Yes: or I want another woman in the house with me'—is met by Miss Hatchard's nervous evasion (17). Her hesitant reply, "The . . . the housework's too hard for you, I suppose?" might, to a generous reader, be meant to be taken up as a coded conversation for the real household difficulties Charity faces, but in Charity's mind, it simply confirms that "Miss Hatchard has no help to give her and that she would have to fight her way out of her difficulty alone" (17). Despite the fact that Miss Hatchard has previously made suggestions—ones she claims Charity is "too young to understand"—that signal her clear understanding of the sexual danger in the Royall household, when she rejects an explicit communication of this understanding, Charity reads her as truly ignorant of these dynamics (14). Indeed, Charity muses that Miss Hatchard has "got to be talked to like a baby" and pities her "long immaturity" so much that she simply acquiesces to Miss Hatchard's query, "Yes, that's it" (17).

Whether Miss Hatchard's parting appeal—"I know Mr. Royall is . . . trying at times; but his wife bore with him; and you must always remember, Charity, that it was Mr. Royall who brought you down from the Mountain"—is meant to undercut any potential female allegiance, it has that effect (19). By imploring Charity to regard it as her duty to abide Lawyer Royall regardless of his transgressions, and in doing so by likening Charity to his wife, Miss Hatchard effectively sanctions Lawyer Royall's incestuous designs via her policy of noninvolvement, leaving Charity "to fight her way out of her difficulty alone" (17). When Miss Hatchard pretends not to know the subtext of a conversation whose subtext she has herself authored, and when she queries Charity in code, she may simply be abiding by the rules of reticence that an ethic of innocence offers to a nineteenth-century woman who would risk her own reputation if she publicly proclaimed too knowledgeably on sexual matters. Yet the net effect—that Charity's isolation is furthered by her need to caretake another woman's naiveté rather than rely on her for support—clearly demonstrates the tenuous nature of choosing not to know for the fin-de-siècle woman. What is an effective individual strategy of survival becomes, when broadened to the social, a failure that further entrenches a threatening status-quo. And our protagonist, who herself embraces an ethic of innocence, is not immune to the critical bias we have seen above when she takes on the role of reader and interpreter. *Summer*'s ultimate feminist failure, then, might be the fact that Charity as reader withholds the very openness toward epistemic alternatives that Charity the agent so relies upon and so desires in those who read her.

Chapter Three

A Failure of Sympathy or of Narrative?

Naturalism's Jaded Women and the Narrative Cycle of Domestic Violence

Most readers of Frank Norris's 1899 naturalist novel *McTeague: A Story of San Francisco* might readily associate the issue of domestic violence in the text with a scene that Jennifer Fleissner calls "among *McTeague*'s most notorious": that in which the antiheroine, Trina McTeague, and her neighbor, Maria Macapa, compete via the injuries sustained through their domestic abuse to see who has endured the most from the crueler husband (214). *McTeague* recounts the story of the marriage and subsequent relationship between McTeague, a brutish laborer masquerading as a dentist, and Trina Sieppe, an avaricious hoarder. The McTeagues' increasingly tense relationship escalates into physical violence when McTeague's masquerade is exposed, he loses his job, and Trina refuses to use her large savings to support the couple. McTeague begins habitually abusing Trina, eventually steals her money, and ultimately murders her. Maria Macapa, the McTeagues' neighbor, works as a maid; her marriage to Zerkow, the junk-shop man, is also marred by material greed—in their case, a set of gold dishes about which Maria constantly speaks and to which Zerkow desires access. Maria is also brutalized repeatedly, and eventually murdered, by her husband.

This scene to which Fleissner refers, in which the narrator describes how the two women bandy descriptions of their injuries back and forth, shocks and troubles due to "the perverse pleasure that Trina and Maria seem to take in their submission" to their husbands' physical brutality (Werner 2). Told in the ironic tone of a distant narratorial perspective, the conversation appears ludicrously over the top and out of place. "Over a cup of tea," the women narrate their domestic abuse as though they were exchanging pleasantries, conflating their husbands' personal histories of violence with tall tales and gossip (Norris, *McTeague* 343):[1]

> They told each other of their husbands' brutalities, taking a strange sort of pride in recounting some particularly savage blow, each trying to make out that her own husband was the most cruel. They critically compared each other's bruises, each one glad when she could exhibit the worst. They exaggerated, they invented details, and, as if proud of their beatings, as if glorying in their husbands' mishandlings, lied to each other, magnifying their own maltreatment. They had long and excited arguments as to which were the most effective means of punishment, the rope's ends and cart whips such as Zerkow used, or the fists and backs of hair-brushes affected by McTeague. Maria contended that the lash of the whip hurt the most; Trina, that that butt did the most injury. (343–44)

The narration of this scene takes place at a seemingly vast distance from the abused bodies of Trina and Maria. The narrator's portrayal of the women's conversation positions the abused women as a common female type: jaded liar. Rather than concentrating on the bodily violations these women experience, abuse here resides only within recounted linguistic description; further, we are urged by the narrator's verbs to consider the abuse as potentially *purely* linguistic: for according to the narration, these women are exaggerators, inventors who trump up stories about their pain with no real intent (even, perhaps, need) to find help. Indeed, the light tone of the scene and its skeptical treatment of the abused women seems oddly out of step within a novel dedicated to depicting the degenerative grotesqueness of modern life. Though details in the text, as well as the novel's trajectory, indicate that these accusations of abuse are serious rather than idle, the rhetorical effect of the scene is to implicate these women as participants in their own abuse and, as such, make it possible to dismiss them.

Why Does She Stay? / Why Doesn't She Leave? Agents and Victims within the Cyclical Tale

Why do women stay with the men who beat them? And how can viewing these choices of women not to know their husbands' brutality within naturalist literature help us answer this question without dismissing such women as merely ignorant? Such a question, emphasizing as it does the choice of the woman to ignore precedent and instead stay fixed within a violent cycle, continues to challenge feminist theorists and literary critics alike. Yet it is crucial to understand the politics of such a question. For even in asking it, we deflect attention from potential societal critique (regarding what men do to her) to the woman's agency (what she *allows* men to do to her). And if we are not careful, this emphasis on female agency can slip very quickly into blame, in which the woman alone becomes the responsible party for her own abuse.

In the previous chapter, I focused on three realist novels about female characters' coming-of-age stories that have caused critics varying levels of discomfort and distress; I argued that in large part, this distress was amplified, if not caused, by these characters' choices not to know, alongside our critical tendency to misunderstand and/or simplify these choices. In this way, I argued that using an ethic of innocence as a lens through which to view these characters' choices could help us attend to critical qualms and reframe discourse more usefully around key feminist political and social values. In this chapter, along with the one that follows, I will turn not to troubling texts, but rather to a troubling social issue that feminist critics have continued to have difficulty treating *which shows up in texts*: female attachment to abusive men. In trying to understand the contours of continuing feminist difficulty here, I will look not only at literary explorations of the cyclical dynamics within violent relationships but also to feminist writings from the later nineteenth century concerning wife abuse, current psychological studies on domestic violence, fin-de-siècle psychosexual research, and the genres of literary naturalism and modernism. In doing so, I seek to pinpoint the usefulness of studying the particular feminist challenge of domestic violence through the fin-de-siècle's focal genre of naturalism.

This is not to suggest domestic abuse is a strictly fin-de-siècle problem; its roots are far longer and deeper than this book can describe adequately. It is, however, an issue we have culturally met with great historical amnesia. Lenore E. Walker's *The Battered Woman* (1979) is, for instance, considered to be a seminal text in the twentieth-century feminist mobilization around domestic abuse, which describes the cyclical nature of domestic violence and theorizes female psychological attachment to their abusers. Walker herself notes the landmark nature of her work; indeed, the book's second sentence tries to make clear how urgent this task is by declaring that "historically, there has never been any public outcry against this brutality" (ix). Yet one reason why I have chosen to make domestic violence the focal issue of two of this book's chapters is because, in the late nineteenth century, feminist activists on both sides of the Atlantic Ocean mobilized around this issue, what was then often termed "wife abuse."[2] In fact, wife abuse was one of the dominant platforms upon which advocates for women's rights sought to express their concern about the laws that protected men at women's expense. Clearly, something odd is afoot when major modes of feminist engagement around the same topic are staged every one hundred years or so, with little to no memory of previous activism around the topic. One of my hopes is that looking at this issue with an ethic of innocence in mind can help us both understand why such amnesia has taken place and also commit current feminist engagement with domestic violence to collective cultural memory.

One reason that domestic abuse continues to engage and vex feminist theory is the complex nature in which women who stay in violent relationships test the boundaries of our understanding of epistemically based action. Nineteenth-century feminists often situated such women as primarily, if not exclusively, agentless victims. Yet this figure—the woman who chooses to stay with her abuser—is also, at the fin-de-siècle, a character to whom blues music, poetry, and modern novels give complicated, yet often overlooked, agency. For example, women's blues has often been critiqued for the way in which it depicts the intertwinement of love and violence; Angela Davis, in *Blues Legacies and Black Feminism*, writes that "women's blues have been accused of promoting acquiescent and therefore antifeminist responses to misogynist abuse" (25). And though Davis goes on to complicate this reading of women's blues, she acknowledges the wealth of female-voiced songs that express affection despite or because of the abuse of men. Indeed, many such songs—Bessie Smith's "Yes, Indeed He Do," "It Won't Be You," and "Hard Driving Papa," as well as Gertrude Rainey's "Black Eye Blues" and "Sweet Rough Man"—fall into a category Davis notes has been described as the "'hit me I love you' tradition of masochistic women's songs" (qtd. in Davis 31). This particular cultural instantiation of the modern cyclical tragedy—one embodied and allowed by excuse-making, absurd woman on behalf of a violent intimate partner—crystallizes some of the issues, both complementary and competing, that this chapter and the one that follows will engage: gendered violence; personal agency (or lack thereof) within violent situations; audience sympathy (or lack thereof) toward the women who experience such violence; and the nexus of aesthetic, affective, and social ideologies that help obscure the legibility within the domestic violence scene of a type of pragmatism that *chooses* mental innocence at the risk of bodily harm.

A key claim undergirding both these chapters is that to focus too insistently on the "she," in terms of both her agency and her affect when deciding to stay, makes it harder to see the social forces that inflect such a decision—forces such as gender expectations, economic limitations, social stigmas attached to separation and divorce, and access to resources and aid. Indeed, as contemporary abused women's advocate Ann Jones puts it, the major problems with even asking the question Why does she stay in an abusive relationship? (or the question's negative, Why doesn't she leave?) is that such a question "transforms an immense social problem into a personal transaction," specifically one in which in which only the woman's agency and actions are debated (131). Such a claim should seem familiar to readers of this books' first two chapters, yet the specific costs of neglecting social forces when trying to comprehend domestic violence's intractability can be deadly. Even though Angela Davis celebrates women's blues for shining the light of public expression of the issue of domestic abuse, she critiques these songs for "lacking . . . analysis of the social forces responsible for black men's propensity (and indeed the male propensity in general) to inflict violence on their female partners" (33). In Davis's treatment of the songs' social effects, she does not discuss their potential ability to spark such analysis in audiences. Instead, she discusses only the songs' ability to make women question their own attachments to violent men—a move that, again, focuses attention on the woman who stays at the expense of attending to the man who batters.

In contrast to such individually focused explorations of domestic violence's continuing cycle, some contemporary studies of abused women privilege structural and material factors in women's decisions to stay. One recent study on domestic violence, for instance, found that "more highly educated woman were less inclined to return to a partner who had battered them"; the study's authors then argued that since "it may be that more educated women have a higher potential for self-sufficiency, which allows them to escape the battering relationship," it seems to follow that "providing opportunities or counseling regarding employment, further education, or high school equivalency testing might be a useful part of aiding spouse abuse victims" (Schutte 609). The logic behind such conclusions suggests that women would choose to leave if they could and that to solve the problem of abuse would require attention to structural inequalities rather than to women's choices or relationship dynamics.

Studies that stress structural and material factors contributing to domestic violence are not new; indeed, such research finds its root in the work many nineteenth-century feminists did on domestic abuse in both

America and England. These nineteenth-century women's advocates, such as Josephine Butler, J. Ellice Hopkins, Lucy Stone, Henry Browne Blackwell, and Frances Power Cobbe, focused on articulating to the public the social ills and oppressions that they viewed as the causes of domestic violence; in particular, Cobbe, an Irish feminist writer and activist, outlined several contributing factors to domestic violence as she understood them in her 1878 "Wife-Torture in England" in the *Contemporary Review*. In the piece, Cobbe lists recent police reports of wife abuse in order to represent the widespread nature of domestic battery in England. She then goes on to enumerate alcohol, prostitution, an impulse to hurt and violate (what Cobbe calls "heteropathy"), and crowded living quarters for the poorer urban classes as key incitements to battery; historians Carol Bauer and Lawrence Ritt are careful to point out, however, that Cobbe finds these social and personal factors explanatorily inadequate unless one takes into account the overarching "broad social context" in which "half of [society's] members were deemed inferior to the other half, and in which women were routinely lumped together with criminals, idiots, and minors" ("A Husband" 108). Gender oppression, for Cobbe, is the scaffolding upon which the commonality of domestic violence rests, and this particular structural scaffolding was one that Victorian-era feminists stressed again and again in their writings.

As I hope is becoming clear, for either nineteenth-century feminist activists or contemporary psychologists, stressing the structural and material factors at work in women's decisions to stay in abusive marriages is one way to make their choices to stay seem reasoned and practical, rather than based on an illusion of hope maintained by a "damaged" individual that her husband will cease his violent ways. In doing so, they deliberately avoid or challenge the psychological emphasis of the kind seen in Walker's "cycle-of-violence" work on battered women. In this "cycle of violence," a once-loving relationship devolves into a stage of tension-building (featuring escalating arguments and episodes of emotional and verbal abuse), culminates in an acute, often physically violent episode of abuse, and is then followed by a period of apologies and promises on the part of the abuser (Walker 55–70). The sense that work such as Walker's depicts women as damaged is exemplified by one recent study on intimate partner violence (IPV), which argues that

> women's explanations of the pros and cons of relationship termination indicate that non-pathological approaches like reasoned action or planned behavior, and investment models, may be

better for understanding this complex and multifaceted decision than theories of learned helplessness, traumatic bonding, and psychological entrapment. (Vatnar 277)

The rejection of a psychological emphasis here seems inseparable from a sense that such an emphasis necessarily pathologizes the motives of the women involved. Certainly, notions of women's "helplessness," "trauma," and "entrapment," which draws on some of Walker's terminology, downplay female agency in favor of medicalizing female attachment to their abusers.[3]

Theorizations that emphasize the psychological perversity over the material/social rationality of the abused woman, or vice-versa, have troublingly called female agency into question. Taken too far, dividing the psychological from the rational implies that the abused woman is not, in fact, healthy enough to be *able to choose* to experience violence. In short, one fear has been that psychological models, rather than presenting women as the dynamic individuals capable of change, offer instead damaged individuals who have no choice other than to remain stuck within their traumatic, repetitious relationships—within the cyclical tale. This is even true about one early to mid-twentieth-century psychological argument about domestic violence to which we will turn later in this chapter: namely, that women enjoyed violence committed against them as a form of masochism that was constitutive of female embodiment and sexuality. While such a theory would at first appear to give women more agency than that of the abused wife as a helpless and damaged women (after all, the female masochist not only desires but might actually *act to seek out* pain), it also dooms these women to the same kind of changeless, futureless agency that the psychologically damaged woman experiences, albeit by naturalizing the cyclical tale from a story of women's victimization to one of women's pleasure. Likewise, overemphasizing the social forces at work in determining women's choices to stay with abusive men also problematically objectifies the woman experiencing abuse, in that such an approach risks portraying women as social constructs rather than as individuals with agency and particular characteristics, affects, and adaptations within their relationships. For instance, while Cobbe made public the deep investments American and British society had in their construction of womanhood, investments that would make ending wife abuse a difficult, if not impossible, task, she also presents such women as primarily, and somewhat uniformly, victims, not only of the men who abuse them but also, and more crucially, of society.

Ultimately, neither psychological nor material emphasis alone has satisfactorily explained the issue of women who choose to stay with abusive men to either nineteenth or twentieth-century activists; as one psychological study puts it, "the most common debate [in contemporary studies of abused women] is [still] whether emotional or practical reasons for return to the batterer prevail" (Roberts 372). Though the social forces at work in determining women's choices to stay with abusive men form a crucial component of the cycle of abuse, it is painfully clear to most who study domestic abuse that women's structural and material circumstances do not completely explain their choice to stay. One scholar thus argues that research stressing the role of external factors "such as economic dependence, lack of safe haven, and fear of further abuse" has "diverted attention from an exploration of the internal factors that influence a decision to return to a battering relationship," a choice many women continue to make today, even as economic resources and safe shelters, to say nothing of women's rights, have become more widely available (Griffing 315, 307). It seems that some account of women's affective stance toward abuse is needed, not only to give more complexity to the psychological portraits of women themselves, but also to explain cases where women stay when there seems to be no material need for them to do so. As Griffing and colleagues write in their 2002 study, we might actually "inadvertently undermine our own efforts to help battered women" by ignoring the psychological or affective elements of their choice to stay (315).

One portrait of the woman who stays for psychological or affective reasons is the romantic dreamer, a hopeful, innocent abused woman often described in psychological studies of domestic violence. Walker outlines, in *The Battered Woman*, the way in which this hopefulness is sustained and used to mitigate male violence by theorizing that cyclical, rather than steady, violence actually helps the abused wife to view staying as a compelling option. In particular, the period of apology after an incident of abuse, according to Walker, allows the woman to return to a "temporary dream state" in which the relationship is romanticized as mostly positive (55–70). Within such cyclical violence, the steepness of the vicissitudes she must stand, the constant demand to wait and stay which makes less and less possible the ever-receding future, do not dull this woman's hopeful countering of facts with dreams. The act of tolerating abuse from the man who loves her can quickly slip, however, under a reader's or critic's watchful eye, into not only "allowing" but actually "authoring" male violence, making victim-blaming of this type of woman dangerously easy. If she gains our sympathy—or more aptly, perhaps, our pity—it is as a victim. Her own significant affect of hope, sympathy, and forgiveness often reads as merely naïve or childlike when juxtaposed with the physical damage done to the body via abuse.

The emphasis on the woman who stays because of her material and affective lack of other opportunities—what this chapter refers to as the "jaded woman" type—is a dominant alternative figure in naturalist literature. She might at first seem to be an appealing counterpart to the romantic dreamer who imagines her husband will change, as the jaded woman stays with her abuser precisely because of her clear-eyedness—her knowledge—about the world and its sad inevitabilities rather than because of her blindness to reality's harshness. This chapter will consider, both conceptually and historically, the alternative to the romantic dreamer of the jaded, knowing woman, both in terms of what is powerful about such a characterization alongside this characterization's limits. For though this jaded portrait of the woman who stays seems to be granted both logic and agency, this is often at the cost of her reader's sympathy. Agency without sympathy posits change only insofar as the abused woman seeks it herself; the scenario requires no global intervention from onlookers, since the abused woman is seen as able to choose to stay or go as she wishes and sees fit. Both our sympathy to and understanding of female agency are needed for any possibility for this cyclical tale to become "unstuck."

Feminist theorist Edwina Barvosa-Carter writes that the "investments and participation of women in cycles of abuse" are "deep but not immutable"; for there to be a chance at mutability, she implies, an acknowledgment of what goes into making a woman a repeated "victim" of domestic violence—a woman who stays—is necessary (182). We should remember that for this project's purposes, literature's sociological weakness—it presents, after all, characters, not people, stories, not lives—is its theoretical strength. These *stories* of abuse (rather than real-life accounts of domestic violence) provide a telling lens through which we can understand not only the stakes of women's pragmatic choices to stay with their abusers—the material and affective dynamics, as well as the risks of such a choice—but also our readers' response, our outside understanding, which determines our sympathies toward such gendered displays of chosen innocence. Fictional texts offer crucial access to the abused woman's own understanding of what is often, in the real domestic scenario, a very private, hidden violence; they can also prompt readers to investigate our own sympathies in response to such stories. Most important, however—and most crucial to an understanding of repetitive violence—literary studies positions us to view such stories of domestic abuse in light of their form as it both fulfills and exceeds the tragedy of the cyclical tale. It is in this way that the specifically naturalist literary works on which this chapter focuses bear the most relevance, and not just because of the genre's intertwining of the natural and the pathological as catalyzed by the female body (which will be discussed in much greater detail later in the chapter).[4] Naturalism's specific generic role in depicting domestic violence in the fin-de-siècle texts we will consider here is crucial, in part because the naturalist genre foregrounds the themes of cycles, determinism, and fate in all facets of modern life—including a modern construction of domestic abuse. But it is my argument that naturalist literature is particularly useful because of the way these texts attend to the *narrative arc* alongside the cyclical—they address the way in which women's lives of abuse not only repeat, but also have the potential to progress, within such repetition, toward a difference. In fact, the genre of naturalism at the turn of the century, like some of the time period's discourse on domestic abuse, presented a much bleaker view of men than women, in which men, more than their female counterparts, were condemned to sheer repetition and an inability to escape from their brutish state. Thus, women, whom some writers accorded the possibility of repetition with a difference, occupied a position that simultaneously held more potential to change their lot in life but also a greater risk of blame and censure if they chose (or "chose") not to do so.

Nineteenth-Century Activism Meets *McTeague's* Battered Women

The scene of female boasting and besting with which this chapter opened is a passing one in *McTeague*, quickly subsumed into the larger tragic trajectory of the novel. Indeed, we find both women, in some sense, dismissed from the narrative after this discussion. Trina McTeague, as Maria F. Brandt points out, literally remains silent throughout this entire scene when "the narrative replaces her voice with its voice": the inventions, lies, and magnifications we are assured that both of the women vocalize are narrated to us rather than quoted as evidence (17). As for Maria Macapa, the scene ends with her description of Zerkow's increasingly brutal obsession with finding her gold—she proclaims "he's just gone plum crazy," and "he'll whale [her] with his whip" and threaten to "do for [her]" if she doesn't tell him where to find it (Norris 344). This description of Zerkow's crazed anger effectively marks Maria's silencing: the next, and final, time she appears in the narrative, it is as a corpse, with "a fearful gash in her throat under her ear" (348). The larger narrative arc of the text thus shows these women ultimately losing their lives as a result of the violence about which they have proudly boasted.

For instance, not only does this neck wound kill Maria, but Norris's explicit description of it posits her death as one that occurs via both body and language—the throat, through which Maria once articulated her husband's crimes, is rendered useless to her by his violence.

It would be, perhaps, comforting to temper the tragically violent demise of Maria Macapa, as well as the similar bloody death that later befalls Trina McTeague—who drowns "face downward" in her own blood spilled by "McTeague's blows"—by seeing in the above scene the archetype of the victimized woman who doesn't comprehend the seriousness of her abuse and who thus dies because of her ignorance (415). More troubling, then, is Norris's re-presentation of this scene in his 1897 short story "Fantaisie Printaniere"—a text published before *McTeague* but written after Norris completed the novel in 1896, in which Trina and Maria's comparison of injuries scene becomes a fulcrum in the lives of the McTeagues and the Ryers (the story's version of Maria and Zerkow). This short story, explicitly framed by way of repetitive cycles and the relation between repetition and difference, is particularly suggestive given domestic violence's cyclical trajectory; in fact, the entire text is framed around the omnipresence of domestic abuse, as well as the women's consistent response to their husbands' battery.

In the opening of "Fantaisie Printaniere," we find that "as part of the existing order of things," the women's husbands, McTeague and Ryer, fought and feuded (2). "Like the reek from the drum and the monthly visit of the rent-collector," the relationship between the men was a constant, as was the way in which "both men thrashed their wives": "McTeague on the days when he was drunk, which were many, Ryer on the days when he was sober, which were few" (2). In fact, the story's action, which consists of the competition between the wives, ushers in only one change: Trina and Missus Ryer, once "intimate," become enemies as a result of the competition at the same time that the men enter into an "unexpected reconciliation," though the story never explains the reason for end of the men's feud (4). At the story's end, the wives' quarrel becomes a part of a new "existing order of things, like the leak from the gas-works and the collector's visits" (5). The final line of the story establishes, however, the through line of abuse connecting the old and new. Norris writes that "one particular custom common to both households remains unchanged—both men continue to thrash their wives in the old ratio—McTeague on the days when he is drunk (which are many), Ryer on the days when he was [sic] sober (Which are few)" (5).

Unlike in *McTeague*, we see the abused bodies and hear the voices of both Trina and Missus Ryer within "Fantaisie Printaniere"—and yet far from appearing victimized by their abuse, their vocalizations seem to confirm *McTeague*'s narrated description of Trina and Maria's competition. In the short story, Trina and Missus Ryer explicitly articulate pride in their ability to withstand abuse—speaking "proudly" and "loftily" of their own injuries while dismissing each other's injuries as "little scars, little flesh wounds," "little love taps," even "nothun" (4). They compare injuries with aesthetic rather than sympathetic eyes: they "critically compare bruises," looking over each other with the "glance of a connoisseur" (3). Their ownership over their injuries, the way they savor their woundability, suggests that Norris's continuing interest in what is a small scene in his novel hinges on a fascination with these female characters' jaded *and knowledgeable* relationship toward their own repeated abuse.

What does one do with such enduringly shocking, such counterintuitive, portrayals of abused women, portrayals that depict women battling to have survived the worst domestic violence rather than to avoid this abuse? What do such texts say about these women's choices to preserve violent relationships, and to what extent can we understand such women, such choices, from a feminist perspective? And what, moreover, do we make of the detached and ironic narration used to present these women and to inflect our understanding of the abuse they endure? For most of these texts' critical lives, our answers to these questions have been depressingly limited. For example, Brandt writes that even though readers of *McTeague* from as early as 1899 acknowledged "the problem of [the novel's] violent content," they have simultaneously "found ways to justify that content, or at least to render the brutality of its representation as natural and deserved" (5). In order to understand this reception history, it is necessary for us to explore the social context of Norris's late nineteenth century, during which several social movements with feminist ties brought domestic violence, particularly the plight of abused married women, into the public eye. In doing so, I will argue that Norris's naturalist fiction can be considered to be a complicated response to these movements' ideologies and investments, particularly to the way that such movements viewed men and women's moral characters as a key component governing progress within modern society.

Frank Norris's works, and indeed perhaps the genre of naturalism itself, are a part of a fin-de-siècle network of responses to Progressive ideologies regarding gender and violence. In the decades preceding *McTeague*'s publication, feminist activists on both sides of the Atlantic mobilized campaigns around the pressing issue of domestic violence. Yet antidomestic violence activism was simply one of several Progressive movements that dealt with human relationship dynamics. These movements, though diverse, all brought an optimistic attitude toward the modern human to bear on the reforms they advocated.[5] Progressive Era reform stressed evolutionary, developmental models of modernity within their social, economic, political, and moral improvement campaigns in an effort to imagine, then realize, a better, more evolved humanity. One arena in which Progressive reform worked was male-female relationships, optimistically seeking to advance connections that would reflect an increasing, if gradual, "civilization" of women and, in particular, of men.

A central stumbling block to the evolutionary improvement between men and women was the prevalence, in the late nineteenth century, of violence within domestic relationships; as such, feminist reformers of the era attempted to fight such abuse in social, political, economic, and moral realms. In fact, historian Elizabeth Pleck notes that "the two decades after 1870 represented a high point of feminist interest in 'crimes against women' not again attained until the 1970s" (88–89). Much of this feminist interest spilled out into protest against the legal discrepancies between the harsh punishments received by those who abused men and the relatively lax punishments meted out to those who abused women.[6] Feminists also concentrated on the way in which perceived male ownership over female domestic partners contributed to social attitudes that left the public content to ignore wife abuse.[7] Indeed, the leniency of sentences imposed on batterers of wives (often a short stay of a few days to a few weeks in jail) in comparison to those given to address crimes against actual property (robbery, for instance, was punishable in the nineteenth century by flogging in England, and by years of imprisonment in America) led some activists to request that physical punishment for wife beaters be reintroduced to deter domestic violence.[8] Campaigns enacted throughout fin-de-siècle Britain and America to introduce the "whipping post" as a punishment for domestic battery testify to the perceived message that light punishments sent—not only was a woman seemingly not as valuable as a man, but she lost even the protection legally allotted to "things" when she was "owned" by the man who beat her.

Even the term "wife abuse" draws attention to the way in which wives, even more than unmarried women, were particularly legally at risk within abusive relationships. As Carol Bauer and Lawrence Ritt note, "women who lived with men who were not their legal husbands often seemed to receive better [legal] treatment than if they had been married to them" ("Wife-Abuse" 199). Wife abuse, then, was not only an issue of concern to feminists because of the gendered prejudice involved in battery cases; it was also concerning because of the specifically vulnerable position that wives found themselves inhabiting in relation to their husbands, both legally and socially.

In these feminists' view, the social subjugation of women to men formed a more general pattern of which the domestic abuse of women was but one version; that female subjugation undergirded nineteenth-century feminists' understanding of the root of domestic violence is evident in the agendas and projects of the movements to which such feminists belonged. Many activists in England and America who worked on passing legislation that would ensure greater safety to abused wives were involved in the temperance movement, the women's suffrage movement, and the social-purity movement, or—often—some combination of the three.[9] And both the temperance movement and the woman's suffrage movement explicitly addressed the issue of domestic violence as a part of their overall agendas. For instance, in America, the temperance movement—through both narrative and image—was, according to Pleck, "the first American reform campaign to [visually] depict for the public the cruelty of domestic violence" in its efforts to control male vice (49). And American-suffrage activists and married couple Lucy Stone and Henry Browne Blackwell, editors of the Boston suffrage periodical *The Woman's Journal*, very explicitly treated domestic violence within their publication; they introduced a column in 1875 that ran through 1876 entitled "Crimes against Women" that documented incidents of wife abuse. These columns, which listed police reports regarding abuses, brutalization, rapes, and murders of women, were often framed by and interpreted through *The Woman's Journal* writers' understanding of the causes of the issue. In Blackwell's words, which tie antiabuse and prosuffrage agendas together, "these horrors [of domestic violence] result inevitably from the subjection and disenfranchisement of women, just as similar outrages used to result from the subjection and disenfranchisement of negroes. Equal Rights and Impartial Suffrage are the only radical cure for these barbarities" (34).

The social-purity movement, by contrast, was much more explicitly concerned with specifically sexual violence toward women and related to gendered violence primarily via extrapolation. The direct implications the social-purity movement had, however, on the ideologies of gender to which naturalist and naturalist-inflected modernist thought responded makes an investigation of the movement's nuances crucial to this chapter. Because the social-purity movement advocated for the self-control and self-restraint of both men and women in their marital and extramarital sexual relations, as well as for the abolition of prostitution, it has often been viewed as simply conservative or representing, in Sheila Jeffreys' words, "a form of [Victorian-era] moral panic" (6). Indeed, the ideologies of gendered behavior that the social-purity movement advocated seem, at times, to stem more from "the principles of chivalry than [from] those of feminism" (13); for instance, women's "corrective" role toward male sexuality was stressed, and men were urged to feel badly about their own desires in the face of their more restrained feminine partner's "theoretically higher and purer" "sexual standard" (Pleck 90). However, this seemingly conservative movement has fascinating overlaps with radical feminist activist strands, and the root motives undergirding the logic of sexual repression that the movement espoused, in interesting ways, not only limited but also advanced female freedom.

The social-purity movement arose in response to England's Contagious Diseases Acts, passed in the 1860s, which permitted compulsory medical examinations of women suspected of working as prostitutes. The acts encountered widespread criticism from feminists who viewed such "regulatory" legislation as the legalized invasion and abuse of women's bodies. Such feminists contended that these acts, which punished women for prostitution, failed to address the real core of the problem—namely, the men who made female employment as prostitutes possible and who transmitted diseases to them in the first place. (Jeffreys 6–8) Underwriting this law, as the social-purity movement's men and women were quick to point out, was a longstanding double "code of morality" in which women, not men, were expected to maintain their chastity outside marriage and in which, for the maintenance of this double standard, a class of "unmarriageable women" was required in order to satisfy male sexual demands (8–9). For the class of women who could marry, their duty was to satisfy their husbands' sexual desires regardless of their own feelings and to avert their eyes from their husbands' sexual indiscretions.

British social-purity activists such as Josephine Butler and J. Ellice Hopkins addressed this double standard and legal subjugation of women by attempting to "transform men's sexual behavior through challenging the idea that men had an urgent sexual need" that "required" women to "service" it (10). Feminists within the social-purity movement refuted this notion through recourse to evolution, arguing that "the male urge was constructed and not a natural endowment of man," and thus could be contained (49). While advocating self-control, social-purity activists also relied upon "the creation of guilt" to "provide internal controls" on male sexual behavior, a negative linkage between sexuality and morality that understandably has caused feminist concern (18). Thus, through its espoused ideologies of masculinity and femininity, the social-purity movement challenged specific norms of nineteenth-century gendered behavior; yet the movement also championed a feminine (and, in some strands, a masculine) moral virtue that modern perspectives typically dismiss as prudish, old-fashioned, and repressive. This odd comingling of the optimistic challenge to its time period's norms with the potentially conservative form such reform took set out a complex gendered worldview.

In part, the social-purity movement's public prominence contributed to a fin-de-siècle optimism in which male self-control became a meaningful social ideal, not only in sexual situations but also in more general gendered power relations that might otherwise erupt into violence or sexual exploitation. Here, the suggestion that men were not beholden to but could control their sexual urges related to a broader progressive view of male agency within late nineteenth-century discussions of domestic violence, in which lack of self-control (not male legal right) came into prominence (del Mar 55). For instance, Gail Bederman writes that in America, "by the end of the century, a discourse of manliness stressing self-mastery and restraint expressed and shaped middle-class identity" (qtd. in del Mar 52). Such evolutionary discourse tended to view deviations from ideal behaviors into vice "in social, not individual terms," in which women, just as much as men, formed a part of the social whole (Leach 35). The logic through which such social ideals were to be met, however, stressed not the structural but rather the *individual's* role in promoting or suppressing gendered violence. Men thus began to perceive domestic violence as their responsibility to stop; yet individuals, not society at large, were chiefly tasked with relinquishing this violence.

As a result, such a shift in the way men perceived their roles within violent relationships did not necessarily result in a safer domesticity for women. Instead, as Pleck observes, the Progressive Era's emphasis on self-mastery resulted in a continued public complacency regarding radical legislative protection for abused women, such as divorce (107). Additionally, the social-purity vision of self-control, modeled as it was on bending males to feminine standards of self-control, continued to portray women as not only one of the responsible parties for abuse, but also the party responsible for increasing male responsibility within abusive scenarios—it insisted "that women had to reshape the traditional family and make men more responsible" (Pleck 107). The social-purity movement viewed sexuality as an area in which women were consistently asked to submit to male desire; by attempting to limit sexual activity to that necessary for reproduction, social-purity advocates hoped to protect women from male abuse. At the same time, however, they evaded discussion of women's own sexual desires and painted women as purely victims of male demands. In these environs, cultural scripts and values that advocated for male individual control resulted, counterintuitively, in an emphasis on exemplary individual female behavior. Such model women were also problematically transformed into the sexually desireless victims of male excess. As with the question Why doesn't she leave? the gendered moral code of social purity placed women as the party responsible for both partners' behaviors, even as it denied them the ability to choose sex or violence within their relationships.

To this optimistic, evolutionary code of individual agency and the glorification of self-restraint that the social-purity movement championed, the naturalist genre responded by presenting a pessimistic view of modernity, characterized by the hampered human: predetermined in action, doomed to degeneration. Naturalist literature, like Progressive ideology, engages evolutionary theory, but rather than charting human improvement, naturalist writers—such as Theodore Dreiser, Stephen Crane, Kate Chopin, Edith Wharton, and later Richard Wright and Ann Petry—emphasize the degenerative link between animal and man. In line with thinkers like Max Nordau (whose popular *Degeneration* was published in America in 1895), naturalist writers engaged the so-called "primitive" strain within modern man—whether that strain be inherent to all human beings or just sparked by the influence of urban life, industrialization, and even "degenerate" art.[10] Whereas social-purity advocates argued that "the man or woman who is incapable of sexual self-control should be walking about on four legs, and not on two, because lack of self-control is incompatible with human nature," the naturalist rejoinder proclaimed the root similarity between the human and the animal: both, in naturalism, are unlikely to surmount, if not incapable of battling, their urges (qtd in Jeffreys 50). And the naturalist woman, far from virtuously embodying man's moral uplifter, is as subject to the animal in the human, those pesky urges, as is the man. This naturalist view of female personhood gives women some power, but does so only within the context of a perverse social whole, a society fundamentally degenerate and pathologized.

The pessimistic or skeptical stance toward modern uplift espoused by naturalism is taken by a wide range of late nineteenth-century writings. Surprisingly enough, it even inflects some of the same feminist work on domestic violence treated above. For example, rather than castigating men for the inability to restrain themselves, the close of one of Stone and Blackwell's "Crimes against Women" columns reassures the reader that "we are not writing to blame men unduly; as Darwin says, they act after their kind" (413). Though the column argues that it is "intent on showing . . . the necessity that women should have increased power, social, civil, legal, political, and ecclesiastical, in order to protect themselves," a list that clearly enumerates the many ways in which nineteenth-century women were disempowered, its caveat about male blame refutes the mainstream social-purity notion that men have the potential to embody self-control (413). Rather, it skeptically suggests that men are inherently brutes, what Frances Power Cobbe called "beating animal[s]" ("Wife-Torture" 64). Rather than placing the burden of male reform on the female partner, this pessimistic naturalist attitude argues that women require protection via social, not individual, form, because it declares the male human animal, to varying extents, essentially nonreformable.

Hence, though the dominant strain of the social-purity movement viewed modernity through optimistic eyes, these "Crimes against Women" columns suggest that a concurrent strain in fin-de-siècle thought concerning gendered relations shared the pessimistic attitude toward humanity's evolutionary potential that the naturalist genre espoused. Indeed, this confluence, it might be argued, also brings forth the latent "pessimism" within even the seemingly optimistic social-purity mainstream. For the controls that the movement would place on desire, sexuality, and relationships between the sexes suggest the fundamentally selfish, excessive, even violent nature of these unchecked "human" characteristics.

Jaded Power, Unsympathetic Agency

Thus, it should not surprise us that within Norris's naturalist fiction, particularly *McTeague*, the same conflict appears as in the "Crimes against Women" column above: men are Darwin's creatures, subject to ordinary animal urges, but men are also human beings whose animality quickly devolves into monstrosity when paired with specifically human desires. "The sudden panther leap of the animal," present in McTeague's lust-filled encounters with Trina from the start of the novel, becomes more prominent, dangerous, and uncontrollable when combined with social ills like idleness and drink (Norris 35). When McTeague begins beating his wife, we are told that though "he never became a drunkard," "the alcohol had its effect for all that. It roused the man, or rather the brute in the man, and now not only roused it, but goaded it to evil" (Norris 338, 339). To intemperance and instinctual brutality is added "a general throwing off of the good influence his wife had had over him in the days of their prosperity," a formulation in which we see a remnant of the nineteenth-century social-purity gender model wherein the responsible, middle-class, self-controlled female presence functioned to keep her man's brutal instincts in line (339). Here, the text's tragedy is ultimately linked with very human (and narrative) choices and indulgences, making McTeague's willful "submission or resistance" to temptation as important as fate in deciding his brutality (Howard 69). Man is horrifying, then, not because he is a beating animal, as Cobbe calls him, but because the animal who beats is, at root, a *man*.

In contrast to the realist narrative of self-making, the naturalist story of the male human, at least in *McTeague*, is ultimately more cyclical than linearly progressive; at the close of the novel, McTeague, handcuffed in the desert to the corpse of his friend that he has just killed, is literally doomed to death by his own brutishness. McTeague ends just as he began, a brute. In contrast, the novel's *female* story generates tension between cyclical sameness and narrative change. Stone and Blackwell's "Crimes against Women" column devotes a few lines to the exploration of women's ongoing negotiations with such men-cum-brutes as McTeague; its author suggests that the social platitude "all women love all men," is "pleasant," but, if true, "it is a love mightily tempered with fear. We should say rather that women fear all men, and love some" (413). It is here, at the crux of love and fear when faced with the predetermined and brutal man, between cycle and narrative, and extending from an excess of the social inequality between women and men, that we are best situated to discuss the way in which Norris incorporates the "pessimistic" aspects of social purity into his naturalist depiction of the abusive *McTeague* marriage. Indeed, I will argue that Norris's depiction of their marriage builds on such pessimism, radicalizing its more negative depiction of relations between the sexes to insist on the latent if not explicit violence inherent within heterosexual relationships in general.

Both the Maria/Zerkow and Trina/McTeague marriages are marked by violence explicit enough to cause fear, at least in Trina's mind. Trina McTeague asserts that she would "be deathly 'fraid of a man" who abused his wife like Zerkow abuses her neighbor Maria (326); here, Trina seems to categorize the two women's husbands differently, even while the narrator describes her own husband as such a man, with his "enormous, red" hands capable of great brutality, particularly whenever "the animal" inside "stirred and woke" (5, 34, 34). Whereas the fear Trina believes Maria should experience appears to follow from logic—that knowledge regarding Zerkow's past behaviors (i.e., "tak[ing] a knife to [her] once") accurately predicts future behaviors (i.e., future abuse)—the fear that Trina experiences at McTeague's hands stems from a much vaguer, even biological strain (Norris 326). As McTeague closes, for the first time, his open palm into "a fist that was hard as a wooden mallet"—the weapon of choice that McTeague will later use to murder his wife—Trina experiences "her ancient terror of him, the intuitive fear of the male" (332). This ancient fear goes beyond an understanding of women's social subordination to men at the fin-de-siècle; instead, it is an "intuitive feminine fear of the male," one that arises in Trina when McTeague first proposes to her, after which she experiences an ill-omened "fit of vomiting" (38). Trina's physicalized fear is here linked to gender: femaleness, in the face of maleness, experiences sickening terror in this novel. Trina's fear exceeds her specific relationship with McTeague to describe a general, gendered dynamic in which fear of the male is the female lot and "her ancient terror of him" is naturalized enough to read generically as descriptive of all heterosexual relationship dynamics (332). This pairing of pathological violence with intuitive fear distinguishes Norris's novelistic treatment of heterosexual marriage from the representation in "Fantaisie Printaniere," in which violence alone remains the inevitable accompaniment to matrimony. Moreover, the *affect* this seemingly intractable fact of violence and the related absence of fear generate in the wives concerned shifts dramatically (from novel to story) in a direction that appears to give them greater control—albeit a problematic control—over their domestic situations.

Rather than fearing the inevitable, biological violence of their husbands that would make femaleness a state of victimhood, "Fantaisie Printaniere"'s Trina and Missus Ryer view damage to their bodies as the means by which they might celebrate their toughness and ability to survive a harsh environment. These resigned women move beyond victim status toward that of jaded celebrators by using their wounds as evidence of their adaptive capacity (3). Both pairings of women live in full knowledge that they will be beaten; yet whereas *McTeague*'s Trina trembles at the thought of what such knowledge must mean to her friend Maria, "Fantaisie Printaniere"'s Trina never does. Instead, she uses the strength of her own survival as a justification for scornfully admonishing her abused friend, declaring that she, Missus Ryer, doesn't "know what a good thrashun is" (4). What such a comment from a jaded woman suggests, unlike the fear expressed by her novelistic doppelganger, is that abuse, even if inevitable, can become a tool, a means of attaining a proud, privileged position over one's peers. Put another way: whereas male enmity and spousal abuse are depicted as constants, the jaded women of "Fantaisie Printaniere" use this limited power and agency to usher in a change in the cyclical landscape of the text.

In contrast to *McTeague*, in which the women habitually discuss their abuse, in "Fantaisie Printaniere," the women "avoided speaking of their husbands" and "feigned to keep the secret [of their abuse] from each other" (2). The novelty of the competitive dialogue over their injuries, perhaps because of its very novelty, initiates the sole deviation from pure repetition in the short story—the switch from male to female feud. Thus, it is the women's actions that overpower the intractable naturalist environs of the story. The fallout from this deviation, however, does not continue to empower the women; rather, it serves to sever the female friendship and isolate the wives from each other, a severance made more isolating because the husbands simultaneously forge an unprecedented friendship. The relationship between battery and the cyclical tragedy of this both natural and social, ambiguous "existing order"—an ambiguity Fleissner calls the story's "open question"—suggests that a dangerous narrative trajectory attends such jaded women's agency in relation to domestic violence (298). The narrative arc within "Fantaisie Printaniere" drives Trina and Missus Ryer into further isolation; their stories deviate from the cycle in a way that might very well enable their immediate survival but that also moves the women away from, rather than toward, another's sympathy.

The way in which the jaded woman's isolated celebration of strength lessens our sympathy toward this character type finds reflection in the critical treatment of *McTeague*'s women. Such criticism has tended to ignore Trina's expressions of individual and gendered fear, instead viewing both Maria Macapa and Trina McTeague as unsympathetic, grotesque misers whose tolerance (via staying) of their husbands' violence is strange at best. Instead of seeing these women as the victims, such readers often appear to recognize Trina and Maria, like Trina and Missus Ryer, as active, and thus unsympathetic, participants in their own abuse. In short, their perceived agency posits these female characters contradictorily as nonvictim "victims." Such naturalist women, who use abuse as a tool to celebrate their toughness and who gain this privilege through withstanding violence, have garnered cool, distanced critical treatment that may be comprehensible but which I find deeply troubling.

The lack of sympathy and concern attending the type of woman who matter-of-factly describes her abuse amid everyday concerns, and the questions such a relationship to abuse provoke about her desire to end it, continues in certain naturalist-inflected strains of modernism, particularly those texts that, like *McTeague* and "Fantaisie Printaniere," use ironic narration to depict female characters experiencing abuse. One notable example is Nathanael West's *Miss Lonelyhearts* (1933), a novel about the disillusionment and subsequent mania of an unnamed male newspaper advice columnist who writes under the moniker "Miss Lonelyhearts"; this novella features several scenes of abuse between intimate partners within the letters that Miss Lonelyhearts receives from the public. One letter writer, who calls herself "Broad Shoulders," narrates years of systematic physical and mental abuse that she has sustained at the hands of her husband, years in which "he threatened [her] life," kept "a hammer, scissors, [and] knife" under his pillow to intimidate her, and "beat [her] up so [she] had to spend over $30 dollars in the dentist" (40, 41). Despite the explicitness of these details of spousal abuse, few critics would argue that West's novel seriously engages the issue of domestic violence—perhaps because of the flatness with which Broad Shoulders refers to her own injuries. Indeed, though Miss Lonelyhearts himself opens the book proclaiming that "the letters [he received as the advice columnist] were no longer funny," and later goes so far as to call them "inarticulate expressions of genuine suffering," the comic language of the novel, the formal containment of the letters in a newspaper advice column, and even the "no longer" itself suggest that funny, in fact, is exactly what these letters are (1, 32).

Quickly, here, I would like to focus on one critical response to these letter writers that makes clear the lack of sympathy afforded to those jaded women who survive, rather than escape, their domestic abuse. This critical response symptomatically expresses some possible consequences of the type of limited female agency expressed within these naturalist depictions. In a 1987 article, John Keyes critiques Broad Shoulders as a woman who is all talk, a verbose gossip whose poorly wrought tale of woe betrays her "childlike . . . tone" and need "to justify herself" (18). Through this and other letters' inarticulateness and inappropriate form (after all, Keyes inexplicably claims, "to write to such a source [as a newspaper advice column] is, then, to express a desire not to seek an answer" [15]), the letters become not depictions of genuine suffering, but rather parodies of pain. Most importantly, though, Keyes's criticism of Broad Shoulders and the other letter writers' suffering centers on the women's failure, like Norris's abused women, to *want* to leave violent men.

Here, Keyes concentrates on the seemingly static nature of the female "victim"; "how can we speak favorably," Keyes asks, "of correspondents who write, less for advice than to continue as they are?" (13). It is this aspect of the letters—the women's choice to ask for help when they have no intention of taking such advice or of helping themselves—that Keyes takes as their genuine flaw. This "passive and victimized," "too common female type" grates on Keyes all the more insistently because her passivity seems disingenuous—she is specifically *not* helpless, but rather *acts* to make her life worse for herself (17). The criticism Keyes levels against Broad Shoulders culminates, unsurprisingly, around the issue of staying with her abuser. Broad Shoulders ends her letter with a plea to Miss Lonelyhearts to "put a few lines in [his] column" to help her answer the final two questions that cap her history of abuse: "Shall I take my husband back? How can I support my children?" (43). Keyes writes that the reader must find these "questions at the end incredibly anticlimactic," then goes on to give the following answers:

> The answer to the first is obvious. It is better not to live with a psychopath. Even she knows this. She has left him four times before. And how can she take him back when she doesn't know where he is? The answer to the second is only a touch more demanding, even given depression America. She has been working, supporting her children because of the failure of her husband. She can continue to do this, with her mother, or a new boarder, to watch mutually over the children. . . . With replies at least so simple in this case, replies she really knows, why, then, does she write? To talk, one must assume. (18)

Though Keyes ends by implicitly disparaging Broad Shoulders for wanting simply to talk, a feminist perspective could suggest that for a woman to talk about abuse is not nothing but rather a first step toward leaving—or at least looking critically at—her relationship. But without such sensitivity, the issue of staying with an abusive partner once again reflects upon the woman's actions rather than upon the man's. For Keyes, Broad Shoulders's very inquiry around staying is illegitimate, a prohibition which implies both that there are no reasons to stay with an abuser and that this truth appears obvious to all, including those directly involved in the scenario. Not only is Broad Shoulders accused of willfully denying the knowledge to which she "really," as a resigned rather than innocent figure, has access, but she is also condemned for positioning her own narrative as a question to a public *who also knows this answer*. Her discourse of abuse is comic, her suffering fake, because she questions whether or not she should stay with her abuser rather than "correctly" asserting that she won't—or just choosing to do, without the burden and bother of public discourse, what we all are presumed to know that the naturalist-modernist worldly, resigned woman *desires* to do anyway: stay.

Female Masochism and Naturalism's Everyday Romance

It is on this question of desire that nonsympathetic readings of women pivot; one senses that behind Keyes's hostility toward Broad Shoulders lies the masochistically inflected fin-de-siècle notion that not only does the jaded woman enjoy talking about her abuse, but she also enjoys the abuse that enables her to talk. And once again, we can return here to Norris's novelistic depiction of Trina McTeague for an exemplary blurring of this fine line between the worldly yet resigned woman who enjoys *surviving* abuse and the talker who enjoys *being* abused. For though the last section of this chapter discussed the way in which *McTeague*'s women compete, like the jaded Trina and Missus Ryer, to display the most serious injuries, Trina's own novelistic experience of abuse is marked not simply by fear, and not simply by pride, but rather, finally and most centrally, by "her perverted love for her husband when he was brutal" (Norris 342). Social-purity discourses position the woman as the victim of male desires, but Trina McTeague takes this further: not merely responding with tolerance but rather with desire and love toward her husband's violence.

Through this "perverted love," Trina exceeds not only the role of the victim that both optimistic and pessimistic social-purity gender ideology would map out for her, but also the role of the resigned survivor to which the wives of "Fantaisie Printaniere," and (to some extent) Maria in *McTeague*, give voice. As *McTeague* progresses from Maria's abuse and death toward a depiction of Trina's eerily similar narrative, the reasons ascribed by the narrator to the female characters' choices to stay in their relationships shift from an ideology of personal power (in which Maria, like Trina McTeague and Missus Ryer from "Fantaisie Printaniere," believes she "can always manage" [Norris 327]) to one of personal desire (in which Trina loves McTeague's brutality). Indeed, much of *McTeague*'s language of abuse used when depicting the McTeague marriage, particularly as the novel develops, is intimately bound with the language of pleasure.

This perversely pleasured depiction of Trina challenges most nineteenth-century feminist theorizations, within both the social-purity and suffrage movements, of the reasons behind women's attachment to violent men. In *The Women's Journal*, one of the key reasons why Henry Browne Blackwell argues that "it is almost impossible to get a wife to testify against her husband" is that a husband is a provider whose means (however small) support his family and without which they would "have to shift for themselves" ("Legal" 20). Trina, by contrast, very pointedly does *not* depend on McTeague for money; her lottery winnings, coupled with her grotesque hoarding behavior and her employment painting figurines, leave Trina both in control of her own finances and in a position to support, rather than depend upon, McTeague. Yet despite Trina's ability to sustain herself economically, her reluctance to speak against her husband mirrors the extent of wild storytelling to which women in the nineteenth century were said to go in order to protect abusive mates. We read, for instance, that Trina chooses to tell her neighbors that her fingers, which McTeague chews on, "had been shut in a door" rather than betray his brutality (342). And while perhaps this does not go to the extremes epitomized by an anecdote recounted by Francis Power Cobbe of a "pitifully ludicrous case cited by Colonel Egerton Leigh in the House of Commons" of a woman who "appeared without a nose, and told the magistrate she had *bitten it off herself*," one has little difficulty in imagining Trina following in Blackwell's wives' footsteps, if McTeague had been arrested for abuse, and "plead[ing] for [her husband's] release" from prison ("Wife Torture in England" 81, original emphasis; Blackwell "Legal" 20). Trina's attachment to her husband thus mimics the nineteenth-century woman's, though her economic independence leads us, from within a materialistic framework, to question why.

In the disjuncture between Trina's similar response and dissimilar circumstances, in her attachment without material need to the nonprovider McTeague, Norris's naturalist depiction of marital violence exceeds the limitations that nineteenth-century suffrage and social-purity rhetoric sets for it. Though nineteenth-century feminists' discussions of domestic abuse often ignored women's agency and instead focused on women's material inability to leave, as well as on their fear of further violence from their husbands if they sought legal separation, *McTeague* shows a new side of why women stay in abusive relationships—because it might be *pleasurable* to both the man *and the woman*. Hence, just as McTeague "found a certain pleasure in annoying and exasperating Trina, even in abusing and hurting her," so too did Trina find "a strange, unnatural pleasure in yielding" (337, 342). Whereas the jaded women express pleasure in winning the comparison of injuries competition—a pleasure rooted in survival—*McTeague*'s Trina finds pleasure within the actions of abuse themselves. This "morbid, unwholesome love of submission" Trina begins to demonstrate in response to McTeague's violence evinces a new, twentieth-century understanding of the woman's role within the domestic violence relationship—that of the female (or feminine) masochist (342).

Naturalism's pain-seeking women—further theorized by early sexological studies conducted between 1890s and World War I—used masochism as an outlet through which women's sexual desires and pleasures could be articulated. Masochism, first coined as a descriptor of a variation of sexual behavior by Austrio-German sexologist/psychiatrist Richard von Krafft-Ebing in *Psychopathia Sexualis* (1886), was developed theoretically by Freud in the early twentieth century to describe a variant in psychosexual behavior with a specifically feminine bent. In "The Economic Problem in Masochism" (1924), Freud outlines three avenues of masochistic expression: "as a condition under which sexual excitation may be roused; as an expression of feminine nature; and as a norm of behavior. According to this one may distinguish an *erotogenic*, a *feminine*, and a *moral* type of masochism" (257).[11] Whereas the first and the third variants of masochism are ascribed to behavioral attitudes, Freud naturalizes the second formulation as inherent to femaleness itself. Indeed, Freud's theorization of feminine masochism (oddly developed while studying not women but so-called "effeminized" men) uses women's roles in sexual situations—both as the sex who is penetrated and as the sex who gives birth—to theorize women's "characteristic" or natural relationship to the desire for pain (Pleck 158; Freud 258).

This normalization of pain in female sexuality was not instantiated by Freud in his 1924 article; his work drew on at least two decades of thought within the burgeoning field of sexology that viewed the woman's role within heterosexual intercourse as indicative that females not only tolerate but take a certain biological pleasure in pain. Havelock Ellis, in his section "Love and Pain" of *Studies in the Psychology of Sex* (1903), culled evidence from his own clinical observation, other psychologists' writings, popular texts, letters from patients, and even literature in order to demonstrate the "certa[in] normal[cy]" of woman's "delight in experiencing physical pain when inflicted by a lover and an eagerness to accept subjection to his will" (74). Not only do such examples help Ellis to argue his own points regarding the normalcy of the pleasure women take in the pain inflicted by their domestic partners, but they also testify to the fin-de-siècle's academic and scientific norm of aligning female pleasure with pain.

So seamless is the relationship between female pain and love within Ellis's work that he quickly rejects any possibility that a "normal" man would purposely subject his female partner to physical pain against her will. At first appearing to acknowledge the potentially problematic normalization of violence that occurs when women's sexual desire is equated with a desire for pain, Ellis writes, "[W]e have to remember that it is only within limits that a woman *really* enjoys the pain, discomfort, or subjection to which she submits" (85, emphasis mine). Rather than preceding to discuss such limits as a way to instruct men to be mindful of their partners' desires, though, Ellis instead relies on men's supposed instinctual care for the women they hurt as the means by which men can determine when women are, in fact, really enjoying pain and when they really are not. Here, Ellis writes not about women's experiences of pain but only about men's *perceptions* of women's reality. He argues that "if a man is convinced that he is causing real and unmitigated pain, he becomes repentant at once" (71). In Ellis's theory of intimate pain, no man is truly responsible for hurting a woman, for if he doesn't repent, "he must either be regarded as a radically abnormal person or as carried away by passion to a point of temporary insanity" (71). Thus, a fin-de-siècle reader would have learned from Ellis's findings not only that normal females enjoy pain when they see it as a sign of love, but also that normal men intuitively know when such pain is no longer acceptable to women and will be able to control themselves accordingly.

Such an encompassing, naturalized understanding of a female desire for pain within intimate relationships was established as a scientific finding with broad-reaching implications in the early twentieth century; before this, however, fin-de-siècle discourse on masochism and female sexuality struggled to distinguish the natural from the perverse. Within Norris's novel, naturalism's generic tendency to depict the whole of society as grotesque calls into question, from the start, McTeague's normalcy. Certainly, a reader of the novel might argue that McTeague is not a normal man, and it is for this reason that he finds himself unable to respect the limits of violence to which Ellis's normal men attend. Trina also is depicted, however, as a character unable to abide by the "normal" relations Ellis depicts—not because of her perverse allowance of pain as a part of her pleasure but because she *sets no limits* on either McTeague's behavior or her pleasure. Thus, as McTeague cannot be expected to respect limits that are never set, the husband cannot logically, within Ellis's formulation, be seen as radically abnormal, and so Trina bears the brunt of the "perversion" label within the McTeague marriage.

Trina's desire for McTeague's love despite his abuse, coupled with her love of her abusive husband—which can be read, as Donald Pizer suggests, as an "abnormal masochism"—is thus shown to be Trina's *choice* rather than her victimization (*The Novels* 69). Whether Pizer means to describe Trina's masochism as an abnormal sexual preference or as an abnormal variant of otherwise normal masochism, her masochism affords Trina a certain emotional depth and agency that at first appears to provide a crucial tweak to the depiction of Norris's other women. But Trina's masochism also troubles; this choice to embrace pain as the central evidence of Trina's agency allows for the trend in Norris scholarship that "condemn[s], if not demoniz[es], the compulsively hoarding Trina" as an abuser who embroils her husband in her masochistic desire and self-denial while viewing McTeague compassionately as the sympathetic "victim of Trina's avarice" (Fleissner 205; Pizer, *The Novels* 78). Interestingly, what critics such as Charles Crow believe earns Trina the unflattering moniker of "miser" is also what Victorian-era feminists would have termed a practical material measure to maintain self-sufficiency (4). And Fleissner, for instance, takes this emphasis on self-preservation further, offering a feminist account of saving in *McTeague* that focuses on the way in which Trina's miserliness includes but exceeds her monetary hoarding to ultimately become a way for her to preserve her self-worth (205). Both above preservation modes—economic and self—have led to more sympathetic understandings of Maria and Trina through feminist analysis. The third type of saving, however—that of Trina's chosen preservation of her violent relationship—is much less easily resuscitated because, once recognized, it counters a logic of victimization crucial to many feminist understandings of domestic violence.

Miserable yet Miserly Womanly Love

Women in *McTeague* are depicted as people who save things—money, dishes, relationships with abusive men—and such saving dooms them to unattractive miserliness. Trina's masochistic desire to stay in an abusive marriage precludes her victimization; more importantly, however, it precludes her husband's responsibility for her pain because it is a pain she willingly accepts and even enjoys. To what extent does this depiction of Trina McTeague affect other representations and understandings of modern female characters and, indeed, modern female women? To some extent, of course, the fact that Trina McTeague is a naturalist character, particularly one of Norris's naturalist characters, helps authorize a belief in Trina's strangeness, her perversity.

Naturalism, for Norris, is not realistic: it cannot exist in the realist's world because it "takes no note of common people, common in so far as their interests, their lives, and the things that occur in them are common, are ordinary" (Pizer, *The Literary* 72).[12] In the naturalist novel, writes Norris, "everything is extraordinary, imaginative, grotesque even, with a vague note of terror quivering throughout" (Pizer, *The Literary* 72).[13] Thus, it is no wonder that Trina McTeague's bodily descriptions—her "course, stunted, and dumpy" figure, her "unkempt, tangled mass, a veritable rat's nest" of hair, and her "swollen," purple-nailed fingers McTeague frequently gnaws—grow more grotesque as her domestic situation becomes increasingly violent. In effect, these bodily descriptions mirror the supposedly escalating perverseness of Trina's pleasurable submission to her husband's brutalities (Norris 371, 342). According to Norris's above explanation of naturalism's nonrealist, romantic strain, Trina is a naturalist character insofar as her masochism transforms her from a housewife into "a strange woman" (Norris 342); when she leaves "our world" in which "we are ordinary" by the route of her "unnatural pleasure," Trina becomes an exceptional, rather than a natural, woman—and thus the jaded, masochistic woman is shown to be an exemplary naturalist, not realist, character (Pizer, *The Literary* 71; Norris 342).

Yet informing Norris's notion of the exceptional, "romantic" facets of naturalism is his simultaneous emphasis on the "truth" such romance contains. In "A Plea for Romantic Fiction," Norris argues that within the type of romance with which naturalism is aligned, we can see beyond "the surface of things"—the arena of realism—to the core of what is human "through the clothes and tissues and wrappings of flesh down deep into the red, living heart of things" (Pizer, *The Literary* 76, 75). Oddly, this bloody description of naturalism's romance is grotesque, not in that it is exceptional but in that it is essential. That is, Norris describes the messy process of naturalist depiction as an excavation of the healthy, biological—if exposed—human body at its most basic level of circulation. This depiction of naturalist characters as rooted in literal, and healthy, human biology (not just literary generic codes) challenges Norris's anxious insistence on Trina McTeague's "strangeness" for combining love and pain, love and fear, within her intimate relationship.

Beneath Norris's assertions to the contrary, there runs the troubling suspicion that Trina's pleasure in pain, like the feminine masochist's, is not, in fact, odd. When Trina's "strangeness" is first introduced in the novel, it is in the context of her love for McTeague's violent abuse; it is here that the reader is first told about Trina's enjoyment of "yielding, in surrendering herself to the will of an irresistible, virile power" belonging to her husband (342). What the narrator terms Trina's "perverted love for her husband when he was brutal" is made analogous, through the adjective "virile," to a love for the masculine sex, whereas Trina enjoys her traditional feminine sexual role of "yielding" and "surrendering," even when such surrender occurs outside of the confines of explicitly sexual activity (342). Yet in the decades after *McTeague*'s publication, as the literature regarding female masochism continued to grow, it became harder to read Trina's purported love of abuse as strange. Rather, she "embodies a problem endemic to the psychological literature on female masochism, which is forced to admit that a perverse 'love of submission' seems in women's case hard to distinguish from normal understandings of feminine sexuality" (Fleissner 208). Indeed, in the 1930s, when Helene Deutsch and Karen Horney sparred in psychoanalytic journals over whether feminine masochism was biologically or socially determined, Deutsch (the proponent of biologically rooted feminine masochism) dominated, erasing any sense of masochism's "strangeness" at all. Rather than considering women's seemingly "perverse" desires "as importantly conditioned by the culture complex or social organization in which the particular masochistic woman has developed," as Horney suggested, Deutsch assured her twentieth-century readers that "masochism is part of the woman's 'anatomical destiny,' marked out for her by biological and constitutional factors . . . lay[ing] the first foundation of the ultimate development of femininity" (Horney 38; Deutsch 52). Masochism was not only normal: in Deutsch's view, it was a female developmental necessity.

What is troubling about Trina's strangeness, then, both as Norris writes it and as it is later available to us as readers, is not perhaps that she is different from other women, but that she—as a representative heterosexual woman, and as the confines of fin-de-siècle heterosexual domesticity demand—desires, loves, and lives in a way that strangely embodies a female norm. Trina McTeague, as the masochistic abused woman, not only presents an extreme version of the fin-de-siècle understanding of the everyday female experience of romance. She also, in this role, depicts one limit case of female agency via the jaded acceptance of male abuse. Her power to choose not only to withstand but also to actively seek out abuse suggests the ultimate untenability of resuscitating the kind of jaded woman who asks to be brutalized for feminist purposes—not because an individual Trina McTeague, the masochist, could not feel pleasure from domestic abuse, but because an increasingly normalized Trina McTeague, the masochistic *type*, suggests no possibility of exiting—no desire to exit—the cyclical tale, except by her own destruction.

Chapter Four

The Legacy of Naturalism, a Cycle of Leaving

Reading Agency in the Passive, Empty Woman

The naturalization of the masochistic woman from the world-wise, jaded one that I traced in the previous chapter, along with the unsympathetic critical response both types garner, marks one potential consequence of a naturalist-modernist antiprogressive, pessimistic worldview: women gain agency and empowerment only insofar as they are also perceived as perverse celebrators of their own abuse. Neither jaded bravado nor feminine masochism, however, depicts for the reader a dynamic site of pragmatic negotiation in which women might turn a blind eye to their abuse and choose to stay with abusive partners for myriad reasons that do not, in consequence, serve to sanction the violence of men. By the 1940s, when modern novels associated with literary naturalism like Richard Wright's *Native Son* (1940) and Ann Petry's *The Street* (1946) were published, public conversations surrounding wife abuse had virtually halted: euphemisms such as "domestic disturbance" and "family maladjustment" replaced explicit language of abuse and battery, newspaper and journal coverage of domestic violence dried up, and "psychiatry, under the influence of Helene Deutsch, regarded the battered woman as a masochist who provoked her husband into beating her" (Pleck 182). Just as the McTeagues move into the Zerkows' old home after Maria's murder and Trina's body literally replaces Maria's, this substitution of female figures anticipates the early twentieth century's emphasis on masochism's defining presence within heterosexual relationship dynamics and renders the women interchangeable. Yet it also, most disturbingly, suggests that the ultimate desire of the now-ubiquitous Trina McTeagues, what the women-cum-masochists want and attain, is their own destruction.

Perhaps this normalization of the masochistic female is one reason why naturalist-modern texts are not often critically treated by focusing on the domestic violence they portray. This lack of attention to the domestic violence they depict, moreover, is not indicative of broader literary trends; the many Victorian literary studies that attend to domestic abuse, for instance, stand in marked contrast to the slight treatment domestic abuse has received in modern literature.[1] In part, the historical gap in public attention and mobilization around the issue of domestic violence during the early twentieth century informs this lack. For though we have seen how late nineteenth-century feminists made the issue of domestic violence a priority, historian Elizabeth Pleck notes that "there was virtually no public discussion of wife beating from the turn of the [twentieth] century until the mid-1970s" (182). Formal aspects of modern literature have also helped focus critical attention away from domestic abuse; modern texts not only often position such abuse as momentary incidents that inform broader themes rather than crucial specifics within in the plot, but the violence often occurs to minor characters and is subordinated by appearing as a scene we hear recounted by the text's characters, rather than as one we witness first-hand in the action of these novels. For example, both verbal and physical violence arise in the marriages of Janie Crawford in Zora Neale Hurston's *Their Eyes Were Watching God* (1937), but the physical violence Tea Cake uses on Janie is subsumed into a romantic storyline of their successful marriage. And Tennessee Williams's play *A Streetcar Named Desire* (1947), though often discussed in terms of Stanley's violent rape of his wife's sister, Blanche, features scenes of domestic violence between not only Stanley and Stella, but also between the Kowalskis' neighbors, Eunice and Steve, scenes that are overshadowed in critical attention by Blanche's story and the violence perpetrated against her.

These scenes, however, are often brief, recounted rather than depicted, and so quickly moved beyond narratively that critics have, at times, overlooked them with what seems a puzzling blindness. For instance, literary critic Amanda J. Davis writes in her article about violence in the homeplace within modern literature that "there is not repeated spousal abuse" in *The Street*; however, several spouses and girlfriends are repeatedly abused throughout the novel (27). In addition to Min's history of abuse, which I will discuss in detail much later, the man Boots (whom Lutie, the main character, kills), is an abuser, and Lutie and Min's neighbor, Bill Smith, throughout the novel "come[s] home drunk again and [beats] up his wife" (Petry 313). Historian Elizabeth Pleck even argues that "very few modern novels contained scenes of marital violence," but, in fact, what is fascinating to me is that many modern novels do contain just that—scenes of (rather than plots concentrated upon) domestic abuse (182). Other canonical modern texts that feature scenes or suggestions of domestic violence include F. Scott Fitzgerald's *The Great Gatsby* (1925), Wyndham Lewis's *Tarr* (1918), Susan Glaspell's *Trifles* (1916), J. M. Synge's *Playboy of the Western World* (1907), Sophie Treadwell's *Machinal* (1928), Katherine Mansfield's "The Woman at the Store" (1912), D. H. Lawrence's *Women in Love* (1916), Ford Madox Ford's *The Good Soldier* (1915), Willa Cather's *My Ántonia* (1918), Edith Wharton's *The Age of Innocence* (1920), Nella Larsen's *Passing* (1929), and Richard Wright's *Native Son* (1940) (a list that's far from complete). And yet, the early twentieth century's lack of political mobilization around the issue of domestic abuse and modern literature's formal sidelining of such violent plots seem to render these scenes critically invisible, while domestic violence disappeared from cultural, even popular, discourse.

Naturalism's Modern Legacy and the Passive Woman Alternative

By the first few decades of the twentieth century, we see established two discrete types of jaded, world-wise women whose destructive pleasure enables them to stay with their abusers—those who accept abuse as a means of establishing their toughness and self-worth (like the women in "Fantaisie Printaniere") and those who masochistically enjoy it (like *McTeague*'s Trina)—though it is ultimately the latter who became more strangely naturalized within modernist discourse. By the late 1920s, for instance, when Langston Hughes published his poem "Beale Street Love," the relationship between women's love for men and love for violence from these men is legible not just as a link, but also as a definition. In the course of this seven-line poem, which depicts the act of a man hitting a woman after the opening "love/ is," love is explicitly, definitionally linked to male violence through the first three lines' metaphor (1–2). This man's fist, both a potential symbol for violence and a literal instrument of domestic battery, furthers the poem's violence through its actions, described in lines 4 and 5, of a physical facial beating. His is not just a fist that, once formed, threatens; rather, it is one that inflicts damage on another's body parts through its activities of "crushing" and "blackening" (4, 5).

These verbs' specificity contrasts starkly with the nonspecificity of the body parts the fist hits. The "lips" and "eyes" that are damaged by love in this poem are, at least in these two lines, parts that remain unattached to a specific face, let alone a specific body and person (4, 5). The gender of the man's victim isn't even made clear until the poem's final word—"Clorinda"—when we learn that the love spoken of in line one is heterosexual and that the bashed body is that of a woman (7). Gender thus becomes the poem's punchline as well as its delayed undercurrent. The majority of the poem's emphasis is placed on the damage that the man's fist—love—wreaks to not just any, but specifically a female, material body.

Hughes's redefinition of the violent damage love does to the lover's body could, of course, be read as a mere physicalized metaphor for the psychic pain of a rocky relationship. In turn, one could couple this general pain with the more localized racial trauma that black eyes—perhaps even eyes when metaphorically "blackened"—witness in Jim Crow American modernity. Yet the ease with which the poem can be interpreted as a strictly realistic depiction of a type of male violence understood as "love" disturbs any merely metaphoric reading. And the poem's final two lines—when Clorinda asks to be hit again—only further such disturbance, demanding that we shift our understanding of the violence in the poem from one of sadistic victimization to one of masochistically permitted, even consensual, violence (6–7). As the poem's only vocalization, these lines force us to confront not the man's fist but rather his fist's victim's own response to the violence inflicted upon her body. With these lines and this name, the scattered body parts to which the nameless man does violence are consolidated in the body of Clorinda. We find that the "lips" that were supposedly crushed have not, in fact, been destroyed: they can and do still speak. Her words and the attributive tag giving her ownership over them suggest that "Beale Street Love" is not simply an ironically titled commentary on a particularly brutal man's version of love that readers are meant to see through and critique. Rather, the poem as a whole asks the reader to consider, simultaneous to such irony, if this poem could seriously be about something called love as long as the cycle of violence it depicts is accepted, asked for, and continued by the abused female character.

I raise the example of Hughes's "Beale Street Love" in connection to the female masochistic character type with a certain trepidation that a reading of what might realistically be called love by two people might continue the blurring into what we as a culture expect or even idealize love to be (a blurring that the normalization of female masochism had already, as noted, begun). I do not, for instance, want a reader of this analysis to accept Clorinda's request to be hit again as a permissive excuse to further general gendered violence. Such a reading's real danger emerges when one ignores individual habits, biological differences, personal predilections, and a history of gendered oppression and inequality in favor of allowing the following reductive argument, one at which a feminist scholar like myself understandably balks: it is okay for men to beat women if they are consenting adults in love. Yet it frightens me more to refuse the risk of analyzing this text, because the alternative is one that would understand Clorinda as a mere victim of the man's fist by simplifying their attachment—and by erasing her voice. Clorinda's closing request, that her beating occur "again," opens up one version of the woman who stays in an abusive relationship through her own active, desirous participation in violence (6). What reading this request as Clorinda's masochistic participation in abuse perhaps obscures, however, is the link that this jaded woman has to the character type of the hopeful innocent.

Another way in which we might understand Clorinda's vocal act of authorizing the violence against herself, aside from as an enthusiastic masochist, would be by reading Clorinda as primarily a victim due to her own extraordinary, absurd sympathy. In such a view, Clorinda the romantic might truly believe the poem's opening metaphor that equates love to a fist and ask for a beating not because she likes pain but because she likes love. For such a Clorinda, her love for the man is absolute and trumps any violence he would do to her. This is, once again, the battered woman who believes her man loves her and finds it easy, even natural to make excuses for and live with his battery. Indeed, feminist theorist Edwina Barvosa-Carter notes that cycles of violence not only can emerge "due to institutional factors, such as the lack of legal, financial, and familial support systems available to battered women," but also persist "because of the discursively inculcated and continually rearticulated belief (repeatedly performed in word and deed) among many battered women that beating signifies love and that their assault is justified by their trespasses against the wishes of men" (182). Such a character type might be holding out hope for a future in which the fist would cease to crush and blacken her face, or else she might see her present relationship similarly to the way in which people in nonviolent situations tend to see theirs—full of both good points and bad, highs and lows—a viewpoint that dilutes the severity of the violence in her life to the mere everyday vicissitudes of intimate relations. And yet, the masochist's insistent return to the site that affords her desire and love, albeit via pain, suggests that the naïve dreamer is not the opposite but rather, often, the complement of the world-wise woman. A hopeful reading of Clorinda, who sees love *despite* a man's abusive fist, here blurs with the worldly, masochistic Clorinda, who apprehends love *because of* that same fist: each Clorinda requests the same battery, albeit for distinct reasons.

Perhaps we might also read Clorinda's request to be hit again as one that signals not her romantic innocence but her world-weary resignation to male violence: here, a modern, racially inflected reading of the impoverished naturalist women Frank Norris depicts in "Fantaisie Printaniere" that the last chapter treated. Within such a reading, the stark depiction of a man empowered by violent domination becomes muddled by the equally stark response of the woman he batters; indeed, Patricia Bonner, a critic who espouses Clorinda's wisdom in an effort to counter her students' frequent "interpretation of Clorinda as a weak, powerless, and submissive victim," argues that Clorinda's final statement "robs [the man] of some of his power" (109, 110). Bonner uses the ambiguity in power relationships that Hughes's ending provides to comment not only on Clorinda's "power" and "wisdom," but also on what she calls "the true and constant source of all of [such women's] blues—unfair treatment of African Americans" (109, 110). In Bonner's reading, both the man and Clorinda are victims of society and an oppressive history of race relations, not victims of one another; she suggests that Clorinda's "request" to hit her again "indicates that she may understand the roots of [the man's] abusive nature and his twisted need to assert himself in this manner" and that one of Clorinda's telling insights demonstrated in this poem is that "love hurts when people hurt inside" (110). In such a reading, then, Clorinda might emerge as the bearer of an enormous sympathy, but a sympathy paradoxically predicated not upon imagining that things might one day turn out differently but upon a world-weary sense—like Trina McTeague and Missus Ryer from Norris's story decades before—that the "existing order of things" is still the best they're ever likely to be (Norris, "Fantaisie" 2).

In contrast to any of these readings of Clorinda, and coinciding with a disappearance of domestic violence discourse in the early twentieth century, I will use this chapter to explore the emergence of yet another version of an abused woman—a kind of uniquely passive character type who appears to others to be drained of affect like an empty shell. She might at first appear as a mere shadow to these more dynamic female character types I have previously treated, for what is initially striking about this final woman-who-stays character type is not how she sees the link between abuse and love, but rather that she appears to choose a sort of passive blindness toward both abuse and love. In doing so, she maintains an emptied-out self who appears to see nothing at all. We can see an example of such a willfully blinded, emptied-out woman in the interaction between Biff and his sister-in-law, Lucile, in Carson McCullers's *The Heart Is a Lonely Hunter* (1940).

In this novel, Lucile, a minor character, has an abusive ex-husband, Leroy, to whom she remains closely attached, despite the relationship trajectory that includes, in Biff's description, the following: "You married this certain party when you were seventeen, and afterward there was just racket between you after another. You divorced him. Then two years later you married him a second time. And now he's gone off again and you don't know where he is" (127–28). Clearly, one element Biff's description highlights is the cyclical nature of the abusive marriage. In Biff's estimation, even without considering Leroy's more personal character failings, this cyclical narrative's "facts" alone should "show [her] one thing—you two are not suited to each other" (128). It is not, however, the cyclical nature of violence but rather the form that Lucile's attachment to Leroy takes—an odd mixture of knowledge about Leroy's brutality, cognizance of her love for him, and an unwillingness to find pleasure in either romance or masochism—that is of most interest to us here in beginning to outline this "emptied" female character type.

Biff cannot comprehend Lucile's continued attachment to Leroy; he asks her, "[D]on't you ever just think a thing through and find out what's happened and what ought to come from that? Don't you ever use logic—if these are the given facts, this ought to be the result?" (McCullers 127). To her negative reply, "[N]ot about him, I guess," Biff retains his incredulity, further pressing her with the question, "[T]hen if he comes back you'll let him stay here and sponge off of you just as long as he pleases—like it was before?" (127, 128). Lucile's response—"Yeah. I guess I would. Every time the doorbell or the phone rings, every time anybody steps up on the porch, something in the back of my mind thinks about that man"—confirms not only her inability but also her disinclination to extricate herself from the relationship (128). To this, Biff responds by "spread[ing] out the palms of his hands" and saying, "There you are" (128). With such a pronouncement, Biff essentially presents Lucile's own logic back at her in an effort to establish the unreasonableness of her attachment to Leroy. This mirroring move may on the surface attempt to convince, but what it also signals is that Lucile's passivity in the face of her affection for her abusive ex is the crucial problem. For rather than take any overt actions against Leroy, all Lucile is willing or able to do is passively hope he "won't ever knock on that door again"; indeed, she is not even open to changing what door he would need to knock on in order to find her (128).

Lucile's striking inability to unstick her cycle—due to either an unwilling passivity or an impossible powerlessness to reject Leroy—is highlighted all the more by comparison with Biff's intervention into their violent relationship.

While Lucile has refused to confront her violent relationship with Leroy, Biff has done so on her behalf, albeit unasked: readers learn that sometime in the past, Biff beat up his brother-in-law for telling the following story: "He said he would come home about once a month and beat hell out of you and you would take it. But then afterward you would step outside in the hall and laugh aloud a few times so that the neighbors in the other rooms would think you both had just been playing around and it had all been a joke" (McCullers 129). Rather than denying this story, Lucile, with "a red spot on each of her cheeks," expresses only embarrassment about her own response to Leroy that this story exposes. She also sees her response not as a mistake, but rather as an inevitable engagement that is also, because of its inevitability, an explanation for her need to reject the world. She tells Biff, "[T]hat's why I got to be like I have blinders on all the time so as not to think backward or sideways" (129). Lucile so distrusts her own patterns of action that she has even rejected all future attempts at romantic relationships, a move that links her ability to withstand and excuse domestic violence for the sake of her love for Leroy to a naturalized tolerance of domestic violence within her relationships with all men. For Lucile fears that to feel "any kind of throbs" toward a man again would risk launching her again into the same sort of abusive relationship (130). Rather than experience empowerment and pleasure through masochism's merge of love and pain, Lucile here chooses agency's negation—a willful annihilation of choice and self.

Lucile's struggle with her attachment to Leroy despite "realizing all along he's a heel," coupled with her passive hope against his return as the only means she can manage to avoid the inevitably violent consequences of her still-existent love for him, creates a self-excluding "innocent" character. This character type's inability to use her knowledge to avoid her abuser is borne as a curse akin to an addiction rather than an excuse or even a joy (128). Not a masochist (for she does not explicitly desire pain) but also not a romantic dreamer (for she does not delude herself about the fact that pain will come if Leroy returns), Lucile chooses to limit her own agency as a way to negotiate an attachment she cannot evade. Her desire that Leroy will be on the other side of the phone when it rings, of the door when there is a knock, is counterbalanced by her "hope" that "he won't ever knock on that door again," a passive cancelation of her own agency to the will of her environment that recalls a surrender to fate (128). As Lucile stands outside herself and calls herself "a fool" due to her attachment to Leroy, she demonstrates a compounding tragedy of the cyclical tale of domestic violence—that one's desires, just like one's insistent return to not-knowing, can be experienced not as self-empowerment but as self-betrayal.

Between these divergent strands of masochism and hope, agency and victimhood, knowledge and innocence, the willfully blinded and passive abused woman likely seems only a bleak shadow to the other women-who-stay types that the previous chapter treated. But it is out of such an abused woman, a Lucile, that Ann Petry, in her naturalist-modernist novel *The Street* (1946), creates the most complex and agential depiction of the abused woman. Petry's minor character Min at first appears to be in much the same, if not a worse, position than McCullers's Lucile. For Min initially appears, too, to be a passive victim of male violence—a pejoratively described "shapeless" woman, so inconspicuous and rife with "shrinking withdrawal" that, when the novel's protagonist first sees her, she is described as being "scarcely distinguishable from the chair" on which she sat (Petry 23–24). When later in the text Min seems to surmount her passive invisibility and manages to leave her abusive partner, Jones, she appears to emerge from the cyclical stasis of abuse into the successful narrative trajectory of a completely different female character, one neither this nor the previous chapter has yet had the luxury of treating—the woman who *leaves*. What I will use a close reading of Min's character to suggest, though, is that attention to the details of Min's full narrative arc in *The Street* provides a much more challenging alternative to the above dichotomy. Min, I argue, does not oppose a cycle of staying with a narrative of leaving; rather, she evinces something closer to a cycle of *leaving*—or a *narrative* of staying.

Challenging the Narrative of Success: A Passive Agency?

The challenge Petry's character Min offers to normative discourse around domestic violence is an especially important, albeit tricky, representation to pin down, particularly since so many stories of domestic abuse are constructed as successes or failures based on whether women leave (meaning they have succeeded) or stay (often understood as a failure). Additionally, Min's narrative trajectory is particularly unusual, as it is included within a novel that is frequently remarked on for its naturalist and determinist tendencies. Though some critics have read Petry's novel through different generic conventions (notably Evie Shockley's reading of the book as a Gothic text), what Clare

Virginia Eby bemoans as the book's "initial circumscription within a narrow definition of naturalist protest fiction" is understandable and requires attention, even as one pushes beyond such confines (33).² From *The Street's* opening insistence on the "violent assault" of the wind that drives and discourages pedestrians, to the "instinctive, immediate fear" felt by the novel's women when in the presence of men, to the narration's prevailing sense that "it was that god-damned street," not characterological action, that was ultimately responsible for the novel's tragic ending, Petry's characters are hemmed in, deprived of agency, and controlled by environmental and natural forces (Petry 1, 20, 436). Despite the widespread social, environmental, and personal factors, both within Petry's novel and in society in general, that entice women to fail to leave abusive men, the critical narratives we tell about domestic violence within literature (when we do tell them), like the questions we ask about it in general discourse, often see only the women who leave when they are unhappy as the ones making a "correct" decision.

The critical treatment of women within *The Street* has not proven exceptional to these trends. Indeed, within this body of criticism, the tragic trajectory of the novel's heroine, Lutie Johnson, is often contrasted with the comparative "success" Min accomplishes. Petry's novel tells the story of Lutie Johnson, a single, black working mother with an eight-year-old son who saves her earnings in the hopes of accumulating enough money to move out of the Harlem apartment she finds in the book's opening pages; moving is a high priority for Lutie, because she feels an urgent need to get out of the way of Jones, the so-called "cellar crazy" building super who openly, creepily lusts after her (Petry 301). Lutie's sexual objectification is not limited to Jones, however, but is continued by all the men around her. For example, when she is offered a job as a singer in a club, Lutie believes it will provide a route out of Harlem, but she later finds out that the proffered job was merely a ploy by the club owner, Junto, to pressure her into sleeping with him. In the course of the novel, about a year, Lutie is sexually assaulted twice, first by her building super, Jones, and next by Boots, a man who works for Junto at the club. She manages to escape in the first instance and kills her attacker in the second. The novel ends when Lutie abandons her son (who is being detained, pending a hearing in Children's Court, for stealing letters—a plot engineered by Jones) and leaves Harlem in order to escape legal prosecution for Boots's murder. Lutie feels that running away and abandoning her son is her only way to protect any kind of future for him.

Min's presence in Petry's novel is a minor one that intersects only fleetingly with Lutie's. As the poor black woman who lives with Jones, Min at first appears to be in worse straits than Lutie. This is particularly the case when Min experiences the brunt of Jones's frustrated lust for Lutie through his emotional, verbal, and physical abuse. The course of the novel, however, challenges this initial assessment. For instance, at one point in the novel, Min goes to a root doctor in order to purchase a spell that will prevent Jones from throwing her out of their apartment—and this seems to work, because at no point in the novel does Jones force Min to leave. Yet toward the novel's end, Min decides that even if she is not thrown out of her apartment, staying with Jones is not worth it because, in her words, "[he] really ain't bearable no more" (369). Thus, she packs her belongings and makes her escape. Both Lutie and Min live in the same impoverished, violent, and segregated Harlem that "blacken[ed]" the eyes of Hughes's Clorinda, and both women are plagued by the sort of racial and gender discrimination that Patricia Bonner uses to assert Clorinda's wisdom and compassion for her racially oppressed, if violent, male partner (Hughes 5). But whereas Lutie's story charts the narrative arc's rise and fall—from the single mother scrapping by, to the hopeful dreamer, to the crushed and criminalized victim—Min's story arc, at least ostensibly, depicts a victim emerging triumphantly from gender, racial, and social oppression upon her humanizing, antiracist, antisexist realization that, again in her own words, "a body's got the right to live" (Petry 368).

Viewed as foils, albeit imperfect ones, the narratives critics tell and rehearse in articles and books of Lutie's failure and Min's success indicate the extent to which such notions of success derive from the implicit assumption that women should leave violent situations and that to have "survived abuse successfully"—both within cultural consciousness and in the ideology of those professionals in positions to aid abused women—ultimately means that a woman has succeeded in "essentially 'breaking' such a cycle" of violence (Glass 104). Carol E. Henderson succinctly articulates this assumption in her comparison of Min and Lutie: "[Min's] movement from invisibility to visibility, submission to self-confidence, and finally voicelessness to voice, provides an unsettling story of triumph and determination as a counter to Lutie's failure" (858). And though critics such as William Scott and Meg Wesling have questioned whether or not Lutie's position at the close of *The Street* ought best to be termed a failure, Min's narrative transformation from the passive victim who tolerates battery to the active woman who refuses it is seldom questioned, even by those critics who analyze textual details that would seem to challenge such a reading.[3]

Critical allegiance to Min's transformational arc is aided by *The Street*'s narrative voice itself; unlike the ironic distance that Norris's and West's naturalist texts from the last chapter maintained, Petry's novel enters Min's consciousness to emphasize the process of change both in Min's self-conception and in her understanding of her relationship with Jones. Indeed, the Street's stream-of-consciousness style in such moments is similar, in some respects, to the strategies that Petry's contemporary, Gwendolyn Brooks, uses in *Maud Martha* (as discussed in chapter 2). This evocation of Min's inner voice dramatically informs a reader's understanding of her character; and yet, though we as readers are confronted early on in the novel with Min's "shapeless" body, a descriptor that haunts her throughout the text and that allows her to disappear both into furniture and from Lutie's consciousness, we actually first encounter Min in the text not as this obscured body but as a voice (Petry 23). Upon Lutie's entrance into the building into which she will soon move, she knocks on Jones's door, and when Jones appears and his dog tries to lunge into the hallway, Jones kicks and abuses the creature "until the dog cringed away from him with its tail between its legs" (9). After the dog's retreat, Lutie "heard the dog whine deep in its throat and then the murmur of a woman's voice—a whispering voice talking to the dog" (9). Though Min speaks in a whisper, her voice is insistently present; her murmuring language, which conjures a soothing, care-giving figure, provides a quiet alternative to the abuse Jones perpetrates in their—Jones's, Min's, and the dog's—household. Min's first act in the novel, then, is one of vocalized, surreptitious comfort doled out to the other abused creature within the apartment, a significant action that we see systematically erased, first when Lutie "completely forg[ets]" Min while still within Jones's apartment and subsequently by the narrative trajectory that depicts Min's growth out of silence into voice, as if, contrary to the above evidence, she is learning to speak for the first time throughout the course of the text (24).

Those critics who emphasize Min's oversimplistic trajectory from voicelessness to voice, in order to focus on Min's increasingly powerful role within the novel, might ignore Min's opening whisper; however, they are forced to confront the circumscribed and limited goals that Min uses her voice to lay out for herself along this trajectory. Henderson writes that rather than pursuing the goals of the American dream (freedom, rights, equality), "Min instead dreams of finding a place—a safe space—to exist free of pain or danger. These attributes make Min an unattractive character for some to analyze because on the surface she seems to embody the typical characteristics of the submissive woman" (854). Similarly, Kimberly Drake reads Min as "a character in flux" who is "initially less interested in breaking rules than in preserving the status quo" (72). Indeed, Henderson confirms the extent of Min's submissiveness by acknowledging that "Min's life, as described in the novel, is one of dependency on others who are often abusive" (855).

The two chapters in *The Street* that are narrated through Min's consciousness paradoxically both challenge and confirm Henderson's estimation of Min. The first of these, chapter 5, opens with Min's acknowledgment that she, along with her intelligence, has been overlooked by Jones: "He don't know me," she thinks. "He thinks I don't know what's the matter with him" (Petry 113). What follows are a series of Min's observations that substantiate her knowledge that Jones lusts after Lutie and is thus displeased with Min, a "paradoxical" assertion of intelligence, in Drake's estimation, as it rests on "[Min's] own awareness that Jones thinks she's stupid" (76). Also, paradoxically, her *assumed* ignorance indicates Jones's *actual* lack of knowledge—or, at the very least, his deep underestimation of his partner. Like McCullers's Lucile, Min clearly understands the dynamics of her intimate relationship and can accurately evaluate the character of her mate; in Min's case, however, her unexpected understanding establishes not herself but rather *her observers* as blind. In sum, the first chapter that features Min's thoughts and interiority not only emphasizes Min's epistemic capacity to contemplate her objectification or her perceived lack of intelligence, but it also, in doing so, gives her an intellectual advantage over her would-be detractors.

Yet this "knowing" portrait of Min is quickly undercut in the same chapter by her own assertions that she has never *acted* upon her knowledge in order to leave Jones—assertions that themselves construe revolution (leaving) as the only type of "action" possible within violent relationships. As she goes to visit the Prophet David, a conjure man, in order to find a way to prevent Jones from kicking her out of her apartment, Min emphasizes her consistently passive rather than active role in life. She thinks that this visit to the Prophet "was the first defiant gesture she had ever made. Up to now she had always accepted whatever happened to her without making any effort to avoid a situation or to change one" (Petry 126). This passivity has included, but was not limited to, her romantic interactions: the previous men she had lived with "had taken her money and abused her and given her nothing in return, but she was never the one who left" (127).

Min's emphasis here upon her own passivity receives critical attention at the price of analysis of textual moments that depict her knowing intelligence. Such selective critical sight helps confirm a narrative developmental trajectory from abuse to freedom that relies on Min's progression from passivity to action. Drake writes that it is only "going to the root doctor" that "has given [Min] the opportunity to reflect on herself, itself a radical change in her behavior" that enables Min's evolution "from a passive person to an active one, from object to subject," despite the fact that Min's initial thought in the chapter ("he don't know me") is a self-aware one (78). Similarly, Clare Virginia Eby writes that Min's articulation of her newfound defiance "captures a woman emerging from resignation into agency," though this again ignores Min's earlier agency-filled action of comfort and self-analysis (39). While such critical tendencies affirm the feminist pleasure with which readers view Min's eventual exodus from her violent relationship, they also obscure the adaptive strategies Min employs both in leaving *and in staying with* Jones. In contrast, I suggest that a careful consideration of Min's knowing passivity, present as she both stays and leaves, should force us to reconsider the assumption that a passive woman equates to a disempowered one.

A central object of passive adaptation and resistance in *The Street* is Min's table, an object she has acquired from one of her employers and that she uses to advocate for her own needs in a particularly material manner—namely, by using the secret drawer in the table to withhold her own earnings from her domestic partners, who had, without the table, always been able to find her money "almost as though they could smell it out" (Petry 116). Like Trina McTeague in Norris's novel treated in chapter 3, Min hoards money against her partner's wishes and knowledge; unlike Trina, however, whose miserliness leads to increasingly grotesque self-deprivation (she, for instance, starves herself for the sake of saving money and is, in the end, killed by McTeague because she will not relinquish money to him), Min's saving tendencies shore up her bodily welfare and ensure her independent survival. With the use of the table, we hear, Min had been able to "frustrat[e]" her last domestic partner, Big Boy (116). The table, for Min, offers safety: the mainstay for which she is looking in anything she calls home.

More radically, the table also protects Min's emotional and psychic needs; as Drake writes, the table "shelters her dreams" because the funds that Min saves in the table are ones set aside to better herself and her situation. When Min's first dream of "a set of false teeth" that will make her more attractive to potential "husbands" is supplanted by her desire to stay with Jones in their apartment, the money she's hidden in the table transforms into her means of affording her visit to Prophet David, the root doctor (Drake 75; Petry 116). More concretely, Min uses the table in order to tolerate any relationship with a man in the first place; with the table in tow, she is able to enter into a relationship with Jones with a measure of security, as she reasons that "if he turned out to be like the others it wouldn't matter, because the table would protect her money" (116). These and other textual details force us to acknowledge that, rather than merely accepting her situation, Min has consistently put adaptive strategies at work within her passive resistance; passivity, for Min, is not only a position she willingly inhabits but also one from which she gains a clear (if also covert) sense of protection, privacy, and strength.

We must also note the affective dimensions of Min's relationship to Jones, which, far from constantly oppressing her, have, in fact, often provided her pleasure. Though Min declares that her abusive men of the past had "given her nothing," in the case of Jones, this at least initially appears not to have been her experience. Jones "never asked her for money" and "invited her to come and live with him" rent free, details that for Min suggest "he had wanted her just for herself, not for any money he might be able to get from her" (Petry 116–17). In fact, "until that young Mrs. Johnson moved in," Min's relationship with Jones was marked by the pleasure she felt in the face of evidence that "he was fond of her and he really needed her" (117). This pleasure, which is described not as masochistic but rather as one based in mutual affection and need, required Min's understanding that she needed to stay out of Jones's way during his emotionally abusive "spells of sullenness" (117). Yet, rather than seeing such a condition as a warning sign or as something to bemoan, we hear that Min "didn't mind" such spells because she had the tools to negotiate them. Instead, on the whole, Min declares that with Jones, "she didn't know when she had ever been so happy" (117). In fact, though Min "hadn't cared at all" when her last man, Big Boy, left her, her noninvestment was directly related to the way in which he treated her—"he was always drunk and broke and hungry" (116). Jones, on the other hand, is a man whom Min, at the novel's start, wants to keep around precisely because she has so enjoyed his companionship.

Thus, when Min decides, in chapter 5, to visit the Prophet David and later, in chapter 15, to leave Jones, such defiant gestures need to be understood within the context not only of Min's increasing agency but also of Jones's changing behavior. Indeed, when Min declares to her neighbor Mrs. Hedges as she is leaving him that "Jones really ain't bearable no more," we might reasonably understand such a statement as a commentary not on Min's changing perception of what is worth putting up with, but on Jones's shifting bearability. Put another way, I suggest that we can read, in this statement, as Jones's violence toward Min increases, not evidence of Min's changing estimation of her self-worth but rather of the continual pragmatic negotiations of a subject who has been involved, through some overt action but more frequently via passive self-protection, in her own self-care all along.

Min's Cycle of Leaving

Not only does the presumed polarized narrative of the passive abuse victim's transformation into the empowered woman who leaves abuse behind contribute to Min's dichotomous representation within critical analysis—in which her assertions of passivity are privileged over evidence of her active resistance—but it also contributes to an oversimplified version of the way in which Min's empowerment (i.e., her exodus from the relationship) will guide her future relationships. Keeping in mind naturalism's propensity for fated, determined, and "stuck" narratives, the final scene in which readers of *The Street* see Min is notable for its potentially cyclical ambiguity. Challenging Marjorie Pryse's assertion of Min's "heroic dignity in deciding to leave Jones" is the problematic detail that Min, fresh on the heels of leaving Jones's abusive apartment, is already searching for another man with whom to live (Petry 126). While following the man who is helping her move her things, including that protective table, Min starts to look favorably upon his strength and to think about the fact that "a woman living alone didn't stand much chance" (370). And though she has just left a lethal relationship, she, unlike McCullers's Lucile, retains a desire to be with a man; she ruminates on the protection such a man might lend her in dealing with landlords, since "with a man around. . . . if he was a strong man like this one, they were afraid to talk roughly" (371). Her penultimate vocalization, "Say, you know anywhere a single lady could get a room?" is said with "a soft insinuation," which immediately counters Min's autonomous act of leaving with a seemingly dependent attempt to form a sexual attachment with, literally, the next man she sees (371).

This return to a man after her triumph of leaving might cause a reader to pause and question Min's intelligence, as well as to ask what kind of sympathy she deserves if this next relationship goes badly; indeed, Pryse views Min's repetitious return to a man as evidence of a static, rather than dynamic, life; for her, this mover represents "yet another" in a line of nonideal relationships (127). This negative view of Min's repetition is further substantiated by a scene directly preceding her decision to leave, in which Min waits for Jones to "probably kill her" in an impending physical altercation (357). While Jones approaches her in hate and rage, Min calmly waits for another thing "she knew"—the way the abuse "would go, for her other husbands had taught her" (357). Rather than fighting for her life, she narrates the physical violence she expects Jones, in the path of the others, to inflict upon her body:

> first, the grip around the neck that pressed the wind pipe out of position, so that screams were choked off and no sound could emerge from her throat; and then a whole series of blows, and after that, after falling to the ground under the weight of the blows, the most painful part would come—the heavy work shoes landing with force, sinking deep into the soft, fleshy parts of her body, her stomach, her behind. (357)

We as readers receive no confirmation that the mover will be any different than these other men with whom Min has lived; indeed, Min's knowledge of violence's sure trajectory likely disconcerts us more than it does Min herself. This scene, in which the waiting Min anticipates, but does not run to prevent, her own death is notable: first, for the incredibly odd, though characteristic, detachment Min uses to speak of her own body (357). At first, her body, pictured in parts, is attended by the impersonal pronoun "the"; indeed, it is only when imagining the "most painful part" of the imagined abuse that Min owns the battered body as "hers." This passive detachment from her body's vulnerability to the inflexible rules of abuse seem at first to put Min at risk not only of Jones's violence but also of taking responsibility for her own annihilation. In fact, rather than blame Jones, the abuser, she chooses to "shut out" his image and think only of her own culpability, for she believes that if she hadn't neglected to keep the Prophet David's protective powder with her, her impending death at Jones's hands "wouldn't have come about" (358).

Min escapes with her life not because of any overt action she takes but because of a sign-of-the-cross gesture she makes, "only half-realizing what she was doing," that miraculously, luckily, deters Jones (358). Her knowledge is coupled with impotence in this scene, as any "agency" she seems to have developed dissolves. She knows what to expect from Jones, yet she is helpless to prevent it; she prevents his violence, but she does so without meaning to do it, conundrums that present Min, even after her decision to leave Jones, as a simplistic victim of his violence. But this emptied-out Min, though seemingly impotent, does not appear so impotent to Jones as she does to others. What threatens Min—her willingness to wait and wonder in the face of abuse—is also, oddly, the thing that saves her. In some way, this odd distance—in which Min can acknowledge the body about to be abused as hers and yet still treat it with detachment—allows her a space of calm blindness in which, "without opening her eyes," she can bless herself with a prayer, a move that signals to Jones not her weakness nor her stupidity but, instead, her power (358).

What is it, if anything, that Min sees and gains when she closes her eyes? Is it luck or design that makes her wait, pray? This odd conflation of knowledge and chance, the mesh of Min's passivity with her salvation—the blind luck that plays a part, next to her strategizing, in her ability to live both upon and after her scene of leaving—trouble a notion that Min's next relationship will be, as Drake writes, "not a blind repetition of previous mistakes but an informed determination of her best option; two incomes provide a safety net" (85). To read Min's exodus from Jones's apartment as an indication of her embrace of an active subject position at odds with her previous passive one is to neglect the troublesome notion that Min's knowing passivity may stay put in the face of abuse and help her survive it, suggesting that her next relationship might be *both* her best option *and* a repetition of the past. Further, if one sets aside the question Why do women stay with abusive men? and instead looks closely at the details *The Street* imparts regarding Min, one is confronted with the uneasy notion that Min has never been blindly doing anything at all.

Indeed, I suggest that for us to view Min as an abused agent worthy of our sympathy, we must first reject the sharp line that divides our assignment of passivity and staying to victimization, action and leaving to agency. We must be willing, instead, to see Min's passivity at moments, like her activity in others, as part of a complex network of negotiated living strategies that privilege the agent's life even as they involve living situations that outsiders such as the novel's readership might well consider unlivable. Neither a masochist nor a victim of either hope or circumstance, Min's story of abuse marks another form of narrative failure. Here, women's choices to stay or leave are determined to be successes or failures not by narrative details or tonal distance but by readerly bias, which renders readers unable to attend to the given textual details because of the overarching discursive norms that constitute their bias. Narratives like Min's are too often overdetermined in such a way as to make our accolades for certain characters as detrimental to a social intervention upon the persistent issue of domestic violence as is withholding our sympathy from others. Min, we must recognize, has always had a mind and body, a voice, with which to deal with abuse—it is only Lutie, Jones, critics, or perhaps we readers, who forget this.

Narrativizing the Cycle, Changing the Question

At the conclusion of *The Street*, we are left pondering the problematic of the cycle that is a choice but also still a cycle—the women who remain in abusive relationships, return to them, or find themselves unable or unwilling to extricate themselves from abuse. Even if we grant that oppressed persons might employ not-knowing strategically—or, as Alison Bailey in *Race and Epistemologies of Ignorance* frames this, as "ways of using the dominator's tools [here, ignorance] that do not replicate dominance"—it has been difficult for us to value something that looks like a woman's real lack of knowledge as part of said strategy (Sullivan and Tuana 86). In fact, Bailey uses the example of a battered woman later in that same essay to demonstrate the distinction between the oppressed's use of strategic ignorance and what she terms "real" ignorance; she writes that "women in violent relationships cannot ignore the shift in body language and tone of voice that signal violence" (Sullivan and Tuana 86). And yet what I hope this chapter has suggested is the importance of honoring the separation, however slight, between ignoring and choosing not to know. Rather than demonstrating female ignorance, pleasure, or passivity, the choice to stay and remain in an abusive relationship might demonstrate an all-too-knowing comprehension of these characters' *real* lack of a possibility they have for any future narrative change in their life circumstances.

This social, rather than individual, stuckness is, nonetheless, deeply epistemically frustrating. Here, the repeated questions Why doesn't she leave? and Why does she stay? alongside their myriad proffered answers, return incessantly to the body and mind of the woman and, in doing so, mystify issues of communal responsibility. These questions perform their alchemy, a kind of social supernatural in which women's choices to live with violence are viewed as both perverse and natural, both foolish and biologically sensible, both passively accepted and actively desired. Through an effort to contain these oppositions in the figure of the woman herself, a material and temporal consideration—literarily, narratively, critically—of actual women is forgotten, leaving a chronic cycle of violence to play over and again, generationally as well as individually.

In such a chronic cyclical replaying of events, we butt up against the limits of a pragmatic ethic of innocence or choice not to know. For the interchangeability of women, the already-known answers, the limits of agency and passivity, and the overdetermined trajectories of violence all challenge our ability to read such stories with the open endings such an alternative epistemology seeks. Naturalist-modern aesthetic and social determinism, as we have also seen, makes it difficult to see possibilities for reading these texts in ways that acknowledge women's deviations from the literary-cultural master narrative: to stay is to fail, and to leave is to succeed. For such individual swervings might include, as in Min's case, evidence that women pragmatically choose to return to relationships that, but for the magic of the unconscious (or religious superstition), we fear may end in the same violent death as did the marriages of *McTeague*'s Maria or Trina. After all, we cannot shake the possibility that, Min's strategy/passivity aside, it is but chance that allows readers to happily see Min leave Jones, for had Jones been less religiously superstitious, less fearful of the cross, Min—like Norris's women—might have simply tolerated her partner's abuse until it also resulted in her death. It is not only, then, our forgetfulness of the woman herself, but also our remembrance of past stories, old endings, and other female character types that makes it difficult for us to read—to hope—beyond domestic violence's sure cyclical tragedy toward a possible future for the woman who stays.

Fleissner argues in *Women, Compulsion, Modernity*, that naturalism's stories of women who preserve and save grotesquely "aler[t] us to the fact that, rather than simply denying the future or acceding to it . . . , these women's stories posit the need for an *alternate* future" (225). If we think of women—such as (from chapter 3) the Trinas, Missus Ryer, and Broad Shoulders, alongside this chapter's Min, Lucile, and Clorinda—as savers, grotesque or no, of violent relationships, regardless of their jadedness, masochism, romanticism, innocence, passivity, or combination of any of these, then the urgency of such a need for alternative futures becomes all the more starkly drawn for us. For without alternative futures, a reader of *The Street* is left to wonder not if but *when* another "husband" will succeed where Jones did not in killing Min, or perhaps—for it is much the same—in murdering a niece or neighbor of Min, if Min herself remains an exception.

Not only do the naturalist-modern texts that I have treated in these two chapters conjure domestic violence's commonplace nature and lateral repetition among the text's characters, but they also depressingly remind us of this violence's generational repetition. Here, I will turn once more to Frank Norris's fin-de-siècle novel *McTeague* (1899) in order to ruminate upon the lingering message left behind by a particularly gruesome scene of violent revelation when the body of the murdered Mrs. Trina McTeague is discovered by a group of schoolgirls. This scene is particularly haunting not just because of the conflation of violence and children, but because of the logical linkage of the two: little girls are the next generation of women. Trina is killed by her estranged husband, McTeague, in the cloakroom of the kindergarten she cleans in the evenings. After McTeague murders his wife, he does not take the trouble to hide her body but instead simply closes the door to this cloakroom behind him as he leaves. So, when the children attending that kindergarten arrive the next morning, they do not see

Trina's body. The small girls—for they are all girls—first discover something is amiss when they notice "a funnee smell" coming from the cloakroom (Norris 416). One little girl, however, is better positioned than the others to understand this smell; her father, we learn, is "a butcher," and she notices that it "smells like my pa's shop" (416). Though the girl's comment can be understood literally, the telling linkage between male spheres of work and violence, between blood and everyday experience, and between the literal and figurative ways in which men "butcher" flesh throughout the novel sets up a normalized expectation of male violence just as surely as it inoculates future women against questioning such an association. The chapter closes with an eerily prescient tableau: "[T]he tallest of the littler girls swung the door of the little cloakroom wide open and they all ran in" (416). Here, the biggest girl ushers her fellow females into a scene of trauma, in which they will come face to face not only with a murder but also with a future that, given the odds of the naturalist novel, they are likely to experience as their own.

Domestic violence's questionable magic, its social supernatural, is what allows a group of "five-year-olds" to see what their future womanhood will hold because the questions through which we have dissected their lives—Why do they stay? Why don't they leave?—cannot conceptualize it otherwise. These women who save their relationships—Petry's Min, McCullers's Lucile, West's Broad Shoulders, Hughes's Clorinda, and Norris's Maria, Missus Ryer, and the two Trinas—have all been waiting for something: some deviation, some voice, some imagination within their cyclical tales to unstick their futures.

It may be that the waiting naturalist women above "might be said to save themselves for a future that their texts cannot yet imagine" (Fleissner 225); in the chapters that follow, I aim to demonstrate such possible futures through the textual imaginings of other texts created in the same temporal fin-de-siècle/modern space as those that the first four chapters have studied. The emphasis in this book's first half has been on figures and texts that have been treated largely in reference to their conservative, realist, and/or naturalist modes; while I have evaluated their female figures' embrace of innocence through a pragmatic engagement with their nonrealist flights of fantasy, Gothic grotesquery, feminine perversity, and contradictory, even self-destructive impulses, I am fully aware that the challenge these female representations pose to epistemic norms operate from within the boundaries of the reigning cultural norms and scripts. In the remaining chapters, the texts from the first half of the book will be joined by the pragmatic fantasies within political protest, satire, fantasy, and film that bend and break such boundaries as part of their prophetic reimagining of such norms and scripts. Indeed, the following chapters extend from the largely character-driven readings within part 1 and go on to consider an ethic of innocence as something that one might see as enacted not only by the characters within a text but also by *the stance of the text itself*. In these chapters, I analyze the "pragmatic fantasies" of such texts in order to understand, first, what knowledge the fantasy text refuses and, second, how this refusal is still tied to a pragmatic engagement with everyday, "realist" realities.

It is my contention, though, that such a future will never be imaginable, nor will such pragmatic fantasies be actualized, for real women without a shift in the questions that govern the politics of staying within violent relationships. Rather than ask why women stay, what the narratives of violence we have considered suggest is that a better question might be What changes—social, material, emotional, personal—need to occur before women will choose, more often than not, to leave and to never return? This question no longer implicitly or explicitly calls women foolishly victimized, hopelessly jaded, masochistically empowered, or passively blind for staying within a compromised reality; rather, it notes the agency that informs their hopeful, resigned, jaded, masochistic, passive, and blinded tendencies alongside the crucial role our sympathy plays in constructing the environment in which such agents act. Indeed, it engages not only with the possibilities allowed by refusing knowledge for innocence, but also with the risks that adhere to this refusal within modernity. We might then own our social role in authoring a collective modern narrative of abuse, one that obscures characters' pragmatic intelligence even as it uses characters'—women's—acceptance of male violence to justify looking the other way.

PART TWO

PRAGMATIC FANTASIES

Chapter Five

Are Women People?

Discourses of (Non)Personhood in Suffrage Poetry and Protest

> Women have not been fully incorporated into the human.
>
> —Judith Butler, *Undoing Gender* (37)

This chapter begins a focus, in the latter half of this book, on ways in which choosing not to know allows female individuals a pragmatic means of moving beyond their current limited realities toward alternative horizons, of either futurity or fantasy. As such, this chapter—like the ones before and after it—situates its meditation via the site of the female body: as it is represented both in art and in life. This particular chapter focuses on early twentieth-century suffrage performance and protest in order to unpack the meaning behind the serious tensions such texts expose between artistic female bodies and real bodies, the varying sociocultural values that attach to each, and the implications regarding women's full or partial humanity (to take up Butler's provocative claim, given here in the epigraph). So, to begin this move toward pragmatic fantasy, let us first pause over a particularly violent confrontation between textual and material bodies: the midmorning in March 1914 when Mary Richardson, a "well-known and highly active militant suffragette," entered London's National Gallery and attacked the body of another woman—the nude, painted form of the *Rokeby Venus* (Nead 34).[1]

At the fin-de-siècle, Velázquez's *Rokeby Venus* (1649–1651) was characterized as "perhaps the finest painting of the nude in the world" by an article in the London *Times*, just before its acquisition by the National Art Gallery and nine years before its vandalism by Women's Social and Political

Union (WSPU) militant suffragette Mary Richardson (qtd. in Nead 36);[2] Richardson's subsequent vandalism of the painting, according to art historian Lynda Nead, "has become one of the most notorious acts of iconoclasm in recent history" (35). In large part, Nead attributes this event's notoriety to the public response and outcry that attended the vandalism of the painting. But though Richardson's act drew extensive critical attention and notoriety, she was not the only suffragette to attack a painting, as Hilda Kean notes in "Some Problems of Constructing and Reconstructing a Suffragette's Life." According to Kean, these other suffragettes "focused upon the financial implications of their actions," whereas Richardson, who emphasized the theoretical and thematic root of her attack, drew the explicit connection to women, aesthetic objectification, and political disenfranchisement, which is of most interest to this chapter (483). This difference—between an action meant to cause financial damage (in the case of the former) and one meant to performatively gesture toward underlying ideological connections between the aesthetic and political realm (in Richardson's case)—suggests we might read Richardson's vandalism of the Venus as not merely a criminal act but also an artistic, performative text. Thus, while a categorization of Richardson's attack on the Venus as "iconoclastic" crime situates her actions in the realm of the ideological/political, I will use this chapter to extend this connection, thinking explicitly about the ways in which Richardson's actions, taken as a whole, constitute an act of performance art with aesthetic and political connections to other forms of suffrage art and protest.

The movement to enfranchise women, spanning the transatlantic in the nineteenth and early twentieth centuries, was a political, rhetorical one that used aesthetics, performance, symbolism, and imagery to great persuasive effect. As Lisa Tickner notes in *The Spectacle of Women*, this requires emphasis if only because the "visual past" can fall victim to category insufficiency: being "too 'artistic' for the interests of political history . . . and too political (and too ephemeral) for the history of art" (ix). And yet art—particularly performance art—often threads the needle between these categories, as I hope the following pages will show. In large part, my justification for reading Richardson's action as a piece of performance art (rather than merely a crime) comes from emphasizing the explanatory discourse she used to contextualize her actions, which combined reference to the visual (art and art history), performance practice and theater, and the rhetorical use of the media to archive and contextualize an ephemeral act. And indeed, Nead's analysis of the unique significance of Richardson's act relies not only on her suffragette status but also, largely, on the legibility of feminist protest in her actions. Nead understands this protest primarily within an artistic-historical context, as one that intervenes in "the dissemination of the patriarchal ideal of the female nude through the institutions of art education and art criticism" (43). And yet, within Nead's discussion of the public outcry against Richardson, she also pinpoints a fascinating, if disturbing, trend of molding aesthetic immortality out of seemingly human flesh that shows how art-historical ideologies breach the confines of the museum, both affecting and being affected by broader gendered discourse.

An extensive article from *The Times*, entitled "National Gallery Outrage" and issued the day after the *Rokeby Venus*'s vandalism, describes the details of Richardson's iconoclasm in a way that acknowledges this breach. The action is narrated as follows, under a section entitled "The Attack on the Picture":

> [Richardson] stood in front of the Rokeby Venus for some moments, apparently in contemplation of it. There was nothing in her demeanour to arouse the suspicions of the uniformed attendant and a police constable who were on duty in the room and were standing within seven or eight yards of her. The first thought of the attendant, when he heard the smashing of glass, was that the skylight had been broken; but a moment later he saw the woman hacking furiously at the picture with a chopper which, it is assumed, she had concealed under her jacket. He ran towards her, but he was retarded somewhat by the polished and slippery floor. The constable reached the woman first and seizing her by the right arm prevented her from doing further mischief. She allowed herself to be led quietly away to the inspector's office. Addressing a few visitors to the Gallery who had meanwhile collected, she said, "Yes, I am a suffragette. You can get another picture, but you cannot get a life, as they are killing Mrs. Pankhurst." ("National" 9G)

Since the "suspicions" of the official "uniformed attendant" and "police constable" were what Richardson first failed to trigger, then went on to provoke, we might easily understand this "mischief" of hers both as defiance of institutional (and male) authority and as a censured crime. Indeed, it would make sense to do so; the gendered response of art galleries in the wake of Richardson's vandalism attests to the way in which suffragette mischief was perceived as a female threat to a male-dominated sphere. Diane Atkinson writes in her book *The Suffragettes in Pictures* that "attacks on works of art prompted the closure of many of the country's art galleries and museums to women, and sometimes to the public completely" (153). Even when complete closure to women was not enforced, various public sites banned the presence of personal items typically exclusively carried by women. And while the British Museum remained open to women, so long as they were "accompanied by men who would accept responsibility for them" or, when unaccompanied, on the condition they could produce "a letter of recommendation from a gentleman who would vouch for their good conduct and take responsibility for their actions," such paternalistic restrictions reinforced the assumption that women's suffrage was an extremist position of only female individuals (153). Here, not only was the broader problem of women's willfulness clearly constructed as a matter in need of male policing, but the male gender's word was also taken to unquestionably support the interest of the state, not the suffragettes.

It would at first seem that Mary Richardson—arrested, jailed, allowed to make a statement—had been punished for committing a clear-cut crime of vandalism against a lifeless painting (Nead 35). Fascinatingly, however, in the weeks following the incident, the question of what, or whom, Richardson's crime was committed against remained, at least in public discourse, ambiguously unresolved. Take, for instance, the *Times* article above. Even preceding the description of Richardson's act of vandalism, we are led by the column title to think of this incident as an "attack," a word which connotes a personal nature to the violence committed against the painting. Though Richardson seems to have sought, in her quoted outburst above, to draw a clear distinction between a replaceable "picture" and a precious "life," primary reports and critical readings of the incident noted the connection without tending to make this same distinction ("National" 9G). Instead, the report above indicates the involvement of three female bodies in the National Gallery incident and also specifies their roles in the crime narrative—Mary Richardson, criminal; Venus, victim; and Mrs. Pankhurst (the jailed suffragette leader of the militant WSPU to whom Richardson explicitly links her actions), motive.

That one of these bodies was painted does not discount the Venus from her status of female victim; rather, albeit counterintuitively, paint seems to solidify the Venus's victim status in cultural discourse. Thomas J. Otten claims in his comments on "the slashing of the Velázquez" that "this practice of categorizing experience and artifacts into 'life' and 'art' only so that those categories may swap attributes are what aestheticism depends on" (298). Thus, to take up Otten's position, it is not in spite of the Venus's position as art, but because of it, that she is able to be seen by the public as a victimized life. Meanwhile, the human bodies of Emmeline Pankhurst, Mary Richardson, and other suffragette activists languished in British prisons for their actions, meant to draw attention to the lack of public value, indeed the partial lives, that their political disenfranchisement enforced.[3]

Are Women People?
Alice Duer Miller's Dual Question

If it seems merely absurd to suggest that the damage to the life of a painted woman was received with a public outrage that was not likewise extended to news of her human counterpart's damage, this might be in part due to our greater comfort in emphasizing the humorous rather than the seriousness within irony and satirical comparison. And yet strategies of ironic comparison, taken to their absurd conclusion, allowed for some of the most radical suffrage texts to exhibit the material effects of disenfranchisement on the fin-de-siècle female body. For instance, American writer and women's suffrage campaigner Alice Duer Miller compiled a Sunday column in the *New York Tribune*, which ran from January of 1914 through 1917. Miller's column focused on the ironies, hypocritical logic, and sexist judgments within "news, quotations, poems, fictionalized conversations, statistics, and cartoons about gender inequalities" in order to showcase the variety of issues at stake in suffrage advocacy (Chapman 59). And yet, Miller gathers these issues together through the central, indeed title, question of her column: "Are women people?" The column, and especially the 1915 collection of poems that grew out of it (published under the similar title *Are Women People? A Book of Rhymes for Suffrage Times*), not only demonstrated the way in which witty rhymes and poetic parodies could be used to advocate for women's political enfranchisement but also made explicit the extent to which Miller's feminist advocacy relied on rhetorically indirect strategies, while all the while, the question "are women people?"—its absurdity, its seriousness, and under which these various collected fragments were housed—hovered overhead.

Miller's column and book use similar methodologies, in which quotation, ventriloquism, and paraphrase function both as argumentation and as mirrors; however, for the purposes of this chapter, I will focus primarily upon her book's collective effects. One of the first aspects of the book one notices is the way in which Miller highlights via quotation aspects of the speeches, legal judgments, and newspaper articles by both antisuffragists and male democratic leaders that appear provocative or even forward thinking. Miller then exposes, organizes, contextualizes, and (at times) comments upon the underlying ironies and hypocrisies within this borrowed language. To contemporary readers, Miller's techniques might call to mind current comedy news shows like *The Daily Show* and *Last Week Tonight*, shows which base their commentary on recontextualizing clips from other media and cultural sources, and yet (as we will see here) this strategy had more contemporary linkages to other forms of subversive female humor writing in the late nineteenth and early twentieth centuries. Through Miller's use of framing, juxtaposition, and parodies of antisuffrage logic/rhetoric, coupled with her imaginary, projected embodiment-via-ventriloquism of the quotations' original speakers within her poems, Miller's book *Are Women People?* exposes a duo of social absurdities that stem from her text's overarching question.

The first of these absurdities—that of the hypocrisy, in relation to gender, contained within America's public and legal language of equality—is legible from *Are Women People?*'s opening poem. Miller's imagined conversation between father and son makes available to the reader the distance between the rhetoric and the reality of gender equality, what critic Mary Chapman describes as "the gap between boasts about the extensiveness of American democracy and the practice of exclusion that refused to acknowledge half of its citizens as people at the polls" (60). The poem runs as follows:

> Father, what is a Legislature?
> A representative body elected by the people of the state.
> Are women people?
> No, my son, criminals, lunatics, and women are not people.
> Do legislators legislate for nothing?
> Oh no; they are paid a salary.
> By whom?
> By the people.
> Are women people?
> Of course, my son, just as much as men are. (Miller 1–2)

This poetic exchange highlights, as Chapman suggests, the way in which women's inclusion within the social category "people" by the American government is neither self-evidently essential nor static, but rather contingent and changing. Miller's poem highlights the disjunction between a collective governmental system in which women are recognized as people (and thus a part of the taxpaying public) and an exclusionary one, in which women are not people (and thus a part of the population unable to vote); that these disparate systems are, in fact, not merely *different* but rather directly *oppositional* attitudes held by the *same* government is a realization that provides the poem's key irony.

Through the poem's absurdly contradictory shifts—its 180-degree pivots between identifying and not identifying women as people—Miller's piece lampoons the particularly monetary context in which female personhood is recognized. This system in which women are only evaluated and valued as people when there is money to be gained, Miller's poem implies, attains its viability and cultural sanction because women's economic obligation directly benefits the government in a way that female voting rights might not. (Indeed, the perception that women's voting rights might harm the government's interests is a key theme in many of Miller's satirical poems, including some later treated within this chapter). Importantly, this governmental stance of women's partial personhood could, arguably, be seen as further subordinating rather than (even partially) empowering the female half of the population. For indeed, although women may make money, when the issue of where their money should go is raised, women in America, according to Miller, find themselves denied their ability to participate as voting citizens. In short, when women's pockets are valued, even as their political voices are silenced, the system that enforces such values forces women to act as economic contributors to their own continued subjugation.

The eerie similarity between this poem's implicit protest on behalf of women's suffrage and such women's colonial ancestors' protest against British rule—the political cry of "No taxation without representation!"—was certainly not lost on Miller or on her suffragist contemporaries; indeed, comparison of women's grievances and arguments for their own suffrage to earlier demands for *male* suffrage and emancipation (during both the colonial and antebellum periods) was a dominant tactic of the women's suffrage movement in both America and Britain in the early twentieth century, as was analysis of the economic interests accompanying enfranchisement. Laura E. Nym Mayhall, in "The Rhetorics of Slavery and Citizenship," even demonstrates the central role that the idiom and analogy of slavery had in the women's suffrage campaign (485–88). And yet, when antisuffrage rhetoric is put in conversation with previous enfranchisement campaigns for both men and formerly enslaved male populations, both at home in Britain and America and abroad, it is unclear why the persuasive and logical argumentation used to fight for the enfranchisement of certain populations would not also, logically, apply to women's enfranchisement. For instance, the British suffragette

Constance Lytton, whose 1914 memoir *Prisons and Prisoners* recounted her political actions on behalf of the militant suffrage organization, the WSPU, noted that when British leaders spoke about other countries, "the assertive claim to the value of voting rights for men, wherever these are denied" in fact functions to "perennially [if indirectly] educat[e] the public to [women suffragists'] contention" about the importance of universal, not just male, suffrage (61). Further, "the drawbacks resulting from laws and customs [in other nations] based on sex bias are also constantly put forward by Anti-Suffragist men themselves" with seemingly little to no reflection on how such assertions would bear on their own nation (61). Lytton, like Miller in the "Are Women People" column and book, concluded from these bizarre confluences, that "to meet the Anti-Woman Suffragist arguments, it is only necessary to quote their own utterances" (62).

It may appear at first, then, that Miller's question "Are Women People?" gains its primary purchase on its audience's imagination as an ironic query. Of course, one might answer, women are people—it is just that some have a vested interest in denying this, for reasons that (as seen above) exceed logics attending personhood arguments used to enfranchise males of certain classes and races. Such irony makes use of what Nancy Walker terms "double text" rhetoric, where texts work subtly to challenge sexist, stereotypical views of women even as they appear "superficially merely to describe" a scene rather than critique it (13). Here, quotation itself is not mere part of but actually constitutes the entire argumentation. Making use of Walker's theory, we can read Miller's *Are Women People* as a text rhetorically designed to first avoid overt politicking as it draws in its reading public and then, once its readers are hooked, force them to do a sort of double-take in the face of the absurdity (and surprising political relevance) of the questions it asks. For instance, Chapman, as a means of explaining why Miller mobilizes humor, parody, and ironic commentary in lieu of "respectful conversation" in the poetic voices within "Are Women People?" argues that quotation and ventriloquism are used as a kind of stand-in for the feminist voice for those individuals who would—if these poems were spoken through an *explicitly* feminist voice—refuse to engage them (66).

Miller's work, in Chapman's view, draws the reader's attention to the "impossibility of conversation" between the suffragists and their opponents, not merely because the suffragists' opponents seem unaware of the implications of their own language but because of their prejudicial inability to engage seriously with the words of someone speaking from a feminist perspective (77). She claims that until these two discrete parties could talk with one another, "quotation and ventriloquism had to function as a substitute for that conversation in order to bring the statements of . . . anti-suffragists into proximity with a suffragist perspective" (77). Within such staged conversations, Chapman argues that the voices of feminist women could "articulate their selves [albeit implicitly] by the ironic, parodic, decontextualization and reframing of these utterances" (66). Miller's "double-text" not only subtly critiques an opponent's position; more importantly, it does so by literally erasing the suffragist as subject and instead speaking "doubly" from one voice—holding a schizoid conversation between interpretations, rather than persons, that cannot easily be rejected on the basis of holding one voice to be an "outsider" position.

It is with this simultaneous erasure yet phantasmagoric preservation within antisuffrage rhetoric of the suffragette/feminist subject that Miller's work, I argue, heralds the second of the "duo" of absurdities to which I earlier referred. Rather than reading Miller's poetry only within the genre of "propagandist satire," as Sophie Blanch terms it, or else as work invested in "pretending to take seriously what is patently ridiculous," as Zita Dresner claims, I want to suggest that a further, more central, absurdity attending the key issue of Miller's book lies in the contradictory truth her poetry exposes: that the absurd opening query—Are women people?—is not so absurd after all (Blanch 9; Dresner 34).[4] Miller's writing is humorous, to be sure, but I contend that her central query about whether women are persons is both deadly serious and, if answered seriously, profoundly pessimistic in outlook. Indeed, Miller's juxtapositions in her opening piece between the father's initial denial of female personhood and his subsequent acceptance of women as people already sets the stage for a reader's realization that, in fact, in important ways women *are not* "people": that is, they do not share the same political and legal rights as men. One might argue that Miller's opening poem shows women to be a sort of half-people, or people half of the time, rather than not people at all. I suggest, however, that the fluctuating contexts and vested interests by and through which women's personhood is here decided, coupled with women's explicit removal from a position of power that would enable them to participate in this decision process, helps us answer the question Are women people? by leaning—via the evidence—toward the negative rather than responding—almost automatically—in the positive.[5]

In what follows, I use the second of Miller's two absurdities as the groundwork for mapping out the impact of the conclusion that women somehow are not people within the feminist "performance" of Miller's transatlantic contemporary Mary Richardson and for tracing this answer's continued relevance today. Miller's poems make clear that in important ways, concerning political and social rights and freedoms, women did not, and do not yet, quite fit into the protective social category of "people"; by placing her work in conversation with other texts that are not only temporally linked but also distinct from Miller's own, I argue that her negative answer not only helps us to understand the political stakes in her own work, but it also provides a rubric by which we might understand the feminist fantasies in texts that this book treats in later chapters. Indeed, I hope to show how this question of female personhood not only haunts Miller's poems and Richardson's performance, but also centrally informs their own and subsequent authors' ethic of innocence—the *way* in which, as well as what, they, like the other characters and women we have looked at thus far in this project, choose not to know.

Miller's and Richardson's pieces are, I argue, pragmatic texts that, in crucial ways, engage the social disavowal of female personhood, despite criticism that has tended to obscure the negative in favor of more romantic, essentialist accounts not only of women's abilities to "be" persons but also of the positive impact such "being" has on female safety in the face of systemic cultural violence. For in these texts, Miller and Richardson do not simply reject the universalist or realist urge to laugh at the absurdity of the question of women's personhood. More crucially, they also reject the knowledge that women's tenuous "subjecthood"—whatever personhood that they *do* have—is what they need more of: a rejection whose stakes become starker and clearer in the latter twentieth century, even as we rely on pragmatism, a philosophy that flourished in the early twentieth century, in order to create this stark clarity.

Pragmatism's Process: Creating, Not Recognizing, Personhood

To seriously embark on such a rereading, we must first ask the following question: Under what circumstances and through what worldview could one seriously argue that certain categories of human beings are not people? When I suggest, as above, that feminist politics and critics have often ignored the negative strain of female personhood that this chapter traces, I do not mean to suggest that they do so without good reason. Indeed, although I am exploring discourses of (non)personhood that I read as influencing the texts of Miller and Richardson, I do not want to avoid the very political and personal stakes of these texts for female "persons," nor do I want such an exploration to deaden their texts' feminist heft. Most critics have tended to read Richardson's protest through the lens of subjecthood (or personhood), which makes much sense given Richardson's own political and aesthetic investments. Like Alice Duer Miller, Mary Richardson was an activist on behalf of women's suffrage; more specifically, Richardson was a member of the WSPU, and her militant activist activities in England on the WSPU's behalf resulted in her serving several prison sentences. Thus, her famous 1914 protest slashing of the *Rokeby Venus* in London's National Gallery is frequently, and sensibly, read and understood in the context of suffragette protest against Britain's disenfranchisement of its female "subjects."

Such discourse on subjecthood that Richardson's performances have traditionally been understood to engage—one that privileges her defense of the female subject—is not negligible to my argument; in fact, it has important political, personal, and even imaginary functions that cannot be ignored. I take seriously, even unapologetically, pragmatist Richard Rorty's somewhat flippant point that "practical politics will doubtless often require feminists to speak with the universalist vulgar" ("Feminism" 47). To the extent that readings of Miller's and Richardson's work as protests against female subjects' mistreatment prove to be persuasive in a political sphere in which women were and still are advocating for their basic political rights or in an aesthetic sphere in which women's bodies in public are all too often viewed purely as visually pleasurable yet nonsentient objects, their engagements with a discourse of subjecthood are invaluable (47). Yet I too, like Rorty, urge the "profit" we might find "from thinking with the pragmatists" about the questions regarding female personhood these performances raise—as well as the question, in Miller, that such pragmatic thinking makes possible in the first place (Rorty, "Feminism" 47).

How, we might well ask, does Miller's work justify her negative answer to the question Are women people? and why might this answer be a pragmatic one? Miller's poem that opens *Are Women People?* ("Father, what is a legislature?", quoted in full earlier in this chapter), begins this justification by joining "criminals, lunatics, and women" into a category of those without personhood, thereby implicitly suggesting that these three types of beings share some characteristic that serves to disqualify them from the title "people"—though it is unclear, from the poem itself, what matrix connects and excludes them (2). Feminist precedent for this line in Frances Power Cobbe's 1868 essay "Criminals, Idiots, Women and Minors" used the connections between these categories to show the absurdity of legal barriers to women's ownership of property postmarriage; indeed, each of these categories of individuals experienced diminished legal freedoms in comparison with men (during Cobbe and Miler's lifetime certainly, but also still, in part, today). However, each found its freedoms diminished for differing reasons. Criminals, for instance, could be excluded from full personhood by virtue of moral transgression—that is, their criminal infractions upon the social order result in their loss of legal privileges that would normally attend their age, race, gender, and social standing. Lunatics, on the other hand, are not so much morally as mentally excluded from personhood; here, the mentally ill are characterized as lacking the intellectual acuity to participate in society as "people." Women, perhaps unsurprisingly, fall somewhat awkwardly between the criminal and the lunatic; the logic that excludes them from full personhood both combines and exceeds the exclusionary tactics employed in the two previous cases. For, although, most explicitly, women have been historically excluded from full participatory personhood based on their gender and other intersectional factors such as race, class, and sexuality, when one looks more closely at the logic evinced by antisuffrage rhetoric, the confluence of mental and moral reasons for such exclusion becomes evident.

Rorty argues that without "full personhood" (a term he borrows from Marilyn Frye's *The Politics of Reality*), women will be treated "like children or the insane, as degenerate cases—as beings entitled to love and protection but not to participation in deliberation on serious matters" ("Feminism" 57). And indeed, portrayals of female criminality, lunacy, and childlike intellect were particularly rife in representations of a specific kind of fin-de-siècle woman, the women who recognized/believed she was not yet fully a person: the suffragette. Indeed, criminals were exactly what women who protested and argued for their suffrage in America and Britain around the fin de siècle became; June Purvis notes that "about 1,000 women" were imprisoned for their suffragette deeds in Britain from 1905 to 1914, and Laura Mayhall argues that over this same period, in cultural and discursive ways, "suffrage militancy, in any true sense, [became] impossible without imprisonment"—that is, reducing women fighting for the right to vote to criminality (*Votes* 135; "Creating" 330).

In addition to being criminalized, suffragettes were frequently depicted as insane or mentally lacking. Angela K. Smith's book *Suffrage Discourse in Britain during the First World War* references a 1912 article in the *Times* in which Sir Almroth Wright, a British bacteriologist, made so-called "'scientific' claims linking suffragism with female hysteria" (9). British suffragettes who participated in hunger strikes as acts of political protest when imprisoned for their militant suffrage campaigning were depicted as "irrational women, deliberately seeking their own torture" (Purvis, "Prison" 104). No mere extremist rhetoric, forcible feeding was, in fact, a torturous process that, according to Caroline J. Howlett, involved the following:

> The hunger-striking prisoner was first held down on a chair or bed by several wardresses. Feeding was then carried out by doctors, either orally or nasally. If the feeding was oral, a gag made of wool or metal was inserted to prevent the mouth from closing; where the patient resisted, a metal gag was generally forced into the mouth, cutting the gums and lips and often breaking the teeth. Once the gag was inserted, it was screwed open to widen the mouth, and a thick rubber tube was inserted into the throat and pressed down into the stomach. Alternatively, a thinner rubber tube was inserted via the nostril, causing severe pain, particularly to the eyes. Food was then poured from a jug into the tube via a funnel; milk and Bovril [a thick, salty meat extract] were two of the commonest ingredients." (5–6)

Indeed, the treatment of forcible feeding was, at the time, a protocol most commonly practiced on those who were mentally ill, and the government (as well as later critics such as Roger Fulford, whom June Purvis references) used the comparison to these mentally ill patients to show that forcible feeding "was not dangerous" (qtd. in Purvis, "Prison" 105). This connection was taken so far that, according to Caroline J. Howlett, "attempts were made by prison authorities to certify individual suffragettes as insane in order to legitimate the practice [of forcible feeding]" (17). The treatment British suffragettes received in prison, most notoriously their forcible feeding, was in large part authorized by reference to the presumed illogicalness of taking part in a hunger strike, a lack of logic attributed to these women's "defective minds" in order to explain their "insane conduct" inside the prison (Geddes 82, 83). Such an attribution can read as not only a critique of these particular women's mental faculties but also as a commentary on the subhuman or childish intellectual capabilities of all women

These acute treatments of suffragette women as criminals, lunatics, and illogical, defective, or child-like adults was made possible in part by more generalized attitudes toward women that engaged this same oppressive triad. For instance, when considering another of Miller's pieces entitled "Our

Own Twelve Anti-suffragist Reasons," from the book version of *Are Women People?* one sees that she depicts, in list form, twelve common rhetorical claims supporting women's disenfranchisement in order to emphasize the contradictory mental and moral assumptions about women upon which such claims were based. These assumptions appealed to women's supposed criminality, childishness, and moral failings at the same time as they appealed to their supposed purity, influence, and naïveté. By cleverly organizing these antisuffrage claims into subtle pairings throughout the list, Miller uses the immediate juxtaposition of their order to expose the underlying contradictory logic informing the movement to deny women the vote, which can be seen in the poem's full text below:

1. Because no woman will leave her domestic duties to vote.
2. Because no woman who may vote will attend to her domestic duties.
3. Because it will make dissention between husband and wife.
4. Because every woman will vote as her husband tells her to.
5. Because bad women will corrupt politics.
6. Because bad politics will corrupt women.
7. Because women have no power of organization.
8. Because women will form a solid party and outvote men.
9. Because men and women are so different that they must stick to different duties.
10. Because men and women are so much alike that men, with one vote each, can represent their own views and ours too.
11. Because women cannot use force.
12. Because the militants did use force. (Miller 17–18)

Both the oppositional logic and the radically oppositional characterizations of women within such logic informs the ironic humor of Miller's piece. And yet, at either extreme of this oppositional logic, women are denigrated. Numbers 5 and 6, for instance, speak to the binary casting of women as either evil or pure; regardless of their seeming opposition, however, the end result of each claim taken *independently* maintains the corrupt status of women. Thus, if each claim were to be taken as true, women's moral inability to participate in the public sphere would go unchallenged regardless of whether they are taken to play the role of the corruptors or the corrupted. It is only by pairing the claims oppositionally that their contradictory logic, their seeming untenability, becomes available to a reader, lending the piece not only its humor and irony, but also its explicit political relevance to the suffrage movement. Once again, though, I want to suggest that this is only the first stage of Miller's irony, for we could also read these claims as coexisting social "facts" or truths, truths that—despite their untenable opposition—nonetheless both, at the same time, retain their core, "de-personalizing" truth and that continue to hold sway in spite of their seeming untenability.

Pushing beyond the initial humor, we are able to notice the commonalities despite opposition—the critical evaluation of women that remains constant despite the binary. For instance, we see that no acknowledgment of women's intelligence ever emerges in the above claims, even in the pairings (3 and 4; 9 and 10) that speak to the dissention in marriages that will occur if women are allowed to vote. Points 4 and 10, for instance, posit women as unthinking beings, who will either be "told" how to vote by their husbands or who so lack any difference or mental independence from men that they do not even *need* to be told what to do to in order accede, inevitably, to their husbands' wishes. In contrast, then, we might expect 3 and 9 to bear witness to women's independent, albeit negatively construed, thought. What we get, however, speaks not to intelligence but to conflict. Three merely remarks on the "dissention" that would occur between domestic partners without commenting on the logic informing women's hypothetical disagreements with their mates, whereas 9 uses women's difference to imply that they do not belong in the realm of politics in general but should instead stick to the stereotypically nonintellectual "duties" of the home to which they have traditionally be assigned. Sharing in the qualities of both criminals and lunatics as creatures who must be sequestered from the world of "people" because of their moral and mental vulnerability, women's disqualification from personhood constructs them as not only differently gendered but also morally and mentally lacking in comparison to their male peers—a triad of oppression that, by virtue of its multiple facets, has no easy, unilateral refutation.

In sum, when I say we might take seriously, consider unabsurd, Miller's query Are women people? I am suggesting that we consider how we might reasonably, logically, and pragmatically answer this question with a no, and what it might force us to attend to if we were to do so. This attention would include querying the extent to which women are *not* fully people, not only as constructed verbally in antisuffragist rhetoric but also—and more crucially—as constructed socially through several diverse avenues that such rhetoric shapes and is shaped by, including institutional, legal, material, and discursive forces and oppressions. If Nancy Walker is right in her argument that "women's humor is an index to women's roles and values, and particularly to their relationship with [national] cultural realities," then Miller's text *Are Women People? A Book of Rhymes for Suffrage Times* offers her "take" not only on reality but also on the "times" in which her text was written (7). Miller's work, as Chapman, Walker, Blanch, and Dresner all note, is feminist and modern in nature; however, the *kind* of modern feminist protest Miller's work instantiates moves beyond a call for women's essential, natural rights to be recognized and respected to what I would argue we can productively view as a more *pragmatic* form of feminism, one that recognizes women's rights as neither inherent nor naturalized, but rather in need of *creation* within a given social sphere.

To explain what pragmatist feminist thinkers might mean when they talk about needing to create rather than simply to recognize women's rights, and to investigate why we might read Miller as one of them, I will turn to Richard Rorty's writings, in which he explores the question of female personhood from a pragmatist perspective. According to Rorty, in pragmatist discourse/philosophy, the question of one's "personhood" is not seen as an "all-or-nothing affair" (either you are or are not a person) but instead as "a matter of degree," in which partial personhood is not only possible but constitutive ("Feminism" 53). This viewpoint is possible because Rorty and other likeminded pragmatists believe that there is no "ahistorical" reality in which women's rights are "intrinsic" but not yet granted as a part of a social reality (44); instead, pragmatists see reality as a kind of social "evolutionary development" governed by the cultural privileging of "things like turns of speech, terms of aesthetic or moral praise, political slogans, proverbs, musical phrases, stereotypical icons, and the like" (45). Not only is this stance sensitive to the constructed nature of our various social arrangements, but it also points a spotlight on the forces—including the literary and linguistic—that are an integral part of this construction (even as they, too, are impacted by other forces).

Put simply then, the social, discursive reality is, for pragmatists, the only reality; any body, including a woman's, has a right to claim only the privileges that the society of which they are a part agrees to grant him or her. Any rights that an individual would wish to have—that is, for our purposes, can *imagine* having—but that the social whole does not recognize or agree on are thus no more than potential. Such rights must be invented or created—in short, materialized—in order to become a part of a future social whole. And in a linguistically centered pragmatism such as Rorty's, in which social evolution is always inextricably linked with linguistic evolution, the space for "creation" of the right to be a person resides, largely, in language.

Within Rorty's pragmatist-linguistic space, personhood can be either created or exposed as underdone by language but never simply claimed as an essential "right." As such, we can understand further implications of the normative thrust behind Miller's comparison between the oppressive nonpersonhood of women and the social category of lunatics. Rorty writes:

> [A]ssumptions become visible as assumptions only if we can make the contradictories of those assumptions sound plausible. So injustices may not be perceived as injustices, even by those who suffer them, until somebody invents a previously unplayed role. Only if somebody has a dream, and a voice to describe that dream, does what looked like nature begin to look like culture, what looked like fate begin to look like a moral abomination. For until then only the language of the oppressor is available, and most oppressors have the wit to teach the oppressed a language in which the oppressed will sound crazy—even to themselves—if they describe themselves *as* oppressed. ("Feminism" 43)

Rather than for such oppression to seem natural (or, in fact, to be made invisible), Rorty argues that for the social construction of women's oppression to become visible, a different language must be found, one that can offer "not just new words but also creative misuses of language—familiar words used in ways that initially sound crazy" (44). Moreover, this voice that speaks in a new language must describe not the wrongs that she has suffered based on her so-called "natural" rights but rather her "previously unplayed role," a future creation she imagines but is currently prohibited from embodying. Keeping Rorty's version of pragmatist feminism in mind, we might consider that Miller does not just liken women to lunatics to exploit, politically, the rhetoric of antisuffragists; rather, the women to whom Miller refers in her poetry might very well actually appear to speak like (and thus resemble) lunatics, particularly while advocating for women's to-be-imagined "rights."

In this sense, it is not coincidental that Miller's genre and tone are comedic; after all, the absurd linguistic challenge *Are women people?* will at first be likely to provoke in an audience a response of laughter. By asking a question about the linguistic terms that govern her oppression, Miller inevitably makes a joke, a joke that functions as much via its flirtation with unintelligibility as seriousness within its contemporary social discourse as through its pointed critique of specific legal disenfranchisement.

Miller's feminist "misuse" of old language to create new roles for women, a language that literally "misuses" others' quotes, does not quite emerge into full-fledged creation. Rather, Miller's poetry, within the genre of comedy, functions as a node along an evolutionary linguistic path suspended between past madness and future sanity. Not merely describing women's violated albeit "natural" rights, nor yet imaginatively inventing a nonironic, right-filled position for future women, Miller's comedic yet deadly serious verse can be seen as participating in a kind of preparatory pragmatic prophecy. When I invoke the term "prophecy" in reference to pragmatism and Rorty, I am aware that I am employing a term that has a history of use in conjunction with pragmatism: specifically, within Cornel West's writings on "prophetic pragmatism." Like West, I use the invocation of "prophecy" to signal a political dynamic within pragmatism that is invested in change; however, I do not mean to imply, by my use of the term, the same particular set of nationalistic, religious/moral, materialistic, or intellectual positionings that West does.[6] Rather, I am interested in the way in which language that straddles the realms of sanity and madness (language that seems mad in that it is dislocated from a context that would have allowed it to make sense) can seem like the language of "prophecy"—a language that melds the mystical with the wise, the "truth" teller with the fool or conwoman. Rorty urges that "we have to stop talking about the need to go from distorted to undistorted perceptions of moral reality, and, instead, to begin talking about the need to modify our practices so as to take account of new descriptions of what has been going on" ("Feminism" 45). I see Miller as engaged in this sort of "new" descriptive work, work that is not rendered illegitimate or foolish because it is difficult to comprehend but rather as avant-garde. Mimicking yet remodeling society's voice, Miller's feminist description of women's vacillating and absent personhood sheds new light on the cultural space surrounding women's fight to gain political access to the social sphere on par with men; she shows women's lack of personhood to be more than just a clever turn of phrase but instead a basic axiom of a current reality under which women's potential humanness is suppressed.

Feminist politics has attempted to create better and better realities for individuals and citizens of all genders, and suffragette protesters worked within this political umbrella. In this light, I argue that Richardson's protest event performs a knowledge, an ethic of innocence, that trumps the audacious, even blasphemous light in which Miller's *Are Women People?* might be viewed, particularly within a feminist landscape that emphasizes "natural," essentialized rights. For Richardson's text not only wonders if women *are* people; it appears to wonder—as Richardson turns away from any easy knowledge of the female subject to de-ironize Miller's key conundrum from within her politicized, feminist position—if women *should* be.

Thinking with the Pragmatists: Aesthetic and Political Value in Mary Richardson's Avant-Garde Protest

By expanding on Rorty's specifically linguistic understanding of feminist pragmatism's creative potential to include performance and protest, we can consider the preparatory, prophetic "languages" in which both Alice Duer Miller's poetry and Mary Richardson's slashing of the *Rokeby Venus* "speak." Indeed, the fact that Richardson's text is not only performative but also uses the artist's own, female body as a core component of the text brings to the foreground both the troubling voice of the protesting woman and the distressing *embodiment* of the woman who speaks her prophecy. Whereas the physical presence of the female body might at first seem to unavoidably accent the way in which women have bodies—and are thus people—like men, I will use the pragmatic-feminist framework that Rorty sets out and that I have used to interpret Miller's work to show how Richardson's protest provided a prescient and thus shocking articulation of the fraught space of the female "person." For one of the strange ironies of "personhood/subjecthood" debates in general Western philosophy/criticism and in art history discourse in particular is that embodiment and the human body are frequently used to accentuate not personhood but nonpersonhood, not subject status but objectification. By gaining access Richardson's act through visual and textual traces, statements made by Richardson about her "work," and public and critical response and reaction to the event, we can investigate the way in which Richardson's protest, though explicitly and personally embodied, nonetheless also grappled with the difficulties of visibly (not just visually) depicting women's lack of personhood or subjecthood, a struggle that is perhaps exacerbated rather than eased by using the body of the woman/artist as the textual vehicle.[7]

For many artists and critics, the modern advent of performance art that centered on the explicit and personalized body of the artist intervened in art history's key metonymic conflation—one that has often allowed "the framed image of the female body, hung on the wall of an art gallery" to stand as "shorthand for art more generally" (Nead 1). This metonym has historically performed an inherent split of mind from body, in which the mindful subject/viewer was positioned in a role of bodiless superiority while viewing the mindless body—absent of personhood—of the object of art. Further, it aligned the superior "subject" with an implicitly masculine position of observation and the looked-on, aesthetic, and embodied nonperson or "object" with the feminine. Such metonymic alignment existed at the expense of the specifically female body's presence within the gallery as an artist and subject, rather than as just a passive object. In light of this cost, Amelia Jones argues in her book *Body Art: Performing the Subject* (1998) that body art, distinct from performance art in general, has a "particular potential . . . to destabilize the structures of conventional art history and criticism" (5). She positions body art against a history of "disinterested" viewing, in which a subject is invited to leisurely observe an art object, without any challenge from the artwork (or absent artist) to interrupt the subject's view (5).

Body art destabilizes the artistic discursive norms attending the female aestheticized body in two crucial ways. First, as Tracy Warr writes, "in the late 1950s and early 1960s, . . . body art [was] largely aimed towards an exhibition of the self in its full embodiment as a way of laying claim to 'being' itself," an art movement in which female artists in particular created works that "propos[ed] fully embedded and socially relevant feminist bodies that [were] also specific 'selves'" (21). Thus, from Warr's point of view, one of body art's important contributions to discourses of art and aesthetics is that it insists that the female body be read as a unique self or *subject*, not just as an object. And Lynda Nead emphasizes the power inherent within performance art to "reveal" particularly the "woman's body as matter and process, as opposed to form and stasis" (63). In both of these interpretations, both the "artist" and the "interpreter" are "marked as contingent," while the latter can no longer "claim disinterestedness in relation to [a particular] work of art" because such "artwork" is always coexistent with the artist's body and his or her (relationally formed) subjecthood (Jones 9). Here—sounding like no one so much as early pragmatist thinkers like Jane Addams, John

Dewey, or William James, who stressed the collaborative, intersubjective, and mutually constructing nature of community—Jones reads body art as a mode that insists on interplay and exchange, rather than on either isolated, unidirectional senses of give and take or interactions entered into by two discrete, unchanging subjects.

In important ways, the aesthetics and politics of suffrage protest align not only with performance art but also, in particular, with body art. Tickner's work on what she terms "suffrage spectacle" emphasizes precedents to these protests (state ritual, Edwardian pageantry, and labor movement iconography), as well as their radical difference from earlier models (56–57). She points out, for instance, that for women to march publicly in the streets was to court an "almost entirely degrading" association between women and sexual promiscuity, so much so that suffragettes needed to take care to balance their gender rebellion with other public markers of traditional femininity (such as art needlework) in order to perform their bodies in a way that the public would not summarily dismiss or objectify (58, 81). These careful maneuverings speak not only to the suffragette understanding of the importance of their engagement, via protest, with the public, but also to the precarious nature of the female subjecthood they performed and embodied. Simply to appear as a female body in public was not only not necessarily to be seen as subject but, in fact, was historically and culturally conditioned to erase female subjecthood. Indeed, Tickner's argument that women's socially marginal status allows their bodies, as representative sites, to "carry any of the meanings that accrue to the other" or to be read merely as "abstract," and that thus one major task of "suffrage art and rhetoric . . . was to reinhabit the empty [female] body," seems to acknowledge the same root issue that body artists, in the critical view above, were contesting: the objectification, and the erasure of the person, from the body of the woman on display (209).

Here, Jones's investment in a theory of artwork that sees "interpretation-as-exchange" (rather than objecthood-rendered-for-viewing-by-a-subject) is useful in reanimating a frequently unarticulated relationship between viewer and viewed; her theory's commonalities with pragmatism, moreover, mark a distinct shift from a Western theoretical and philosophical tradition that emphasizes discrete, even static individuation or personhood (9). Jones's conception of performance art, by contrast, theorizes the relationship between audience and art as a dynamic one marked by mutual, and continual, (re)constitution—the viewer creates, interacts with, and changes both art and artist just as the art and artist create, interact with, and change the viewer. Lest such pragmatism give way to idealism, however, Jones notably avoids a theory of performance art that is simply transformative. She argues that "body art does not strive toward a utopian redemption but, rather, places the body/self within the realm of the aesthetic as a political domain," a domain that is inherently neither positive nor negative but instead always contingent upon the exchange's specifics (13). This is in keeping with broader claims about the potentially powerful platform for speech that women could harness within their own bodies. For instance, Caroline J. Howlett, argues that "the female body is a prime ground for signification; if as a woman you want to be read you must write what you have to say there" (34). And yet, as Mayhall makes very explicit in "Creating the 'Suffragette Spirit,'" such power comes with clear risks: "[U]nintended consequences follow women's production of themselves as spectacular; only a very limited reading of those practices would have it that women always control the reception of images they produce about themselves" (333) It is the ambivalence of this power, coupled with the specifics of both gendered and aesthetic discourses attending the "intersubjective exchange" that offers both voice and risk to women, at which I would like to take a closer look.

That the exchange prompted by body art between the subject/viewer and the art/artist is both necessitated and complex seems undeniable from a pragmatist perspective; what I would wish to question, then—and where I think recourse to Miller's work can be of service to our reading of Richardson—is not the exchange itself that body art prompts but rather its necessary (and recognizable) *intersubjectivity*, or the assumed *subject status* of those who partake in the exchange. For it does not seem to me at all a given that the conflation of artist and artwork would necessitate a viewer's recognition of this artist/artwork as a subject. It seems that even if we comprehend "the art 'object' [in body art] as a site where reception and production come together" to create something that could be recognizable as a unique object "in all of its sexual, racial, and other particularities," this object would still not necessarily be recognizable to the viewing subject as a simultaneous subject (Jones 14, 5).

Whereas Jones's intersubjective exchange revises aesthetic theory along some pragmatist principles, the more radical pragmatics of *Are Women People?*—of Miller and indeed of Rorty—can help us to read Richardson's performance in light of the issue of personhood itself. In her statement to the press quoted at the start of this chapter, Richardson explicitly categorizes the *Rokeby Venus* as a *picture*; public discourse, however, quickly transformed the painted Venus into a sort of tenuous subject. As Lynda Nead argues, the newspaper coverage of the painting's damage treated the Venus not as a work of art but as a live victim; she compellingly demonstrates, for instance, how such reports "represented the attack on 'The Rokeby Venus' in the visual and written language usually reserved for the sensation murder" (38). So, from the *Times*, we hear of a painting that was "attacked" and "mutilated" ("National" 9G). The "cuts" are described meticulously, as in an autopsy, in which Richardson's actions are "blows" from a "weapon" that "caused a cruel wound in the neck," a "severe cut," a "gash," and "a broad laceration starting near the left shoulder" ("National" 9G). These more ambiguous words like "cut" are infused with fleshy significance by terms normally associated with criminal acts against the human body, such as "mutilation" and "wound." Indeed, the specific kinds of criminality associated with Richardson's act are reflected in the nicknames she was given: Nead notes that she was called "the 'Ripper'" and "the 'Slasher'" (38), and these links persist even in Richardson's obituary, where we are reminded that she has "[won] for herself," through her actions, "the sobriquet 'Slasher Mary'" ("Miss" 15D). These descriptive names, though literally reminiscent of the "ripping" and "slashing" damage her weapon did to the *Rokeby Venus*, also connect to cultural memories and depictions of Victorian-era murders of public female bodies, further solidifying the discourse surrounding the incident by linguistically modulating a crime of vandalism into a crime of murder.

The conflict that arises as the aesthetic object is attacked, infringed upon, and even "re-author[ed]" through the act of vandalism into a murdered being has been read by Nead as a "breakdown of the genre of the female nude" (41–42) Yet rather than view the "fleshy" descriptions of the Venus as an indication of genre breakdown, I suggest we can view this link of flesh and art as the ultimate indicator of the genre's coherence and success: as the logical, if extreme, extension of a genre that sees beautiful women as ideal art, ideal art as beautiful women. After all, such Richardson sobriquets, resurrecting as they did the cultural residue of the Jack the Ripper murders, sensationalized the Venus's flesh as both human and object by aligning the Venus's victim status with another female victim type—a prostitute—whose actual human body was also aestheticized and commodified. Perhaps the most blatant linguistic fusion of flesh and art in the Venus's slashing adheres in the description of "the seventh and most important injury," described by *The Times* as "a ragged bruise" (1914). A canvas may be cut, but certainly the word choice of bruise is out of place in a two-dimensional aesthetic vocabulary. Nead's thorough reading of this particular description capitalizes on these spatial discrepancies. She writes that "to refer to the damage on 'The Rokeby Venus' as a bruise is instantly to confuse the distinctions between hardness (the canvas) and softness (the signified female body)" and, further, that such an account describes "damage to a woman's body rather than to a picture" (39). On one hand, Nead seems undeniably correct—a canvas cannot bruise while a body can, and so what is being depicted in *The Times* is not an object of art but a human subject: thus, a transmutation has occurred. But, looked at literally, in context, the account does not describe a woman's body at all—it is explicitly a description of the damage to a picture. The tension between these two seeming incompatibles defines what we might view as the Venus's tenuous subjecthood: the endgame of the "female nude" genre in which the beautiful flesh of the human body becomes also simultaneously, albeit not logically, the aesthetically beautiful immortal substance of art and a body-object capable of being bought, sold, and owned as a thing within the global market.

What can it mean to view a picture as a subject, and what kind of subject would this be? An emphasis on the real possibilities of the Venus's "subjecthood," as opposed to the representational manifestations such a merge implies as metaphor or metonym, requires a substantial refiguring of much of art discourse. Indeed, this mode in which both paint and cells form a kind of female flesh calls up a third question: How different, if at all, is the body of the Venus from that of a fleshy human body used in performance art contemporarily and in the coming decades? The question has epistemic dimensions as well; for instance, Rebecca Schneider notes that within the realm of performance art, "the question becomes one of how to apprehend—with the double connotation that word bears of both 'know' and 'fear'—such an embodied space [. . .] after/in/aware of the history of objectification" (157). Though this history is obviously essential to an understanding of the dangers incumbent upon positioning the female subject as an aesthetic body, it seems that this history of objectification is necessarily just as much a history of *subject formation*—the conditions according to which bodies and flesh are made subject.

It does not make sense to take subjecthood as a given from which objects can be made without recognizing that the opposite can occur—that in the vandalism of the *Rokeby Venus*, a subject with a human body has been formed from the art object. This would force us to consider the Venus, in some sense, to be murderable: not to consider that the public necessarily believed the Venus was made of flesh, but that the *value* they placed on the Venus was akin to the value—and not merely within discourse—of human life. Correspondingly, then, we must query the terms and ways that human life itself was and is valued. For the fact that a distinction between the two versions of the Venus—fleshy subject, painted art—is clearly *not* being defined seems essential to our understanding, not only of the positioning of the *Rokeby Venus* but also of the way that the live female bodies—Richardson's and Pankhurst's—are discussed.

The body of Emmeline Pankhurst, invoked by Richardson upon her arrest, cannot be divorced from the scene of vandalism/murder attending the painted Venus. Instead, Richardson's mention of Pankhurst works to realign a sense of value that she maintains has gone awry in society. Nead views the incident as a media-produced discourse surrounding "two opposed forms of femininity: the patriarchal ideal (the Venus) and the deviant (the militant suffragist)" (37). And yet certainly this binary of patriarchal ideal and deviant, the one Nead emphasizes in her book, is not the only oppositional reading these bodies provoke. Ideas of passivity versus activity, silence versus speaking, and nude versus clothed not only contour and complicate the ideal female and deviant female bodies that Nead sees evinced in the *Rokeby Venus* slashing, but they all accrue to inform the more basic distinction I see at work within Richardson's act: the distinction between the subject and the object (the person and the nonperson). According to Richardson, paintings and lives should not be equated in value; paintings are replaceable, but "another life" to replace Pankhurst's cannot be attained ("National" 9G). A statement that Richardson sent to the WSPU makes more explicit her pronouncement of Pankhurst's comparative rarity; however, to articulate this rarity, she parleys in aesthetics. In her statement of rationale, Richardson joins the two bodies with the term beauty: "I have tried to destroy the picture of the most beautiful woman in mythological history as a protest against the Government for destroying Mrs. Pankhurst, who is the most beautiful character in modern history" ("National" 9G). Richardson links ideal, two-dimensional physicality to unique, human personhood via the term "beauty," which moves the subjecthood of Mrs. Pankhurst—and the means by which Richardson evaluates her fitness as a human being—into the realm of the aesthetic. Just as the Venus is praised for the rarity of her "flesh" that can bruise, so Mrs. Pankhurst is valued for the rarity of her soul, which is beautiful. Aesthetics here become a bridge between the two women, but its invocation levels rather than denotes privilege to Pankhurst, since emphasis on Pankhurst and the Venus's like beauty suggests that Pankhurst, like the Venus, has had a price placed on her head.

Value as leveling device becomes key, then, not only in terms of the artwork's cultural estimation but also in terms of its economic worth. For far from highlighting an opposition between art and life, we find that the humanizing terms applied to the Venus go hand in hand with her object value, since cultural and economic worth are conflated within the field of aesthetics. Despite all the violent language of attack and murder that seems to privilege the Venus's subjecthood, the "outrage" of the vandalism is linked inextricably with the depreciation, once the painting was damaged, in its monetary value "by as much as $50,000 to $75,000"—a language of economics most often associated with objects or the objectified (*The New York Times* "Militant" 4). In fact, the painting had been bought by and for the British nation. Because the painting was not only a piece of art but instead an artwork with an owner, the assertion that, postvandalism, "it has become a broken thing" was perhaps most keenly or personally felt as a loss of individual possession—and thus control—over items owned ("Militant" 4). Here, in an eerie echo of previous centuries' rape law and discourse, the Venus's own bodily damage transforms not her but rather her owners into the recognizable victims of her body's lost value (Stewart 213).

Interestingly, this same sense of personal loss is evident in Richardson's rationale for both her act of vandalism and her invocation of Pankhurst. At the time of the vandalism, Pankhurst was "on a hunger and thirst strike in Holloway Prison" (Gamboni 94). Richardson implied that her own actions were designed to highlight the plight of Pankhurst's body as a call to "the public" to "cease to countenance human destruction" ("National" 9G). However, the human destruction Richardson points to is not explicitly or entirely female *bodily* destruction. The "Cat and Mouse" Act, by which self-starving suffragette prisoners were released before their health deteriorated to the point of putting their lives at risk, was in place specifically to preclude physical, self-imposed destruction of the body, while (importantly) also avoiding governmental responsibility for such destruction (Nead 35). Indeed, J. F. Geddes notes that "prison officers would be liable if a prisoner succeeded in starving herself to death, and suicide in any case was a crime" (82). Thus, not only did the government have an interest in preventing deaths for which they could be held accountable, but they also had the legal recourse to prevent such deaths, in that a deliberate attempt to kill the self was considered criminal behavior that could be punished.

Richardson, too, was subject to these laws; following her arrest and her subsequent hunger strike, the *New York Times* reported that she was "being forcibly fed" ("Forcibly" 4). The article goes on to quote Home Secretary McKenna, who claimed that "every care [was] being taken by the medical officers in Holloway Prison to prevent the prisoner from injuring herself, but it is their plain duty to feed her even at some risk rather than permit her to commit suicide by starvation" (4). McKenna's statement makes clear that the steps of forcible feeding, or ultimately the prisoner's release, were taken by the government in order to prevent what was viewed as her sure death from self-starvation (4). Yet forcibly feeding the suffragette prisoners was often injurious to these women's health and was viewed by many as excessive, cruel, dangerous, and even lethal. Caroline J. Howlett, for instance, calls the practice "life-threatening," particularly if food was accidentally poured into the lungs (5–6). According to June Purvis, Mary Richardson herself became ill while being forcibly fed and was only released in order to have an operation for appendicitis that would save her life (*Votes* 147).[8] In addition, critics like Geddes—who argue that forcible feeding was dealt out to the suffragettes as punishment, not as treatment—find corroboration in contemporaries of the suffragette such as Dr. C. W. Mansell-Moullin, who saw, according to a speech delivered at Kingsway Hall on March 18, 1913, that "the real object" of forcible feeding was "to bend or break that prisoner" (Jorgensen-Earp 309). Thus, we might suggest that it is not only, nor even primarily, the suffragette woman's life that is at risk of what Richardson terms destruction; rather, what Richardson might be protesting is the state of her female subjecthood that transformed such risks and degradations as imprisonment and forcible feeding into commonplaces or "duty"-driven treatments. It is perhaps only in this light that we can understand the particularly gendered implications of some such "degradations" that attended the forcible feeding of the suffragettes: June Purvis reports in *Votes for Women* that some women, such as Frances Gordon and Fanny Parker, were "fed through the rectum or [in Parker's case] vagina" (149). That such "feeding" methods were medically questionable and, in the case of the latter, anatomically unconnected to the digestive track make clear the unnourishing message of bodily violation and vulnerability the suffragette prisoners received through this treatment.

As subjects of the state of England in the early twentieth century, Richardson and Pankhurst were subjugated by laws and subjected to a loss of control over their bodies, even their lives. Here, human and body are not separable constructs; for Richardson's body to be saved even as her will—to not eat, to kill herself—is revoked seems the stricture under which this female, human subject must live. She, as a live body, was saved, not due to any aesthetic valuation or devaluation, but because the state had a selfish interest in not being responsible for her death—a view corroborated by Alice Duer Miller herself, who, in an article published in the *New York Times* on July 6, 1914, argued that "the reason for preserving the women's lives [who are being forcibly fed] is one of political expediency, not of exaggerated chivalry" (6).[9] Richardson's and Pankhurst's bodies were valuable to the state; as such, their individual, unchecked wills were threats. Instead of presuming the protest behind the *Rokeby Venus*'s vandalism to concern the objectification of women (or their fall from full subjecthood) under the patriarchic hegemony of early twentieth-century England, it seems that Richardson's protest more accurately concerns women's subjectification—the way in which the structures surrounding them construct and help determine their embodied experience of (gendered) subjecthood.

In her explanation of her actions, Richardson anticipates the public's vehement response to her act of vandalism while also staging her own interjection into this discourse: "If there is an outcry against my deed, let everyone remember that such an outcry is a hypocrisy so long as they allow the destruction of Mrs. Pankhurst and other beautiful living women" ("National" 9G). Richardson here seems fully aware that her act will induce others (including the ambiguous "they") to respond, and her charge of hypocrisy—by way of comparing the public's response to the Venus's destruction with their response to Pankhurst's imprisonment and forcible feeding—highlights the ironies within both public discourse and her own intervention. For while Richardson's words clearly mark the discrepancy between the treatment of the art object and the human subject, as well as the linguistic irony of attributing more "humanity" to the wounds of a canvas woman than to the wounds of the suffragette wasting away, or being force-fed, in jail, this statement also marks the connection that such discrepancies have to issues of control over the female body. Inflecting humanity on the Venus in order to express its value proved beneficial to the government, while attributing humanity to Richardson or Pankhurst, though beneficial to the government who would not be responsible for the deaths of its subjects, could only limit the women regarding their political aims, along with their individual, willful voices.

Therefore, it is crucial for us to note that the hypocrisy that Richardson references might not refer to the public's supposed concern for human lives and subjects—a concern that, in the end, was proved false by the attention they paid to the Venus's body at the expense of Mrs. Pankhurst's. Though such logic is compelling, I want to suggest that, alternatively, Richardson could be critiquing the public's assumed attribution of inherently positive value to subjecthood in general, an assumption that a comparison between Mrs. Pankhurst and the Venus suggests is unfounded. Put more simply, the deep irony of Richardson's statement is not that her comparison of painting and flesh begs the question of why Mrs. Pankhurst, as a subject, is not treated better. The irony is that, essentially, her statement forces us to ask why Mrs. Pankhurst, human subject, is not treated as a painting: at root, why she is not treated—and valued—like an *object*.

Realist art has often been positioned as an unbalanced metaphor for life, in which life can be compared to art but always ultimately trumps it; this is what Mary Richardson's statements to the WSPU suggest *should be true*. If one chooses to refrain from habitually reducing art to life's inferior mirror, however, then our investigation of the discourse produced in response to Richardson's slashing of the *Rokeby Venus* is better primed to note the irony inherent in the humanization of art. Humanization and discussion of flesh in regard to the *Rokeby Venus* might be seen not as recognition of what is human about a work of art but rather as merely *vocabulary*, by which we, as subjects, express our valuation of aesthetic objects that depict the female form. Of course, such a reframing of the relationship between life and art has commonalities with the nineteenth-century aestheticism movement; however, though the privileging of art over life in the aestheticism movement functioned importantly to disconnect art from the political or moral realms, the reading I am suggesting here acknowledges art's superior position *in order to* query its moral and political message. Because, when applied to human women (as in Miller's opening poem), this vocabulary of humanization often serves to hurt, not help, the women it characterizes.

Creating the Female Person: Where a Pragmatist Might Go from Here

That the *Rokeby Venus* slashing occurred in a museum space is hardly arbitrary; it is this act's very position within the museum that allows for the narratives surrounding Richardson's vandalism to expose the privilege given by the public to aesthetics and art objects over human lives. This privilege remains visible, even as Richardson's act was subsumed into broader suffrage protest as a challenge enacted by and on behalf of female subjects. My analysis is not meant to suggest that Mary Richardson sought to objectify women via her performance. Rather, my reading highlights the normative force of discourse itself and the need to increase the urgency and seriousness with which we consider the implications this incident has for the way in which we discuss and conceive of objectification and the status of the female subject—her nonpersonhood—within the modern era. What these texts' pragmatism might teach us is to see personhood—both its possibility and positivity—as something that, for women, is still significantly in need of creation. Richardson's performance evinces the same foundational irony evident in Miller's poetry; not only are women, in very important ways, not considered to be people, but the ways in which they *are* considered to be people serve not to empower but rather, contradictorily, to hamper and restrict them. For this tendency—which has long outlasted the "suffrage times" that Miller originally composed her verses to address—to truly change, not only would a subject need to be visible to art's audience from within the form of an aesthetic object, but also a recognized status of subjecthood, of personhood, must become a safe position to occupy for any, but especially the female, body.

For a woman to seek recognition as a subject, these texts suggest, has been and is still a dangerous attempt, one that does not carry with it any innate assurance that to be seen as a subject will protect her from harm. Rather, by comparing the discursive treatment of the *Rokeby Venus* with that of the suffragettes like Mrs. Pankhurst who were fighting to be seen as subjects equal to men, one is confronted with the chilling evidence that the aesthetic female body receives better treatment—and more public demand for protection—than the live one. Of course, this is not to say that subjecthood in its ideal, utopian formation would be a dangerous position to occupy. Rather, it is to argue with the pragmatists that until such a utopia is reached, until this imagined future is created and obtained in reality, the different meanings "subject" takes along the lines of gender (and race, class, sexuality, etc.) determine the danger or safety attending such a position.

Even if we believe that in many important ways women are not yet persons, this belief does not mean that no injustice has been done to their personhood. Indeed, Rorty argues that while we might pragmatically abandon a notion of male oppression's "injustice to past actuality," we can still cite its "wrongness" in the form of a "suppression of past potentiality" ("Feminism" 54). A woman's lack of achievement of full subjecthood, then, does not mean that she is in no way a subject, nor that she is not able to achieve full subjecthood. Rather, it means that the social conditions under which she currently lives construe her "subjecthood" as less than full—and suppress her potential to reach full subjecthood through various means, not the least of which involves terming her partial-personhood her "subjecthood" and erasing the distinctions between the varying powers and privileges a word like "subject" implies based on a being's gender.

That women like Richardson, Mrs. Pankhurst, and the women about whom Miller's poetry speaks are suppressed in *potential* is a crucial conceptual shift; if the suffragette hunger striker were to be seen as only a vacant body in need of saving, the government's choice to ignore her will to choose not to eat would not register, for there would be no validity to such "will" in the first place. On the other hand, by reverting to the romance inherent within universalist or realist tendencies, and outside of the context of pragmatism, we might recognize her as a human subject and say, naively, that it is due to a quality of her recognized personhood that she was saved from starvation, which would ignore the other interests (governmental self-interestedness, economic investments, sexism) that were also at work. If, however, we consider one's personhood to be designated, in full or part, by social rather than essential norms, the romance of mutual subject recognition easily gives way and exposes instead the violent failure of equal exchange. A museum, a government, or a public must not only be responsible for the subjects and positions it disappears through its binaries, but also the lack of subjecthood and personhood its politics and prejudices—its system of aesthetics and commodities—allows, even necessitates, though it also masks these lacks.

Richardson's and Miller's texts materialize the objectified female body as evidence of a kind of modern "haunting." Here, feminist engagement with the power of "objecthood" is the ghost that runs counter to the more full-bodied feminist engagement with female subjecthood. This ghost, we must realize, is not a benign spirit we can effectively ignore; rather, what I hope in these final paragraphs to show is the importance of acknowledging this ghost's presence in our modern discourse in order for the feminist political goals with which this chapter started to be realized—or, even, realizable. It is my hope that by acknowledging this failure of equality—that "subject" is *not* a universal term with universal meaning, that we *do not* inherently value "subjects" over "objects"—we can usher in an understanding of intersubjectivity (in both performance art and in broader public response) that is not reducible to the monolithic sense of a "mutual transformation" of mutual subjects (Phelan 575). When we embrace these texts' radical choice not to know that women are people, we can then confront the circumstances that create our fraught relationships with other subjects, ones that make such positive intersubjective exchange both circumstantial and hesitant. It is a fallacy, these texts ultimately suggest, to think that our subjecthood is inherently regarded as valuable, or as "full," to others. Thus, insisting on a recognition of full and equal subjecthood in all human beings, regardless of difference, frequently does not ward off violence as we think it will. Rather, we must continue the work these texts begin of speaking differently, of creating new avenues by which such a recognition of subjecthood can be deployed to acknowledge a value that ensures its subject's safety, even when in exchange with another subject.

Discourses of feminist epistemology can benefit from a consideration of not only these texts' creation of new descriptive language regarding the personhood of women but also the perceived "craziness" of their "language" in the eyes of the public. We might think about Miller's linguistic misuses as bits of language that help to pave the way for new descriptions of women, misuses that highlight women's social plight as not-yet-people in an effort to campaign toward a future in which the question Are women people? not only would be merely absurd, but also would never need to be asked—nor even thought—at all. Such a future is in keeping with Rorty's vision that "at some future point in the development of our society guilty relief over not having been born a woman may not cross the minds of males. . . . [T]hat would be the point at which both males and female had *forgotten* the traditional androcentric language" ("Feminism" 58, original emphasis). This future interestingly embeds its own sense of choosing not to know—the rejection of a past language in which outmoded distinctions between genders become not only obsolete but mere gibberish.

We must learn, it seems, how to both counter and work within a social discourse of aesthetic value and commodity in order to make our subject selves indispensable to those other subjects we encounter. We must find a means to articulate a subject's value not as essence nor as aesthetic commodity but as a *contribution*, a being with an ability to further the social collective if her potential is given the opportunity to be reached. Though Miller's language does not yet articulate this new female person, her experiments with language do help to make legible other linguistic expressions that more radically critique women's present social position through their outlines of and recourse to an imaginary future. In this book's next chapter, I will turn to some thinkers, writers, and artists who have imagined such a future and "spoken" it into being through their art; I will discuss the ways in which, through this art, we can sustain the hope of seeing alternative futures emerge from individual imaginations into community consciousness. This chapter's dedication to the more preparatory "texts" of Miller and Richardson are ones that pave the way for new avenues of expression—and, indeed, the more radical terms of their not-knowing—that those in the next chapter engage. But their preparatory language, their prophecy, is not without hope. Though their perspective on female personhood is skeptical at best, Miller's and Richardson's texts provide pragmatic openings to rethink our core assumptions on the path to creating, someday, "a better set of social constructs than the ones presently available and, thus, . . . the creation of a new and better sort of human being" (Rorty, "Feminism" 60).

Chapter Six

Making Women, Making Humans

Fantasies of Melancholic Mourning in Modern Sex Changes and Sex Losses

> [H]ow might we encounter the difference that calls our grids of intelligibility into question without trying to foreclose the challenge that the difference delivers? What might it mean to learn to live in the anxiety of that challenge, to feel the surety of one's epistemological and ontological anchor go, but to be willing, in the name of the human, to allow the human to become something other than what it is traditionally assumed to be? This means that we must learn to live and to embrace the destruction and rearticulation of the human in the name of a more capacious and, finally, less violent world, not knowing in advance what precise form our humanness does and will take.
>
> —Judith Butler, *Undoing Gender* (35)

What I called in chapter 5 the preparatory, prophetic languages in which the texts of Miller and Richardson speak can perhaps more accurately be viewed not as transparently communicative tongues but rather as linguistic primers, ways of speaking that depend on the studious dedication of their audiences to realize their communicability. The new avenues of expression that chapter 5's texts make possible, in short, are only "possible" inasmuch as their audiences collude to hear them *as expressive*. Thus, the hope that these texts hold out for a new discourse, one in which a "better set of social constructs" can create this "new and better sort of human being" that chapter 5's conclusion left us contemplating depends deeply on what happens (if it happens) in the translation from tongue to ear, from syllable to word, from speaker to audience: from individual imagination to community consciousness (Rorty, "Feminism" 60). In other words, for such speech to function pragmatically and create alternative futures, an account of its movement from fantasy to the social real is needed, one that is, also and at once, an account of the movement from a unique individual to communal other.

This chapter turns to modern texts that treat imagined futures, each of which work to negotiate the two yoked axes I reference above: the fantasy-to-social-reality axis and the individual-to-community axis. These three texts—Virginia Woolf's *Orlando: A Biography* (1928), Sherwood Anderson's "The Man Who Became a Woman" (1923), and Katharine Burdekin's *Proud Man* (1934)—not only engage in what I will argue can be viewed as feminist pragmatist fantasies through their stance of innocence toward social knowledge. They also do so by choosing not to know one of burgeoning modernism's most common fictional stories, as well as this book's most relied-upon tales: that two primary and distinct sexes of human beings exist that we call "man" and "woman." Each text, in its own way, takes on the topic of biological sex and sex change in order to speak beyond the bounds of what the previous chapter deemed mere prophecy. And by doing so, these texts "realize," if at times only fleetingly, alternative worlds that might move us beyond the reality of binary sexed bodies—a reality that, I will argue, these texts posit as a major component of modern affects of loss and melancholia. They do so, however, in complex ways that do not always succeed in balancing the axes above to provide both the utopic idealization and the concomitant material plan so necessary to the feminist pragmatic version of futurity this chapter is invested in thinking toward.

To most clearly chart these texts' attempts and failures to balance the fantasy/social real and individual/community axes, I will read their fantasies of "sex change" with regard to a third, final axis—the comedy/tragedy axis. Here, tragedy will take on several valances that include failure, grief, mourning, and melancholia. I use all these terms in an effort to sort through the various ways in which modern literature has often depicted not only sex change but also sex loss, as I argue that the loss, not the change, is the more constitutive element of modernity's affect toward embodied sex. Whereas chapter 1 investigated the hopeful open-endedness that pragmatism could bring to seemingly realist "tragedies" at the fin de siècle, this chapter will investigate the productive pragmatic work that tragedy's "negative" emotions can lend, via fantasy, to this realism a mere decade later.

One final note before embarking on this investigation: the texts that this chapter will treat are engaged with the embodied fantasies of characters that only uneasily, temporarily, and with great debate might fit into the category of "woman." One, then, might reasonably ask why such texts and such a chapter on them have a place in a project concerned with the modern female subject. In answer, I argue that in order to present a pragmatic reading of "female" subjects, it is crucial for us to engage in the seemingly back-to-basics work of breaking apart the apparent binary of male/female and re-imagine what it is even *to be* a woman. Indeed, part of what is at stake in this chapter is the claim that underlies all my textual arguments: that re-imagining "being" woman is not a mere intellectual exercise but rather the central pragmatic work we need to engage in for any change in sex and gender dynamics—both within literature and in the world—to occur.

This chapter's epigraph quotes Judith Butler's "ethical query," which challenges us to "be willing, in the name of the human, to allow the human to become something other than what it is traditionally assumed to be" (*Undoing* 35). In light of chapter 5's argument that, in a crucial sense, women are not yet "human," Butler's challenge becomes even more significant. For the redefinition of "human" might also allow us to begin creating such a definition with both male *and female* bodies in the mix. In part, then, this chapter will query the book's focus on women by pointing to the limitations of knowledge-based "realistic" portraits of women and favoring instead the freedoms fantasy can allow for "female" characters. But it will also emphasize the ways in which this work of redefining "humanity" is not just the work of the women, the oppressed, or the other folks that the category of "human" currently excludes. This chapter will show the extent to which such redefinitions affect the spectrum of excluded and included: the human as well as the subhuman, nonhuman, not-quite-human, woman, and, perhaps surprisingly, even the man.

Unbound Sex, Transformed Society: *Orlando: A Biography*

It seems only fitting to begin our discussion of modern sex changes and sex losses with the troublingly clear first word of a troublesome text filled with troubled embodiment: *Orlando*'s opening gambit "he" (11). This oft-remarked-on first word, along with its following assurance set off from the sentence's verb "was" by em-dashes, "he—for there could be no doubt of his sex, though the fashion of the time did something to disguise it—was," reads for critics such as Amikó Imre not as a comforting assurance but rather as a destabilizing "invit[ation] to a joke," one in which we're invited, through the defense of a commonplace pronoun, to query the commonplace of sex (Woolf 11; Imre 178). For most critics, the story that follows this opening—a tale that depicts, in satirical biographical style, the coming of age of the novel's protagonist, Orlando, who lives for more than three hundred years and changes sex from a man to a woman—confirms their common understanding of what the joke lambasts (dichotomous treatment of gender and sex). Much disagreement, however, still reigns about what is, after all, the joke's ultimate punchline.

As a way to make sense of the protagonist's sudden sex change—the single event in Orlando's extraordinary biography that has garnered the most critical treatment—and to understand the way in which this sex change influences the reading of sex and gender in the novel as a whole, critics have alternately termed Orlando's gender defiance as a matter of transsexuality, transvestism, or androgyny. While all three retain a sense of gender mixing or blurring, the implications for Orlando's anatomical sex, on the one hand, and gender identity—both in terms of how Orlando identifies and is read by others—on the other, vary greatly from term to term. Many critics have positioned *Orlando* in relation to Woolf's famous statements in the contemporaneously written *A Room of One's Own*: "[I]t is fatal [for a writer] to be a man or woman pure and simple; one must be woman-manly or man-womanly"—that is, a compilation, an androgyne, a mix of the sexes rather than one or the other (104). As such, they have read the character of Orlando as a utopian, if fantastical, portrait of this androgynous ideal, a physical manifestation of Woolf's push toward intellectual androgyny.[1] Then, too, many critics have commented on what appears to be a heterosexual nonconformity or "gender fluidity" on Orlando's part that would suggest Woolf's investment in depicting a queerly desiring individual (Carstens 40).[2] Despite this, some critics have read *Orlando* as an essentially feminine, not just feminist, text, stressing Orlando's final state of, or development into, femaleness rather than the blurring of boundaries that the text as a whole suggests.[3] Some of Woolf's insistence on gender fluidity might not stem from disinterested intellectual theory; rather, much work has been done autobiographically to connect Orlando to Woolf's same-sex desire and her lover Vita Sackville-West's own life.[4] And the question of costuming—of clothes masking, modifying, and making Orlando's gender—has been central to many critics' investigations of Woolf's articulation of the links between a body and its covering—a transgressive articulation that invokes but also moves beyond transvestism as conventionally understood (dressing as the sex opposite from one's own) to tap into the multivalent possibilities of "trans."[5]

To definitively label the gender-bending aspects of Orlando—and indeed *Orlando*—has proved elusive, perhaps impossible; the critical debates on this subject that were launched over eighty years ago show no signs of slowing or coming to consensus. In one aspect of reading *Orlando*, however, critics do seem to agree: the text's tone is comic, triumphant, celebratory, and utopic.[6] Yet it is not *Orlando*'s engagement with sex and gender that lacks seriousness; indeed, when contrasted with Woolf's gendered reality, and even our contemporary treatment of gender, the lightness of her novel—a book which ends, after all, in its protagonist's happiness—presents a significant critique (via implicit comparison) of a cultural ideology that too often views gender as an essentialized outcropping of genital sex, the female gender as hierarchically inferior to the male, and any notion of "trans" as, at minimum, a danger, if not a perversion. Instead, when I speak of the text's utopic, comedic dimension, I seek to highlight the way in which the text's world presents its most explicitly fantastical moments—Orlando's long and seemingly endless life, the sudden change in sex—as events with surprisingly slight consequences and very little concern. If Woolf's fantasy engages what is possible for the human, if it works, as Judith Butler claims in *Undoing Gender,* to "mov[e] us beyond what is merely actual and present into a realm of possibility, the not yet actualized or the not actualizable," then it does so by gesturing toward that which outpaces our imagination. This "not yet" that is still impossible to conceive within human reality as we know it is, here, Orlando's singular, untroubled, and extraordinary existence that resides, without censure or cultural disavowal, alongside others' normative sexed existences (28).

What critical discourse has bypassed in the attempts to sort out the particular kind of gender-bending Orlando represents is that Orlando, as a comic character, embodies a fantasy of sex change that relies chiefly on nonrepresentative status: his, then her, insistent individuality. Indeed, the social scene of the text more often than not bends itself to Orlando's extraordinary circumstances; Woolf's fantasy text skews heavily toward individual exception. A primary example of this telling individuality arises in the treatment of the legal ramifications of Orlando's sex change from male to female. Halfway through the novel, Orlando arrives back in eighteenth-century England after spending time in Turkey during the seventeenth century; upon her return, she learns that "she was a party to three major suits" (124). Further,

> the chief charges against her were (1) that she was dead, and therefore could not hold any property whatsoever; (2) that she was a woman, which amounts to much the same thing; (3) that she was an English Duke who had married one Rosina Pepita, a dancer; and had had by her three sons, which sons now declaring that their father was deceased, claimed that all property descended to them. (124)

Though the Turkish gypsies had accepted Orlando into their way of life, one which allowed her to live in comfort while "scarcely giv[ing] her sex a thought," upon returning to England, Orlando's unusual relation to time and genital embodiment will (it seems) finally have some ramification (113).

No such ramification, however, materializes. It may take a century to decide the court cases (which are never mentioned in the text after their initial appearance until they are decided), but their ultimate decision results in the annulment of her Turkish marriage, the declared illegitimacy of her sons, and the pronouncement "indisputably, and beyond the shadow of a doubt" that her sex is "Female" (186–87). Orlando is then allowed to enter "into the undisturbed possession of her titles, her house, and her estate" (187). Not only does this legal decision render Orlando the social beneficiary of an officially sanctioned sex change, but the amount of time it took for the courts to reach this decision works in her favor, as by the time she is granted a decision, the sex she has changed into can inherit property, whereas in the previous century, when the lawsuits were launched, "she" could not have done so.

Orlando's gender ambiguity thus helps rather than harms or limits her; moreover, we are told in the eighteenth century that "pending the legal judgment, she had the law's permission to reside in a state of incognito or incognita as the case might turn out to be," a permission that allows her to exist for a century in a state of androgyny without fear of consequence (125). And when the case is ultimately decided, the legal judgment results not in outrage or confusion among the townspeople of Orlando's home, but rather in "rejoicings" (187). The extensive, excessive, and comically absurd nature of such celebrations is depicted by Orlando's biographer as follows:

> The town was illuminated. Gold caskets were securely sealed in glass cases. Coins were well and duly laid under stones. Hospitals were founded. Rat and Sparrow clubs were inaugurated. Turkish women by the dozen were burnt in effigy in the market place, together with scores of peasant boys with the label "I am a

base Pretender," lolling from their mouths. The Queen's cream-colored ponies were soon seen trotting up the avenue with a command to Orlando to dine and sleep at the Castle, that very same night. Her table, as on a previous occasion, was snowed under with invitations from the Countess of R., Lady Q., Lady Palmerston, the Marchioness of P., Mrs. W. E. Gladstone, and others, beseeching the pleasure of her company, reminding her of ancient alliances between their family and her own, etc. (187–88)

Of note in this passage is not only that Orlando's gender change is accepted and celebrated by the masses, but also that this social acceptance is authorized by the very traditional process of legal sanction; this legal decision, moreover, necessitates both a "winner" of the judgment (Orlando) and a "loser"—here, the Turkish woman whom Orlando had married and the boys he had fathered when he was still a man.

It is important and telling that the racial, national, and class particularly of these "losers" clearly mark them as "other" to the white English nobility Orlando represents, albeit complexly. It is instructive to recall that the tail end of the first line of the novel, which I did not quote above, does more than merely gender Orlando as male-identified; since he is engaged in "the act of slicing at the head of a Moor which swung from the rafters," this opening gambit teaches us not only about sex and masculine behavioral expectation, but also about the not merely accepted but indeed expected violence enacted against the racialized other that implicitly marks Orlando as white and landed. Later, we learn that such permissive violence is not only contemporarily but also generationally sanctioned: the head, we find out, is a familial trophy brought back from Africa by one of Orlando's male ancestors. Here again, as in the text's opening line, Orlando's body enacts its privileged existence by trampling the personage (literally and figuratively) of the exoticized modern other. And yet, I do not want to overlook, in understanding the intersectional oppressions at work here, the oddly similar way in which the celebration's excesses accompanying both the "winning" and "losing" side might be read. The celebration passage above is replete with over-the-top gestures, grotesque in their grandiosity as well as their caricature. The "losers'" bodies are fashioned into parodic dolls that are formally immolated, whereas the "winner" is lauded by fashioning gold caskets and sealing them away from usability, by literally throwing money away underneath stones. Both extremes present images of empty labor, scenes of objects created only to be destroyed or made useless. The comedy of Orlando's sex change comes at the expense of the labor, bodies, and resources of the townsfolk in Orlando's society: society and its norms are here made subservient to the individual Orlando.

As a confirmation of Orlando's superior position over her society, the entirety of the above quoted passage is literally enclosed within brackets. Orlando's fictional biographer explicitly interprets these brackets into which this story has been put for the reader, declaring that the details of the celebration are "properly enclosed in square brackets, as above, for the good reason that . . . it was without any importance in Orlando's life. She skipped it, to get on with the text" (Woolf 188). Orlando neither values nor even acknowledges these celebratory gestures; rather than attending the celebration, "she was in the dark woods with Shelmerdine [her lover, and then husband] alone" (188). That Orlando can make the choice to ignore the townsfolks' celebration makes the celebration at once entirely meaningless and wholly meaningful. Indeed, the ultimate signal of Orlando's extraordinary position of unique superiority is exhibited by her stance of ignorance toward the crucial social shifts that have had to occur in order to authorize, allow, and even welcome her embodiment.

Grieving Communities: Sex Losses within Sex Changes

Prisoner to neither context nor sex, Orlando never finds the need to grieve for what a cultural boundary will not permit. This emphasis on Orlando's exceptional, individual status suggests once more the telling importance of the novel's first word—which is, of course, not just any pronoun, but a singular personal pronoun—though it does so by ignoring the word's gender in favor of its singularity. The male and female Orlando both occupy a space of privilege throughout the text that allows for the fantasy of mutable sexuality and sex change to go unchecked by a reality that might otherwise have tempered it. Such a fictional space provides a place of joyful and comic imagining for its readers, but it also runs the risk of appearing inaccessible. Orlando's privilege is explicitly marked off in the text as particular to Orlando's own life, history, and experience, and the "innocent" stance the novel takes toward embodied sex might easily be read as a stance only feasible if one refuses to engage with reality and its grown-up knowledge that males and females have different bodies and are not interchangeable. The same far-reaching future vision that allows *Orlando* to outpace our current conceptions of body, sex, gender, and relationality also allows it, by virtue of its distance from the present, to be easily dismissed or laughed off as lighthearted fun by a society not yet ready to heed a full-fledged social critique in a comedy—a critique that would take on not only the way in which we conceive of gender but also the ways in which we understand bodily sex, including the costs that such divisions between gender and sex might have for the individual person within society.

The liminal fantasy *Orlando* presents, which uses comedy to straddle the line critically between radicality and conservativeness, risks critical oversimplification by virtue of its joyful tone and its full-fledged departure from reality. The important interventions this text makes into thinking through embodied sex can be seen in their complexity, however, by considering other modern texts that temper their related fantasies with a melancholic acknowledgment of reality's limitations. What structuralist Tzvetan Todorov used as a defining quality of the "fantastic" genre—its ability to leave open the question of whether or not its fantastic or nonrealist moments occur—suggests we might view fantasy as a mode of writing that maintains a grief-tinged acknowledgment of its own genre (25). This understanding of fantasy—a text that is aware of its state of dreaming even as it persists in this dream—presents a version of knowing innocence, in which fantasy marks not only the extent of its imaginings but also the important work within reality that such imaginings do. For such texts also take care to acknowledge the problems that ensue when we leave such fantasy, for an adult investment in reality "as is," behind.

Though the potentially unbounded genre of fantasy might initially appear at odds with reality's serious limitations, grief, and even death, Judith Butler's pragmatically inflected queer and feminist theory gives us a way to think about the necessary connections between the two. Butler's work, particularly in *Undoing Gender* (2004), emphasizes what might easily appear to be realist concerns about allowing people, regardless of race, class, sex, gender, or embodiment, to live a life that is valued and recognized in the social sphere. Butler articulates fantasy and grief as not in excess of, but in fact what helps to author such value and recognition. And here, in fact, is where we see the connection between fantasy and grief most fully. Butler asks, "how do the contours that we accept as the cultural frame for the human limit the extent to which we can avow loss as loss?" (24). I use this chapter's other two texts—Sherwood Anderson's "The Man Who Became a Woman" and Katharine Burdekin's *Proud Man*—in order to flesh out both these contours and limits in relation to embodied sex. Butler provides a link between the radical and the fantasizer in that both, according to her definitions, yearn for something outside the cultural frame—outside current reality. She argues that such an individual can "use, as it were, one's unreality to make an otherwise impossible or illegal claim" and that this "interven[tion]" is one way in which one might "disrupt what has become settled knowledge and knowable reality" (*Undoing* 27). "Fantasy," Butler writes, "is part of the articulation of the possible," and its articulation—its form and content—is governed by the limits of reality that both grief and the ungrievable mark (28). This chapter takes seriously Butler's assertion that "possibility is not a luxury; it is as crucial as bread" as it plumbs the ways in which these stories of sex change mark, via melancholia, their continued hope for making what is socially impossible possible, as well as acknowledge, via mourning, their recognition that reality does not yet recognize the possibilities they articulate as anything more than the product of an overactive, idealist, and even childish imagination (29).

Sex Difficulties:
Male Modernity's Resistance to Loss, Reluctance to Mourn

Critics of literary modernism have long acknowledged the central concern with gender difference and ambiguity that many writers—in particular, many male writers—of the early part of the period had. This concern was frequently explored via gender-bending, sex-changing characters; indeed, in addition to Woolf's *Orlando*, two other pillars of canonical modernist literature—James Joyce's *Ulysses* (1922) and T. S. Eliot's *The Waste Land* (1922)—prominently feature a male character who undergoes a sex change, as well as an exploration of the unique and conflicted perspective that such a change brings. These two texts, however, are far from the only modernist textual experiments with mutable sex; Nathanael West, Sherwood Anderson, and Djuna Barnes, for instance, address versions of sex change, transsexualism, and/or transvestism in their works.[7]

Writing about this array of modernist sex changes, Sandra M. Gilbert and Susan Gubar argue that male modernists portrayed "sexchanges" as fundamentally troubling, using these representations "to reinscribe traditional gender hierarchies" while also rendering the nausea and revulsion of transgressing sex ("Sexchanges" 773). And in their second volume of *No Man's Land*, they argue that this male "obsession" with enacting sex change only to reinscribe the traditional binary divisions between men and women had its root in "the emasculating terrors of the war" (343). World War I's core-shaking experience, they suggest, led male modernists to anxiously cling to gender "truth" as "the ultimate reality underlying history," a truth that could distinguish between gender's "false and true costumes" (*No* 343).

One of the texts by a male modernist that has traditionally received critical treatment in line with the rubric above is a short story by Sherwood Anderson entitled "The Man Who Became a Woman," which first appeared in his 1923 collection of stories, *Horses and Men*. "The Man Who Became a Woman" recounts the circumstances leading up to and surrounding an extraordinary experience in the youth of the narrator, Herman Dudley: one night, when he was nineteen and working as a racehorse groom or "swipe," he turned into a woman. His sex change first manifests to Dudley in the mirror of a local bar. Then, after he retreats in horror and fear to the sanctity of the stables and the racehorse he loves, he is awoken from his sleep by two drunken, black, male coworkers, who also take him, even in his naked form, for a woman and attempt to rape him. Terrified, Dudley runs wildly to escape their assault and only regains his composure—and his male sex—when he falls into and gets tangled up in the bones of a horse lying on the grounds surrounding an old slaughterhouse. These events, recollected by an older, settled, and married Dudley, still haunt him; Dudley describes his transformation into a woman as a story that has "been on [his] chest" for years, and he claims that he has "often dreamed about the happenings in it" (190).

This memory troubles beyond its mere staying power; Dudley inflects his memory with guilt as well as horror, declaring that "to tell" the story "will be kind of like confession," a way to "clea[n] up the room [he] live[s] in" (189–90). Thus, when Dudley writes of his sex change, he also writes about the other aspects of his life that have contributed to producing a "pretty messy" room: his rambling youth as a tramp and swipe, his "love" for fellow swipe Tom Means, his loneliness after Means leaves race track life, his youthful lack of sexual experience and discomfort around women, and his feeling of distance from the other swipes due to Dudley's attitude toward women, as well as to his racial difference (as, save Dudley and Means, most of the other significant swipes in Anderson's story are black) (190).

In deference to the complexity of Anderson's portrait of Dudley and to the wealth of issues going on in the text (sexual maturation; homosocial, homoerotic, and even perhaps homosexual desire; a growing awareness of the social codes of heterosexual, white masculinity), Gilbert and Gubar acknowledge that "Anderson's analyses of sex roles are complex and conflicted";

nonetheless, they stress Dudley's "horror" upon finding himself transformed into a woman as a sign of Dudley's (and Anderson's) sexism ("Sexchanges" 773). The emphasis on Anderson's conservative view of sexual difference, even his "nostalgia for a supposed golden age of sexual relations" in which "man" and "woman" were discrete, differentiated, and stable identities, is continued more recently by Mark Whalan and Joyce. R. Ladenson.[8] Yet this argument eschews what I find most fascinating in Anderson's text: the way that such cultural and (perhaps) authorial anxieties about modern man's effeminization are at odds with Herman Dudley's emotional experiences within both the process of his sex change and his discursive wanderings as he repeatedly contemplates, worries over, and eventually decides to tell the story of his transformation. To me, it is within such affective descriptions that Anderson's "The Man Who Became a Woman" presents a much more complicated and even transgressive view of the cultural and personal stakes of not only becoming a woman, but also—and perhaps even more centrally—becoming a man. Anderson's story offers a fantasy of sex change alongside a realistic narrative of the loss of sexed *possibility*; it employs both grief and melancholia to explore a loss that moves beyond and counter to Gilbert's argument about her lack of surprise at male modernist penchants for "want[ing] the consolidation of orthodoxy" in regards to gender ("Costumes" 218). For within Herman Dudley's emotional attitude toward not sex *change* but rather sex *loss*, the pragmatics of Anderson's fantasy—as well as Dudley's failed choice not to know—can be glimpsed.

Uncomfortable Gender, Disallowed Sex: "The Man Who Became a Woman"

As in Woolf's *Orlando*, throughout "The Man Who Became a Woman," the protagonist's individuality—his status as not *the* man but as *a*, and *a particular*, man—is essential; the throughline in both texts that connects both the male protagonist and the female he comes to embody is their sense of division from those around them. Whereas Orlando's individuality is presented as privilege, however, Dudley's is presented as the result of an extreme emotional state of isolation and loneliness. Dudley's first impressions of his "girl's face" is that it is a face that looks "lonesome and scared" (207). Rather than attributing such loneliness and fear to the shock of sex change, it seems more accurate to see Dudley's interpretation of his girl's face as part of his extensive history of loneliness that he shares with his readers before narrating his sex change.

We might consider Dudley's feminine-inflected affective excess to not only figuratively separate him from the more "thoroughly" male swipes but to also render him vulnerable to such a literalized becoming.[9] Dudley's loneliness is fueled in part by his inability or unwillingness to access women as intimate partners in the way other men do. Critics have often read Dudley's "inability" as evidence of his homosexual desire for his male friend Tom Means, but it seems more likely that Dudley's block against the kind of sexual intimacy the text constructs as typical is about sexual repression rather than sexual preference.[10] Corroborating this reading are the details Dudley gives of his dreams, in which he "kept seeing women's bodies and women's lips" and would wake "feeling like the old Harry" (197). The dreams—the desires—that in Dudley's waking mind made him feel comparable to the devil are, importantly, heterosexual desires (which does not exclude his desire for men but, rather, excludes an exclusively homosexual desire); moreover, Dudley's devilish dreams require seeing women as sexualized parts (bodies and the sexually connotated "lips") rather than as human beings. If the performance of masculinity around the racetrack requires that men "do not go without women," Dudley is out of place in this landscape, not because he lacks sexual desire for women but because he disavows in his waking life the fragmentation of the other (female) sex that his sexual desire—within the codes of masculinity that he understands—would require (195).

Such a prohibition of a sexual desire based on acknowledgment of the other and a fear of the other's forced fragmentation risks seeming overly sentimental, antiquated, and effeminate to his fellow swipes. Dudley himself acknowledges that even his closest friends, Tom Means and Burt, "used to laugh at [him] about [his inability to date and sleep with women] sometimes" (196). However, it seems important to note that this "femininity" in Dudley does not seem to bother him until after Means leaves. He describes the feelings "Tom's talk" evoked in him as physical nourishment comparable to pork chops that "stick to the ribs," a shared language that "started something inside you that went on and on," enabling both "splendid dreams" and a feeling of "fine[ness]" upon waking (197). After Means left, Dudley writes, his "body seemed all right and just as good as ever but there wasn't no pep in me" (201). This lack of mental "pep" contributes to Dudley's loneliness, and he finds himself disassociating from the physical world. Dudley's dissociation brings with it behavioral change; he "got lazy and mopey and had a hard time doing [his] work" (196). It is tempting to read such descriptions as Dudley's recollections of his slow mental unhinging, but I think it also essential to emphasize that what Lonna M. Malmsheimer describes as Dudley's "acute mental illness," his "hysteria" is, to Dudley himself, a "fix" of the mind that importantly could be, if not cured completely, at least ameliorated by communion with another (as it was with Tom Means) outside of social—and gendered—mandates (19).

For instance, Dudley's closeness to the horses in his care sparks not only longing but also respite in him. Dudley writes about interacting with his favorite horse, Pick-it-boy: "I wished he [the horse] was a girl sometimes or that I was a girl and he was a man. It's an odd thing to say but it's a fact. Being with him that way, so long, and in such a quiet way, cured something in me a little" (200). Though such a wish privileges heterosexual intimacy, it interestingly does not privilege Dudley's association with maleness. Indeed, the sex he takes seems entirely negligible—being a girl or being a man are presented as two equally weighted options separated only by an "or." Rather, it is the extended period of connection, the quietness, and the "way" in which the two were joined—as two creatures simply *being*—that Dudley treasures. The horse for Dudley functions like Tom Means did; we hear that "after an evening like that [with Pick-it-boy] [Dudley] slept all right and did not have the kind of dreams" that fragmented women and haunted him upon waking (200). This cure, however, is not sustainable because it requires, at least socially, a type of heterosexual human transformation of both himself and the horse in order to legitimate it. Whereas the gender that Dudley himself adopts appears negligible to him, that a gender must be adopted to break through his social isolation and difference is not. Dudley's awareness of the social proscriptions that mandate his heterosexuality and thus his intimacy with an appropriate body (here, a woman) makes the "cure" he's identified impossible to sustain, even though he finds the socially acceptable "cure" proffered to him—sex with random women—personally impossible.

Thus, what appears to be Herman Dudley's hysteria or madness might more accurately be seen as an expression, almost illegible, of a man taking on one of the most fundamental sites of presumed knowledge—that of gender and sex—a site fundamental not only to society, but also to himself. Dudley's insistence on his body's core wellness, coupled with the dreams of women's bodies that so disturb him, suggests that it is not Dudley's sexual appetite or his physical ability to act on such desire that has gone awry, but rather his conscious, willed, even intellectualized desire that troubles, isolates, and ultimately singles out Herman Dudley for a change in sex. Dudley's desires for women's bodies, to be with a woman "up to the hilt," would require, in his conscious life, "such a woman as [he] thought then [he] should never find in this world" (198, 202). That this woman would have "something in her like a race horse" suggests that Dudley's ideal woman would embody the simplicity, the "just being," that enables his peaceful connections with both the racehorse Pick-it-boy and his friend and fellow swipe Tom Means (202). The world, not Dudley's imagination or his desire, stands in the way of such a hope for a female intimate. Lonna M. Malmsheimer suggests that Dudley is "unable to accept his role in terms of maleness as socially defined" and that "he refuses to conform to the male stereotypes which are part of his experiences" (21); while these refusals certainly form aspects of Dudley's objection to the "world," part of what I am arguing is that, to Dudley, "maleness" means nothing in isolation, and he rejects masculinity only in that it defines one half of an unsatisfactory, and unequal, binary with the pairing "woman."

Malmsheimer goes on to posit that what she terms Dudley's "mental" sex change provides evidence that suggests that not only would he "rather be a woman than accept maleness as it is defined by his available role models," but that his ultimate—if failed—"want" was "to be totally human and to carry into adulthood all the attributes of his humanity, even those regarded as stereotypically female" (21, 23). But what precedes Dudley's sex change is not just his disgust with masculinity but, in fact, his disgust with humanity. Looking at the dirty, crowded, and unappealing town in which Dudley finds himself, he speaks to the superior aesthetic sense of the animal: "[A] race horse isn't like a human being. He won't stand for it to have to do his work in any rotten ugly kind of a dump the way a man will, and he won't stand for the smells a man will either" (204). Directly before entering the bar in which he changes sex, Dudley experiences extreme aversion to humanity, declaring:

> The sight of it all, even the sight of the kind of hell-holes men are satisfied to go on living in, gave me the fantods and the shivers right down in my liver, and on that night I guess I had in me a kind of contempt for all men, including myself, that I've never had so thoroughly since. Come right down to it, I suppose women aren't so much to blame as men. They aren't running the show. (206)

The subtle slippage in these two passages from "human being" to "man" (as a word signaling, arguably, humankind) to "man" (as a sexually specific designator placed in opposition to woman) creates a funneling down of meaning that ultimately makes "humanness" and "maleness" into interchangeable signifiers. For Dudley, I want to suggest, the problem is not that the ideal of total humanness must give way to a more limited maleness, but rather that to be human is, in some key sense, to be *male*, with all of the hellish compromise attending it.

Dudley's realization and dread of this meaning behind the male mandate of "human," a maleness that encourages cowering in "hell-holes" away from possibility, sets the ground for his sex change; when Dudley watches a man stomp on and break another man's shoulder because the other man was showing off by mocking him, Dudley finds himself "so sick at the thought of human beings . . . [he] could have vomited" (214). As the "scared young girl" who he sees in the barroom mirror, Dudley does not experience femininity as an escape from the maleness that so appalls him; instead, he experiences an extreme disidentification with himself as well as with the other humans in the bar. So just as "the men, the miners, . . . the red-faced bartender, the unholy looking big man who had come in and his queer-looking kid . . . all of them were like characters in some play, not like real people at all," Dudley experiences, via sex change, a sense of "[him]self, that wasn't [him]self" (209). Femaleness, then, is not a state of being that Dudley welcomes; rather, it indicates the lack of easiness he feels with his identity, as a human, in general.

The dissatisfaction Dudley feels with "humanness" physically sickens; by contrast, the respite he feels after leaving the bar as a woman when he enters the stall of the nonhuman Pick-it-boy is extreme. In fact, Dudley declares that finding himself alone with the horse "was one of the best and sweetest feelings [he's] ever had in his whole life" (214). Importantly, though, it is not just the horse himself that gives Dudley this good feeling; rather, it is also the fact that Pick-it-boy's presence allows him access to *memories*, and specifically to memories that present alternative versions of women that are closer to Dudley's ideal fantasies than to his disturbing nightmares. These women that Pick-it-boy calls to Dudley's mind are not the "mean and low and all balled-up and twisted-up human beings" that "even the best of [women] are likely to become" in the world as Dudley knows it (215). Instead, the dream woman who has become explicitly and physically linked to the body of the horse as Dudley seeks comfort in Pick-it-boy's stall is, like "queens in fairy stories," fantastically unattainable (215). Indeed, Dudley's only means of access to such a woman is literally through the horse's body, which might help us to understand the stakes of the scene that follows the sex-change in the bar, perhaps the most sexually explicit in the text.

Ushered in by Dudley's "queer feeling" that he and the horse inexplicably "understan[d] each other," he narrates the following scene of nonhuman communion (217):

> I went over to where he [the horse] stood and began running my hands all over his body, just because I loved the feel of him and as sometimes, to tell the plain truth, I've felt about touching with my hands the body of a woman I've seen and who I thought was lovely too. I ran my hands over his head and neck and then down over his hard firm round body and then over his flanks and down his legs. His flanks quivered a little I remember and once he turned his head and stuck his cold nose down along my neck and nipped my shoulder a little, in a soft playful way. It hurt a little but I didn't care. (217)

If we read this exchange as a type of surrogate sex scene, as the slip for Dudley between the horse's and a woman's loveliness urges us to do, what perhaps most deserves note is the way in which such a comparison figures each party's role in sex as not only nonheterosexual, but also nonpenetrative. The emphasis falls, instead, on touching the whole of the body; pleasure for the horse is demonstrated by his quivering, for Dudley by the pain about which he does not care. Both include a sense of being shaken and affected but do not specifically or clearly align with or refer to genital experience. In effect, by channeling Dudley's sex scene with the dream woman through the body of Pick-it-boy, the reader is left with an image of Dudley's ideal sexual encounter that, though it would occur between members of the opposite sex, does not appear normatively heterosexual, not only due to Dudley's "sex change," but also because of the way in which the biological sex, even the physical anatomy, of the participants is diminished in importance in both the imagined *and* actualized interaction above.

Thus, for us to understand the terror of the following scene, in which Dudley is mistaken for a woman (even while naked) by two of his fellow swipes and is almost sexually assaulted, we need to consider his body as a site that might both be recognizable as a woman's and also require none of the specific anatomy and biology that being a "woman" conventionally suggests. And though this scene, for critics like Babb and Malmsheimer, presents the apex of Dudley's disidentification with masculinity and his preference for femaleness, I think it is more accurate to view this scene—if we consider that Dudley's chief disidentification is not with masculinity but with humanity—as one that gains its horror not from its continued rejection of these "masculine" traits but rather from its exposure of Dudley's core identification, despite his best intentions, with humanity (and its ultimate "maleness").

On what grounds can I justify claiming Dudley's core identification is with humanity, and that this humanity is, moreover, at root a male humanity? To begin with, we must look closer and query the narrative of sex change we are given by Anderson's story: though Dudley may turn into (in his imagination, in some kind of fantastical reality) a woman, the woman he becomes is not a particular, unique woman but rather his (male) construction. He claims that "all my life . . . I had been dreaming and thinking about women, and I suppose I'd always been dreaming about a pure innocent one, for myself, made for me by God maybe"; indeed, according to Dudley, "men are that way. . . . [T]hey've always got that notion tucked away inside themselves, somewhere" (220). Dudley literally places this notion at the male core—he calls it "a kind of chesty man's notion" (220–21). He then tells us more about the "kind of princess" he "invented": a woman "with black hair," a "slender willowy body," "shy and afraid" (221). This dream woman is the model upon which Dudley's transformation is based: the "puzzler" to him is that he "now . . . was that woman, or something like her, [himself]" (220, 221). Given Dudley's explanation that all men have in their chests a notion of a woman like this, we might imagine that though the woman Dudley transforms into might appear particular, she is not unique; though another man might form another version of this woman with different characteristics, she would still be the male notion of woman—not woman herself.

We can further see the horror at the root of Dudley's realization that his mysterious sex change might have been orchestrated by his own masculine desires rather than by his anti-masculine sentiments by looking at Dudley's escape from his would-be rapists. We as readers are not presented with a character who perceives himself as a victim lucky to escape his attackers; rather, Dudley identifies in turn both as a victim and as the pursuer—the raped and the rapist. He describes himself as being "full of terror" while running from the two men; yet rather than holding them accountable for their actions, Dudley, upon reflection, rationalizes his attack (222). Black men, he claims, are "up against it in this country"; they lack easy access to prostitutes, as racial prejudice allows whites to "have negro women fast enough" but does not let black man succeed "the other way around" (219). Interestingly, Dudley's response to this scenario cannot develop a coherent reading that is sensitive to the inequality experienced by both women and black men; by terming the latter response the "fai[r]" one, his ultimate allegiance of logic tips the balance toward his male, rather than female, identification, regardless of the racial difference between himself and the other swipes (219). In short, Dudley views his colleagues as "justified in what they did," an attitude that, despite the affective horror Dudley feels when he is victimized, appears to blur the boundaries between prostitutes and women in general, suggesting the male right to sexual access of any woman (219). And as Dudley runs from his would-be rapists, he hears "something strange and scary, a steady sound, like a heavy man running and breathing hard, right at my shoulder," but rather than attribute this sound to the men pursuing him, Dudley believes instead that "it may have been [his] own breath, coming quick and fast" (222). In pursuit of himself, Dudley—the image of woman—runs "like a crazy man" from the man this image represents (224).

I see this circuit of self-pursuing/self-pursued, this failure of idealized disidentification, as an experience so distressing to Dudley that it might help contextualize the deathlike experience he describes at the close, for him, of being a woman. Dudley runs from his pursuers, himself, until he falls forward into the middle of the ribs of a horse skeleton. While holding onto the bones, Dudley experiences "a new terror" that he likens to "a big wave," one that "knocked you down and rolled and tumbled you over and over and washed you clean, clean, but dead maybe" (225). It is this perception of mortality—the experience when Dudley "seemed to [himself] dead"—that, in his words, "burned all that silly nonsense about being a girl right out of [him]" and that finally allowed him to "screa[m] at last" in vocalization of his terror (225). Some critics read this moment of death as one in which Dudley grows up, or in which he finally accepts the social role of maleness that society offers (or imposes upon) him;[11] rather than reading the moment as a death of the self, however, I think the above details most clearly point to a death of the *dream to get outside of the self he already is*—a death that, cleanly and tragically, signifies his inability to be other than the male human, or even to imagine himself in a different role.

Toward a Melancholic Mourning, or a Mournful Melancholia

Of what value, then, is the sex change that is not a sex change—the man who fantasizes himself as a woman, who may even fantastically turn into one, only to discover that this "woman" is a mere chimera of his own, inevitable, inescapable maleness? Crucially, I think, its value lies less in the success of the sex change than in the affective response to the entire experience. For what Dudley is, he attempts to disavow; finding this impossible, he experiences a sort of living death. "The Man Who Became a Woman" may be, more accurately, a story about a man who stays a man, but in documenting Dudley's poignant attempt to do otherwise, it presents us with the question of where we are left if a male character who is lonely, different—someone who is sympathetic, to some extent, with women—*cannot be* other than male. Dudley forces us to consider this question by insistently returning to this narrative after years have passed, and only after several attempts to explain why the story (in his mind at least) still needs to be told. The physical exodus "out of the race-horse and the tramp life for the rest of my days" that Dudley so neatly charts in the story's final words butts uncomfortably against the insistent return of these days in the life of his psyche (228). In what we might best describe as a sort of haunting, the story has maintained a presence in Dudley's life that has not been benign—Dudley writes that he "often dreamed about the happenings in it, even after [he] married Jessie and was happy" (190). Marriage to a woman, happy heterosexuality, a secure relationship, communion with another—all of these were dreams that the younger Dudley longed to fulfill; yet even after achieving them, Dudley still "screamed out at night" while returning psychically to the events in his tale (190).

The story's lack of forward motion does not preclude it from serving as the kind of reality-based model for readers that Woolf's text could not be. For it is most useful for us to note that the point in Dudley's narrative at which he screams is not when he finds himself transformed into a woman in the bar, not when he witnesses the beating, not when he experiences his solace with Pick-it-boy, not when he is assaulted by the two men in the barn, not even while running from his assaulters. He screams, according to his own remembrance of the events, directly after the woman "nonsense" is "burned" out of him (225). The situatedness of this scream signals to us as readers that Dudley's dreams become nightmares not when he remembers being transformed into a woman, but when he remembers this possibility extinguishing. At risk, at root in his scream, then, is the extinguishing of his melancholia: a haunting of possibility lost but not yet fully grieved, gone but not yet fully surrendered, that—in the wake of his inability to become a woman—marks his repeated remembrance that he once, still, found it necessary to try.

The kind of grief that Herman Dudley experiences is realized both during the actual events "The Man Who Became a Woman" recounts and in the remembrance of these events that he, as an older narrator, makes reference to throughout; his reported experience of continual engagement with a sort of "lived death" might best be explicated in light of Sigmund Freud's definition of melancholia. I have suggested earlier in this chapter that texts of sex change engaging the tragic side of the comedy/tragedy axis evince a turn-of-the-century affect toward embodied sex, an affect rife with melancholia. Though melancholia and melancholy affect have long been terms used to describe negative, depressive, or sad emotions and affects, recent criticism has used the Freudian definition of "melancholia" as a way to explain and explore a particular modern affect in which straightforward grief over someone or something "lost" is neither possible nor socially preferable.[12] In his paper "Mourning and Melancholia" (written in 1915 and published in 1917), Freud draws a distinction between the more healthy mourning and the "pathological mourning" of melancholia on the basis of whether or not the subject is able to let go of its love object after this object rejects the subject (587). For Freud, mourning occurs normally (and as mourning) when a person, after being slighted by a loved object or finding this object otherwise "lost," is able to enact a "withdrawal of libido from this object and a displacement of it on to a new one, but something different" (586); in opposition, melancholia's pathology results from the subject's inability to withdraw. Instead, the melancholic subject increasingly identifies with this lost object to the point that the object becomes incorporated into the subject as a part of himself or herself.

Critics have used this understanding of melancholia—as a loss "ungrieved"—to think about issues as diverse as national identity,[13] American race relations,[14] and performative malady.[15] More generally, some critics, such as David L Eng, David Kazanjian, and Jonathan Flatley, have engaged melancholia to describe the embodied experiences of modern humans.[16] In these works, we see two key trends of contemporary critical treatments of melancholia, both of which Judith Butler's work helped to instantiate: the move toward considerations of melancholia as a socially inflected affect and the willingness to think through productive elements of melancholia.

Both trends significantly contravene a Freudian understanding of melancholia's individuated pathology. For though Freud's subsequent work in *The Ego and the Id* (1923) on melancholia and mourning calls into question the stark opposition between the two terms, any amelioration of his judgment of melancholia's supposed "pathology" is based on his newly conceived notion of the usefulness that melancholic incorporation has for the establishment of the individual ego, not on any sort of reconsideration of the theory that one needs to move on from loss by refocusing on the self (not the other).[17] Both of Freud's discussions of melancholia read the rejection experienced by the melancholic subject as one that, either in reality or imaginatively, marks a break from a previous, more halcyon period of nonrejection; however, when the term is taken up by Judith Butler in *Gender Trouble*, her article "Melancholy Gender—Refused Identification," and *Bodies That Matter*, the loss experienced by the subject is increasingly written about as a loss without a history of nonloss: a loss that could have never been otherwise.

Butler's reading of melancholia links two important themes that we see in Anderson's text: the nonpersonal but instead socially determined loss and gendered, embodied experience. Indeed, Butler uses melancholia to understand the formation of gender identity on the part of the subject. She argues that the cultural prohibition against homosexual desire requires that subjects "lose" the ability to desire a certain sex as a love object but cannot acknowledge this "loss" as a loss; consequently, the subject melancholically incorporates the "lost" desire into the self and uses this loss to create its own gender identification. Though critics have rightly taken issue with some of the details of Butler's "gender melancholia," her broader emphasis on the social dimension of melancholia has not yet been mined for its full potential.[18] The fact that the "losses" Butler discusses are contingent upon not personal predilection but rather on cultural prohibitions leads to a kind of melancholia that arises in the subject before he or she even has a chance to experience desire, love, and loss. She suggests that the kind of melancholic loss that interests her "might be better understood on the model of foreclosure," a word she uses "to suggest that this is a preemptive loss, a mourning for unlived possibilities" ("Melancholy" 165, 170). Loss, for Butler, is not personally but culturally constructed; the melancholic being experiences his or her "pathological" inability to grieve, his or her troublesome tendency to incorporate and identify, because of social, not personal, standards.

While Butler uses the model of melancholia proposed by Freud to investigate the loss of a potential love object, we might also view melancholia, in light of the bodily sex changes this chapter discusses, as a way to refuse to acknowledge the loss of a potential body. If we see melancholia as, at root, a mode of dealing with socially necessitated loss—a loss that occurs when limits are drawn, conclusive differences acknowledged, and possibilities made impossible—then I would suggest that the above reading I have proposed of Anderson's story invokes such melancholia; however, instead of demonstrating the "gender melancholia" that Butler outlines, I suggest that Herman Dudley best exhibits a sort of "sex melancholia" in which the ungrieved loss is not the loss of a potential category of lovers (for Dudley freely admits his love for another man), but a potential category of (sexed) self. In short, we might read Dudley's fantasized femaleness, as well as his reoccurring nightmare of his failed sex change, as his melancholic refusal to acknowledge and grieve his inability to be other than a man. Here, I do not mean to suggest that Dudley would rather be a female; instead, and crucially, Dudley's sex melancholia is, like Butler's gender melancholia, born of a cultural experience of foreclosed, pre-empted loss. If melancholia is experienced by the subject as the sense of being, in the words of Butler, "inhabited or possessed by phantasms of various kinds," and if such ghosts are born of lost, unlived possibilities, then it makes sense to see Dudley's melancholic loss as the loss of being not only *other than* but also *more than* male—in other words, to be more than one, in addition to an alternative, sex (*Gender* 93).

By considering melancholia's social dimension, we highlight the relationship between the melancholic and the social, while leaving the specter of Freud's "pathology" suspended as a question in the gap between them. Whereas Freud (and melancholia's critics) construes the melancholic affect as pathological, the modern social melancholia we see in Anderson's text and elsewhere indicts society, not the melancholic, as the problem. Such an indictment is made possible by these texts' seemingly imperfect depiction of melancholia and its melancholics—for the modern melancholics I treat here, such as Dudley, fail to avoid grief. In this sense, one might question whether we can truly call Dudley a melancholic; after all, melancholia is about the refusal to grieve via incorporation, whereas I hope the above analysis has shown how much evidence exists that Dudley does grieve, and grieve heavily, when he finds himself to be, in the end, only a man. And indeed, within traditional Freudian melancholia, we might not find the best descriptor for Herman Dudley. Even Butler, who seeks to link the processes of melancholia and mourning more closely than Freud, suggests that melancholia is still a way to "keep [loss] at bay, to stay or postpone the recognition and suffering of loss" ("Melancholy" 167). For both Butler and Freud, the melancholic act of internalizing loss is at odds with recognizing and suffering from said loss. Dudley, at the close of "The Man Who Became a Woman," seems to be both suffering from the knowledge of lost possibility (he rejects the "silly nonsense" of being a woman, he experiences a sense of living death) while also, and at the same time, still sustaining via incorporation the possibility that loss precludes (in his dreaming of and retelling of the incident of becoming a woman). One might suggest that Dudley insists on the facticity of having "become" a woman so that he might experience a loss of being rather than a pre-empted loss of possibility that would cast him as lost before he had even begun. More interesting, though, might be the suggestion that Dudley is able to both suffer and sustain, to both acknowledge and refuse loss, through the purposeful belief in fiction: an ethically innocent faith in fantasy.

Poised between mourning and melancholia, Dudley provides a model of a mournful sex melancholic who acknowledges the limitations of cultural constrictions while also challenging, via sustained faith in alternative possibilities, the strength of the cultural forces that have foreclosed his own possibilities. Moreover, Dudley's expression of melancholic mourning offers us a model of community and relationship to the "other" that moves beyond Freud's insistent individualism, on one hand, and Butler's surrender to social forces, on the other. By both mourning a lost "other" and also still refusing to relinquish the fantasy of not having lost it, the version of melancholia that Dudley demonstrates challenges the idea that the culturally pre-empted loss is impossible to openly grieve. His fantasy sustains and, more importantly, communicates, both his possibility and his loss, even as his belief in the fantasy authorizes his perception of loss as legitimately grievable rather than simply as mad. But for his melancholic mourning to work, Dudley requires an audience; he requires a community of others to embark after him on his project of purposeful belief. For we can legitimate his grief within a broader cultural context—and thus challenge its pre-emptive loss—only if we, too, have faith in his fantasy.

An Image, a Path, and an Opening:
Proud Man

The texts this chapter has treated thus far present two incommensurable versions of a response to the problem of biological and social "sex" that we might categorize as forms of "knowing innocence"; moreover, the division between these versions hinges on the tonal stance along the comedy/tragedy axis that these texts take toward their fantasies of androgyny or sex change. In Woolf's *Orlando*, we are presented with an almost entirely fantasized scene of bodily sex. Orlando may mourn throughout the text for various losses (the betrayal of his first love, the dashing of his literary hopes, the limitations Victorian gender roles place upon her body and spirit), but the key issue of sexual differentiation is never experienced by Orlando as a loss at all—not because Orlando does not see the need to be either male or female *as* a loss, but because Orlando remains, throughout the course of the text, immune to this need. Orlando purchases the freedom to be sexually ambiguous as a right of moneyed, landed, gentrified privilege, a privilege that claims its birthright at the expense of the bodies and lives of other racial and class minorities within the community. Attending to the circumstances surrounding Orlando's fantastic exception to sex, we might rightly view Woolf's appealing fantasy as a tantalizing image that her nonexceptional readers have no hope of approaching. *Orlando*'s knowing innocence might provide an alternative to sexual realities as we know them, but it provides no path through knowledge toward such innocence that we—who have lost and mourn—might follow.

In contrast to *Orlando*'s investment in fantastic exception, Anderson's story weights its approach toward sex change and sexual ambiguity on the side of a culturally accepted reality, despite its fantastic elements. Anderson's narrator, Dudley, begins his reminiscence by thinking about his attempts to escape his "lonely life"; this somber note carries throughout the text, informing all of Dudley's remembered actions and proving to be an inescapable feeling for both narrator and text (Anderson 185). Though Dudley refuses to give up parts of his fantasy of sexual oneness or ambiguity through recourse to melancholia, the strength of his inevitable return far exceeds that of his resistance. A far cry from the joyful celebration in *Orlando*, Anderson's story both sustains and mourns its fantasy, but at the price of fully embodying it. Whereas *Orlando* could not provide its readers with a path to the alternative version of sexual embodiment it depicts, "The Man Who Became a Woman" more closely depicts the type of knowing innocence that is available to us all—a shadowland of fantasy we can never quite reach, even if texts can convince us that the fantasy is worthwhile.

What is needed, then, is a version of chosen innocence toward sexual embodiment that might merge the fantasy with the path, all while balancing our three axes of fantasy/reality, individual/community, and comedy/tragedy.

Asking for this version might, of course, prove to be too much; we might bear in mind Rorty's caution that the pragmatic path to making a dream a reality is one that depends on the ability of the dreamer to communicate and convince a social body to develop in a common direction, and that such communication is fraught with the risk of sounding crazy, of lacking language with which to vocalize such a dream (Rorty, "Feminism" 43). But just as Dudley's mourning does not extinguish but only dampen his hopes, the difficulty in finding a fully articulated path toward a new sexual embodiment that could stand as a general rule rather than just an exception should not extinguish our efforts to search for a path that is perhaps partially paved. It is with this in mind that I want to turn, finally, to a brief consideration of British writer Katharine Burdekin's novel *Proud Man* (1934).

First published under Burdekin's male pseudonym Murray Constantine, *Proud Man* tells the story of an unnamed "Person" who, while in a "dreamlike and unreal" state, goes at the behest of a group of "human beings" to live among the "subhumans," who, the human beings posit, "might possibly be [their] ancestors" (Burdekin 13, 15, 14).[19] Quickly, readers come to understand that this nameless and sexless Person is a being from either the future or a more evolved state of the present (for the Person believes these subhumans to be "on the same planet in another time") and that the "subhumans" are what Burdekin's readers would have recognized as the human occupants of earth in the 1930s—or, indeed, would still recognize as earthlings today (15). The unnamed Person—who is called by various subhumans first Verona, then Alethea Gifford Verona, then Gifford Verona—is first taken by the text's characters to be a woman; however, the Person goes on to live not only as a woman but also as both a man and a being without sex. As such, the Person's story does not merely engage our own contemporary understanding of sex and gender through the roles that the Person learns to inhabit; it also exceeds these and gestures toward a completely different understanding of human sexual embodiment by depicting "an entity independent of others both physically and emotionally, who is self-fertilizing and can produce young, if it wishes to, alone and without help" (Burdekin 22–23). Furthermore, the Person positions male/female dyadic sexual development (and interdependence) as the midpoint on evolution's progress "from a single-sexed unconscious being, such as an amoeba, to a single-sexed fully conscious being" (22). It is this aspect of *Proud Man*'s presentation of embodied sex that most interests me, for this evolutionary model provides the very confluence of image and, if not an explicit, at least a suggested path toward a different imagining of sex that the texts of Woolf and Anderson lack.

Interestingly, this social evolutionary model of sexual dyadic development from a place of sexual oneness has a mirror within the story that not modern fiction but rather modern science tells about individual bodily development in utero. Biologically, sexual differentiation takes place as a process of six variables, including chromosomal sex, sex-specific gonad development, and internal/external sex organs. Within the complexities of this process, it is now evident that at most stages, male or female differentiation at one variable does not causally mandate like differentiation at the following (Hyde 105–13).[20] As a result, in approximately 2 percent of births, the sex indicated by some of the variables disagrees with that of other variables (Hyde 111). Also, given the increasingly sophisticated possibilities of technological influence on the body, it is possible manually to affect gonadal differentiation.[21] What this scientific story of the body suggests is that it is not mere nonsense for Dudley to have "lost" the possibility of being a woman, or of being a sexually undifferentiated body: the latter is a lost bodily reality, science tells us, and the former a lost bodily possibility.

In addition to, and perhaps more important than, the evolutionary model, however, is the way in which Burdekin's text portrays not only its characters but also its *readers*. As a narrative, the story is pitched to a never-specified "you," although from the opening chapter, a reader understands that this "you" is not a subhuman but rather another human being, one who, like the Person, is single-sexed, fully-conscious, and entirely independent (14–15). As Daphne Patai notes in her introduction to *Proud Man*, "readers are constantly interpolated by the narrator as more evolved beings," a narrative mode that places *Proud Man*'s readers in a curious position, in which they are both detached from their actual subjectivities and forced, by way of address, to inhabit another's (xv). Not only, then, does *Proud Man* use the imaginative choice of innocence to provide a fantastic alternative to sexed reality, but its narrative stance makes its readers into the bridge that renders this fantasy legible. Rather than simply reading a story about another's attempts to joyfully, mournfully, or melancholically embody an alternative version of sex, Burdekin's readers are forced, via the act of reading, to take on this posture of innocence themselves and to experience a double consciousness: both as "humans" who share the Person's realities and as recognizable "subhumans" in the Person's eyes. Or, put differently, both as beings constructed/constricted by current sexual truths and as fellow Persons with bodies that suggest that a wholly other sexual truth is not only possible but *has been realized*. Just as the Person travels back in time to immerse itself in subhuman culture and live as the subhumans do, we as readers are invited to see a potential future of our own reflected in this Person—to see ourselves as a part of the human culture to which the Person so often refers.

Proud Man is broken up into four parts; part 1, "The Person," is written as a sort of anthropological study of the "subhuman" culture in 1930s England, whereas the following three parts ("The Priest," "The Woman," and "The Man") tell the stories of the Person's experience living with, learning from, and helping three different "subhumans": Andrew Gifford, a male priest; Leonora Simons, a female novelist; and Gilbert Hassall, a male murderer. Part 1, "The Person," provides the study of modern gender issues, which form a cornerstone of Burdekin's distinction between "subhumans" and "humans." The Person introduces the subhuman distinction along sex lines in its following observation:

> The idea that one individual should be both male and female, wholly and practically and conveniently within itself, was repugnant to them, even though their bisexuality was the cause of unbelievable pain, discomfort, and grief. They were not *persons*, and they did not want to be *persons*; they were *males* and *females*, or, as they preferred to call themselves, *men* and *women*. (23)

Not only does this passage present a utilitarian version of sexual oneness (practical, convenient), but the subhuman relationship to sexual oneness that it portrays is, moreover, one that hinges on the ambiguous use of the term "bisexuality." We might understand this reference to "bisexuality" not as a statement about sexual desire for both males and females but rather as a way to signal the fundamental seed of human oneness (that is, the male/female jointure) that is present in the "male" and "female" subhumans, despite their desire not to be human persons. From the perspective of the Person, the main reason why this "bisexuality" causes subhumans pain and grief ("the root cause of all the subhuman wretchedness") is their knowledge of it: "*because they have become conscious of [bisexuality]*" (23). Knowledge here becomes a trap for the subhumans, not because of the contents of the knowledge itself but because of the constraints (social, bodily, interpersonal) that prevent them from fully embracing and embodying this knowledge.

The Person's sense that subhuman consciousness or "knowledge" breeds their discontent maps quite easily onto traditional, perhaps even biblical, notions of the harm knowledge does when placed in "subhuman" hands; this also corresponds with the glorification of the pure state of "unknowing innocence" before knowledge of both biological and relational "sex" takes hold, which this project has been so invested in questioning. Importantly, though, Burdekin departs from this traditional understanding of knowledge's corrupting force on the innocent. The Person writes that "it is not possible to say that the misery of subhuman life [that is, life after knowing] is either good or bad; it is, if evolution is a fact, necessary" (24). In the Person's view, the miserable consciousness of bisexuality must, if subhumans are to become human, give way through "fear and doubt, . . . [and] jealousy" to "leisure, and the heightened consciousness" that will accompany evolutionary development (24). Counterintuitively, then, in order to re-see the knowledge of their bisexuality as a productive epistemic good rather than an ill to be repressed, the subhumans must turn away from—or reject—the other thing they know: that to be a normal human is to be either a man or a woman, not both or neither. For Burdekin's Person, the answer to subhuman suffering is not a reversion to innocence but a move through knowledge to, via choosing not to know, a different conception of the first knowledge: a *knowing differently* that would allow them to grasp their "bisexuality" as a convenient, practical whole in which they might find peace. In this sense, Burdekin provides us with an evolutionary model through time of what an ethic of innocence might both *look like* and *create*. This innocent "knowing," this form of hope for change in future knowledge, is what we as readers are invited to imbibe, so long as we can suspend our disbelief and respond to the Person's interpolating "you" as a similarly evolved member of its species. From this vantage, then, we are challenged to ask with the Person not How do we make sense of one being with both male and female sex? but rather How do we make sense of the limit of *two* sexes? The "naturalness" of dyadic sex is challenged by the text's certainty that human beings not only can and will live without it but also will be better off when it is surpassed.

We see seeds of this betterment in the text itself. For though the Person states that the subhumans it encounters do not wish to be persons like it, when the Person first arrives in England and stays with a family of subhumans, it finds that they behold it, even when read as a female (the sex that the Person notes is viewed by the subhumans as inferior and nondominant) with much envy and even desire for "[the Person's] superiority"

(78). This "superiority" is demonstrated not only by the Person's physically and aesthetically superior body but also by its intellect, which surpasses any within the subhuman household. Interestingly, the men of the household behold the Person with desire and lust, wondering "how [the Person] managed to be so very much more beautiful than any woman [they] had ever seen in the flesh, or in representations" (78–79). This male desire for the nonfemale, but also nonmale, body suggests another interesting way in which we might understand the fundamental "bisexual" desire of subhuman (and human) beings: not that men (or women) might desire both male bodies and female bodies, but that men (or women) might actually desire an individual who evinces a sort of combination male/female body.[22] As such, though the subhumans may not yet desire *to be* persons, they clearly still envy and desire the Person (though along the normative and often heterosexual lines that their version of sexed bodies permits), suggesting that the barrier they feel toward becoming Persons falls along epistemic rather than erotic or affective lines.

The initial ruminations on "subhuman" dyadic sex that the Person presents so anthropologically to the reader, as well as the way its observations are borne out within the scene of the Person's first encounter with a subhuman household, are complemented and complicated by the three sustained relationships with subhumans that the Person goes on to experience in the text. Each subsequent part of *Proud Man* concerns itself with a key subhuman stumbling block on the road to the evolution into personhood that the Person helps the respective subhumans to explore. First, the Person (as Verona) helps Andrew, the priest, to tackle ideas of God, virtue, and vice. Next, the Person (as Alethea) helps Leonora, the woman, to challenge both her ideals and her perceptions regarding male/female relations. Finally, the Person (as first Gifford, then rechristened as Paris) helps Gilbert, the man, to explore his own psychological traumas that have allowed him to murder three little girls. Though each section of *Proud Man* touches on the issues of sex division, the Person's experiences with Leonora tackle it most directly. That the section that deals most explicitly with sexual difference is the section in which the Person is living as a "woman" with a subhuman woman should come as no surprise. After all, Leonora, as an observer of sex relations from the less privileged sex, is able to critique both women and men for the parts they play in perpetuating the system.

Both Andrew and Leonora quickly recognize the truth of the Person's sex: it is neither man nor woman, but rather something that seems to work outside the binary system they know. Leonora, however, is not prepared to adopt the Person's as the better model, though she is quite critical of the sexism she experiences in her day-to-day life. For Leonora, the problem is not one of sexual difference but of the cultural meanings that those differences have come to indicate. She explains to the Person that her ideal of perfect communion between men and women would require them to be quite different: they "must stop being masculine and feminine, and become male and female. Masculinity and femininity are the artificial differences between men and women. Maleness and femaleness are the real differences" (178). Moreover, this real difference is (for Leonora) not an impediment to a relationship but rather the means by which one can "make the love and the work and the unit" out of the two (179).

The Person counters that the "artificial differences are . . . the result of the old original mess," that they "have arisen to console men from the real differences, and a complete change in the *human* character must take place before they can be broken down" (179). When the Person goes on to suggest that the children who would come out of the unions that Leonora wants, the ones who would use real difference as a means to "perfect understanding," might take a further evolutionary step and be "in time born" in such a way that "united the whole natures of the lovers in themselves, even to their sexes," Leonora balks at such an idea, crying that "then there would be no more lovers, and the children would be cold, cold" for "without sex there is no passion or feeling of any kind. No evil, but no good either" (192). The Person calls this reaction childish, a wish on Leonora's part to never "grow up," but Leonora stands firm in her position that to imagine a world in which the sexes were united and thus had no passion or love for another body would be "terrifying" (192).

In this exchange, Leonora and the Person best express a thread of critique to the Person that runs throughout the text: the cost to subhuman ideals that the Person's version of humanity represents. For the Person is repeatedly described by various subhumans, but particularly Andrew, Leonora, and Gilbert, as being cold and without love. Andrew thinks of this lack as evidence that the Person "ha[s] no need of love" (127). This, however, does not mean that the Person is selfish; on the contrary, readers find out quite early in the text that the Person operates under an ethic that requires it to risk its own well-being to save another. The Person calls this not an ethic of sacrifice but rather a "self-preservation instinct," as the Person's version of the self is extended to all other living things that feel pain, be it another Person, a subhuman, or even a mouse (126). For Andrew, this idea of self-preservation, though it might look like love and sacrifice, is without the warmth for another that those "subhuman" emotions signify; it indicates, to him, that the world of the Person is "cold, still, icy, green-pillared beautiful . . . like the North Pole" (127). The life he imagines for People, in short, seems closest to a life without life at all. Likewise, Leonora chides the Person for having "no heart of fire" and calls it an "old cold mountain," and Gilbert proclaims that "glaciers are not more cool than [it]" (171, 289). For this reason, both Andrew and Leonora, when they leave the Person, resolve to stop their relationship. Andrew describes it best, saying that if the Person were to write him letters, he "couldn't bear their coldness" (150). For him, the Person's physical presence, its "beauty and [its] sinlessness and the peace [he] gets from [it] make [him] forget, when [he's] with [the Person], that [it] ha[sn't] the faintest feeling of love for [him]" (150). Neither Andrew nor Leonora can imagine a deep connection to another without love, or indeed any emotion whatsoever, and thus their vision of the Person's world, enabled by its whole sex, seems to them both perfect and terrible.

Toward a Human Woman

As readers positioned between identities—interpolated as Persons, but coming to the book with the biases of the "subhuman"—we are left without easy answers to the conundrum the Person's sexless world posits for our sexed selves. Part of the strength of *Proud Man*'s exploration of embodied sex is that it presents the Person's future as a conversation rather than as an idealized given. The narrative allows the distance necessary for us to critique the Person's "superior" position, even as this position is offered to us as a way out of the grief and oppression of dyadic sex. Indeed, within a framework of melancholia and mourning, we can view the Person's embodiment as radical melancholia, in which the other becomes so incorporated into the self that every pain-feeling living being becomes a part of it; however, rather than evincing an image of ultimate love for the other, the Person presents a version of extreme individuality.

Andrew describes the Person's ethic as coming close to something like "unselfish individualism, which would make the whole world one corps," but, in a sense, the world this ethic describes is also nothing but selfishness, as there is only self (149). In this world of the single body, in which there is no yearning for another, there is also no sense of progress nor of time nor, really, of change. When Leonora asks the Person if its society is still evolving, it replies that "it's impossible to say" since they have "completely lost all interest in what [subhumans] call *history*" (194, 195). Moreover, the Person suggests that humans in its society have reached a sort of end point, declaring that "it seems likely that they are now fully evolved, adult, and therefore perfect" (195). This unselfish and yet all-self world of entire human independence/interdependence that the Person represents provides a version of community that is not, in fact, communal at all; the Person is entirely at peace in itself and has no outside other to challenge it and from which it might learn. The ultimate image of full personhood *Proud Man* presents, of one body containing both male and female sex, is an image of each human being recognizing itself as larger than its individual body; existing in perfect, cold peace; and leaving the others of itself alone for the duration of its existence.

That *Proud Man* does not come down on one side or the other, that we are positioned by the text's narrative voice to partake in Personhood even as we experience our subhumanity, allows for a critical space in which we as readers are invited to contemplate the image and path that Burdekin draws for us. The process of evolution itself is, tellingly, never disclosed: the subhumans have no sense of how to get to the position of the Person, and the Person has no sense of what its people's existence was like before their humanity (or even if there was such a before). One might be tempted to read this gap as the author's necessary cop-out, a mark of the limits of fantastic fiction that imagines and designs alternative lives for us without being able to make the blueprints for us to really accomplish this design. However, I think it is possible to read this gap in a much more hopeful light. In her afterward to *Proud Man*, Daphne Patai remarks that in creating the Person, Burdekin, by "imagining a world without imagination," "ironically displays her own abundant inventiveness" (Burdekin 343). Not only, though, does Burdekin demonstrate a feat of imagination as a writer, but she also implicitly argues for the importance of imagination in us all. If imagination, as Patai claims, is what allows Burdekin to "envision alternative paths" to a troubling reality, then it also is what prevents her, perhaps, from dooming humanity to the radical melancholia of the Person, who knows no loss, no past, no other, and no future (343).

For the Person, who returns to its own reality after it awakes from its dreamlike stay with the subhumans, the experiences it had with Andrew, Leonora, and Gilbert are "of no importance whatever" (317). The Person, who is sure in its personhood, concludes by stating that the subhumans' "possible attainment of humanity depends on how far they can become and remain, no matter what assaults are made on them, individuals"

(318). Though the Person opposes the individual to the mass rather than to community in general, the "terror of being alone" that it perceived in subhumanity (a terror that contributes to what we might think of as both negative and positive ideas of community) leads it to believe that "it does not seem probable that [the subhumans] were [its] ancestors" (318). Without imagination, the Person cannot comprehend the link between subhumanity and its own society. Rather than seeing this judgment as a negative reflection on subhuman (our "human") society, however, the text makes room for a reader to find the experience of personhood-by-proxy *of importance* and to perhaps be happy, to some extent, that the version of humanity that the Person represents is not likely to be one that subhumanity (our humanity) ultimately embraces.

In this study of modern fantastical treatments of sex change, sex loss, mourning, melancholia, and moments of happiness, I have suggested the ways in which attending to the affective character of such fantasies can help us to plumb these representations not only for their escapist spaces but also for their knowledge. Anne Anlin Cheng ends her introduction to *The Melancholy of Race* with her hopes for the productive power of writing melancholia for an audience; she argues that "if we are willing to listen, the history of disarticulated grief is still speaking through the living, and the future of social transformation depends on how open we are to facing the intricacies and paradoxes of that grief" (29). What I hope this chapter accomplishes—through a description and use of the axes along which such intricacies and paradoxes regarding sex melancholia reside—is a sense of how melancholia can make future transformation possible; that it can do so only when coupled with fantasy, with community, and—yes—with mourning should be seen as its strength, not its weakness. Burdekin's narrative engages melancholia, individuality, community, the social real, fantasy, and a touch of levity and mournfulness; as such, it provides both an alternative version of our future *and* an incentive for us to continue to imagine other versions. Though the Person concludes its narrative—half study, half memoir—by declaring that it does not believe "the future story of that [subhuman] race will be very different from its past," we subhumans—as mourners and melancholics, as bodies who experience both loss and hope—retain not only the imagination to disagree that we won't change but also, and most importantly, the imagination to create a divergent image and path for such change to follow (318).

Chapter Seven

Allowing Innocence?

Belief, Knowledge, and the Modern Community

> But as his mind came out of the control he exposed their lie that they were dealing with a mere breakdown of the normal process by pushing away this knowledge and turning to them the blank wall, all the blanker because it was unconscious, of his resolution not to know.
>
> —Rebecca West, *The Return of the Soldier* (67)

Of what use to us is an ethic of innocence, and indeed, how far can its imaginative engagement with potentiality over "knowledge" take us? As I attempt to address these concluding questions in the following pages, I find I must first tackle the most contentious word in the above statement, at least from a feminist/poststructuralist standpoint: "us." When I write "us," I do not mean you, I, or any reader happening across this text—no, what I refer to is that elusive, collective (though not uniform) us that the pragmatists attempt to evoke out of the diverse individuals, families, and social units that make up a society. This is the us that Jane Addams and Ellen Gates Starr strove to emphasize when they created Hull House to express, in Addams's words "the growing sense of the economic unity of society" and their faith that "social relation is essentially a reciprocal relation" (*Twenty* 59). It is the us that William James, in *Pragmatism: A New Name for Some Old Ways of Thinking*, feels comfortable claiming that pragmatism embraces—a unity of us that forms a "one[ness] by as many definite conjunctions as appear . . . [but is] also NOT one by just as many definite DISjunctions," and in which "the oneness and the manyness are absolutely co-ordinate" (91, 85). It is the us that Judith Butler, in *Undoing Gender*, sees not only in social relationality but in the very idea of "self" when she argues that "as bodies, we are always for something more than, and other than, ourselves . . . [which] suggests . . . that 'association' is not a luxury, but one of the very conditions and prerogatives of freedom" (25–26). And it is the us that Richard Rorty, riffing on John Dewey, defines not as pragmatism's "philosophical search for commonality" but rather the connection that might stem from "focus[ing] instead on our ability to make the particularly little things that divide us unimportant—not by comparing them with the one big thing that unites us but by comparing them with other little things" (*Philosophy* 86).

This us that the above pragmatic thinkers help define—one that joins without erasing difference, one that constitutes not only the social but also the individual—is the field of inquiry to which I suggest that we, at the close of this book, now turn, in order to help us think about the role that choices not to know have within an interactional social sphere of exchange and mutual dependence. In this book, we have considered narratives of "innocence" in which individuals and characters have refused (to others and to themselves) to know a variety of things in order to mentally survive their daily traumas and toils; to better survive materially and emotionally through harsh conditions; to protest their subjugation to reality's oppressive circumstances; and to sustain personal hopes and fantasies of being "other" than the ways in which society (and even, at times, they themselves) have perceived and described them as being. We have also looked at texts and authors who engage such chosen "innocence" in order to imaginatively/rhetorically correct material actions they have committed for the sake of "knowledge," to question common social assumptions, and to create not only the new worlds toward which we might strive, but also the new paths that we might take there.

Key to all of these narrative interventions is the replacement of normative conceptions of knowledge with something much more provisional, something that "innocence" has permitted these narratives to embrace. As a way to name this provisional space, we might make use of one of Richard Rorty's formulations of alternatives to knowledge. Rorty suggests that "we can, in politics, substitute *hope* for the sort of knowledge which philosophers have usually tried to attain" (*Philosophy* 24). If we look at this book's narratives of epistemic innocence with Rorty's claim in mind, it becomes possible to view these texts' substitution of future-oriented choices not to know for more stagnant knowledge, not as mere hopeless dreaming but rather an epistemology with a crucial political function. As well, viewing such narratives in light of Rorty's claim, as well as with regard to the pragmatist "us," affirms the connections between reality and fantasy that the texts this book studies have relied upon, a connection that previous criticism of such texts has not always emphasized.

I have shown that these epistemic refusals of knowledge—by individuals, characters, authors, and texts—have been particularly devalued in the fin-de-siècle/modern gender context, in which epistemology and discursive gendered norms are closely intertwined. As such, these refusals to know have met with a skeptical audience, one that has at times charged them with backward, conservative, and/or sentimental shrinking from both reality and forward progress. If we take Rorty's pragmatist claims seriously, however, we might view the switch from a mindset of "gaining knowledge" to one of "gaining hope" as a switch that invites us to see such innocence, even in the hands of female characters and feminist texts, as a powerful alternative to views of modernity's progress that have tended to reinforce traditional, masculinist norms of knowing even as women gained ground publicly and institutionally as epistemic beings. Rorty writes that pragmatists

> see both intellectual and moral progress not as a matter of getting closer to the True or the Good or the Right, but as an increase in imaginative power. We see imagination as the cutting edge of cultural evolution, the power which—given peace and prosperity—constantly operates so as to make the human future richer than the human past. Imagination is a source both of new scientific pictures of the physical universe and of new conceptions of possible communities. (*Philosophy* 87)

In this definition, Rorty not only resuscitates the imagination (or hope) as a site where legitimate and real social "growth" might originate; he also uses "imagination" to join scientific exploration—a pursuit traditionally yoked to the rational and "modern"—with the utopian hope for social progress that might otherwise be relegated to the idiotic province of the pipe dreamer. Such yoking challenges an easy distinction between epistemic and emotional pursuits, in that the imagination is positioned to generate new knowledge that is simultaneously a new possibility beyond the bounds of knowing's former constraints. But for such imagination to spark cultural, not just scientific, revolution, recourse to the pragmatic "us" is needed. Whereas a scientist might make a discovery, the truth about which he or she might then be able to convince the world, the power of the interactional-based pragmatist depends not only on inspiring community imagination, but also on inciting—which is much more challenging—the *communal agreement* to imagine, to hope, and to believe in order to instigate meaningful, lasting change. And, as I hope my book has shown, the challenge of the latter is deepened considerably by the gendered dynamics within modernity that allow, or prevent, such agreements from being communally reached.

Thus, it seems not only fitting but pragmatically necessary, as we approach the end of this project, to shift our focus from the individual agent (be it a character, author, or text) of an ethic of innocence to the communities that surround these "innocent" individuals. Of course, parts of all of the preceding chapters have invoked and analyzed some sense of such communities: Addams as both character in and author of *The Long Road of Woman's Memory* becomes a community member with the power to either sanction as truth or dismiss as fiction her Hull House clients' stories; critical engagement with early twentieth-century *bildungsromans* have circumscribed our ability to read female agency in compromised conditions; the advocates, theorists, and general public confronting tales of real and fictional domestic violence create, through their readings, the character types and tropes that continue to authorize and/or challenge abusive cycles; the public response to Richardson's protest, and suffragette action more broadly, helps constitute the network of participatory belief that authored her performance; and the modern refusal to acknowledge dyadic sexual difference, and the freedom this refusal provides for characters and authors to mourn their singular adult "sex," complicates modernity's continued engagement with the fraught sociobiological categories of male and female.

Indeed, we have been talking about epistemic communities all along: communities not only of knowledge but also of belief or the refusal to believe in epistemic alternatives; the type of choice not to know that this book theorizes is, at root, a categorization dependent upon interpretation. So when I suggest a turn in this project's conclusion toward "us," toward community, I see this turn not as a departure but rather as an avenue to more fully flesh out the stakes of some of the earlier gestures toward community that this project has made. I will do so through the consideration of a final pair of modern texts that stage, as their central concern, the interaction between an "innocent" dreamer and this dreamer's community: British modernist writer Rebecca West's novella *The Return of the Soldier* (1918) and the recent American film written by Nancy Oliver and directed by Craig Gillespie, *Lars and the Real Girl* (2007). That one of these texts clearly exceeds the bounds of the fin-de-siècle/modern period will allow me to demonstrate, at this project's close, the way in which this book's focal problem—the female choice not to know—has continued to trouble our twenty-first-century understanding of epistemology, in spite of feminism's increasingly mainstream integration into our intellectual and social lives.

Allowing "Innocence": The Dreamer and the Community

Despite their temporal and spatial dislocation, *The Return of the Soldier* and *Lars and the Real Girl* share certain striking similarities: both focus on male "innocents" who are depicted as mentally ill due to their seeming rejection of reality, and both rely on a specifically female community in order to embrace these men's rejections and also, at times paradoxically, to enact these men's "cures" from their choices not to know. Both texts, that is, explore a particularly female ability to extend epistemic agency and authority to male characters whom others deem delusional, as well as the reasoning these women use to justify activating this ability. It is in some part due to this focus on the female sustenance of individual (male) choices not to know that I include these two stories in the conclusion to a project concerned with women and innocence. For though both focus on a male character's engagement with "innocence," these final two texts pointedly suggest that the work of sustaining "innocence" for the male character falls under a female province, marking their engagement with "performative" or "ethical" innocence as femininely inflected.

The Return of the Soldier and *Lars and the Real Girl* both engage these male choices not to know within generic and environmental boundaries that are overtly feminized. *The Return of the Soldier* is famous among modern literary studies of World War I for its depiction of the mental, not physical, trauma of war; it focuses on British soldier Chris Baldry, who returns home to Baldry Court from the warfront with amnesia that renders him unable to recall the past fifteen years of his life.[1] West's depiction of Baldry's shell shock is significant for its early engagement not only with a debate within medical and military circles over its "biological or psychological" origins, but also for shell shock's discursive link to what "was often considered [a] 'feminine,'" pseudohysterical response to war (Bonikowski 514; Cowan 297).[2] Yet far more interesting, perhaps, is where this depiction of mental, if feminized, war trauma meets domestic romance—for Chris Baldry's amnesia has led him to forget the existence of his current wife, Kitty, and has returned him to a time, fifteen years earlier, when he was in love with, and still courting, Margaret Allington—a woman who has also subsequently married and made a life with another. The bulk of the novella, then, depicts the uncomfortable effects that Chris's amnesia—what the other characters ultimately term a "madness"—has on Margaret, Kitty, and Chris's cousin Jenny (also the text's narrator) who lives with Chris and Kitty at their family estate, Baldry Court. *Lars and the Real Girl*'s protagonist, Lars Lindstrom, also suffers a traumatic wounding, though his trauma stems from the death of his mother during childbirth rather than the trauma of war. He, like Chris Baldry, engages a form of what others consider to be madness within the domestic-romantic realm. However, rather than resurrecting a past romance as Chris does, Lars procures a "Real Doll" online (a made-to-order, life-sized sex doll) and introduces her to his family as his girlfriend, Bianca. The film's narrative arc focuses on Lars's relationship with his family, his doctor-cum-therapist, and the town in which he lives as he embarks on, has, and ultimately ends a relationship with Bianca.

As such, the worlds of both *The Return of the Soldier* and *Lars and the Real Girl* are, to significant extents, carefully constructed by female characters to nurture, protect, sustain, and cure the central male characters' dissatisfaction, unhappiness, and illness. In West's novella, Jenny and Margaret—though each with a somewhat different agenda—organize around Chris, initially to promote his happiness despite his amnesia, just as Kitty and Jenny worked to promote his happiness before it. Despite their reluctance, both Jenny and Chris's wife, Kitty, agree to bring Margaret Allington to Baldry Court to help soothe the stressed, lost, and verging-on-suicidal Chris; her subsequent weekly visits sustain and fuel Chris's happiness despite her obvious physical difference from the youthful girl Chris once courted. In fact, that he does not seem to notice this distinction—and that Margaret, for her own reasons, engages him on his own terms—allows him, as Susan Varney writes, to "return . . . to a time of innocence . . . before any disappointments in love" (261). In Lars's case, his sister-in-law, Karin, his coworker Margo (who has a not-so-secret crush on Lars), and a local elder, Mrs. Gruner, all step in to respond to his physician's orders to tolerate Lars's delusion and let it run its course. Each woman mobilizes her own circle of influence (the home, the workplace, the town) not only to tolerate Bianca's presence but also to accept her into local town life. Eventually, Bianca is given a job (modeling clothes) and a volunteer position (sitting with/"reading" to kids), and she accompanies Lars to a party at a co-worker's home that he otherwise would not have been psychologically able to attend. In both texts, the women who care for Chris and Lars cultivate a safe environment in which their refusals to know go unchallenged, at least until the men are more able to engage such challenges for themselves.

Yet these texts are no purely utopian spaces of belief; when these two modern men embrace innocence over knowledge, rather than wholeheartedly celebrating this embrace (as other turn-of-the-century fictions and their critical receptions do), the discourse in each of these novellas—whether or not the characters are really innocent, whether they are choosing not to know or unable to know—links them much more closely to the female-centered narratives that previous chapters of this book have treated. Indeed, the question of whether these men "know" that their delusions are delusional remains explicitly—suggestively—open-ended in both texts. Lars's "innocent" faith in Bianca's realness is described at one point by his brother Gus as not a hallucination (a false perception) but a delusion (a false belief). In making this distinction, Gus seeks to emphasize that it is not Lars's *perception* of reality but rather his *interpretation* of it that is in question during the course of the film. But whether or not the "false belief" in Bianca's realness that Lars manifests externally equates to what Lars "really" believes, in his inner consciousness, is an interior experience that the film never attempts to tap. Thus, we as an audience are left to question whether the delusion Lars experiences is something that happens to him, something he chooses, or something he embraces alongside a more normative understanding of Bianca's doll-like status. Similarly, Chris's amnesia is never explained by biological or neurological injury, facts that a reader could take as proof that he "really" doesn't remember. And, in fact, his wife, Kitty, maintains at various points in the novel that Chris's amnesia is a mere excuse, that it is "all a blind" and that "he's pretending," a significant point to which we will later return (West 31). In sum, the very question of whether or not these two characters' innocence is a choice or a defect, an act of agency or a signal of mental aberration, demarks these texts as ones that follow a "feminine" rather than "masculine" modern model of performing innocence, one in which the agency, intelligence, and will of the "innocent" are key areas of question or contention.

Yet just as these texts raise the question of the truth of these characters' innocence, they also present these characters as members of communities that, at least in part, also invest in turning away from these questions. Here, the multiple layers of innocence that take place in these texts strike me as particularly rife for analysis at this book's conclusion. For while these texts treat male innocence as an issue deeply enmeshed with female community, both texts also invoke a community of women who, with varying levels of enthusiasm or reluctance, create and sustain their own refusals to know as they "play along" with the delusions of the central male characters. Margaret's visits to Chris, Karin's serving of food to Bianca at the dinner table, Margo's conversations with Bianca, and Mrs. Gruner's intervention in an argument between Lars and Bianca that defends Bianca's independence from him are not mere absurdities but rather acts of epistemic generosity toward Chris and Lars that also, consequently, change these women's own epistemic understandings of what they do and do not know. As such, these female characters embody the figure of the "knowing innocent" more overtly than any other characters we have considered thus far. No one encountering either *The Return of the Soldier* or *Lars and the Real Girl* can doubt that at least some members of the female community involved "know" differently, even better, than the beliefs that they help sustain—that Chris is fifteen years younger, without wife or dead child, or that Lars's girlfriend, Bianca, is made of flesh and blood, not plastic.

The medical language of "cure" in each text belies these texts' investments in and explorations of affect; healing via communion with others; and—yes—that most romantic of romance sentiments, love, all of which mark these texts' departures from traditional realist, modern modes of depiction. And yet, ultimately, the cure that functions in each text as both the promise that fuels their narratives and the goal toward which they tend troubles the (partial) communal embrace of innocence, or at least this embrace's staying power. The conversations around cure in each text join a medical paradigm with a fantastic, romantic one, a juncture that blurs the genres of both texts; yet, ultimately, cure is aligned more with reality than innocence, with traditional epistemology rather than alternative forms of knowledge. *Lars and the Real Girl* has been critiqued by Ryan Gilbey, among others, for its abandonment of satire (man loves doll) in favor of what he calls "an ingratiating celebration of small-town togetherness" (it is okay in the eyes of the town that man loves doll), which devolves into a "cutesy-pie package" (42).[3] But the film still ends with Bianca's funeral, at which a composed Lars stands over her grave and prepares to go for a walk into the real with his (human) love interest, Margo. Likewise, critic Steve Pinkerton notes the disdain that West's critics have had for the love story between Margaret and Chris, finding it not realistic but rather a "putatively contrived 'romantic' dimension of an otherwise compelling tale of trauma and the home-front," even though the "trauma" Chris endures at war could, arguably, be said to return him to a happy state. This reading could suggest that it is not war but rather the bursting of what Pinkerton terms Chris's "amnesiac bliss" that both cures the original trauma and perpetrates another, ultimate, trauma of return to reality (2).[4] Indeed, the site at which Chris and Margaret met in the past and to which both of their imaginations and desires tend is described by Marcella Soldaini as a "utopian dimension of reparation, a mythical timeless world where the mind can recover"—a blissful site of romance that lacks key boundaries of reality such as time and space, but which is ultimately shown to be mere temporary respite (112–13).

As we continue an investigation of these texts' engagements with community and cure—with the power of the imagination to create and shift, pragmatically, a social sphere to embrace not only reality but also a hope for difference—I will return to focus on the way in which each of these texts engages fantasy and sociality as a component of cure. I will also, moreover, analyze the distinctions between the two models of cure that *The Return of the Soldier* and *Lars and the Real Girl* depict. For, despite all the similarities noted above, a crucial difference in the trajectory of the two texts, of their engagements with innocence, remains. West's modern novella ends with Kitty's triumphant vocalization, " 'He's cured!' " upon finding her husband's amnesia has gone and the soldier has "returned" a second time (90). As Jenny depicts it, "cure" in West's novel is an ambiguous term, one that signals Chris's emergence from amnesia but also his doomed downfall; this mode of cure is at odds with health and happiness, not just fantasy, and it shatters the sense of rest and peace in the text that Chris gleans from his time ensconced in his innocence with Margaret. *Lars and the Real Girl*, by contrast, pictures "cure" as something that fantasy does not oppose but rather helps one work toward. Even at the end of the film when Bianca has "died," neither Lars nor the other townsfolk are forced to recognize any sort of essential truth about Bianca's "life" (or lack thereof). Indeed, Lars's increased ability to connect with Margo, his family, and the other members of the community never hinges on him being brought back into a reality in which Bianca is only a doll (though it does, importantly, require the doll's demise); rather, he controls, directs, and modifies his fantasies to enable himself to let Bianca go without ever denouncing his "innocence" and learning to "know" more normatively.

It may be that in this difference, we can note a shift in modern representations of not-knowing that we, like the pragmatists, might find hopeful. For though over ninety years ago, as West's text argues, reality functioned as a "draught that we must drink or not be fully human," Gillespie's film suggests that, today, being fully human might depend, at least in part, on staving off drinking such a draught (West 87).

To Be or Not to Be Human: A Pragmatist's Dilemma

The Return of the Soldier, as narrated through the worldview of Jenny Baldry, depicts the innocence of Chris's amnesiac idyll as being at odds with or in opposition to a state of full humanity. This controversial claim is made in the closing pages of the novel, when Jenny contradicts some of her earlier statements praising Chris's innocence—what she provocatively refers to at one point as his "unconscious" "resolution not to know"—in order to ultimately present the above binary to readers (West 67). However, Jenny initially describes Chris's amnesia as an intellectual triumph, remarking that she "felt a cold, intellectual pride in his refusal to remember his prosperous maturity and his determined dwelling in the time of his first love, for it showed him so much saner than the rest of us, who take life as it comes" (65). This "act of genius" that Jenny "had always expected from Chris" is here posited as a rejection of reality that betrays not madness but the depths of his sanity; her initial description of Chris aligns higher degrees of "sanity" with an agential capacity to imaginatively seek to transform one's life, not just passively receive it (65). That Chris's "sanity" might be a product of the mind but not the conscious will is a fascinating possibility and impossible conundrum that Jenny's description of Chris's amnesia holds out. For how does one unconsciously (without overtly willed action) resolve (will) *not* to know what one's mind does, in fact, appear to already know (or to have known)? Chris is not described here as forgetful; in Jenny's depiction, he uses his agency against his consciousness to act ingeniously in service of a sanity that hopes for a future by throwing away the past.

Whereas at first this "choice" on Chris's part strikes Jenny as daring, savvy, and above the normal ken, her later evaluation of this same act appears radically altered (65). When it becomes clear that Margaret knows how to "cure" Chris—indeed, that such a "cure" is possible—Jenny views the "act of genius" that Chris has performed not as an intellectual success but rather as only "the trivial toy of happiness" (88). Further, she sees her own and Margaret's roles in helping to provide this toy as an act "utterly negligent of [Chris's] future" and one "blasphemously careless of the divine essential of his soul" (88). The rejection of reality the Jenny had previously praised is now depicted by her as a "delusion" that, if continued, will "tur[n] to a senile idiocy" (88). This rhetoric posits Chris's choice not to know not only as an act against God but—perhaps worse in his female relations' eyes—as an act that puts his full personhood at risk. As a result, Jenny believes that the beloved man whom she, Kitty, and Margaret so admire will become "queer-shaped" and "would not be quite a man" if he continues to embrace epistemological innocence (88). Likewise, the final decision to cure Chris is portrayed by Jenny as a sort of "righteousness," and though it is Margaret who punctuates this decision with her pronouncement that "the truth's the truth . . . and he must know it," Jenny confirms Margaret's attitude as, ultimately, the only tenable one within the modern purview (88).

The question of Chris Baldry's "cure" and "return" to a seemingly more human (yet perhaps less sane) embodiment of the memories that his bout with amnesia erased at the close of *The Return of the Soldier* has remained central to most critics of West's text. Critical response to the novella generally falls into two camps: those who believe, like the female characters in the novella ultimately do, in the necessity of the "cure" for Chris's ultimate well-being; and those who find these characters' belief in the inevitable cure to be a question the text asks its readers to grapple with, not a statement it asks them to accept. Illustrating the extremity of the first position, Margaret Stetz sees Jenny's second stance as the more "mature understanding of what modern life demands of us"—that "suffering and danger must be confronted directly" and that one gains "truth" at the (reasonable) price of "safety" (75, 77). Conversely, several critics (particularly ones with feminist investments) read Jenny's closing endorsement of Chris's "cure" and subsequent return to full masculinity as a signal of female complicity in male modes of violence and gendered oppression.[5] These essays use critical readings of the women's final kowtowing to "cure" as opposed to happiness as evidence that such women "take an instrumental role in ensuring the continuation of male violence" both socially and personally (MacKay 134). Jenny and Margaret's final act of "curing" Chris, which is read by Stetz as a meaningful, mature sacrifice on the part of the women, is seen by these writers as an indictment of women who foolishly participate in their own oppression. Interestingly, one of these latter critics, Laura Cowan, reads the closing return/cure in a way that aligns West's own authorial investments most closely with the attitude not of her book's female characters but of Chris Baldry. Cowan writes that West's "stance towards the central social issues of her time," such as suffrage for women, was one that emphasized not change but "transformation," one in which a "new social system" would "demand a new imaginative vision of its citizens" (303). This picture of West as one who, like Chris, finds "the world in 1916 [to be] inadequate" and thus rejects the present, appears as yet another version of the act of refusing to know—an act, we might recall, that Jenny first calls "genius" and that a reading like Cowan's might suggest is the way in which West (not Jenny) would have us ultimately evaluate Chris's innocence (304).

With such a reading in mind, we might view Chris Baldry, a performer of an "ethic of innocence," as the most feminist character in the text; the irony, of course, that his feminism is at least in part made possible by the privilege of his maleness is not insignificant. And yet of more significance to this project is the realization that his ultimate failure to sustain his innocence prompts: his performance—indeed, his feminism—depends on the complicity of his audience. I think it is possible for us think about Jenny's two reactions to Chris's innocence—a genius act of extreme sanity, a delusion suffered by a queer-shaped half-man with his soul at risk—not as contradictions but rather as complicated depictions of the same troublesome space of refusing to know. For Chris's amnesia and his entrenchment in a past hope that "reality" has already foreclosed for him resonates with other depictions of the not-quite-mad, not-typically-sane folk this book has considered, the folk who speak a pragmatic language of possibility that sometimes sounds like madness to a less hopeful audience. And we could read Jenny's evaluation that an amnesiac Chris would be queer and not-quite-a-man as a judgment that might be accurate, given the reality that Chris mentally rejects but yet must still physically abide. There is, after all, no possibility that the "innocent" Chris would be allowed to go back to war; as long as he were to walk "loose-limbed like a boy," he would be able to avoid not only the war itself but also the "harsh and diffident masculinity" of the soldier, the British modern man, who Jenny both dreams of and dreads to see return after Chris's "cure" takes effect (West 90, 89).

In fact, the history of her cousin that Jenny provides early in the novella not only signals why Chris's "genius" rejection of knowledge was something in keeping with his innate character; it also shows how the above portrait of soldierly masculinity was likely one that Chris worked to construct/adopt rather than naturally embodied. Chris is described by Jenny as one who is "not like other men," an assertion that she supports via recourse to his childhood activities and attitudes (West 7). She says that as a child, "he had always shown great faith in the imminence of the improbable," and she saw in him a "stronger motion of the imagination" than in most children (7, 8). This "faith," Jenny claims, "persisted into his adult life," when he continued to engage, according to her, the necessarily "hopeless hope" of adulthood: "becoming completely reconciled to life" (8). Chris emerges as a pragmatic dreamer and, thus, a perpetually queer man because he dares to hope for an alignment between life and himself. His is, moreover, a portrait of one whose attitude toward reality has always been fraught and who, in an attempt to become "reconciled" to life, might have adopted the performance of masculinity that his country, wartime, and indeed, the women in his life, demanded.

Viewing Chris Baldry as queerly oriented toward reality—as embodying a type of pragmatist-feminist presence by embracing, not relinquishing, something that society deems a "hopeless hope"—can highlight the failure of this queerness and feminism not in light of modernity itself but rather in light of *modern community*. Chris's character evinces a predisposition toward dreaming, toward alternative considerations of reality, and toward the kind of feminist pragmatism that pushes potentiality toward actuality; he fails, however, to move forward to this new real and instead must "return" to a traditional reality of husband and soldier because of the way in which his community reads and critiques his innocence. As long as Jenny and Margaret protect his state of amnesiac innocence, he is able to exist as if in a "magic circle" (West 88). But it is explicitly not his own continued amnesia that allows him to stay there; rather, his cognitive and physical space of respite is anchored by the (female) community that surrounds him—the women who "gathered the soul of the man into [their] soul[s] and [are] keeping it warm in love and peace so that his body can rest quiet for a little time" (70). Though such romantic language idealizes the feminine-maternal role, we might view the attitude of protective enabling such a passage describes within a broader pragmatic viewpoint as one that any individual, of any gender, could inhabit. Thus, we might see Jenny's two, seemingly opposing, evaluations of Chris's innocence as not only complementary but also as evidence of a telling, necessary shift in the trajectory of the book. When Jenny admires Chris's refusal to know, he can sustain it; when she deems it a cruelty that puts his ultimate welfare at risk, his dream is shattered (regardless of whether or not this shattering is actually crueler in Chris's (or our) own view). West's novel implies, via its insistence that Chris be cured when all (not just one or two) of the women around him desire it, that when the ethic of innocence is involved, the "hopeless hope" is only hopeless to the extent that society—not the hoper—evaluates it as such.

The Romance of Community: Can It Be Real[ized]?

While *The Return of the Soldier* forecloses the communal support of Chris's delusion/genius in order to enact his "cure," the small, northern, rural community in which Lars Lindstrom lives tackles the problem of its man's "madness" by mobilizing its network of support, a choice that critic Randolph Dreyer terms "colluding with delusion" (301). In doing so, the townsfolk essentially allow Lars's "innocence"—his "belief" that Bianca is a real woman with whom he has a relationship, rather than a sex doll that he purchased to satisfy his own desire—to become not simply a personal but rather a communal "reality" in which both Lars and the townsfolk share. Indeed, after the conversation among town elders in which the plan to "collude" with Lars is reached, the townsfolk never look back—they fully commit to the knowledge that Bianca is real, though they, as Dreyer notes, also "know [she] is a doll" (302). Whereas Dreyer suggests that it is this latter "knowledge" that marks the townsfolks' difference from Lars, the film (as mentioned above) is coy in regards to affirming or denying what it is, exactly, that Lars *really* knows. In the scene immediately following the town leaders' decision-making meeting, Lars attends church with Gus, Karin, and Bianca (who sits in a wheelchair); after the service, a townsperson gives Bianca a leftover flower display from church. Lars's response to this gift—"Those are nice, huh? They're not real so they'll last forever. Isn't that neat?"—indicates that Lars not only can distinguish reality from illusion in some venues, but also that he has a clear rationale for privileging illusion. His logic here can easily work metaphorically as a justification for a *chosen* refusal to "know" that Bianca, like the flowers, is a fake; as such, the statement further clouds any clear adjudication of Lars's interiority. What is clear, though, is that the remainder of the town easily recognizes Bianca's "fake" status but yet adopts an attitude, in direct contradiction to this knowledge, that she is real.

As such, the townspeople of *Lars and the Real Girl* perform an ethic of innocence as a part of their efforts to eventually fold Lars back into a pre-Biancan reality. They, like the women in *The Return of the Soldier*, ultimately desire a cure that requires some kind of return to the real world; however, what the course of the film suggests is that "cure," for Lars's community, is accomplished not through his simplistic "return" but through a process of transformation in which the experience of "reality" for both Lars and the townsfolk is changed. Further, this change in reality, this transformation, is accomplished not due to Lars's "innocent" dreaming, nor by the ethic of innocence the town displays while believing him, but through the confluence of the two: the unabashed acceptance of an agent by his audience that allows for collective innocent imagining to pave the way for *actual* change. For at the close of the film, when Lars "cures" himself of Bianca by admitting her "death" and burying her, the Lars who stands over her grave—proud though sad, not alone but comfortably encompassed by a group, bold enough to suggest a social encounter with a human woman—is not the only "changed" character. The townsfolk themselves come to understand that though accepting Bianca might not be a big deal, folding Lars into their social whole is.

Though characters indicate this realization in various ways and at various times (a colleague's glee that he attends her birthday party though it means bringing Bianca, the enthusiasm of a group of men to find Lars out bowling with Margo), the effects of Lars's community inclusion or exclusion are made particularly transparent through the character of Gus, Lars's brother. For Gus, Lars's "delusion" first presents a terrifying and off-putting realization that his brother is insane. This thought is so difficult for Gus to accept that he stays home from work the day after Lars brings Bianca home, claiming that he all-encompassingly "do[esn't] feel good." After Gus and his wife, Karin, decide to heed the doctor's advice and go along with Lars's delusion, the film depicts Gus's efforts to engage with Lars and Bianca, as well as to educate the men he works with about the nuances of Lars's condition. Later, Gus's full acceptance of Lars—despite the delusion—allows him to admit his own feelings of guilt and culpability in contributing to Lars's loneliness and mental problems; we find out that Gus left home when Lars was very young to escape their father's depression after their mother died during Lars's birth. In one of the film's key scenes, Gus apologizes to Lars for leaving him with their father and suggests he should never have done so, given their father's mental state. He explains: "I shouldn't have left you alone with him. He was too sad, it scared me, and I just . . . I just ran. And that was selfish. And I'm sorry." Lars's response—a slow smile, a long look, and finally a shrugged "That's okay"—initiates reparations to the brothers' distant relationship. At the close of the film, Gus stands alone while at Bianca's funeral and cries, admitting to Lars's doctor (who comes over to ask him if he is okay) that he is proud of his brother: "[H]e's unbelievable" is Gus's final pronouncement on Lars, a statement that could easily be used to describe Lars's "madness" but that, due to Gus's emotion, thankfulness, and happiness, instead indicates that Gus can now see Lars's specialness as a gift, not a curse.[6]

The film's insistence on collective transformation through the embrace of fiction is the root of *Lars and the Real Girl*'s power for some critics, just as it is the basis of critique for others. Indeed, the "ethical" dimension of the film's embrace of innocence seems to be the pivot on which these praises and critiques rest. For instance, Mark Moring of *Christianity Today* praises the film on the basis of its perceived message, "Love can conquer just about anything," which he sees demonstrated in the behavior of Lars's "family, friends, and fellow churchgoers" who "accept him unconditionally" (72). Conversely, Ryan Gilbey equates the films' proclaimed hope with a too-good-to-be-true religiosity, writing that "if the director, Craig Gillespie, really believed in the broad-church world-view that he's flogging, he wouldn't feel the need to keep reassuring us, through his film's overstated jauntiness, that everything is tickety-boo" (43). More neutrally, Randolph Dreyer speaks to the film's morality outside of an explicitly religious context, commenting that "this is not really a film about mental illness; it is an allegory about acceptance and generosity" (303). And Brian D. Johnson sees *Lars and the Real Girl* as one of a few recent films that feature "innocents—naïve outsiders putting their own oddball spin onto American family values"; this comment locates the film's ethic as an extension of nation-specific attitudes that, interestingly, coincides with Richard Rorty's own argument that pragmatic hope is a particularly democratic/American philosophical mode of being (50).

Whether we view such an ethic as religiously, morally, philosophically, or even nationally motivated, what seems important to me in these various strands of criticism is the way in which the film's happy ending seems to be read by all critics (those both pro and anti the film's trajectory and tone) as idealized. The utopic vision of rejecting, manipulating, and transforming reality that shatters at the close of the modernist novella *The Return of the Soldier* does not, in *Lars and the Real Girl*, undergo any such disillusionment. Instead, the characters in *Lars and the Real Girl* seem to find their utopic vision (which, we might do well to recall, is also a pragmatic vision) both immediately useful as a coping mechanism and also protective of future potential and possibility.

The skepticism shown by critics who praise the film as an allegory or who denounce it as saccharine rests on the difficulty both sets of critics have in seeing practical coping and imaginative transformation as two aspects of the same act—in seeing the link between pragmatism and utopia. In refusing this link, both sets of critics increasingly dichotomize reality and fantasy, further split the practical from the prophetic, and contribute to the critical difficulty conceiving of the kinds of individual and collective acts of innocence that both these texts portray as politically motivated interventions upon the status-quo. Such criticism threatens to preclude the questions with which this conclusion opens—Of what use to "us" are these ethical choices against knowledge? How far can such performances take us?—through the implication that as long as the "us" is a "real" us, who lives in the "real" world, the domain of choice discussed here and to which these narratives belong can never intrude upon reality as anything more than a hopeless hope.

Ambiguous Innocence:
Its Warning, Its Hope, Its Charge

In answer to the critical tendencies above, I offer a feminist pragmatist version of an ethic of innocence as a way to breach the gulf between the "real" us and our utopic fantasies. Moreover, I think that in the progression from *The Return of the Soldier* to *Lars and the Real Girl*, we can see incremental progress in textual efforts to close this gap. After all, we have moved from West's 1918 portrait of the necessary or inevitable shattering of Baldry's feminist-sympathetic dreams to Nancy Oliver and Craig Gillespie's 2007 portrait of a feminist community that transforms its members by sustaining such dreams. Where these texts do their most significant work in terms of identifying a modern mode of negotiating innocence is, I think, in their ultimate suggestion that the modern "ethic of innocence" is already always a transitory state, an ethical stance that, dependent as it in on the collusion of a community, does not and can never authorize utopias that the community views as merely idiosyncratic. Lars the dreamer is sustained by his community, and thus he can sustain his innocence, whereas Chris Baldry's individual utopia, judged by his community as outside the bounds of the allowable, shrivels and dies. In true pragmatist form, these community-dependent models of innocence suggest that our imaginative capacity, our possibility for change, is only ever as possible as the collective allows—a democratic, community-centered model of change that is both hopeful and pessimistic.

Indeed, the model of transformative community we see in *Lars and the Real Girl* is far from perfect; just as the romantic portrait of Chris's lover, Margaret, has been condemned by feminist critics for not being an "apt or workable mode[l] or idea[l] of female identity," the idealized Bianca—the plastic sex doll transformed via the male imagination into a chaste Brazilian missionary—falls short of either aptness or workability (Cowan 304). Certainly, part of the humor of the title of the film is located in its playful engagement with the term "real." Bianca, we know, comes from the "Real Doll" site, but in what sense is she a "real" girl, and what does her "realness" tell us about the role women have in helping to sustain male "innocence"? Moreover, why is there not a *Bianca and the Real* (insert gendered noun here) film instead, in which a human woman gets to choose not to know with likewise idealized outcomes? With this in mind, Bianca's root status as a sex doll becomes problematic in a way that the film never explicitly addresses: though Lars may not "use" Bianca for sex, his "use" of Bianca to establish connections with the "real" people in the film—most specifically with the human "real" girl Margo—might too closely mimic the way in which women have been historically used, not as dreaming beings themselves, but only as tools by which others might achieve their dreams. And the fact that Lars transforms and re-enters reality at the expense of Bianca's ability to continue to exist—the fact that he creates her death in order to emerge anew into his life—might stand as a warning to any too-facile appropriations of the film's narrative as a model for communal feminist praxis.

In important ways, and in ways I by no means want to obscure, using pragmatism as a mode of feminist political and social engagement must always be a fraught project. If we recall from this book's first chapter, William James writes in *Pragmatism* that "at the outset, at least, [pragmatist philosophy] stands for no particular results. It has no dogmas, and no doctrines save its method" (38). Such a method-centered philosophy is both pragmatism's great strength as a political force (for it allows for conversation, compromise, and progress) and also its weakness as a theory that would seek to promote any particular world view (for it allows compromise via conversation and progress only inasmuch as a community is willing to collectively call for it). In a similar vein, Richard Rorty suggests thinking of pragmatism not as a theory with a coherent set of principles but rather "as primarily therapeutic philosophy—therapy conducted on certain mind-sets" (*Take* 125). Rorty may be willing to claim that "insofar as pragmatism privileges the imagination over argumentation, it's on the side of the Romantics" and "insofar as it prizes intersubjective agreement, it's on the side of plain ordinary democratic politics"; Rorty follows in James's footsteps, however, by avoiding claiming for pragmatism any particular purchase on political investments, social attitudes, or activist stances that could easily be construed by theorists and critics as radical or revolutionary (particularly when critics and readers demand that such revolutions must work in opposition to a conservative status-quo) (135). This is not to suggest that pragmatist methodologies do not have radical or revolutionary elements—indeed, the kind of toppling of older ideologies that pragmatism recommends can be viewed as both radical and revolutionary (indeed, I hope my book suggests as much). However, the *nature* of the pragmatist revolution or radicality is not something that can be easily or simply aligned with the kinds of political and social movements we traditionally think of as "radical/revolutionary" methodologies. As such, if theorists or critics have feminist political or social goals in mind, reading the epistemics of innocence—the choice not to know—via a lens of pragmatism may not always work in service of these goals, in part because the pragmatist methodology of innocence this book explores can be used to express not only the human desire to progress forward and imagine differently, but also the very real and pragmatically valid desire to stay put.

As a final caveat, then, for future critics to keep in mind if they might be interested in using either the alternative epistemology of an ethic of innocence as I have theorized it or general pragmatist methodologies to analyze literature, social values, and political actions, I want to turn briefly to the figure of Kitty Baldry in West's *The Return of the Soldier*. Though I have given a lot of attention to this novella in terms of Chris's "innocence" and the performances of "not-knowing" by Jenny and Margaret that, for at least a short while, allow him to sustain it, it is worth considering the way in which Kitty's own performance of innocence uses a similar methodology of not-knowing to opposite effect. For though we have read Chris's cure as a return to reality that is ushered in by a failed communal performance of innocence, in a crucial sense, his failure and return are made possible only by Kitty's own, more successful, refusal to know.

Kitty's first response to hearing about Chris's "wound" of amnesia is disbelief. To Jenny's insistence that "Chris is ill," Kitty responds skeptically, "[Y]ou're saying what [Margaret] said," by which she implies that Chris's "illness" is not fact but rather a rumor substantiated by an interested, unreliable party (17). Throughout the novella, Kitty considers his amnesia as not a war injury but rather a choice constituting a "breach of trust," a "blind" by which Chris is simply "pretending" to have lost his memory and through which he has shown himself to be "a man like other men," caught up in an affair with a "bad woman" (17, 31). Kitty's treatment of Margaret, poor from the start, worsens as the narrative continues; she "wept" upon witnessing Chris's happiness when he first encounters Margaret, refuses thereafter (as much as possible) to see Margaret when she comes to Baldry Court (despite the fact that she has allowed her to do so), and behaves rudely to her when she does have to meet her (59, 75). Fascinatingly, this insistent refusal to know has been treated by critics alongside the model Charles Mills proposes in "White Ignorance" as a move available to the hierarchically empowered to reject the disenfranchised: here, white, wealthy, heterosexual, and *male* rationality.[7] For example, Melissa Edmundson has argued that Kitty Baldry's treatment of Margaret evinces a sort of "unforgiving, masculinist mindset that led England into war" by considering the way in which Kitty herself best embodies the martial attitude throughout the text that she promotes for her husband (493). And though Jenny later claims that Kitty was forced, eventually, to recognize that Chris's illness "was no pretence," Kitty's statements to Dr. Anderson, the psychiatrist treating Chris, that directly precede Chris's cure—that she believes he could cure himself "if he would make an effort"—suggest that she clings, despite "knowing" in some fashion that he is ill and that he is not pretending, to the idea that he is not and he is (61, 79).

Then, too, it is only through Kitty's insistence that the slew of doctors, ending finally with Dr. Anderson, come to Baldry court to examine Chris at all: he is perfectly content with his new life of seeing Margaret once a week. One suspects that without Kitty's insistence, Chris might have been left untreated and remained blissfully "innocent" forever. For Kitty, her own performance of innocence to Chris's mental "wound" is what allows her to hope for and keep attempting to find his cure while also permitting her to disparage Margaret and the kind of happiness that this other woman provides to Chris as a sort of tawdry, stolen thing (62). Whereas Chris uses his "innocence" to imagine a better reality for himself, Kitty uses her "innocence" to disparage his imagined reality and return her husband, at the close of the text, from his ideal world (from which she finds herself excluded) to the real world that she privileges.

Though the text, as narrated by Jenny, villainizes Kitty as "the falsest thing on earth," it nonetheless seriously depicts the way in which Kitty suffers as she faces the loss of her husband to another woman (87, 89). Reading with an ethic of innocence in mind asks us to attend to this pain, not merely that which the text's villain creates in others but also that which she herself fees; it further urges us, via acknowledging the authenticity of Kitty's "suffering" that drives her refusal to know, to connect Kitty to the other women this project has treated, even while noting her distinction. In short, such a reading forces us to recognize that the imagined reality that brings Chris such happiness simultaneously alienates and oppresses Kitty. And significantly, Jenny notes that it is her own and Margaret's acknowledgment of Kitty's "suffering" that forcefully "remind[s] [them] of reality" and helps to usher in Chris's cure" (87). This concluding clash between Chris's innocence and Kitty's, which resolves via the other characters' acknowledgement of Kitty's misery in the face of Chris's happy idyll, goes beyond suggesting that Chris's choice not to know requires communal support to be sustainable. Ultimately, it suggests that one must attend to those that one's stance of innocence excludes, even as it also suggests epistemic conservatism: that performances of innocence that sustain reality are likely to win out over those that would change it.

The complexity that a comparative consideration of Chris and Kitty Baldry displays here—the way in which an "ethic of innocence" in *The*

Return of the Soldier can be used to advance both an imagined future utopia and a stasis in reality via the same methodology, should signal to us both the usefulness and limits of pragmatism's methodology for an emancipatory feminist theoretic. Again, here, the gender dynamics at work are provocative; the male-bodied Chris Baldry's choice not to know is effeminized along the female innocent model, critiqued for its lack of mental acuity, and fails to be sustained, in contrast to the more typical male modernist refusals of knowledge that this book's introduction invoked. Meanwhile Kitty's innocence—though chosen from a female body—does not carry the stigma of female fin-de-siècle choices not to know that this book as a whole as treated; it is more in line with the oppressive refusal to know that typically aligns with masculinist privilege and the power status quo it seeks to maintain (à la Mills). Both *The Return of the Soldier* and *Lars and the Real Girl* not only expose the powerful promise of communal acts of not-knowing, but also show the limitations, risks, and dangers of too quickly assuming that this promise is all we need to imagine, then actualize, better worlds for ourselves.

What I hope my readings of these texts, as well as the book's arguments as a whole, might signal is not that we must privilege the choice of innocence over the choice to know. For one thing, I hope I have suggested that in many ways a choice not to know is not a rejection of knowing all together but rather a mode of seeking out alternative forms of knowledge. And for another, I hope that the amount of difficulty, violence, critique, censure, and devaluation that the female enactors of an ethic of innocence have endured as described in this book alone would warn that the search for epistemic alternatives for the modern woman have had real, serious, and lasting consequences. Instead, I merely insist that we learn to read these modern female "innocents" more closely, read their rejections of knowledge as motivated rather than vacuous, and query their positioning within communities, in order to better understand the ways in which both knowing and not-knowing, what one knows and does not know, contribute to the gendered modern narratives of progress, stasis, and even devolution.

What this book's counter to a simple "knowledge-equals-progress" narrative of modernity might suggest is that we have a continued need for more ethicists of innocence—more agents who engage with and question knowing rather than simply promote knowledge, and whose choices to engage the former do not result in their social devaluation. To this last point, this book's ultimate aim in seeking to more fully account for women who choose not to know in turn-of-the century literature and culture is to argue that we—as readers, art consumers, and citizens—have a communal responsibility to consider these innocents, and their alternative epistemologies, seriously. For if communities, such as in *Lars and the Real Girl*, have the power to allow innocence to become new knowledge, we must also acknowledge how such knowledge itself, even when fueled by a refusal to know, is, like pragmatism, a morally empty term, one that can just as easily promote a return to the old—which is sometimes (not always) something we might view as the negative, the backward, or the oppressive. Our responsibility, *An Ethic of Innocence* suggests, is to invest in this cycle of knowledge production/refusing to know by constantly critiquing what we claim we "know" and what we claim we "don't know." To think about the former as, sometimes (but not always), the risk to our most revolutionary aims, while seeing the latter's innocence as, at times, the more fruitful.

Notes

Introduction

1. See here Cynthia Townley's *A Defense of Ignorance* introduction, as well as Robert N. Proctor and Londa Schiebinger's edited collection *Agnotology: The Making and Unmaking of Ignorance* (2008).

2. See, for instance, Anne McClintock's *Imperial Leather: Race, Gender and Sexuality in the Colonial Contest* (1995) for a detailed analysis of the complex interaction between these three within the British imperial project. For an introduction not only to the tradition of Native American women's writing, but also to the critical traditions at stake in obscuring or contouring this tradition, see Jodi A. Byrd's "The Stories we Tell" (2012). And for more on the relationship between African American women's writing, enslavement, autobiography, and other forms of writing, see John Ernest's "Nineteenth-Century African American Women Writers" (2012). These are, of course, mere starting points within these critical conversations.

3. While I have signaled ways in which the trope of female innocence that I treat extends to—and is complicated and challenged by—intersectional approaches to female identity throughout this manuscript, I hope future scholarship might give more robust accounts of female choices not to know within particular intersectional communities: both ones included within this manuscript and ones outside its purview.

4. Much of the critical conversation about *The Portrait of a Lady* has circled around what we are to make of James's characterization of Isabel Archer: to what extent she seeks freedom/independence; whether she is a rebel from social mores or ultimately expressive of conservative ideals of domesticity, marriage, and "ladyship"; and how to interpret the ambiguous ending of the text. See, for instance, Joel Porte's introduction to his edited collection, *New Essays on* The Portrait of a Lady (1990), which focuses on the critical complexities presented by Isabel Archer's characterization, including the tendencies critics have had to overemphasize the dichotomy between innocence and experience within her representation. For more on the way Isabel Archer maintains conservative Victorian norms while also manipulating these

to her advantage, see Annette Niemtzow's "Marriage and the New Woman in *The Portrait of a Lady*" (1975) and Mary S. Schriber's "Isabel Archer and Victorian Manners" (1976). For more on the "infamously vague conclusion" of the novel, see Tessa Hadley's "'Just you wait!'" (2002) and Kimberley Lamm's "A Future for Isabel Archer" (2011) (Lamm 256). And though I do not agree with Robert Weisbuch's assertion that "Isabel's final choice, to return to her marriage, is her triumph," I find his underscoring of the critical readership's "wish to deny this"—indeed, the readership's own ethical and emotional stakes in decrying Isabel's decision—a useful parallel to the work I present here (610).

5. See Annete Niemtzow's "Marriage and the New Woman in The Portrait of a Lady" for an extended analysis, including a social analysis, of Isabel's attitudes toward marriage and a reading of why, after refusing so many suitors, Isabel decides to marry Osmond. Recent work, such as Patrick Fessenbecker's "Freedom, Self-Obligation, and Selfhood in Henry James" (2011), continues to grapple, albeit more critically, with the seemingly absurd choices Isabel makes throughout the novel, most specifically to marry and stay with her abusive husband.

6. See here also Millicent Bell's essay "Isabel Archer and the Affronting of Plot" (2018), which also highlights the importance of "the act of choice" as central to Isabel's character, though Bell emphasizes that this investment in choice is "theoretical" rather than acted upon (599).

7. I specify here that this is *Isabel's* marital reality, not the reality of marriage in the late nineteenth century in general. For an excellent introduction to the wide variety of courtship and marital models available in the nineteenth century, with attention to intersectional identity, see Melissa Adams-Campbell's *New World Courtships* (2015).

8. See, for instance, Xiomara Santamarina's essay "Black Womanhood in North American Women's Slave Narratives" (2007), which—though not about innocence directly—demonstrates the way in which the rhetorical choices black women made in their narratives of enslavement showed keen awareness of, and responsiveness to, public biases that saw such women as either "de-gendered . . . because they performed field and manual labor" or "oversexed because of their sexual vulnerability" to whites (232). This not only parallels the pattern of the enslaved exploiting bias to their own advantage, as in the Frederick Douglass example above, but also highlights the distinct sexual and gender expectations that contour American black female experiences differently than the experiences of their white counterparts.

9. See Miranda Fricker's *Epistemic Injustice: Power and the Ethics of Knowing* (2007).

10. See chapter 4 of Townley's *A Defense of Ignorance*.

11. See William James's "Pragmatism and Humanism" in *Pragmatism* for a discussion of pragmatism as a humanistic philosophy.

12. Despite this insistence on pragmatism's methodological focus, much of the work that has been done concerning pragmatism and literature had primarily focused

on historical connections between pragmatism and writers. The James brothers are popular topics here (see Jonathan Levin's *The Poetics of Transition* (1999) and Richard Poirier's *Poetry and Pragmatism* (1992)), as are experimental writers (Michael *Magee's Emancipating Pragmatism* (2004)). James Livingston's *Pragmatism, Feminism, and Democracy* (2001) draws together elements of great interest to this project, but from a primarily historical lens. A few exceptions to this trend of engaging pragmatism primarily historically are David Kadlec's *Mosaic Modernism* (2000), which focuses on radical modern texts and anarchism; Brian May's *The Modernist as Pragmatist* (1997), which reads E. M. Forster's work as a compromise between liberal idealism and modernist skepticism; and Lisi Schoenbach's *Pragmatic Modernism* (2012), which, while focusing on modernist writers engaged with pragmatism, also configures an alternative strand of modernist aesthetics around the concern with habit. There is also a small literature of feminist pragmatist treatments of science fiction/fantasy texts. See Tom Moylan's *Demand the Impossible* (1986), Erin McKenna's *The Task of Utopia* (2001), and Ellen Peel's *Politics, Persuasion, and Pragmatism* (2002).

13. See here Eduardo Mendieta's introduction to *Take Care of Freedom and Truth Will Take Care of Itself* (2005), where he describes the "two central virtues" of Rorty's work as "respect and hope," or, more specifically, a "profound respect for ordinary citizens" and a "utopian hopefulness that social justice is a worthy project to devote our lives to, even if we have no guarantees that we will succeed and that our gains will not be rolled back" (Rorty xii).

14. See Rorty's "Feminism and Pragmatism," as well as this book's fifth chapter, for more detailed analysis of the meaning and ramifications of this suggestion.

15. See Ann Clark's essay in the *Hypatia* special issue on feminism and pragmatism, "The Quest for Certainty in Feminist Thought" (1993), Keith's "Feminism and Pragmatism" (1999), Miller's "Feminism and Pragmatism" (1992), Sullivan's *Living across and through Skins* (2001), and Livingston's *Pragmatism, Feminism, and Democracy*.

16. See this book's first chapter for a more comprehensive discussion of pragmatist tenets and their relationship to feminist philosophy. Also see the 1993 special issue (8, no. 2) of *Hypatia*, which is dedicated to a discussion of the relationship between these two schools of thought.

17. See Frances Power Cobbe's 1869 treatise, "Criminals, Idiots, Women, and Minors" for more on the Victorian infantilization of women.

18. See here Robin Bernstein's *Racial Innocence*, which hinges on the key claim that innocence within the nineteenth-century American context "was raced white" and that racist depictions of black children as unable to feel pain became a way in which such children were "defined out of childhood" (4, 20). Also see Claudia Nelson's work on Victorian age inversion in *Precocious Children and Childish Adults* (2012), which discusses child-women as well as precocious girls within the social values of Victorian domesticity, marriage, and childrearing; Nelson points to class complexities, as well as political complexities, that make such representations of the

relationship between innocence, childhood, and women both vexed and productive (particularly in chapters 3 and 4). For more on the relationship between class and sexuality, see Susan David Bernstein's "Dirty Reading" (1994).

19. See, in particular, Felski's chapter "Visions of the New: Feminist Discourses of Evolution and Revolution," in *The Gender of Modernity*.

20. See, for instance, the ending choices against knowledge made by three male protagonists in three canonical modern novels: Edith Wharton's *The Age of Innocence* (1920), when Newland Archer chooses not to go into his former love's apartment and find out what she has become; D. H. Lawrence's *Women in Love* (1920), when Rupert Birkin refuses to "know" that he cannot maintain a loving, intimate relationship with both a man and a woman; and E. M. Forster's *A Passage to India* (1924), when Professor Fielding refuses give up on a friendship with the Indian doctor Aziz, despite its social impossibility.

21. In the conclusion to this book, I provide textual evidence to suggest that whether or not Chris does "actually" return to innocence is a question that *The Return of the Soldier* asks rather than answers.

22. See Leo Bersani's "Is the Rectum a Grave?" (1987) and Lee Edelman's *No Future* (2004).

23. See chapter 6 of Faye Halpern's *Sentimental Readers* (2013) for more on this tension.

24. See, in particular, James's lecture "Pragmatism and Common Sense" (lecture 5 in *Pragmatism*).

Chapter 1

1. See Marilyn Fischer's "Trojan Women and Devil Baby Tales: Addams on Domestic Violence" (2010), which links Addams's invocation of the "primitive" to evolutionary theories about race memory.

2. See here Christopher Hager and Cody Marrs's "Against 1865: Reperiodizing the Nineteenth Century" (2013), in which they argue that current prevailing periodization structures have "tend[ed] to posit, or at least tacitly promote, a chronology of phased evolution that is belied by the fluid and multilinear patterns of literary history. The literature of the nineteenth century is an archive not of progressive displacements but of coeval mixtures, piebald genealogies, promiscuous exchanges, and uncanny retrievals and durations" (266).

3. Sean Epstein-Corbin's useful article "Pragmatism, Feminism, and the Sentimental Subject" (2014) does great work in aligning pragmatist philosophy to the genre of moral sentimentalism and, through this alignment, to feminist politics. This article charts the way in which both male and female pragmatists made use of this generic tradition and serves as an important indicator that it is the specific confluence of authorial gender, gender of subject, and gendered genre in Addams's writing that we must attend to, not merely one or two of these prongs.

4. A very useful, brief run-down of the key aspects of U.S. Progressivism can be found in Scott Herring's first chapter of *Queering the Underworld: Slumming, Literature, and the Undoing of Lesbian and Gay History* (2007). See pages 26–27 in particular. For more information on the foundation of Hull House, see Mina Carson's *Settlement Folk*, especially pages 1–9.

5. See the forward by Henry Steele Commager of Addams's *Twenty Years at Hull-House* (x–xi).

6. According to DeKoven, this all-female workforce was only temporary: "quite early on, a men's residence was added" (328).

7. See, in particular, pages 109–19 of Carson's *Settlement Folk*.

8. For comments on the patronizing nature of early Hull House aid efforts, see Charlene Haddock Siegfried, *Pragmatism and Feminism*, 78–79; for a debate on the assimilationist tendencies within the Hull House project, see Lissak's *Pluralism and Progressives* and Shannon Sullivan's response to Lissak's charges in "Reciprocal Relations between Races: Jane Addams's Ambiguous Legacy" (2003).

9. See Carson, pg. 54, for further support that the rhetoric of residential benefit was consciously scripted and developed by both Addams and Starr from the opening of Hull House.

10. Thayer refers to Peirce's "How to Make Our Ideas Clear," published in 1878 in *Popular Science Monthly*.

11. Excerpted by editor John. J. McDermott from Dewey's *Creative Intelligence: Essays in the Pragmatic Attitude*.

12. For more on Dewey and James's use of Addams and praise of her work, see *The Social Thought of Jane Addams* (Christopher Lasch, ed.) and Ellen Condiffe Lagemann's "The Plural Worlds of Educational Research" (1989).

13. Addams endured a childhood bout with tuberculosis of the spine, which left its mark on her both physically and through recurrent painful episodes (Hotaling 34). In addition, she dealt with psychological illness. For Addams's account of her own period of psychological malaise, see *Twenty Years at Hull-House*, chapter 4.

14. See, for this view, Marianne DeKoven's "Excellent Not a Hull House."

15. For the few other exceptions to the text's critical neglect, see Maurice Hamington's *The Social Philosophy of Jane Addams* (2009), 57–58, Duffy's "Remembering Is the Remedy: Jane Addams's Response to Conflicted Discourse" (2001), and Marilyn Fischer's "Trojan Women and Devil Baby Tales: Addams on Domestic Violence."

16. For more information on Peirce's particular version of pragmatism, see Ross Posnock's *The Trial of Curiosity* (1991) and Neil Gross's article in Craig Calhoun's *Sociology in America: A History*, especially page 190.

17. For feminist literary-critical work that emphasizes textual gaps, see work by Sandra Gilbert and Susan Gubar such as *The Madwoman in the Attic* (1979), Catherine Gallagher's *Nobody's Story* (1994), Anne-Lise François's *Open Secrets* (2008), and classic works in reader-response theory such as Louise M. Rosenblatt's *The Reader, the Text, the Poem* (1978). For works that more specifically engage literal

"silences" within texts, see the following: Patricia Laurence's *The Reading of Silence* (1991), Janis P. Stout's *Strategies of Reticence* (1990), Sanford Budick's *Languages of the Unsayable*, (1989) and Leslie Kane's *The Language of Silence* (1984).

Chapter 2

1. Feminist difficulties engaging women's choices to stay with abusers will be more fully developed in chapters 3 and 4 of this book.

2. For a critical essay that also links the two fruitfully, although ultimately arguing that they should be considered separately, see Barbara White's "Edith Wharton's *Summer* and 'Women's Fiction.'" Also, see Jennie A. Kassanoff's *Edith Wharton and the Politics of Race* (2004), 128–29.

3. For more on reception history, see also Delia Caparoso Konzett, "Getting in Touch with the True South."

4. See also Elizabeth Ammons, *Edith Wharton's Argument with America*.

5. See Deborah Hecht's "Representing Lawyers" and Kathryn Voorhees-Whitehead's "'The Long Flame' of Edith Wharton's *Summer*."

6. See Grafton's "Degradation and Forbidden Love in Edith Wharton's *Summer*" and Hecht's "Representing Lawyers."

7. See Susan L. Hall's "The Death of Love" and Nancy Walker's "Seduced and Abandoned" for competing interpretations of Charity's choice not to tell Harney about her pregnancy.

Chapter 3

1. Throughout this chapter and the next, all quotes from *McTeague* will be drawn from the 2002 Modern Library edition of Norris's text.

2. Throughout this and the following chapters, I will use the terms "domestic violence," "domestic abuse," "wife abuse," "domestic battery," and "intimate-partner violence (IPV)"; each subtly differs in meaning. "Domestic violence" and "domestic abuse" are general terms that describe violence within domestic, intimate relationships (often, though not always, sexual relationships). "Wife abuse" is the nineteenth-century term for domestic violence, privileging the marriage relationship in its scope. "Domestic battery" is largely a legal term defining a particular type of battery. IPV is the term currently preferred by the social sciences, as it provides an umbrella for a broader category of relationships than does "domestic." I will most often prefer "domestic violence" or "domestic abuse," however, as they are terms that conjure the intimate, relational settings with which these chapters are concerned.

3. See Lenore Walker's *The Battered Woman* for more information on the theory of learned helplessness. See Dutton and Painter's "Emotional Attachments in Abusive Relationships" (1993) for more on traumatic bonding.

4. For more on the centrality of the female figure to the genre of naturalism, see Jennifer Fleissner's *Women, Compulsion, Modernity.*

5. See Steven Mintz's *Moralists and Modernizers* (early nineteenth century) and Richard Hofstadter's *The Age of Reform* (Progressive Era).

6. This strategy, though used by late nineteenth-century and turn-of-the-century feminists as a part of their campaigns for women's justice in domestic abuse situations, continued into the twentieth century just as the concerns for "crimes against women" continued. See Sheila Jeffreys, *The Spinster and Her Enemies*, 58.

7. See Pleck, *Domestic Tyranny,* 91.

8. See Bauer and Ritt, "Wife-Abuse, Late-Victorian English Feminists, and the Legacy of Frances Power Cobbe," 199, regarding punishment of robbery in England. See Lawrence Meir Friedman's *Crime and Punishment in American History* (1994), 108–13, regarding punishment of robbery in America.

9. See Pleck, chapters 3 and 5 of *Domestic Tyranny.*, as well as Jeffreys, 28–35, for those involved in both the social purity and the suffrage movements.

10. See Fleissner's *Women, Compulsion, Modernity*; Daniel Pick's *Faces of Degeneration: A European Disorder, c. 1848–1918* (1993); and June Howard's second chapter of *Form and History in American Literary Naturalism* (1985).

11. Original publication information is as follows: "first published in Zeitschrift, Bd. X., 1924." See Freud 255.

12. From Norris's "Zola as a Romantic Writer," anthologized in Pizer's *The Literary Criticism of Frank Norris.*

13. From Norris's "Zola as a Romantic Writer."

Chapter 4

1. See, in particular, Marlene Tromp's *The Private Rod: Martial Violence, Sensation, and the Law in Victorian Britain* (2000); Kate Lawson and Lynn Shakinovsky's *The Marked Body: Domestic Violence in Mid-Nineteenth-Century Literature* (2002); and Lisa Surridge's *Bleak Houses: Marital Violence in Victorian Fiction* (2005).

2. See also Meg Wesling's "The Opacity of Everyday Life," in addition to Evie Shockley's "Buried Alive" and Clare Virginia Eby's "Beyond Protest."

3. See William Scott's "Material Resistance and the Agency of the Body in Ann Petry's *The Street*" and Meg Wesling's "The Opacity of Everyday Life."

Chapter 5

1. The terms "suffragist" and "suffragette," though both used to identify supporters of women's suffrage movements in the late nineteenth and early twentieth centuries, are not interchangeable. Mayhall explains the difference as follows: "the term 'suffragist' includes all women in late nineteenth- and early twentieth-century

Britain engaged in the campaign for women's parliamentary enfranchisement, and the term 'suffragette' describes those women who had come to believe that resistance to existing government provided the only legitimate means of redressing women's exclusion from the franchise" ("Rhetorics" 488). In short, all suffragettes are suffragists, but not all suffragists are suffragettes. In order to highlight the generally accepted distinction between the two, however, I have used the term "suffragette" throughout to apply to those suffrage supporters who used militancy to fight for women's voting rights, and "suffragist" for those who did not campaign militantly.

2. *The Times*, December 14, 1905, 9.

3. Emmaline Pankhurst's daughter, Christobel Pankhurst, made explicit this threat to the lives of women who agitated for enfranchisement in a 1908 speech at St. James's Hall on the militant methods of suffragettes; she argued that "by denying [women] the vote and applying methods of coercion to us, they are placing us in danger of life and limb every day that we live" (Marcus 46).

4. See Sophie Blanch's "Taking Comedy Seriously: American Literary Humor and the British Woman Writer" (2007) and Zita Dresner's "Heterodite Humor: Alice Duer Miller and Florence Guy Seabury" (1987).

5. In distinct yet similar terms, during a speech given in New York in 1913, Emmaline Pankhurst describes the "only [explanation] [she] can think of" for men's inability to understand women's desire for the vote as akin to their own as follows: "to men women are not human beings like themselves" but rather "superhuman" or "sub-human" (Marcus 160).

6. For more on West's use of prophetic pragmatism, see his *The American Evasion of Philosophy* (chapter 6) and the evaluations of this theory contained in George Yancy's edited *Cornel West: A Critical Reader* (2001).

7. Though there are certainly differences, both connotatively and within their history of usage, between subjecthood and personhood, as well as lack of personhood and objecthood, I am using these terms interchangeably to help facilitate a bridge between a pragmatist discourse that focuses on issues of personhood and the feminist, art, and body-art discourses that focus on issues of subjecthood/objecthood.

8. For more information, see J. F. Geddes's article "Culpable Complicity" and June Purvis's article "The Prison Experiences of the Suffragettes in Edwardian Britain."

9. For a defense of the government's actions and a condemnation of the WSPU's hunger strike campaign, see C. J. Bearman's "An Army without Discipline?" (2007).

Chapter 6

1. See Esther Sánches-Pardo González's "What Phantasmagoria the Mind Is" (2004), Pamela L. Caughie's "Virginia Woolf's Double Discourse" (1989), Cécile Ladjali's "When I Write, I am Sexless" (2005), and Francette Pacteau's "The Impossible Referent" (1986), 82.

2. See the essays by Gilbert and Delgi-Esposti, as well as Nancy Cervetti's "In the Breeches, Petticoats, and Pleasures of *Orlando*" (1996) and Judy Little's "(En)gendering Laughter: Woolf's *Orlando* as contraband in the age of Joyce" (1988).

3. See Nathaniel Brown's "The 'Double Soul': Virginia Woolf, Shelley, and Androgyny" (1984), James J. Miracky's "Regen(d)erating the Modernist Novel" (2002), and Ruth Parkin-Gounelas's "The Other Side of the Looking Glass" (1993).

4. See Rachel Warburton's "Nothing Could Be Seen Whole or Read from Start to Finish" (2007).

5. See Johanna X. K. Garvey's "If We Were All Suddenly Somebody Else" and Rachel Warburton's "Nothing Could Be Seen Whole or Read from Start to Finish."

6. See Johanna X. K. Garvey's "If We Were All Suddenly Somebody Else" (1994), Nancy Cervetti's "In the Breaches, Petticoats, and Pleasures of Orlando," Judy Little's "(En)gendering Laughter," Pamela L. Caughie's "Virginia Woolf's Double Discourse," Ruth Parkin-Gounelas's "The Other Side of the Looking Glass," Sophie Mayer's "The Mirror Didn't Crack" (2008), Esther Sánchez-Pardo González's "What Phantasmagoria the Mind Is," and Ralph Samuelson's "Virginia Woolf, *Orlando*, and the Feminist Spirit" (1961).

7. See West's *The Dream Life of Balso Snell* (1931) and *Miss Lonelyhearts* (1933), as well as Barnes's *Nightwood* (1936).

8. See Mark Whalan's *Race Manhood, and Modernism in America* (2007) and Joyce R. Ladenson's "Gender Reconsiderations in Three of Sherwood Anderson's Novels" (1977).

9. See also Michael North, 191.

10. See here Howard S. Babb's 1965 article entitled "A Reading of Sherwood Anderson's 'The Man Who Became a Woman'" (1993) an early interpretation of the text that is cited and reworked by most other critics of the story.

11. See Howard S. Babb's "A Reading of Sherwood Anderson's 'The Man Who Became a Woman,'" Christopher MacGowan's "The Heritage of the Fathers in Sherwood Anderson's 'The Man Who Became a Woman'" (1993), and Lonna Malmsheimer's "Sexual Metaphor and Social Criticism in Anderson's 'The Man Who Became a Woman'" (1979).

12. For information regarding the history of melancholia in literature, see Jonathan Flatley's *Affective Mapping: Melancholia and the Politics of Modernism* (2008), chapter 1.

13. See Mitchell Breitwieser's *National Melancholy: Mourning and Opportunity in Classic American Literature* (2007).

14. See Anne Anlin Cheng's *The Melancholy of Race* (2001).

15. See Christina Wald's *Hysteria, Trauma, and Melancholia: Performative Maladies in Contemporary Anglophone Drama* (2007).

16. See David L. Eng and David Kazanjian's anthology *Loss* (2003) and Jonathan Flatley's recent *Affective Mapping: Melancholia and the Politics of Modernism* (2008).

17. See Butler's *Gender Trouble*, chapter 2, for more discussion of Freud's modified understanding of melancholia as a part of mourning.

18. See John Hood-Williams and Wendy Cealey Harrison's "Gendered Melancholy or General Melancholy?" (2000).

19. For more on the pseudonym's history and identification of Burdekin with Murray Constantine, see chapter 11 of *Rediscovering Forgotten Radicals*, edited by Angela Ingram and Daphne Patai (1993).

20. At the first level or variable, a potential future sex is suggested by the chromosomal karyotype in the zygote (the initial cell produced by sexual reproduction that will become the fetus); the majority of genetic females have a karyotype of 46, X and the majority of genetic males have a karyotype of 46, XY. At the next variable of sexual differentiation, sex-specific gonads develop in the fetus from bipotential primordial gonads. One would expect that a body with the karyotype 46, XY would automatically develop testes, but this is not necessarily the case. A gene on the Y chromosome called SRY is responsible for testes development, which in turn triggers H-Y antigen, a hormone that causes the gonads to differentiate as testes. This gene was discovered when researchers looked at the seemingly contradictory "adult women who had XY sex chromosomes and were infertile" and found that these bodies "were missing a section of the Y chromosome, precisely the section containing the SRY" gene (Hyde 108). The complexities and conflations accumulate through the subsequent variables of differentiation—those involving hormonal processes, the formation of internal reproductive organs, the formation of external reproductive organs, and, finally, the brain.

21. For example, introducing H-Y antigen into a 46, X body will result in testes development, while introducing drugs to block H-Y antigen into a 46, XY body will allow the gonads to develop into ovaries, introducing additional variables into the already complex biological system (Hyde 105–13).

22. A similar scenario in which men, believing they desire the most beautiful "woman," are actually desiring a body that is not differentiated in a fully "female" way can be found in the 2006 episode "Skin Deep" of the television show *House*.

Chapter 7

1. See Laura Cowan's "The Fine Frenzy of Artistic Vision" (1998) and Marcella Soldani's "Violated Territories" (2007) for more on the particular historical significance of this text.

2. See Bonikowski's "The Return of the Soldier Brings Death Home" (2005) and Cowen's "The Fine Frenzy of Artistic Vision."

3. Tanner Stransky for *Entertainment Weekly* similarly comments on the town's "Capraesque" quality (51).

4. Wyatt Bonikowski, in a similar vein, terms the whole novel a "deceptively simple romantic tale" (531).

5. See Marina MacKay's "The Lunacy of Men, the Idiocy of Women: Woolf, West, and War" (2003), Wyatt Bonikowski's "The Return of the Soldier Brings Death Home," and Laura Cowan's "The Fine Frenzy of Artistic Vision."

6. This is in the parlance, of course, of another modern media oddball, Adrian Monk of the USA Network's television series *Monk*.

7. Included in Robert N. Proctor and Londa Schiebinger's edited collection *Agnotology: The Making and Unmaking of Ignorance* (2008).

Works Cited

Adams-Campbell, Melissa M. *New World Courtships: Transatlantic Alternatives to Companionate Marriage*. Hanover, New Hampshire: Dartmouth College Press, 2015.
Addams, Jane. *Democracy and Social Ethics*. 1902. Urbana: University of Illinois Press, 2002.
———. *The Long Road of Woman's Memory*. 1916. Kessinger Publishing reprint. New York: MacMillan.
———. *The Social Thought of Jane Addams*. Ed. Christopher Lasch. Indianapolis: Bobbs-Merrill, 1965.
———. *The Spirit of Youth and the City Streets*. 1907. Ed. Allen F. Davis. Urbana: University of Illinois Press, 1972.
———. *Twenty Years at Hull-House*. 1910. Forward by Henry Steele Commager. New York: New American Library, 1961.
Alcott, Louisa May. *Little Women*. 1868–69. Ed. Elaine Showalter. New York: Penguin, 1989.
Ammons, Elizabeth. *Edith Wharton's Argument with America*. Athens: University of Georgia Press, 1980.
Anderson, Sherwood. *Kit Brandon*. New York: C. Scribner's Sons, 1936.
———. "The Man Who Became a Woman." In *Horses and Men: Tales, Long and Short, from Our American Life*. New York: B.W. Huebsch, 1923. 185–228.
Atkinson, Diane. *The Suffragettes in Pictures*. Forward by Glenda Jackson. Gloucestershire: Sutton, 1996.
Austen, Jane. *Pride and Prejudice*. 1813. New York: Bantam, 2003.
Babb, Howard S. "A Reading of Sherwood Anderson's 'The Man Who Became a Woman.'" *PMLA* 80.4 (Sept. 1965): 432–35.
Baccolini, Raffaella. "Gender and Genre in the Feminist Critical Dystopias of Katharine Burdekin, Margaret Atwood, and Octavia Butler." In *Future Females, the Next Generation: New Voices and Velocities in Feminist Science Fiction Criticism*. Ed. Marleen S. Barr. Lanham: Rowman and Littlefield, 2000. 13–34.

Barnes, Djuna. *Nightwood*. 1936. London: Faber and Faber, 1963.
Barvosa-Carter, Edwina. "Strange Tempest: Agency, Poststructuralism, and the Shape of Feminist Politics to Come." In *Butler Matters: Judith Butler's Impact on Feminist and Queer Studies*. Aldershot, Hampshire, England: Ashgate, 2005. 175–89.
Bauer, Carol, and Lawrence Ritt. "'A Husband Is a Beating Animal': Frances Power Cobbe Confronts the Wife-Abuse Problem in Victorian England." *International Journal of Women's Studies*. Ed. Sherri Clarkson 6.2 (March/April 1983): 99–118.
———. "Wife-Abuse, Late-Victorian English Feminists, and the Legacy of Frances Power Cobbe." *International Journal of Women's Studies*. Ed. Sherri Clarkson 6.2 (May/June 1983): 195–207.
Bearman, C. J. "An Army without Discipline? Suffragette Militancy and the Budget Crisis of 1909." *The Historical Journal* 50.4 (2007): 861–89.
Bell, Michael Davitt. *The Problem of American Realism: Studies in the Cultural History of a Literary Idea*. Chicago: University of Chicago Press, 1993.
Bell, Millicent. "Isabel Archer and the Affronting of Plot." In *The Portrait of a Lady*. Ed. Michael Gorra. Norton Critical Edition. New York: W. W. Norton, 2018. 585–604.
Berlant, Lauren. *Cruel Optimism*. Duke University Press, 2011.
———. *The Female Complaint: The Unfinished Business of Sentimentality in American Culture*. Durham: Duke University Press, 2008.
Bernstein, Robin. *Racial Innocence: Performing American Childhood from Slavery to Civil Rights*. New York: New York University Press, 2011.
Bernstein, Susan David. "Dirty Reading: Sensation Fiction, Women, and Primitivism." *Criticism* 36.2 (Spring 1994): 213–41.
Bersani, Leo. *A Future for Astyanax; Character and Desire in Literature*. Boston: Little, Brown, 1976.
———. "Is the Rectum a Grave?" *October* 23 (Winter 1987): 197–222.
Blackwell, Henry Browne. "Crimes of a Single Day." *The Woman's Journal*. January 29, 1876. 34.
———. "Legal Redress for Assaulted Wives." *The Woman's Journal*. January 18, 1879. 20.
Blair, Emily. *Virginia Woolf and the Nineteenth-Century Domestic Novel*. Albany: SUNY Press, 2007.
Blanch, Sophie. "Taking Comedy Seriously: American Literary Humor and the British Woman Writer." *Studies in American Humor* 3.15 (January 2007): 5–17.
Boehm, Beth A. "Fact, Fiction, and Metafiction: Blurred Gen(d)res in *Orlando* and *A Room of One's Own*." *Journal of Narrative Technique* 22.3 (Fall 1992): 191–204.
Bonikowski, Wyatt. "The Return of the Soldier Brings Death Home." *MFS: Modern Fiction Studies* 51.3 (Fall 2005): 513–35.

Bonner, Patricia. "Hughes's 'Beale Street Love.'" *Explicator* 57.2 (Winter 1999): 108–10.
Bourke, Angela. *The Burning of Bridget Cleary: A True Story.* New York: Penguin Books, 1999.
Brandt, Maria F. "'For His Own Satisfaction': Eliminating the New Woman Figure in *McTeague*." *American Transcendental Quarterly* 18.1 (March 2004): 5–23.
Breitwieser, Mitchell. *National Melancholy: Mourning and Opportunity in Classic American Literature.* Stanford: Stanford University Press, 2007.
Brooks, Gwendolyn. *Maud Martha.* 1953. Chicago: Third World, 1993.
Brown, Nathaniel. "The 'Double Soul': Virginia Woolf, Shelley, and Androgyny." *Keats-Shelley Journal: Keats, Shelley, Byron, Hunt, and Their Circles* 33 (1984): 182–204.
Bryan, Mary Lynn McCree and Allen F. Davis, eds. *100 Years at Hull-House.* Bloomington: Indiana University Press, 1990.
Budick, Sanford. *Languages of the Unsayable: The Play of Negativity in Literature and Literary Theory.* New York: Columbia University Press, 1989.
Burdekin, Katharine. *The End of This Day's Business.* New York: Feminist Press at the City University of New York, 1989.
———. *Proud Man.* 1934. Forward and Afterward Daphne Patai. New York: Feminist, 1993.
———. *Swastika Night.* 1937. Old Westbury, New York: Feminist, 1985.
Butler, Judith. *Bodies That Matter: On the Discursive Limits of "Sex."* New York: Routledge, 1993.
———. *Excitable Speech: A Politics of the Performative.* New York: Routledge, 1997.
———. *Gender Trouble: Feminism and the Subversion of Identity.* 1990. New York: Routledge, 1999.
———. "Melancholy Gender—Refused Identification." *Psychoanalytic Dialogues* 5 (1995): 165–80. *PEP: Psychoanalytic Electronic Publishing.* January 13, 2010. <http://www.pep-web.org/document.php?id=PD.005.0165A>.
———. *Undoing Gender.* New York: Routledge, 2004.
Byrd, Jodi A. "The Stories We Tell: American Indian Women's Writing and the Persistence of Tradition." In *The Cambridge History of American Women's Literature.* Ed. Dale M. Bauer. Cambridge: Cambridge University Press, 2012. 11–29.
Calhoun, Craig, ed. *Sociology in America: A History.* Chicago: University of Chicago Press, 2007.
Carson, Mina. *Settlement Folk: Social Thought and the American Settlement Movement, 1885–1930.* Chicago: University of Chicago Press, 1990.
Carstens, Lisa. "The Science of Sex and the Art of Self-Materializing in Orlando." In *Virginia Woolf out of Bounds: Selected Papers from the Tenth Annual Conference on Virginia Woolf.* Ed. Jessica Berman and Jane Goldman. New York: Pace University Press, 2001. 39–46.

Cather, Willa. *My Ántonia*. 1918. Oxford: Oxford University Press, 2006.
Caughie, Pamela L. "Virginia Woolf's Double Discourse." In *Discontented Discourses: Feminism/Textual Intervention/Psychoanalysis*. Ed. Marleen S. Barr and Richard Feldstein. Urbana: University of Illinois Press, 1989. 41–53.
Cervetti, Nancy. "In the Breeches, Petticoats, and Pleasures of Orlando." *Journal of Modern Literature* 20.2 (Winter 1996): 165–75.
Chapman, Mary. "Are Women People?' Alice Duer Miller's Poetry and Politics." *American Literary History* (2006): 59–85.
Cheng, Anne Anlin. *The Melancholy of Race*. Oxford: Oxford University Press, 2000.
Chi, Wei-jan. "The Power of the Imagination in 'The Man Who Became a Woman.'" *Fu Jen Studies: Literature and Linguistics* 21 (1988): 61–72.
Clark, Ann. "The Quest for Certainty in Feminist Thought." *Hypatia* 8.3 (1993): 84–93.
Clark, Suzanne. *Sentimental Modernism: Women Writers and the Revolution of the World*. Bloomington: Indiana University Press, 1991.
Cobbe, Frances Power. "Criminals, Idiots, Women, and Minors." *Victorian Women Writers Project Library*. Ed. Perry Willett. Transcribed copy from Pitt Theology Library, Emory University. Library Electronic Text Resource Service (LETRS), Indiana University Bloomington. August 23, 2009. <http://www.indiana.edu/~letrs/vwwp/cobbe/criminal.html>.
———. "Wife-Torture in England." *The Contemporary Review* 32 (April–July 1878): 55–87.
Comprone, Raphael. *Poetry, Desire, and Fantasy in the Harlem Renaissance*. Lanham, MD: University Press of America, 2006.
Conway, Jill. "Women Reformers and American Culture, 1870–1930." *Journal of Social History* 5.1 (1971): 164–77.
Cowan, Laura. "The Fine Frenzy of Artistic Vision: Rebecca West's *The Return of the Soldier* as a Feminist Analysis of World War I." *The Centennial Review* 42.1 (1998): 285–308.
"Crimes against Women." *The Woman's Journal*. December 25, 1875. 413.
Crow, Charles. "Gnawing the File: Recent Trends in *McTeague* Scholarship." *Frank Norris Studies* 13 (Spring 1992): 1–5.
Crowley, John W. "The Unmastered Streak: Feminist Themes in Wharton's *Summer*." *American Literary Realism* 15.1 (1982): 86–96.
Cutler, Edward S. *Recovering the New: Transatlantic Roots of Modernism*. Hanover: University Press of New Hampshire, 2003.
Davis, Allen F., and Mary Lynn McCree, eds. *Eighty Years at Hull-House*. Chicago: Quadrangle Books, 1969.
Davis, Amanda J. "Shatterings: Violent Disruptions of Homeplace in *Jubilee* and *The Street*." *MELUS* 30.4 (Winter 2005): 25–51.
Davis, Angela. *Blues Legacies and Black Feminism: Gertrude "Ma" Rainey, Bessie Smith, and Billie Holiday*. New York: Pantheon Books, 1998.

Dawson, Melanie V., and Meredith L. Goldsmith, eds. *American Literary History and the Turn toward Modernity*. Gainsville: University of Florida Press, 2018.
Deegan, Mary Jo. *Jane Addams and the Men of the Chicago School, 1892–1918*. New Brunswick: Transaction Books, 1988.
DeKoven, Marianne. "'Excellent Not a Hull House': Gertrude Stein, Jane Addams, and Feminist-Modernist Political Culture." In *Rereading Modernism: New Directions in Feminist Criticism*. Ed. and Intro. Lisa Rado. New York: Garland, 1994. 321–50.
Delgi-Esposti, Cristina. "Sally Potter's *Orlando* and the Neo-Baroque Scopic Regime." *Cinema Journal* 36.1 (Fall 1996): 75–93.
del Mar, David Peterson. *What Trouble I Have Seen: A History of Violence against Wives*. Cambridge, MA: Harvard University Press, 1996.
Deutsch, Helene. "The Significance of Masochism in the Mental Life of Women." *International Journal of Psycho-Analysis* 11 (1930): 48–60.
Dewey, John. *Liberalism and Social Action*. 1935. Amherst: Prometheus Books, 2000.
———. *The Philosophy of John Dewey: The Structure of Experience*. Ed. and Intro. John J. McDermott. Vol. 1. New York: G. P. Putnam's Sons, 1973.
Dewey, John, and Arthur Bentley. *Knowing and the Known*. Boston: Beacon, 1949.
Donovan, Josephine. *New England Local Color Literature: A Woman's Tradition*. New York: Frederick Ungar, 1983.
Drake, Kimberly. "Women on the Go: Blues, Conjure, and Other Alternatives to Domesticity in Ann Petry's *The Street* and *The Narrows*." *The Arizona Quarterly* 54.1 (March 1998): 65–95.
Dresner, Zita. "Heterodite Humor: Alice Duer Miller and Florence Guy Seabury." *Journal of American Culture* 10.3 (Fall 1987): 33–38.
Dreyer, Randolph. "Lars and the Real Girl (review)." *Perspectives in Psychiatric Care* 44.4 (October 2008): 301–3.
Duffy, William. "Remembering Is the Remedy: Jane Addams's Response to Conflicted Discourse." *Rhetoric Review* 30.2 (2001): 135–52.
Dutton, D. G., and S. Painter. "Emotional Attachments in Abusive Relationships: A Test of Traumatic Bonding Theory." *Violence and Victims* 8.2 (1993): 105–20.
Eby, Clare Virginia. "Beyond Protest: *The Street* as Humanitarian Narrative." *MELUS* 33.1 (Spring 2008): 33–53.
Eckel, Leslie Elizabeth. *Atlantic Citizens: Nineteenth Century American Writers at Work in the World*. Edinburgh: Edinburgh University Press, 2013.
Edelman, Lee. *No Future: Queer Theory and the Death Drive*. Durham: Duke University Press, 2004.
Edmundson, Melissa. "Complicating Kitty: A Textual Variant in Rebecca West's *The Return of The Soldier*." *Notes and Queries* 55.4 (December 2008): 492–93.
Eliot, George. *Middlemarch: A Study of Provincial Life*. 1871–72. New York: Signet Classic, 1964.

Ellis, Havelock. *Studies in the Psychology of Sex: Analysis of the Sexual Impulse, Love and Pain, the Sexual Impulse in Women.* 1903. Philadelphia: F. A. Davis, 1908.

Elshtain, Jean Bethke. "A Return to Hull House: Reflections on Jane Addams." *Cross Currents: A Yearbook of Central European Culture* 38.3 (1988): 257–67.

Eng, David L., and David Kazanjian, eds. *Loss: The Politics of Mourning.* Berkeley: University of California Press, 2003.

"The English Militants." *New York Times.* July 6, 1914. ProQuest Historical Newspapers *The New York Times (1851–2003).* Indiana University Libraries. Bloomington, Indiana. 16 June 2009. <http://proquest.umi.com>.

Epstein-Corbin, Sean. "Pragmatism, Feminism, and the Sentimental Subject." *Transactions of the Charles S. Peirce Society* 50.2 (2014): 220–45.

Ernest, John. "Nineteenth-Century African American Women Writers." *The Cambridge History of American Women's Literature.* Ed. Dale M. Bauer. Cambridge: Cambridge University Press, 2012.273–92.

Felski, Rita. *The Gender of Modernity.* Cambridge, MA: Harvard University Press, 1995.

———, ed. *Rethinking Tragedy.* Baltimore: The John Hopkins University Press, 2008.

Fessenbecker, Patrick. "Freedom, Self-Obligation, and Selfhood in Henry James." *Nineteenth Century Literature* 66.1 (June 2011): 69–95.

Fischer, Marilyn. "Trojan Women and Devil Baby Tales: Addams on Domestic Violence." *Feminist Interpretations of Jane Addams.* Ed. Maurice Hamington. University Park: The Pennsylvania State University Press, 2010. 81–105.

Fitzgerald, F. Scott. *The Great Gatsby.* 1923. New York: Chelsea House, 2006.

Flatley, Jonathan. *Affective Mapping: Melancholia and the Politics of Modernism.* Cambridge: Harvard University Press, 2008.

Fleissner, Jennifer L. *Women, Compulsion, Modernity: The Moment of American Naturalism.* Chicago: University of Chicago Press, 2004.

"Forcibly Feeding Mary Richardson. *New York Times.* April 3, 1914: 4. ProQuest Historical Newspapers *The New York Times (1851–2003).* Indiana University Libraries. Bloomington, Indiana. February 13, 2006. <http://proquest.umi.com>.

Ford, Ford Madox. *The Good Soldier: A Tale of Passion.* 1915. London: Folio Society, 2008.

Forster, E. M. *A Passage to India.* 1924. San Diego: Harcourt Brace, 1952.

François, Anne-Lise. *Open Secrets: The Literature of Uncounted Experience.* Stanford: Stanford University Press, 2008.

Frazier, Valerie. "Domestic Epic Warfare in *Maud Martha.*" *African American Review* 39.1–2 (Spring–Summer 2005): 133–41.

Freud, Sigmund. "The Economic Problem in Masochism." 1924. *Sigmund Freud, M.D., LL. D. Collected Papers.* Vol 2. Ed. Ernest Jones, M.D. Trans. Joan Riviere. 6th edition. London: Hogarth, 1949. 255–68.

———. *The Ego and the Id.* 1923. Trans. by Joan Riviere. Revised and Edited by James Strachey. New York: W.W. Norton, 1962.

———. "Mourning and Melancholia." In *The Freud Reader*. Ed. Peter Gay. New York: Norton, 1989. 584–89.

Fricker, Miranda. *Epistemic Injustice: Power and the Ethics of Knowing*. Oxford: Oxford University Press, 2007.

Friedman, Lawrence Meir. *Crime and Punishment in American History*. New York: Basic Books, 1994.

Frye, Marilyn. *The Politics of Reality: Essays in Feminist Theory*. Trumansburg, NY: Crossing, 1983.

Gallagher, Catherine. *Nobody's Story: The Vanishing Acts of Women Writers in the Marketplace, 1670–1820*. Berkeley, University of California Press, 1994.

Gamboni, Dario. *The Destruction of Art: Iconoclasm and Vandalism since the French Revolution*. New Haven: Yale University Press, 1997.

Garvey, Johanna X. K. "'If We Were All Suddenly Somebody Else': *Orlando* as the New *Ulysses*." *Women's Studies* 23 (1994): 1–17.

Gates, Jr., Henry Louis, and K. A. Appiah, eds. *Zora Neale Hurston: Critical Perspectives Past and Present*. New York: Amistad, 1993.

Geddes, J. F. "Culpable Complicity: The Medical Profession and the Forcible Feeding of Suffragettes, 1909–1914." *Women's History Review* 17.1 (February 2008): 79–94.

Gerber, Nancy. *Portrait of the Mother-Artist: Class and Creativity in Contemporary American Fiction*. Forward by Andrea O'Reilly. Lanham: Lexington, 2003. 23–37.

Gilbert, Sandra M. "Costumes of the Mind: Transvestism as Metaphor in Modern Literature." In *Writing and Sexual Difference*. Ed. Elizabeth Abel. Chicago: University of Chicago Press, 1982. 193–219.

Gilbert, Sandra M., and Susan Gubar. *The Madwoman in the Attic: The Woman Writer and the Nineteenth-Century Literary Imagination*. 2nd edition. New Haven: Yale University Press, 2000.

———. *No Man's Land: The Place of the Woman Writer in the Twentieth Century*. Vol 2: *Sexchanges*. New Haven: Yale University Press, 1989.

———. "Sexchanges." *College English* 50.7 (Nov. 1988): 768–85.

Gilbey, Ryan. "Meet the Girlfriend." *New Statesman*. March 24, 2008, 43.

Gilmore, Leigh. *Tainted Witness: Why We Doubt What Women Say about Their Lives*. New York: Columbia University Press, 2017.

Glaspell, Susan. "Trifles." 1916. In *Plays*. Ed. C. W. E. Bigsby. Cambridge: Cambridge University Press, 1987. 34–45.

Glass, Dee Dee. *"All My Fault": Why Women Don't Leave Abusive Men*. London: Virago, 1995.

González, Esther Sánchez-Pardo. "'What Phantasmagoria the Mind Is': Reading Virginia Woolf's Parody of Gender." *ATLANTIS* 26.2 (December 2004): 75–86.

Grafton, Kathy. "Degradation and Forbidden Love in Edith Wharton's *Summer*." *Twentieth Century Literature: A Scholarly and Critical Journal* 41.4 (Winter 1995): 350–66.

Griffing, Sascha, Deborah Fish Ragin, Robert E. Sage, Lorraine Madry, Lewis E. Bingham, and Beny J. Primm. "Domestic Violence Survivors' Self-Identified Reasons for Returning to Abusive Relationships." *Journal of Interpersonal Violence* 17.3 (March 2002): 306–19.

Hadley, Tessa. "'Just You Wait!': Reflections on the Last Chapters of *The Portrait of a Lady*." In *The Portrait of a Lady*. Ed. Michael Gorra. Norton Critical Edition. New York: W. W. Norton, 2018. 613–27.

Hager, Christopher, and Cody Marrs. "Against 1865: Reperiodizing the Nineteenth Century." *The Journal of Nineteenth-Century Americanists* 1.2 (Fall 2013): 259–84.

Hall, Susan L. "The Death of Love: Sexuality, Secrets, and Settings in Wharton's *Summer*." *Edith Wharton Review* 21.2 (2005): 10–17.

Halpern, Faye. *Sentimental Readers: The Rise, Fall, and Revival of a Disparaged Rhetoric*. Iowa City: University of Iowa Press, 2013.

Hamington, Maurice. "Jane Addams." *The Feminist eZine—Philosophy*. The Lilith Gallery Network. June 7, 2006: 14 pages. June 4, 2008. <http://www.feministezine.com/feminist/philosophy/Jane-Addams.html>.

———. *The Social Philosophy of Jane Addams*. Champaign: University of Illinois Press, 2009.

Haskell, Thomas L. *The Emergence of Professional Social Science: The American Social Science Association and the Nineteenth-Century Crisis of Authority*. Urbana: University of Illinois Press, 1977.

Hawthorne, Nathaniel. "The Birthmark." 1843. In *Great Short Works*. Ed. Frederick C. Crews. New York: Harper and Row, 1967.

Hecht, Deborah. "Representing Lawyers: Edith Wharton's Portrayal of Lawyers and Lawyering in *The Touchstone* and *Summer*. In *Literature and Law*. Ed. Michael J. Meyer. Amsterdam: Editions Rodopi B.V., 2004. 83–97.

Hekman, Susan J. *Gender and Knowledge: Elements of a Postmodern Feminism*. Cambridge: Polity, 1992.

Henderson, Carol E. "The 'Walking Wounded': Rethinking Black Women's Identity in Ann Petry's *The Street*." *MFS Modern Fiction Studies* 46.4 (Winter 2000): 849–67.

Herring, Scott. *Queering the Underworld: Slumming, Literature, and the Undoing of Lesbian and Gay History*. Chicago: University of Chicago Press, 2007.

Hofstadter, Richard. *The Age of Reform: From Bryan to F. D. R.* New York: Vintage Books, 1955.

Hood-Williams, John, and Wendy Cealey Harrison. "Gendered Melancholy or General Melancholy? Homosexual Attachments in the Formation of Gender." *New Formations* 41 (2000): 109–26.

Horney, Karen. "The Problem of Feminine Masochism." 1935. In *Psychoanalysis and Women*. Ed. Jean Baker-Miller, M.D. Middlesex, England: Penguin Books, 1973. 21–38.

Hotaling, Debra. "The Body of Work: Illness as Narrative Strategy in Jane Addams's *Twenty Years at Hull-House*." *Auto/Biography Studies* 6.1 (Spring 1991): 33–39.
Howard, June. *Form and History in American Literary Naturalism.* Chapel Hill: University of North Carolina Press, 1985.
Howlett, Caroline J. "Writing on the Body? Representation and Resistance in British Suffragette Accounts of Forcible Feeding." In *Bodies of Writing, Bodies in Performance.* Ed. Thomas Foster, Carol Siegel, and Ellen E. Berry. New York: New York University Press, 1996. 3–41.
Hughes, Langston. "Beale Street Love." In *Fine Clothes to the Jew.* 1927. New York: Alfred A. Knopf, 1929. 57.
Hummel, William E. "My 'Dull-Witted Enemy': Symbolic Violence and Abject Maleness in Edith Wharton's *Summer*." *Studies in American Fiction* 24.2 (1996): 215–36.
Hurston, Zora Neale. *Seraph on the Suwanee.* 1948. New York: Harper Perennial, 1991.
———. *Their Eyes Were Watching God.* 1937. New York: Harper Perennial Modern Classics, 1994.
Hyde, J. S., and J. DeLamater. *Understanding Human Sexuality.* New York: McGraw-Hill, 2003.
Hypatia: Special Issue on Pragmatism and Feminism 8.2 (1993).
Iker, Karen. " 'The Bit of Art, That Could Not Come from Any Other': Gwendolyn Brooks's *Maud Martha* and the *Bildungsroman* Revised." *In Process: A Graduate Student Journal of African-American and African Diasporan Literature and Culture* 1 (Fall 1996): 91–111.
Imre, Amikó. "Twin Pleasure of Feminism: *Orlando* Meets My Twentieth Century." *Camera Obscura* 54 or 18.3 (2003): 177–210.
Ingram, Angela, and Daphne Patai, eds. *Rediscovering Forgotten Radicals: British Women Writers, 1889–1939.* Chapel Hill: University of North Carolina Press, 1993.
Jackson, Shannon. *Lines of Activity: Performance, Historiography, Hull-House Domesticity.* Ann Arbor: University of Michigan Press, 2000.
Jaggar, Alison M., and Susan Bordo, eds. *Gender/Body/Knowledge: Feminist Reconstructions of Being and Knowing.* Rutgers: Rutgers University Press, 1989.
James, Henry. *Daisy Miller: A Study.* 1878. Intro. David Lodge. London: Penguin Books, 2007.
———. *The Portrait of a Lady.* 1881. Intro. Fred B. Millett. New York: Random House, 1951.
James, William. "Address at the Emerson Centenary in Concord." 1903. February 14, 2008. *Arisbe: The Pierce Gateway.* Joseph Randsell, website architect and coordinator. January 19, 2009. <http://www.cspeirce.com/menu/library/aboutcsp/james/1903em.htm>.
———. *Pragmatism: A New Name for Some Old Ways of Thinking.* 1907. Filiquarian, 2007.

Jeffreys, Sheila. *The Spinster and Her Enemies: Feminism and Sexuality 1880–1930.* London: Pandora, 1985.
Jones, Amelia. *Body Art/ Performing the Subject.* Minneapolis: University of Minnesota Press, 1998.
Jones, Ann. *Next Time, She'll Be Dead: Battering and How to Stop It.* Boston: Beacon, 1994.
Jorgensen-Earp, Cheryl R., ed. *Speeches and Trials of the Militant Suffragettes: The Women's Social and Political Union, 1903–1918.* Madison: Fairleigh Dickinson University Press, 1999.
Joslin, Katherine. "'Experimental Moralist': Jane Addams as Storyteller." *Excavatio: Nouvelle Revue Emile Zola et le Naturalisme International* 10 (1997): 1–8.
———. *Jane Addams, a Writer's Life.* Urbana: University of Illinois Press, 2004.
Kadlec, David. *Mosaic Modernism: Anarchism, Pragmatism, Culture.* Baltimore: John Hopkins University Press, 2000.
Kane, Leslie. *The Language of Silence: On the Unspoken and the Unspeakable in Modern Drama.* Rutherford, NJ: Farleigh Dickinson University Press, 1984.
Kassanoff, Jennie A. *Edith Wharton and the Politics of Race.* Cambridge: Cambridge University Press, 2004.
Kean, Hilda. "Some Problems of Constructing and Reconstructing a Suffragette's Life: Mary Richardson, Suffragette, Socialist, and Fascist." *Women's History Review* 7.4 (1998): 475–93.
Keith, Heather E. "Feminism and Pragmatism: George Herbert Mead's Ethics of Care." *Transactions of the C. S. Pierce Society* 35.3 (Spring 1999): 328–44.
Keyes, John. "'Inarticulate Expressions of Genuine Suffering?' A Reply to the Correspondence in *Miss Lonelyhearts.*" *University of Windsor Review* 20.1 (1987): 11–25.
Knight, Louise W. "Jane Addams and the Settlement House Movement." In *Against the Tide: Women Reformers in American Society.* Ed. Paul A. Cimbala and Randall M. Miller. Westport, CT: Praeger, 1997: 85–98.
Konzett, Delia Caparoso. "'Getting in Touch with the True South': Pet Negroes, White Crackers, and Racial Staging in Zora Neale Hurston's *Seraph on the Suwanee.*" In *White Women in Racialized Spaces: Imaginative Transformation and Ethical Action in Literature.* Ed. Samina Najmi and Rajini Srikanth. Albany: State University of New York Press, 2001. 131–46.
Krafft-Ebbing, Richard von. *Psychopathia Sexualis: with Especial Reference to Contrary Sexual Instinct: A Clinical-Forensic Study.* Ed. and Intro Brian King. 12th edition. Burbank, CA: Bloat, 1999.
de Laclos, Choderlos. *Les Liaisons Dangereuses.* 1782. Trans. by P. W. K. Stone. London: Penguin, 1961.
Ladenson, Joyce R. "Gender Reconsiderations in Three of Sherwood Anderson's Novels." *Massachusetts Studies in English* 6.1–2 (1977): 90–102.

Ladjali, Cécile. "When I Write, I Am Sexless." *Diogenes*. 208 (2005): 82–93.
Lagemann, Ellen Condliffe. "The Plural Worlds of Educational Research." *History of Education Quarterly* 29.2 (Summer 1989): 184–219.
Lamm, Kimberley. "A Future for Isabel Archer: Jamesian Feminism, Leo Bersani, and Aesthetic Subjectivity." *The Henry James Review* 32 (2011): 249–58.
Lars and the Real Girl. Dir. Craig Gillespie. Writ. Nancy Oliver. Perf. Ryan Gosling, Emily Mortimer, Paul Schneider, Kelli Garner, Patricia Clarkson. Metro-Goldwyn-Mayer, 2007.
Larsen, Nella. *Passing*. 1929. New York: Modern Library, 2002.
Lattin, Patricia H., and Vernon E. Lattin. "Dual Vision in Gwendolyn Brooks's *Maud Martha*." *Critique* 25.4 (1984): 180–89.
Laurence, Patricia Ondek. *The Reading of Silence: Virginia Woolf in the English Tradition*. Stanford: Stanford University Press, 1991.
Lawless, Elaine J. *Women Escaping Violence: Empowerment through Narrative*. Columbia: University of Missouri Press, 2001.
Lawrence, D. H. *Women in Love*. 1920. Ed. David Farmer, Lindeth Vasey and John Worthen. Intro. and Notes Mark Kinkead-Weekes. London: Penguin Books, 2000.
Lawson, Kate, and Lynn Shakinovsky. *The Marked Body: Domestic Violence in Mid-Nineteenth-Century Literature*. Albany: State University of New York Press, 2002.
Leach, William. *True Love and Perfect Union: The Feminist Reform of Sex and Society*. New York: Basic Books, 1980.
Levin, Jonathan. *The Poetics of Transition: Emerson, Pragmatism, and American Literary Modernism*. Durham, Duke University Press, 1999.
Lewis, R. W. B. *Edith Wharton: A Biography*. New York: Fromm International, 1985.
Lewis, Wyndham. *Tarr*. 1918. Oxford: Oxford University Press, 2010.
Lissak, Rivka Shpak. *Pluralism and Progressives: Hull House and the New Immigrants, 1890–1919*. Chicago: University of Chicago Press, 1989.
Little, Judy. "(En)gendering Laughter: Woolf's *Orlando* as Contraband in the Age of Joyce." *Women's Studies* 15 (1988): 179–91.
Livingston, James. *Pragmatism, Feminism, and Democracy: Rethinking the Politics of American History*. New York: Routledge, 2001.
Lueck, Beth L., Sirpa Salenius, and Nancy Lusignan Schultz, eds. *Transatlantic Conversations: Nineteenth-Century American Women's Encounters with Italy and the Atlantic World*. Hanover: University Press of New Hampshire, 2016.
Luria, Salvador. Untitled Talk. National Symposium on Genetics and the Law. Copley Plaza Hotel, Boston. May 20, 1975: 6 pages printout. *The Salvador E. Luria Papers*. February 28, 2008. <http://profiles.nlm.nih.gov/QL/B/B/H/V/>.
Lyon, Janet. "Women Demonstrating Modernism." *Discourse* 17.2 (1994–1995 Winter): 6–25.
Lytton, Constance. *Prisons and Prisoners*. 1914. Ed. Jason Haslam. Peterborough, Ontario: Broadview Editions, 2008.

MacGowan, Christopher. "The Heritage of the Fathers in Sherwood Anderson's 'The Man Who Became a Woman.'" *Journal of the Short Story in English* 21 (1993): 29–37.

MacKay, Marina. "The Lunacy of Men, the Idiocy of Women: Woolf, West, and War." *National Women's Studies Association (NWSA) Journal* 15.3 (Fall 2003): 124–44.

Magee, Michael. *Emancipating Pragmatism: Emerson, Jazz, and Experimental Writing.* Tuscaloosa: University of Alabama Press, 2004.

Malmsheimer, Lonna M. "Sexual Metaphor and Social Criticism in Anderson's 'The Man Who Became a Woman.'" *Studies in American Fiction* 7.1 (Spring 1979): 17–26.

Mansfield, Katherine. "The Woman at the Store." 1912. In *Katherine Mansfield's Selected Stories.* New York: W. W. Norton, 2006. 27–36.

Marcus, Jane, ed. *Suffrage and the Pankhursts.* London: Routledge & Kegan Paul, 1987.

May, Brian. *The Modernist as Pragmatist: E. M. Forster and the Fate of Liberalism.* Columbia: University of Missouri Press, 1997.

Mayer, Sophie. "The Mirror Didn't Crack: Costume Drama and Gothic Horror in Sally Potter's *Orlando*." *Literature/Film Quarterly*. 36.1 (2008): 39–44.

Mayhall, Laura E. Nym. "Creating the 'Suffragette Spirit'; British Feminism and the Historical Imagination." *Women's History Review* 4.3 (1995): 319–44.

———. "Household and Market in Suffragette Discourse, 1903–14." *The European Legacy* 6.2 (2001): 189–99.

———. "The Rhetorics of Slavery and Citizenship: Suffragist Discourse and Canonical Texts in Britain, 1880–1914." *Gender and History* 13.3 (November 2001): 481–97.

McClintock, Anne. *Imperial Leather: Race, Gender, and Sexuality in the Colonial Contest.* New York: Routledge, 1995.

McCullers, Carson. *The Heart Is a Lonely Hunter.* 1940. Boston: Houghton Mifflin, 2000.

McKenna, Erin. *The Task of Utopia: A Pragmatist and Feminist Perspective.* Lanham, MD: Rowman and Littlefield, 2001.

Michaels, Walter Benn. *The Gold Standard and the Logic of Naturalism: American Literature at the Turn of the Century.* Berkeley: University of California Press, 1987.

"Militant Hacks Rokeby Venus." *New York Times.* March 11, 1914: 4. *ProQuest Historical Newspapers The New York Times (1851–2003).* Indiana University Libraries. Bloomington, Indiana. 13 February 2006. <http://proquest.umi.com>.

Miller, Alice Duer. *Are Women People? A Book of Rhymes for Suffrage Times.* 1915. Kessinger Publishing Reprint.

Miller, Marjorie C. "Feminism and Pragmatism." *Monist* 75.4 (Oct 1992): 445–57.

Mintz, Stephen. *Moralists and Modernizers: America's pre–Civil War Reformers.* Baltimore: Johns Hopkins University Press, 1995.

Miracky, James J. "Regen(d)erating the Modernist Novel: Literary Realism vs. the Language of the Body in D. H. Lawrence and Virginia Woolf." *D. H. Lawrence Review* 31.1 (2002): 29–50.

"Miss Mary Richardson." *Times*. November 8, 1961: 15D. *The Times Digital Archive 1785–1985* Indiana University Libraries. Bloomington, Indiana. February 9, 2006. <http://web6.infotrac.galegroupcom>.

Monk. Created by Andy Breckman. Perf. Tony Shalhoub, Ted Levine. USA Network. 2002–2009.

Moring, Mark. "Inflatable Love. Seriously." *Christianity Today* 52.4 (April 2006): 72.

Moylan, Tom. *Demand the Impossible: Science Fiction and the Utopian Imagination*. New York: Methuen, 1986.

"Mrs. Pankhurst in Jail." *New York Times*. March 11, 1914: 4. *ProQuest Historical Newspapers The New York Times (1851–2003)*. Indiana University Libraries. Bloomington, Indiana. February 13, 2006. <http://proquest.umi.com>.

"Mrs. Wharton's Story of New England." *New York Times*. July 8, 1917. 58. *ProQuest Historical Newspapers The New York Times (1851–2003)*. Indiana University Libraries. Bloomington, Indiana 5 June 2008. <http://proquest.umi.com>.

"National Gallery Outrage." *Times*. March 11, 191 4: 9G. *The Times Digital Archive 1785–1985*. Indiana University Libraries. Bloomington, Indiana. February 9, 2006. <http://web6.infotrac.galegroupcom>.

Nead, Lynda. *The Female Nude: Art, Obscenity, and Sexuality*. New York: Routledge, 1992.

Nelson, Claudia. *Precocious Children and Childish Adults: Age Inversion in Victorian Literature*. Baltimore: The John Hopkins University Press, 2012.

Ngai, Sianne. *Ugly Feelings*. Cambridge, MA: Harvard University Press, 2005.

Niemtzow, Annette. "Marriage and the New Woman in *The Portrait of a Lady*." *American Literature* 47.3 (November 1975): 377–95.

Norris, Frank. "Fantaisie Printaniere." Project Gutenburg Consortia Center's World Public Library Collection. (1896). November 21, 2008. <http://www.netlibrary.net/eBooks/WorldeBookeLibrary.com/fantaisie.htm>.

———. *McTeague: A Story of San Francisco*. 1899. Intro. Alfred Kazin. New York: Modern Library, 2002.

———. *McTeague: A Story of San Francisco. An Authoritative Text, Background and Sources, Criticism*. Ed. Donald Pizer. New York: W. W. Norton, 1977.

North, Michael. *Reading 1922: A Return to the Scene of the Modern*. Oxford: Oxford University Press, 1999.

O'Malley, Seamus. "*The Return of the Soldier* and *Parade's End*: Ford's Reworking of West's Pastoral." *Ford Madox Ford's Literary Contacts* (2007): 155–64.

Ostman, Heather. "Patterning Daughterhood, Anticipating Adulthood: Constructing the Self in the Autobiographies of Jane Addams and Emma Goldman." *Pennsylvania English* 27.1 (Fall 2004–Spring 2005): 60–78.

Otten, Thomas J. "Slashing Henry James (On Painting and Political Economy, circa 1900)." *The Yale Journal of Criticism* 13.2 (2000): 293–320.

Pacteau, Francette. "The Impossible Referent: Representations of the Androgyne." In *Formations of Fantasy.* Ed. Victor Burgin, James Donald, and Cora Kaplan. London: Routledge, 1986. 62–84.

Parkin-Gounelas, Ruth. "The Other Side of the Looking Glass: Women's Fantasy Writing and Woolf's *Orlando.*" *Gramma: Journal of Theory and Criticism* 1 (1993): 137–53.

Payne, Kenneth. "Grania, 'A Mad Woman . . . Doomed to Attempt the Impossible': Imagining Utopia in Katharine Burdekin's *The End of This Day's Business.*" *Lamar Journal of the Humanities* 30.2 (2005): 33–42.

Peel, Ellen Susan. *Politics, Persuasion, and Pragmatism: A Rhetoric of Feminist Utopian Fiction.* Columbus: Ohio State University Press, 2002.

Petry, Ann. *The Street.* 1946. Boston: Houghton Mifflin, 1974.

Pfeiffer, Kathleen. "*Summer* and Its Critics' Discomfort." *Women's Studies* 20 (1991): 141–52.

Phelan, Peggy. "Marina Abramović: Witnessing Shadows." *Theatre Journal* 56 (2004): 569–77.

Pick, Daniel. *Faces of Degeneration: A European Disorder, c. 1948–1918.* Cambridge: Cambridge University Press, 1993.

Pinkerton, Steve. "Trauma and Cure in Rebecca West's *The Return of the Soldier.*" *Journal of Modern Literature* 32.1(Fall 2008): 1–12.

Pizer, Donald, ed. *The Literary Criticism of Frank Norris.* Austin, University of Texas Press, 1964.

———. *The Novels of Frank Norris.* New York: Haskell House, 1973.

Pleck, Elizabeth. *Domestic Tyranny: The Making of American Social Policy against Family Violence from Colonial Times to the Present.* Urbana: University of Illinois Press, 2004.

Poirier, Richard. *Poetry and Pragmatism.* Cambridge, MA: Harvard University Press, 1992.

Porte, Joel, ed. *New Essays on The Portrait of a Lady.* Cambridge: Cambridge University Press, 1990.

Posnock, Ross. *The Trial of Curiosity: Henry James, William James, and the Challenge of Modernity.* New York: Oxford University Press, 1991.

Proctor, Robert N. and Londa Schiebinger, eds. *Agnotology: The Making and Unmaking of Ignorance.* Stanford: Stanford University Press, 2008.

Pryse, Marjorie. "'Pattern against the Sky': Deism and Motherhood in Ann Petry's *The Street.*" In *Conjuring: Black Women, Fiction, and Literary Tradition.* Ed. Marjorie Pryse and Hortense J. Spillers. Bloomington: Indiana University Press, 1985. 116–31.

Purvis, June. "The Prison Experiences of the Suffragettes in Edwardian Britain." *Women's History Review* 4.1 (1995): 103–33.

Purvis, June, and Sandra Stanley Holton, eds. *Votes for Women.* London: Routledge, 2000.

Roberts, James C., Loreen Wolfer, Marie Mele. "Why Victims of Intimate Partner Violence Withdraw Protection Orders." *Journal of Family Violence* 23 (2008): 369–75.
Rorty, Richard. "Feminism and Pragmatism." In *Psychoanalysis, Feminism, and the Future of Gender.* Joseph H. Smith, M.D., ed. and Afaf M. Mahfouz, Ph.D., associate ed. Baltimore: The Johns Hopkins University Press, 1994. 42–69.
———. *Philosophy and Social Hope.* London: Penguin Books, 1999.
———. *Take Care of Freedom and Truth Will Take Care of Itself: Interviews with Richard Rorty.* Ed. and Intro. Eduardo Mendieta. Stanford: Stanford University Press, 2006.
Rosenberg, Rosalind. *Beyond Separate Spheres: Intellectual Roots of Modern Feminism.* New Haven: Yale University Press, 1982.
Rosenblatt, Louise M. *The Reader, the Text, the Poem: The Transactional Theory of Literary Work.* Carbondale: Southern Illinois University Press, 1978.
Samuelson, Ralph. "Virginia Woolf, *Orlando*, and the Feminist Spirit." *Western Humanities Review* 15.1 (Winter 1961): 51–58.
Santamarina, Xiomara. "Black Womanhood in North American Women's Slave Narratives." In *The Cambridge Companion to the African American Slave Narrative.* Ed. Audrey Fisch.Cambridge: Cambridge University Press, 2007. 232–45.
Sawaya, Francesca. "The Authority of Experience: Jane Addams and Hull-House." In *Women's Experience of Modernity, 1875–1945.* Ed. Ann L. Ardis and Leslie W. Lewis. Baltimore: The Johns Hopkins University Press, 2003. 47–62.
Schoenbach, Lisi. *Pragmatic Modernism.* Oxford: Oxford University Press, 2012.
Schneider, Rebecca. "After Us the Savage Goddess: Feminist Performance Art of the Explicit Body Staged, Uneasily, Across Modernist Dreamscapes. In *Performance and Cultural Politics.* Ed. Elin Diamond. New York: Routledge, 1996.
Schriber, Mary S. "Isabel Archer and Victorian Manners." *Studies in the Novel* 8.4 (Winter 1976): 441–57.
Schutte, Nicola S., John M. Malouff, and Johnna S. Doyle. "The Relationship between Characteristics of the Victim, Persuasive Techniques of the Batterer, and Returning to a Battering Relationship." *The Journal of Social Psychology* 128 (1998): 605–10.
Scott, William. "Material Resistance and the Agency of the Body in Ann Petry's *The Street.*" *American Literature* 78.1 (March 2006): 89–115.
Sedgwick, Eve Kosofsky. *Epistemology of the Closet.* 1990. Berkeley: University of California Press, 2008.
Seigfried, Charlene Haddock. *Pragmatism and Feminism: Reweaving the Social Fabric.* Chicago: University of Chicago Press, 1996.
Shockley, Evie. "Buried Alive: Gothic Homelessness, Black Women's Sexuality, and (Living) Death in Ann Petry's *The Street.*" *African American Review* 40.3 (2006): 439–60.

Shotwell, Alexis. *Knowing Otherwise: Race, Gender, and Implicit Understanding.* University Park: Penn State University Press, 2011.

Showalter, Elaine. *Hystories: Hysterical Epidemics and Modern Culture.* New York: Columbia University Press, 1997.

"Skin Deep." *House M.D.* Fox. 20 February 2006. Television.

Smith, Angela K. *Suffrage Discourse in Britain during the First World War.* Hants, England: Ashgate, 2005.

Smith-Rosenberg, Carroll. "The Female World of Love and Ritual: Relations between Women in Nineteenth-Century America." *Signs* 1.1 (Autumn 1975): 1–29.

Snediker, Michael D. *Queer Optimism: Lyric Personhood and Other Felicitous Persuasions.* Minneapolis: University of Minnesota Press, 2009.

Soldaini, Marcella. "Violated Territories: Monkey Island, Baldry Court and No Man's Land in Rebecca West's *The Return of the Soldier.*" In *Literary Landscapes, Landscape in Literature.* Ed. Michele Bottalico, Maria Teresa Chialant, and Eleonora Rao. Rome: Carocci, 2007. 109–16.

Spillers, Hortense J. "'An Order of Constancy': Notes on Brooks and the Feminine." *The Centennial Review* 29.2 (1985): 223–48.

St. Clair, Janet. "The Courageous Undertow of Zora Neale Hurston's *Seraph on the Suwanee.*" *Modern Language Quarterly: A Journal of Literary History* 50.1 (March 1989): 38–57.

Stetz, Margaret Diane. "Drinking 'The Wine of Truth': Philosophical Change in West's *The Return of the Soldier.*" *Arizona Quarterly* 43.1 (Spring 1987): 63–78.

Stewart, Mary White. *Ordinary Violence: Everyday Assaults against Women Worldwide.* 2nd edition. Santa Barbara: Praeger, 2014.

Stout, Janis P. *Strategies of Reticence: Silence and Meaning in the Works of Jane Austen, Willa Cather, Katherine Anne Porter, and Joan Didion.* Charlottesville: University Press of Virginia, 1990.

Stevenson, Pascha Antrece. "Ethan Frome and Charity Royall: Edith Wharton's Noble Savages." *Women's Studies* 32 (2003): 411–29.

Stransky, Tanner. "Guys and Dolls." *Entertainment Weekly* 987 (April 18, 2008): 51.

Sullivan, Shannon. *Living across and through Skins: Transactional Bodies, Pragmatism, and Feminism.* Bloomington: Indiana University Press, 2001.

———. "Reciprocal Relations between Races: Jane Addams's Ambiguous Legacy." *Transactions of the Charles S. Peirce Society* 39.1 (Winter 2003): 43–60.

Sullivan, Shannon, and Nancy Tuana, eds. *Race and Epistemologies of Ignorance.* Albany: State University of New York Press, 2007.

Surridge, Lisa. *Bleak Houses: Marital Violence in Victorian Fiction.* Athens: Ohio University Press, 2005.

Synge, J. M. "Playboy of the Western World." 1907. In *Modern Irish Drama.* Ed. John P. Harrington. New York: W. W. Norton, 1991. 73–188.

Tate, Claudia. *Psychoanalysis and Black Novels: Desire and the Protocols of Race.* New York: Oxford University Press, 1998.

Thackeray, William. *Vanity Fair.* 1847–48. Ed. John Carey. London: Penguin, 2003.
Thayer, H. Standish, ed. *Pragmatism: The Classic Writings.* New York: Mentor, 1970.
Tickner, Lisa. *The Spectacle of Women: Imagery of the Suffrage Campaign 1907–14.* Chicago: University of Chicago Press, 1988.
Todorov, Tzvetan. *The Fantastic: A Structural Approach to a Literary Genre.* Ithaca: Cornell University Press, 1975.
Townley, Cynthia. *A Defense of Ignorance: Its Value for Knowers and Roles in Feminist and Social Epistemologies.* Lanham, MD: Lexington Books, 2011.
Treadwell, Sophie. *Machinal.* 1928. London: N. Hern, 1993.
Tromp, Marlene. *The Private Rod: Marital Violence, Sensation, and the Law in Victorian Britain.* Charlottesville: University Press of Virginia, 2000.
Varney, Susan. "Oedipus and the Modernist Aesthetic: Reconceiving the Social in Rebecca West's *The Return of the Soldier.*" In *Naming the Father: Legacies, Geneologies, and Explorations of Fatherhood in Modern and Contemporary Literature.* Ed. Eva Paulino Bueno, Terry Caesar, and William Hummel. Lanham: Lexington Books, 2000. 253–75.
Vatnar, Solveig Karin Bo, and Stål Bjørkly. "An Interactional Perspective of Intimate Partner Violence: An In-Depth Semi-Structures Interview of a Representative Sample of Help-Seeking Women." *Journal of Family Violence* 23 (2008): 265–79.
Wald, Christina. *Hysteria, Trauma, and Melancholia: Performative Maladies in Contemporary Anglophone Drama.* New York: Palgrave MacMillan, 2007.
Walker, Lenore E. *The Battered Woman.* New York: Harper and Row, 1979.
Walker, Nancy A. "'Seduced and Abandoned': Convention and Reality in Edith Wharton's *Summer.*" *Studies in American Fiction* 11.1 (Spring 1983): 107–14.
———. *A Very Serious Thing: Women's Humor and American Culture.* Minneapolis: University of Minnesota Press, 1988.
Warburton, Rachel. "'Nothing Could Be Seen Whole or Read from Start to Finish': Transvestism and Imitation in *Orlando* and *Nightwood.*" In *Styling Texts: Dress and Fashion in Literature.* Ed. Cynthia Kuhn and Cindy Carlson. Youngstown, NY: Cambria, 2007. 269–90.
Warr, Tracey, ed. *The Artist's Body.* London, Phaidon, 2000.
Washington, Mary Helen. "Plain, Black, and Decently Wild: The Heroic Possibilities of *Maud Martha.*" In *The Voyage In: Fictions of Female Development.* Hanover: University Press of New England for Dartmouth College, 1983. 270–86.
———. "'Taming All That Anger Down': Rage and Silence in Gwendolyn Brooks' *Maud Martha.*" *The Massachusetts Review* 24.2 (1983): 453–66.
Webster, Brenda S. "Helene Deutsch: A New Look." *Signs* 10.3 (Spring 1985): 553–71.
Weisbuch, Robert. "Henry James and the Idea of Evil." In *The Portrait of a Lady.* Ed. Michael Gorra. Norton Critical Edition. New York: W. W. Norton, 2018. 604–13.
Werner, Mary Beth. "'A Vast and Terrible Drama': Frank Norris's Domestic Violence Fantasy in *McTeague.*" *Frank Norris Studies* 19 (Spring 1994): 1–4.

Wesling, Meg. "The Opacity of Everyday Life: Segregation and the Iconicity of Uplift in *The Street*." *American Literature* 78.1 (March 2006): 117–40.
West, Cornel. *The American Evasion of Philosophy: A Genealogy of Pragmatism*. Madison: University of Wisconsin Press, 1989.
West, Nathanael. *The Dream Life of Balso Snell*. Paris: Contact Editions, 1931.
———. *Miss Lonelyhearts & The Day of the Locust*. New York: New Directions, 1962.
West, Rebecca. "On 'The Return of the Soldier.'" *Yale University Library Gazette* 57.1–2 (October 1982): 66–71.
———. *The Return of the Soldier*. 1918. Intro. Samuel Hynes. New York: Penguin Books, 1998.
Whalan, Mark. *Race, Manhood, and Modernism in America: The Short Story Cycles of Sherwood Anderson and Jean Toomer*. Knoxville: University of Tennessee Press, 2007.
Wharton, Edith. *The Age of Innocence*. 1920. Ed. and Intro. Cynthia Griffin Wolff. New York: Penguin Books, 1996.
———. *Summer*. 1917. Intro. Candace Waid. New York: Signet Classic, New American Library, 1993.
White, Barbara. "Edith Wharton's *Summer* and 'Women's Fiction.'" *Essays in Literature* 11.2 (1984): 223–35.
Woolf, Virginia. *Orlando: A Biography*. Ed. Mark Hussey. Annotated and Intro. Maria DiBattista. Orlando: Harcourt, 2006.
———. *A Room of One's Own and Three Guineas*. New York: Book-of-the-Month Club, 1992.
Wright, Richard. *Native Son*. 1940. New York: Harper Perennial Modern Classics, 2005.
Yancy, George, ed. *Cornel West: A Critical Reader*. Afterward by Cornel West. Malden, MA: Blackwell, 2001.

Index

Addams, Jane, 22–23, 37–73, 87, 101, 178, 227, 230
  and the Devil-baby, 30, 37–41, 43–44, 52–62, 64–66, 68–73
  and Ellen Gates Starr, 42, 227
  and Hull House, 22, 30, 37, 39, 41–47, 53, 56, 58, 60–61, 64, 68–70, 101, 227, 230
  and *The Long Road of Woman's Memory*, 30–31, 37–41, 52–73, 230
  and *Twenty Years at Hull-House*, 42, 50–52
agnotology, 15. *See also* epistemology of ignorance
Alcoff, Linda Martin, 10
Anderson, Sherwood, 29
  and "The Man Who Became a Woman," 32, 194, 201, 203–13, 215–19

Bailey, Alison, 10, 153
Barvosa-Carter, Edwina, 113, 139
Bauer, Carol, 110, 117
Bederman, Gail, 120
Berlant, Lauren, 26, 28
Bernstein, Robin, 16, 21
Bersani, Leo, 25, 79
Blackwell, Henry, 111, 118, 121, 123, 129

blues music, 108–9
body art, 178–80
Bonner, Patricia, 140, 145
Brandt, Maria F., 114, 116
Brooks, Gwendolyn, *Maud Martha*, 24–25, 31, 73–77, 80–83, 87–94, 100, 146
Burdekin, Katharine, 29
  and *Proud Man*, 32, 194, 201, 218–26
Butler, Josephine, 111, 119
Butler, Judith, 15, 32, 193, 195, 197, 201–2, 213–16, 227

Calhoun, Craig, 45–46
"Cat and Mouse" Act, 184
Chapman, Mary, 163–64, 166–67, 174
Cheng, Anne Anlin, 226
Clark, Suzanne, 49–50
class (social), 1–4, 6, 11, 16, 19, 21, 23–25, 29, 31, 41–45, 51, 54–55, 58–59, 62, 72–73, 87, 110, 120, 123, 144, 166, 170, 188, 199, 201, 217
  and classism, 1, 11, 41–44, 53, 82, 199, 217
Cobbe, Frances Power, 16, 111, 122–23, 129, 169–70
Comprone, Raphael, 80, 95

279

Contagious Diseases Acts, in England, 119
Conway, Jill, 51–52
Cowan, Laura, 231, 237–38, 243
"Crimes Against Women," newspaper column, 118, 121–23
Crowley, John W., 79, 82

Davis, Amanda, 136
Davis, Angela, 108–9
degeneration, 106, 121, 170
del Mar, David Peterson, 120
Deutsch, Helene, 134–35
Dewey, John, 14, 46–48, 179, 228
domestic violence, 51, 106, 107–18, 120–21, 125–26, 130, 132, 135–37, 140–45, 152–54
  and cyclical nature of, 107–10, 112, 115, 138, 141–45, 153–54
  as occurs in modern canonical literature, 137
Douglass, Frederick, 11
Drake, Kimberley, 146–48, 152
Dreyer, Randolph, 240, 242

Eby, Virginia, 144, 148
Edelman, Lee, 25
Edmundson, Melissa, 245
Eliot, George, *Middlemarch*, 19–21
Ellis, Havelock, 130–31
ephebophilia, 74
epistemology, 1–2, 8–13, 15–16, 18, 27, 30, 47, 51, 73, 92, 153, 190, 228–29, 231, 234, 245
  feminist, 2, 47, 87, 190
  of ignorance, 1–2, 9, 11–12, 14–16, 27–28, 33, 75, 92, 153, 245
ethic of innocence, 3–4, 15, 17, 19, 23, 28–30, 33, 40, 52, 72–73, 75, 83–84, 86, 101, 103, 108–9, 153, 156, 168, 177, 221, 227, 230, 238–39, 243, 246–47. *See also* not-knowing

fantasy, genre of, 15, 17, 29–30, 32, 60, 62, 79, 85, 88–89, 91, 155–56, 194–95, 197, 200–1, 204, 216–17, 219, 226, 229, 235, 242
Felski, Rita, 22, 68
feminism, 2, 11–15, 16, 18–19, 21–29, 40–41, 47, 53, 68, 70, 72, 79, 108, 127, 134, 160, 166–69, 196, 229, 238–39
  and activism/politics, 31, 47, 75, 77, 94, 107–10, 116–22, 163, 176–78, 189, 243–44
  and antifeminism, 2, 29, 74, 80, 103, 107–8
  at the fin-de-siècle, 21–23, 31, 107–10, 116–22, 128–29, 132, 136, 169, 174
  and pragmatism, 14, 30–31, 40, 47, 52, 68, 71–72, 94, 174–75, 177, 194, 239, 243
  and scholarship, 2, 9, 11–12, 14–15, 23–29, 31, 33, 52, 61, 70, 72, 74–75, 80, 84, 94, 98, 107, 113, 132, 139–40, 168–69, 174, 190, 201, 227, 237, 243–44, 247
fin-de-siècle, 13, 17–18, 21, 31, 42, 55, 107, 116–17, 120, 122, 128, 131, 134, 155, 229–30, 247. *See also* turn-of-the-century
  and literature, 13, 15, 111, 114, 154
  and women, 2, 4, 8, 11, 23, 24, 71, 78, 103, 163
Fleissner, Jennifer L., 105, 125, 132, 134, 154–55
forcible feeding, of British suffragettes, 171, 185
Frazier, Valerie, 74, 76, 77

Freud, Sigmund, 130, 213–16

Geddes, J. F., 171, 184–85
Gerber, Nancy, 80, 88–89, 91–93
Gilbert, Sandra, 202–4
Gilbey, Ryan, 234
Gillespie, Craig, 230, 235, 242–43. See also *Lars and the Real Girl*
gothic, genre of the, 49, 59, 61, 65–66, 143, 155
Grafton, Kathy, 74, 82
Gubar, Susan, 202–4

Hall, Susan L., 78
Halpern, Faye, 26
Henderson, Carol, 145–47
Hopkins, J. Ellice, 110, 119
Horney, Karen, 134
Hotaling, Debra, 50
Howard, June, 123
Howard, Lillie, 81, 99
Howells, William Dean, 49
Howlett, Caroline J, 171, 180, 185
Hughes, Langston, "Beale Street Love," 137–40, 155
humor, women's writing and, 164, 166–67, 172–74, 234, 243
Hurston, Zora Neale and *Seraph on the Suwanee*, 31, 73–77, 80–83, 94–100
  and *Their Eyes Were Watching God*, 77, 80–81, 136
hysteria, 95–96, 170, 206

Iker, Karen, 24–25, 27, 81, 87, 91, 93–94
Imre, Amikó, 195–96

James, Henry, 4, 18–20, 23
  and *Daisy Miller*, 20–21
  and *Portrait of a Lady*, 4–8, 18–19, 23

James, William, 13, 33, 47–49, 57, 179, 227, 244
  and *Pragmatism*, 13, 47–49, 227, 244
Jeffreys, Sheila, 119, 121
Johnson, Brian D., 242
Jones, Amelia, 32, 178–80
Joslin, Katherine, 51–53

Kassanoff, Jennie A., 79
Kean, Hilda, 160
Kelley, Florence, 44
Kenney, Mary, 45
Keyes, John, 126–28
Knight, Louise M., 46
Konzett, Delai Capraroso, 77, 80
von Krafft-Ebing, Richard, 130

Ladenson, Joyce, 204
Lanthrop, Julia, 44
Lars and the Real Girl, 32, 230–35, 239–44, 247–48
Lattin, Patricia H. and Vernon E., 76, 89
Leach, William, 120
Lissak, Rivka Shpak, 42
Livingston, James, 14, 47, 49, 57
Luria, Salvador, 8–9, 12–13
Lytton, Constance, 166

MacKay, Marina, 237
Malmsheimer, Lonna M., 206–7, 210
masochism, female, 31, 111, 130–35, 138–39, 141–43, 152
Mayhall, Laura, 165, 170, 180
McCullers, Carson, *The Heart is a Lonely Hunter*, 140–43, 147, 150, 155
Mead, George Herbert, 46
melancholia, 194, 202, 204, 213–17, 224–26

Miller, Alice Duer, *Are Women People?*, 29, 32, 163–74, 176–77, 180, 188–91, 193
Mills, Charles, 9–10, 245, 247
modernism, genre of, 17, 25, 29, 39, 50, 53, 74, 76, 108, 126, 135, 137, 194, 202–4, 230, 242, 247
myth, genre of, 29, 31, 37–40, 48, 58–59, 63, 69, 70–71, 91, 183, 235

naturalism, genre of, 29, 31, 49, 51, 106–8, 114–18, 121–35, 140, 143–45, 150, 154–55
Nead, Lynda, 15–16, 161–62, 178, 180–84
"New Woman," 5, 22, 51–52, 70
Ngai, Sianne, 74, 78
Nordau, Max, 121
Norris, Frank, 133
  and "Fantaisie Printaniere," 115–16, 124–26, 137, 155
  and *McTeague*, 31, 105–6, 114–16, 122–26, 128–35, 137, 154–55
not-knowing, 1–3, 6, 8–12, 15–18, 23–24, 27, 32–33, 40, 53, 63–65, 67, 81, 83, 90, 92, 101, 143, 153, 190, 194, 221, 233, 235, 245, 247. *See also* ethic of innocence
  in late eighteenth- and nineteenth-century female characters, list of, 19

Oliver, Nancy, 230, 243. See also *Lars and the Real Girl*
Ostman, Heather, 50
Otten, Thomas J., 162–63

Pankhurst, Emmaline, 161–63, 183–89
Patai, Daphne, 219, 225

Peirce, Charles Sanders, 46, 53
performance art, 29, 30, 32, 160, 178–80, 182, 189
Petry, Ann, *The Street*, 31, 121, 135–36, 143–55
Pfeiffer, Kathleen, 74–75, 79
Phelan, Peggy, 189
Pinkerton, Steve, 234–35
Pizer, Donald, 132–33
Pleck, Elizabeth, 117–20, 130, 135–36
pragmatism, philosophical, 2, 13–15, 28, 30, 33, 40–41, 43, 46–49, 51, 53, 57, 66, 71–72, 94, 108, 168, 175–79, 188–89, 194, 227–28, 239, 242, 244, 247–48
primitive, 27, 38–39, 43–44, 47, 72, 121. *See also* race and racism
privilege (identity-based), 3, 6, 10–11, 21, 44, 47–48, 50, 77, 124, 170, 174, 183, 187–88, 199–200, 204, 206, 217, 222, 238, 247
Proctor, Robert N., 9
Progressive Era, 39–45, 49, 116–17, 120–21
prostitution, 21, 42, 51, 64, 85, 111, 118–19
Pryse, Marjorie, 150

race, 1–2, 4, 6, 9, 11, 16, 21, 23–25, 29, 31, 74, 76, 166, 170, 188, 197–99, 201, 203, 211, 213, 217, 226
  and antiracism, 77, 88–95, 145, 153
  and racism, 1, 9–10, 12, 24–25, 27, 37, 73–74, 76–77, 80, 87–94, 100, 197–99, 211, 217
Rainey, Gertrude, 108
rape, 10, 73, 80–83, 96–99, 118, 136, 184, 203, 210. *See also* sexuality and violence

realism, genre of, 29–30, 49, 63, 70–73, 75, 78–79, 94, 101, 108, 123, 133, 155–56, 187–89, 194–95, 201, 204, 234
Richardson, Mary, 32, 159–63, 168–69, 177, 180–91, 193, 230
Ritt, Lawrence, 110, 117
Rokeby Venus, 15, 32, 161, 169, 177, 180–83, 186–88. *See also* vandalism
Rorty, Richard, 13–14, 32, 94, 169–70, 180, 228–29, 242, 244
and "Feminism and Pragmatism," 14, 174–77, 188, 190–91, 194, 218
Rosenberg, Rosalind, 22, 46

Sand, Kathleen M., 68
Schiebinger, Londa, 9
Schneider, Rebecca, 182
Sedgwick, Eve, 10, 27–28
Seigfried, Charlene Haddock, 14, 44–45, 47–49
sensationalism, genre of, 51–52
sentimentalism, genre of, 16, 26, 49, 50–52, 62–63, 67, 70, 72, 79
settlement-house movement, 30, 41–43
sexism, 25, 54, 75, 80, 82, 97, 99, 145, 163, 166, 189, 204, 223
sexology, 31, 130
sexuality, 2, 10, 15, 19, 21, 22, 23, 25, 27–29, 51, 111, 123, 134, 138, 170, 188, 196, 200–1, 203, 205–6, 209, 212, 222, 245
and queerness, 2, 25–28, 42, 79, 196, 201, 209, 237–39
and violence, 31, 80, 83, 97, 99, 102, 118–20, 124, 128–32
Shelley, Mary, *Frankenstein*, 12
Small, Albion, 46
Smith, Bessie, 108

Smith-Rosenberg, Caroll, 22
Snediker, Michael D., 25–26
social-purity movement, 31, 118–23, 128–29
sociology, beginnings of professional, 30, 39, 45–46, 51
St. Clair, Janet, 75, 77, 97, 100–1
Stetz, Margaret, 237
Stevenson, Pascha Antrece, 77–78, 82
Stone, Lucy, 111, 118, 121, 123
suffrage movements, 15–16, 118, 128–29, 162–71, 173, 179, 188, 237
Sullivan, Shannon, 10, 14, 153

Tate, Claudia, 76, 82, 99
temperance movement, American, 118
Tickner, Lisa, 160, 179
Todorov, Tvetzen, 201
Townley, Cynthia, 1, 12
Toynbee Hall, 42
turn-of-the-century, 14, 22, 31, 41, 43, 72, 213. *See also* fin-de-siècle
and literature, 233
and women, 4, 19, 52

University of Chicago, 45–47

vandalism, 15–16, 161–62, 181–84, 186–87. *See also* suffrage movements
Voorhees-Whitehead, S Kathryn, 79

Walker, Lenore E., 107, 110–12
Walker, Nancy, 76, 79, 166, 174
Warr, Tracy, 178
Washington, Mary Helen, 76, 80, 89, 91
West, Cornel, 14, 176
West, Nathanael, 126, 145, 202
and *Miss Lonelyhearts*, 126–28, 155

West, Rebecca, *The Return of the Soldier*, 23, 32, 227, 230–40 243, 245–47
Whalan, Mark, 204
Wharton, Edith, *Summer*, 31, 73–87, 94, 100–3
  and *The Age of Innocence*, 137
  and *Ethan Frome*, 76–78
White, Barbara A., 83–84, 101

wife abuse, 107–11, 117–18, 135. *See also* domestic violence
Williams, Tennessee, *A Streetcar Named Desire*, 136
Woolf, Virginia, *Orlando*, 32, 194–204, 217
Wright, Richard, 121, 135
WSPU, 16, 159–60, 162, 166, 169, 183, 187. *See also* suffrage movements

www.ingramcontent.com/pod-product-compliance
Lightning Source LLC
Chambersburg PA
CBHW020327240426
43665CB00044B/789